Aerospace Power: A Comparative Study of India-China and Pakistan

AEROSPACE POWER

A Comparative Study of India-China and Pakistan

Dr. Bimal Chandra Kumar

PRASHANT PUBLISHING HOUSE
DELHI-110094

Published by :
PRASHANT PUBLISHING HOUSE
C-34, 28 Foota Road, Gali-3,
West Karwal Nagar, Delhi-110094
Phone : 011-22963970, Mob. : 9810396373, 8826258746
e-mail.: prashantpublishinghouse@gmail.com

Aerospace Power: A Comparative Study of India-China and Pakistan

First Published 2019

ISBN : 978-93-88526-22-7

PRINTED IN INDIA
Published by Mr. R.K. Jha M/s Prashant Publishing House and Published at H.S. Offset House Press, Delhi.

Preface

Airpower or air power comprises the application of military strategy and strategic theory to the realm of aerial warfare. Airpower began with the advent of mechanized flight early in the 20th century. Airpower represents a "complex operating environment that has been subjected to considerable debate". British doctrine defines airpower as "the ability to project power from the air and space to influence the behaviour of people or the course of events."

The Air Force operates tens of thousands of machines from aircraft and missiles to refueling trucks and jet engines. Making sure all this equipment is regularly maintained is the job of Maintenance Management Production specialists.

Airpower effectiveness clearly depends on training, equipment, organization, and strategy, but comparative studies of airpower tend to focus on just technical and material factors. Social, political, and organizational factors can also determine airpower's value as an instrument of power, either amplifying or attenuating its material potential. Scholarly studies of the sensitivity of military power to political culture tend to focus on armies—the arms of conquest prized by authoritarian states—so there is much to learn in this field, far more than one brief chapter can disclose. Authoritarian states have repeatedly found airpower's utility as an instrument of the state limited by their political institutions, often gaining only a small return for their airpower investments. Some have even found their military treasure working against the interests of their regimes. Even technically adept authoritarian states demonstrate this tendency. The Soviet Union and Nazi Germany devoted considerable resources (largely in collaboration) to develop airpower in the 1930s. While they developed advanced air arms for the time, these governments also impaired these forces with doctrines that improved their adherence to the exclusive party in power but curbed their service to the state. Recent wars provide further and clearer evidence of this trend.

Today, it has acquired independent strategic missions, most notably including those of nuclear deterrence and retaliation, and it is a diversified fighting force with manifest ambitions toward global reach and status. It also is a full-spectrum combat air arm with a precision conventional strike capability, fielding not only fourth-generation multirole fighters, but also force-extending tankers, a recently acquired airborne warning and control system capability, intertheater airlifters, unmanned aerial vehicles equipped with multispectral sensors for longdwell strategic and tactical reconnaissance, and the beginnings of a military space surveillance capability.

This is a reference book. All the matter is just compiled and edited in nature, taken from the various sources which are in public domain.

It is hoped that the book will be immensely helpful for all officers and airmen of the technical and logistics branches of the air forces of all the developing as well as underdeveloped countries for optimizing the inventory and utilizing the savings thus accrued for further modernization.

—Editor

Contents

1

Introduction

COMMAND OF THE AIR AND AIRPOWER

As a primary element of national power, military force must be able to set the conditions for its successful application. For air, land, and sea power that means first establishing command of their respective element. Command of an element is the ability to use power for desired purposes and to prevent an enemy from using that same power within that element.

Because airpower is the only form of military power that operates exclusively above the surface of the planet, its element encompasses a massive cubic area, something noted by Slessor over 70 years ago. Thus, command of the air must be tailored to meet every individual situation, based upon the overall policy guiding the use of military force. Command of the air is best viewed as similar to Julian Corbett's concept of command of the sea. Command can be local (limited in area) or general (less limited in area) and either temporary (limited in time) or permanent (less limited in time). An example of general permanent control of the air is the airspace over the continental United States (although local command of the air was lost over New York City and Washington, DC temporarily in September 2001). A local temporary condition could exist in a target area where attacking forces seize the airspace over a target to protect attacking aircraft from being attacked.

Command of the air has two elements: using the air for desired ends and preventing use of the air by adversaries for their desired ends. As such, command of the air need not be contested to be obtained. During Operation Desert Storm, Coalition air forces seized command of the air from the Iraqis, facilitating the success of both the air and ground offensive campaigns. After the cessation of hostilities, following the imposition of the United Nations-mandated no-fly zones, the Coalition maintained command of the air over

Iraq south of the 32d parallel and north of the 36th parallel for years during Operations Southern Watch, Northern Watch, and Provide Comfort.

For the vast majority of those operations, this command of the air was not challenged by the Iraqis, but Coalition forces maintained it nonetheless. Coalition air forces could operate as desired within the no-fly zones, and the Iraqis were prevented from using the same area for their own purposes. During peacetime, when command of the air is not contested, command of the air means using the third dimension as you wish, without interference. Airpower and command of the air are inseparable. Airpower is that which allows you to gain, maintain, and exploit command of the air.

Douhet and Sherman held different views about the path to gaining command of the air. Douhet believed in bombing airfields and aircraft on the ground. Sherman (and Mitchell) believed command of the air could also be gained by challenging the enemy air force in the air. Both methods can and should be used as the circumstance dictates. This, however, can begin to cloud the definition of what constitutes airpower. Unquestionably, a B-2 dropping joint direct attack munitions on a runway, preventing enemy air forces from taking off is airpower. A special forces team that accomplishes the same thing from the ground may not be airpower, but that is immaterial. The intent of the mission is to keep the enemy from using the third dimension and to gain command of the air. A similar situation exists with air defence artillery. Ground based missile systems cannot fly or float, so they seem to be land power forces. However, their very reason for existence is to maintain local command of the air. The importance of these distinctions lies in the question of command and control of forces.

Exploiting Command of the Air

Exploiting command of the air is the first and most critical role for airpower.

Once gained, airpower can be applied as is required to attain the ultimate goal in the conflict. Airpower's application is defined through where it can apply influence (targeting) and how it can apply influence (missions).

Targeting

Airpower has certain unique strengths that make it appropriate for use in modern conflict. It provides access and is fast and precise in application.

- Access. Since air covers the earth, airpower can reach any target on its surface. No other force has the degree of access to the globe that airpower has. Past limitations in the amount of distance that can be covered due to limited aircraft fuel supply have been mitigated by more efficient engines and aerial refueling. With aerial refueling, aircraft can remain in the air almost indefinitely. With adequate aerial refueling resources, the human flying the aircraft becomes the flight duration limitation. In spite of technological improvements such as aerial refueling, aircraft remain limited by the amount of fuel that they can carry. Airpower still remains the fastest form of military power. However, as Sherman pointed out, airpower is a fundamentally different form of military power. Because it is unique, the principles of war do not apply in the same way that they do for land power or sea power. When applying them to airpower, we must think of the principles differently. Airpower's speed and reach has created the persistent threat of the use of destructive force, enabling it to exert influence over a much wider geographic area, land or sea, in a way that other, slower forms of military cannot.

- Fast and Precise in Application or Response. Airpower is a technology-based capability. As time has progressed, that capability has vastly improved. The speed and range of aircraft have both increased dramatically since Douhet, Sherman, and Slessor wrote. Aircraft can travel fast, and with aerial refueling can cover great distances. Aircraft flight paths are not limited by geography. The fact that aircraft can fly a straight line from departure to their destination means that they can take the shortest and fastest route. Aircraft fly faster than any land or sea based force, and air forces can respond more quickly to any point on the globe than any other force, short of one that is already deployed to the point of crisis. Sovereign countries may refuse permission to fly through sovereign airspace, but airpower has the ability to fly around these denied areas. Land and sea power are affected much more negatively by access denial. In the lead up to Operation Iraqi Freedom, the Turkish government denied the Coalition permission to stage the US 4th Infantry Division from Turkey. This eliminated the ability to attack Iraqi forces from the north, a major piece of the Coalition ground strategy. Airpower remains the fastest way for decisionmakers to apply power. Precision is one of airpower's unique strengths. Precision helps mitigate a limited ability to mass, in the conventional sense of the principle of war. John Warden's concept of strategic paralysis by parallel attack illustrates the point. Because weapons can be delivered with precision, fewer are needed to destroy targets. This makes more assets available to attack more targets across the entire spectrum of the enemy's capability and ability to resist. "Parallel attack deprives (the enemy) of the ability to respond effectively and the greater the percentage of targets hit in a single blow, the more nearly impossible his response." This, again according to Warden, comes close to the Clausewitzian concept of ideal war by striking the enemy at numerous points simultaneously.

Missions

Airpower is particularly well suited for combat operations and the projection of military power. Every theorist since Douhet has improved the way that airpower is used in combat. This improvement has been possible because of airpower's inherent flexibility. It has the ability to apply different forms of influence with the same platforms, the same people, and the same doctrine and training. From force application, aerial defence, reconnaissance and surveillance, and airlift, airpower can be tailored to serve many objectives. Air forces are designed to be flexible. An F-16 can transition from flying no-fly zone enforcement sorties, enforcing United Nations sanctions, to dropping bombs on terrorist training camps on the next mission. This transition can occur within the same day, with the same aircrew flying the same aircraft. That kind of capability defines flexibility. No other force exhibits the same inherent flexibility as airpower.

The US Army is, by necessity, becoming very accomplished at counterinsurgency operations. This new capability has come, however, at the expense of conventional combat capability. Discussions of whether we need, now or in the future, a strong conventional ground force are immaterial. Proficiency at one mission has come at the expense of another capability. Air forces are not subject to the same limitation. The same ability to drop precision weapons in major combat operations can be used in counterinsurgency operations. Working in close coordination with ground troops, as Jack Slessor envisioned, aircraft can strike singular, high value targets, even in an urban environment. This level of integrated capability was impossible 25 years ago. The same aircraft, weapons, personnel, and skill set can be used for operations ranging from low-intensity to high-intensity conflict without any loss of operational capability.

Airlift is the one unique mission that was ignored by all of the airpower theorists examined in this chapter. Airlift, along with aerial refueling, is among the most critical capabilities that airpower provides. It gives decisionmakers many options with regard to the type of influence that can be exerted on a given situation. In February 2008, the US Air Force delivered more than 225,000 pounds of food, medicine, and cold weather supplies to the People's Liberation Army in China to help relieve suffering caused by severe cold weather. In 2005, the US Air Force conducted "the largest humanitarian relief effort since the Berlin Airlift in 1947" to help the victims of a tsunami in Southeast Asia. Airpower was not the only instrument used in the tsunami relief operation, but as with the China relief mission, airpower was able to get the relief to the point of need the fastest. The ability to provide this type of assistance is a form of influence in itself, one that is not available with other forms of power.

Airpower has another key attribute that makes it far more flexible than ground or sea power. Because of its temporary nature, air forces are not generally viewed as occupation forces. The Coalition air forces enforcing the United Nations sanctions enjoyed a level of international tolerance that would not have existed if they had been forces on the ground in Iraq. This aerial occupation was not seen in nearly the same negative light in which United States' ground occupation forces are currently viewed. Boots on the ground, while possibly desirable for the type of operation now underway in Iraq and Afghanistan, seems to represent a more committed action on the part of the United States. Occupation of sovereign territory is a more significant action than penetration of sovereign airspace. Similarly, penetration of sovereign waters by naval forces carries much of the same negative connotation. Airpower gives decisionmakers more flexible options if they desire to deliver force.

The Use of Airpower

As a form of power, airpower provides access, speed, precision, and flexibility available from no other form of power. Power, however, is only as useful as the policy that guides its use. It is incumbent upon airmen, as the ones who understand the nature of conflict and the strengths and limitations of airpower, to advise policymakers on its use. Once the decision is made to use airpower, it is up to the airman to develop a strategy with the available capabilities and resources that best supports that policy. Airpower can be applied across the spectrum, from peace to conflict, and as a tool of all three instruments of statecraft: economic, diplomatic, and military. Airpower can enforce aerial blockades, such as no-fly zones. Its inherent speed can aid the diplomatic process by moving people and intelligence rapidly to points of crisis. It can provide great diplomatic and humanitarian assistance by delivering critical relief supplies to a disaster-ravaged area. It can strike nearly any target located on the face of the earth with relative speed. As capable as airpower is, though, it is most effective when used in concert with other elements of power.

Airpower, as with each other element of power, has strengths and weaknesses, but it alone is uniquely suited to apply influence across all levels of warfare: strategic, operational, and tactical. At which level airpower is used is not defined by the type of platform that exerts the influence. To understand this, we need to break the convention started by Douhet that strategic airpower equals big bombers, attacking the enemy's war making capacity far behind the battle front. Strategic targets are ones that, if attacked, have the most direct effect on the enemy's decision whether to continue fighting. They may be located within range of and vulnerable to attack from smaller aircraft or systems. John Warden understood this as he constructed his model of the enemy as a system. It is the enemy itself, and its inherent weaknesses, that defines which targets are strategic, not the type of aircraft that can reach or destroy them.

The ability to rapidly reach out to almost any point on the earth and influence a target is a tremendous capability. As our ability to gather knowledge about a particular situation continues to increase, airpower's strengths will make it a force of choice, but we must make sure that force is appropriate. The relative ease with which we can apply influence through the air with little perceived risk may incline some to advocate the use of airpower when it is not the appropriate force or force is inappropriate. In the vast majority of cases, airpower must be employed in conjunction with other elements of power. While the application of airpower may be an excellent strategic tool, there are situations where the ability to strike a target rapidly may be needed in support of another form of power. Jack Slessor was absolutely correct when he advocated the strategic application of airpower while acknowledging the possibility of operating in support of ground forces. That operation, though, must remain in the hands of airmen so that airpower is applied in accordance with its strengths and not compromised by its weaknesses. It is critical that we continue to work together with land and sea forces, improving our ability to work together to maximize our capability.

FUTURE OF AEROSPACE POWER

Let me start by being the devil's advocate and making two points to this audience. One: that this seminar is about "Aerospace Power" and not "Air Force Power". The army and the navy, therefore too, have a stake in it, even though it may be a relatively small one.

History has repeatedly confirmed that air power is decisive in conflict, and there can be little doubt that "aerospace power" will certainly dominate the battlefield. However, by itself, airpower has not been able to prevail in any conflict. Look at WW II, Vietnam, Gulf Wars I and II, Afghanistan and lately in Lebanon. A major limitation of air power is that it is inherently transient; you can operate "through" the medium of air but not "from" it. Therefore, in a conflict, you cannot do without what the army calls "boots on the ground" and the navy refers to as "forward presence". We all, therefore, need to move together participatively or jointly.

While the Arab-Israeli wars and the conflicts on our own subcontinent contributed a great deal to the repository of air warfare knowledge and experience, it is the deployments of air power in the Balkans and the Persian Gulf that opened a radically new chapter in air power.

We cannot look at the world through monochromatic lenses, because each nation and each region is faced by its own set of challenges. And just as there is no single panacea for all problems, we need to define a future for aerospace power that is relevant to our conditions and environment.

Aircraft were used in offence for the very first time in 1911, when the Italians bombed the Turks in Tripoli from the air. And WW I was only three weeks old when the first aerial combat took place over France.

This war was to be the first and last major conflict of the 20th century in which infantry made horrendous sacrifices for gaining or losing a few yards of territory; the total casualties of this war, to machine gun fire, poison gas and barbed wire, exceeding those in all previous conflicts put together. Although extensively deployed, aircraft played a generally defensive and not very crucial role in the outcome of war, perhaps due to lack of doctrine and experience. All too often in history, the conclusion of each conflict has served as a prelude to the next one, and so it was with WW I. The script of WW II was said to have been written in June 1919, in the peace Treaty of Versailles, and the inter-war years were spent by strategists working out ways to fight future wars with minimum casualties. And of course, air power offered the greatest promise in this area.

Few events in the history of air power, which can be termed as defining moments because of the momentous impact they had on the course of aerial warfare; World War I and its aftermath are:-

- The merger of the RFC and RNAS in 1918 produced the world's first force, independent of army or navy command for the conduct of air operations; the RAF.
- Naval air power became an established reality, with the first aircraft carrier being completed in 1918, thus giving impetus to a new branch of air warfare with profound implications in the years to come.
- Air power captured the imagination of military theorists like Guilio Douhet, Billy Mitchell and Hugh Trenchard, who staunchly advocated strategic bombing of the enemy heartland to shatter his morale, cripple his war fighting ability: and thus obtain early victory, with the least casualties.

Asymmetric wars involving terrorism, low intensity conflict, and insurrections are going to be far more frequent than conventional wars between nation states. A major challenge for air forces will, therefore, be to adapt some of the advanced capabilities at their disposal to sub-conventional applications

Between the Great wars there were many wars. The French, Italians and the British experimented with air power to put down insurrections in their colonies. Interestingly, as far back as 1922, the RAF was practicing a concept called "air control" in Iraq to avoid committing ground troops against the local tribes. The Spanish Civil War and the Sino-Japanese wars were the proving grounds for new flying machines as well as new aerial tactics.

All this was a useful prelude to WW II. Three different events during World War II which were to have far reaching implications with regard to employment of air power are:-

- The first one, which heralded the opening campaign of WW II, was the German concept of Blitzkrieg or lightning war. Fast moving armoured columns on the ground, supported by furious air assault by the Luftwaffe resulted in the swift conquest of half of Europe in a few months, and set the bar for future army-air cooperation.
- The second was the commencement of a new phase in 1940, of strategic bombing in the hope of breaking the enemy's will to fight and bringing the war to an early conclusion. While the bomber offensive certainly caused immense damage to life and property, and also to German morale, whether its impact was enough to shorten the war remains a hotly debated issue.
- The third was the two atomic bomb detonations over Hiroshima and Nagasaki in August 1945. Both bombs were delivered by a single B-29, and their destructive power was enough to result in instant capitulation by the Japanese. This heralded a terrifying new capability of air power, and ensured a place for the manned bomber in the armoury of nuclear powers for many decades to come.

The Vietnam War constituted a watershed for deployment of air power in the 20th century and beyond. It saw a decade and a half of slowly escalating conflict, in which huge air assets were committed and the US lost over 8500 aircraft and helicopters. Smart weapons were tried out for the first time, and tactics evolved for jet fighters, bombers and attack helicopters, which were to transform air warfare.

The defining moments that have been highlighted were significant in that they contained seminal lessons, both positive and negative, and were instrumental in the formulation of air power doctrines and strategies, and in shaping its future. Most of these lessons were learnt and internalised by practitioners of air power, but humans are imperfect; and there are probably still many mistakes, which get repeated, and many lessons that are re-learnt again and again.

The army and the navy presume that air power is just an extension of their artillery, and the air force, should therefore be the handmaiden of land and maritime forces.

The Kosovo operations and the recent Israeli campaign against the Hezbollah in Lebanon, with the subsequent resignation of the Chief of Defence Staff Lt Gen Dan Halutz would possibly throw up their own lessons.

Closer home, the growth of our own air force has remained intimately linked with India's evolution as a nation state, and her slow but steady graduation from somewhat utopian ideologies in the early years after independence, to the harsh world of realpolitik today.

INDIAN ARMY ALONE CANNOT MEET THE TWIN THREATS OF PAKISTAN AND CHINA

After half a century, the Indian Army (IA) is once again radically increasing its numbers. Both times it was to cater for threat from China. After the 1962 rout, six new divisions were raised; two infantry and four mountain divisions, and the Officer Training Academy in Madras were established. Now, between 2009 and 2011, the IA raised two mountain divisions and the third artillery division, and a new Officers Training Academy has been set up in Gaya. A corps headquarters and two more mountain divisions will be raised in the 12th defence plan (2012 to 2017). Huge amounts will be spent on building infrastructure, accommodation, equipment and ammunition storage facilities against China. And by the 14th defence plan (2022 to 2027), the IA hopes to have its first air assault division; 54 mountain division has been earmarked for this role. The once-again threat from China provokes two pertinent questions: What happened to post-1962 preparedness? And, is India bracing itself enough this time to dissuade adversaries from military adventurism, and fight a successful war, if needed?

For 14 years after the ignominious 1962 debacle, India had no relations with China. After the Chinese unilateral troops' withdrawal from Indian territories, a 320km Line of Actual Control (LAC) came up in Ladakh where the IA had given a reasonable account of itself. The eastern sector, called McMahon Line, where the IA performed abysmally, remained a 'frontier' rather than a 'border.' The word 'frontier' denotes the limit of a nation's political and military influence, while 'border' is defined as the territorial limit of national sovereignty. While diplomatic relations were restored with China in 1976, domestic political upheavals delayed the initiation of a military build-up against China until 1980 when Prime Minister Indira Gandhi returned to power. In 1980, the army chief, General K.V. Krishna Rao presented a strategic military plan called Operation Falcon to the Prime Minister which she accepted. Repudiating Nehru's 'forward policy,' in a step-by-step approach over 15 years, the army's planned heavy deployment on the Chinese front where forward build-up would keep pace with infrastructure development along with viable lines of communications. Arunachal Pradesh, north Sikkim and trans-Ladakh range were to get special attention, and the Prime Minister made it clear that in a future conflict with China, Tawang should not fall. Recalling his deliberations with Mrs Gandhi, General Rao in a detailed interaction with FORCE in August 2005 confirmed that the Prime Minister took great interest in the army's initiative. Issues like would China get provoked by India's military preparedness and start a conflict and the possibility of it using nuclear weapons were discussed threadbare. The plan could well be called a top-down approach. Keeping with times, the plan did not cater for a two-front war, and was an amalgamation of first and second generation warfare with the Indian Air Force (IAF) in a tactical support role. The first generation warfare reflected the tactics of line and column, while the second generation relied on massed firepower. The concepts of air-land battle and active defence had yet not been borrowed from the United States; a mere co-ordination rather than jointness between the IA and the IAF was the need of the hour.

In a show of goodwill, India under Prime Ministers Rajiv Gandhi and P.V. Narasimha Rao abandoned Operation Falcon in 1988, just when China focussed on its neglected west and commenced furtive military infrastructure build-up in Tibet Autonomous Region (TAR) against India. New Delhi's decision was taken without consulting the IA, which was informed that the external affairs ministry would engage China by diplomacy. The Indian defence forces were told to instead concentrate on Pakistan. All lessons of the 1962 conflict were forgotten and it was business as usual. India signed the 1993 and 1996 agreements with China; both worked to India's military disadvantage. The first re-named the entire disputed border as the LAC which by definition meant it could be altered by military force, and the second ensured that no division and high formation army exercises would be held close to LAC. Even for a brigade exercise involving 3,000 troops, India will be required to inform China well in advance.

Meanwhile, the Peoples Liberation Army's (PLA) military plans were unfolding quietly. After India's 1998 nuclear tests, the PLA started pushing LAC inside India by its aggressive patrolling, and whenever India objected, the concerned pockets were added to the increasing list of 'disputed areas' by China. Giving the high altitude and harsh climatic conditions on TAR, the PLA did not intend to station troops close to the LAC and hence it had little need to conduct exercises in location. It instead concentrated on building Rapid Reaction Forces (RRF), 30 divisions of which, in Indian estimate, can be brought from nearby Chengdu and Lanzhou military regions to TAR in one season against India. Excellent border management and mind-boggling infrastructure on TAR would support the PLA divisions to fight a war on Indian territories. In comparison, India lacks RRF capabilities, and is building defences along the LAC to keep its troops perched on high altitudes holding ground. The IA started feeling the heat of PLA's regular transgressions by the turn of the century. In March 2001, Prime Minister A.B. Vajpayee allocated funds and cleared construction of 73 strategic roads on the Chinese border to be completed in a decade. Nothing much happened on the ground. In December 2011, defence minister A.K. Antony informed the Parliament that 13 out of 73 strategic roads had been built and massive allocations have been made for infrastructure construction to include bunkers and storage facilities.

Today, the IA, the fourth largest in the world after the US, Russian and Chinese, is already 13,00,000 strong. It has 37 divisions, five force headquarters for counter-insurgency operations (each equivalent of a division), 10 independent brigades (over three divisions), higher field formations' headquarters, and various combat support arms elements. Of these, 12 divisions and three independent brigades are pitted against China, the rest are meant for Pakistan. According to the IA, it no longer thinks in terms of threats from Pakistan and China, but has chiselled a larger role for itself under the rubric of transformation. It is transforming from a threat-based to a capability-based force to meet challenges of the entire spectrum of war below the nuclear threshold. From conventional to sub-conventional war (terrorism), capabilities to secure island territories, out-of-area (intervention) capabilities to protect India's interests and provide assistance to friendly neighbours, including humanitarian help and disaster relief, and participation in UN operations. The driver for the transformational thinking is not the government, but IA's own assessment that it needs to absorb the technology revolution underway in the world, and given India's rising economy, it should possess capabilities to meet the nation's strategic reach aspirations.

Considering that threats from Pakistan and China have increased and not diminished, isn't transformation oxymoronic? Not at all, says a general associated with IA's perspective planning. The government has kept the defence forces on the fringes of national security policy-making. Neither understands one another. But as the force with boots on ground, the IA has to be prepared for all contingencies, was the firm reply. Notwithstanding denial, one can easily detect IA's rivalry with the other two defence services. While being the largest of the three defence forces, in terms of numbers and capital expenditure, the risen profile of the IAF and the Indian Navy (IN) may have spurred the IA to seek its own transformation. In the larger sense, if the three defence services had been united, the Chiefs of Staff Committee (COSC), which was declared ineffective by the Group of Ministers' report in February 2002, would have worked better. So well, that they would not have missed opportunities to be part of national security policy-making.

The first came in the Fifties. On 25 March 1955, Prime Minister Jawaharlal Nehru announced in Parliament the change of the designation of the Commander-in-Chief of the three defence services to Chiefs of Staff. He added that his government was going into the matter of integration of the defence ministry and the three services headquarters. The Prime Minister intended to be fair. While dismissing the need for a military advisor to the Prime Minister of independent India, he desired the defence forces to be part of national security policy-making. The defence services failed to hold the Prime Minister to his promise missing the point that integration of defence services with the defence ministry would position them as the more knowledgeable partner able to influence policy-making. Nehru was persuaded by the wily bureaucracy in 1961 to designate the three service headquarters as 'Attached offices of the Department of Defence' under the Government of India 'Allocation of Business Rules.'

The next opportunity had to wait for the subcontinent's security status quo to get altered with the 1998 nuclear tests by India and Pakistan. Within a year, after the 1999 Kargil conflict, the K. Subrahmanyam headed 'Kargil Review Committee Report' noted that:

'India's is perhaps the only major democracy where the armed forces headquarters are outside the apex government structure. The Chiefs of Staff have assumed the role of operational commanders of their respective forces rather than that of Chiefs of Staff to the Prime Minister or defence minister. They simultaneously discharge the roles of operational commanders and national security planners/managers, especially in relation to future equipment and force postures.'

Following the Report, the Arun Singh-led task force on 'Defence Management' recommended the creation of the Chief of Defence Staff (CDS), and integration of defence services headquarters with the defence ministry. Both suggestions were watered down before acceptance by Group of Ministers report announced by the Deputy Prime Minister, L.K. Advani in February

2002. Instead of the CDS, Advani suggested a step-by-step approach; while holding out the promise of the CDS, a Vice-CDS was formed, which was subsequently re-named as the Chairman of Integrated Staff to Chairman (CISC), Chiefs of Staff Committee (COSC). The three services' headquarters were cosmetically re-designated as 'Integrated Headquarters of Ministry of Defence', without actual integration.

While all this was happening, what did the defence services do? It is an open secret that the Indian Air Force (IAF) opposes the CDS. Unlike the tactical air force that it was, since the arrival of Su-30 aircraft, it talks about strategic reach. Moving away as a support service to the IA, the IAF is building capabilities for effect-based operations. This implies an emphasis on offensive counter-air operations, which would by its effect assist land operations. The IAF fears that a CDS from the IA may seek to curtail its offensive posture. While it is debatable if this would happen, the argument was welcomed by the bureaucracy worried by the Arun Singh committee recommendation of the CDS becoming the Military Advisor to the defence minister. In 2010, the matter was finally settled, when the bureaucracy amended the 'Allocation of Business Rules', with the defence secretary made responsible for the 'Defence of India and every part thereof'. Ironically, the three service chiefs in 2011 in turns (not together) deposed before the Naresh Chandra task force set up by the government to review the decade old GOM report. The three service chiefs sought a formal say for themselves, individually, in security policy-making. Shouldn't they have approached the Prime Minister together years ago to seek integration of the services headquarters with the defence ministry? If they could do so for the Sixth Pay Commission, surely this issue that has implications at the strategic, operational and tactical levels deserved fuller attention. Unfortunately, the intense rivalry between the services has played into the hands of the bureaucracy.

Learning from Past

Armies, it is said, prepare for the last war. The IA seems to be no exception. Since 1990, when Pakistan-supported proxy war started in Jammu and Kashmir, senior army commanders have been conscious that unlike the 1971 war, little preparatory time would be available next time around. A trigger in J&K could easily escalate into a full-fledged war, and the IA would have to fight with whatever wherewithal it has. Another truism became evident after the 1998 nuclear tests by India and Pakistan: the next conflict, if it is to achieve meaningful military aims, would have to be short, swift and intense; anything between seven to 10 days, after that a mix of enormous international and nuclear weapons spectre would loom large. During the 1971 war, the army chief,

General Sam Manekshaw had sought six months of preparatory time for war from Prime Minister Indira Gandhi. The military posture against Pakistan was: strategic defence with operational level offence(s). It was appreciated that after three to four weeks, military results would start showing in favour of India being the larger force. This military thinking has been drastically altered by three factors: nuclear weapons, ballistic missiles, and Pakistan Army's ability to use irregulars (terrorists) as its first line of offense. A going back to 1971 is nothing short of suicidal.

Yet, in all recent conflicts, the IA does not seem to have grasped the realities. During the 1999 Kargil conflict (Operation Vijay), the IA was caught completely off-guard. Overnight, flights were sent to Russia and Israel to procure stores and ammunition; the artillery was moved from various theatres, creating operational gaps in the event of an escalated all-out war, to reinforce firepower in Kargil; guns were employed in direct firing role, a near impossibility in case of a total war; and the army chief admitted major equipment shortcomings by saying: "We will fight with whatever we have." All this happened when the Pakistan military did not even join the war; its Mujahids, and the then paramilitary force (Northern Light infantry) did the fighting.

The next crisis, Operation Parakram, when the two armies stood facing one another for 10 months, from 18 December 2001 to 16 October 2002, was no better. The IA took 22 days for its build-up of offensive (strike) forces, and according to the government, 800 lives were lost/debilitated during preparatory phase. There are two other frightening little-known facts about this crisis. Insiders have confirmed to FORCE that once mobilisation for war was ordered, the then Northern army commander (responsible for J&K, the supposed trigger for a full-fledged war), Lt. General R.K. Nanavaty told the army chief, General S. Padmanabhan, that he needed preparatory time as troops lacked essential stocks of ammunition, stores and spares. The IA ineptness got covered up by disingenuous political naivety. It was believed that international pressure, especially from the US, during the IA's preparatory phase, dissuaded the Vajpayee government from going to war with Pakistan. The truth is devastating. The then US National Security Advisor (NSA), Condoleezza Rice has confirmed in her recent memoir: No Higher Honour, that it was the other way round. The US had resigned to a war between India and Pakistan, when India's NSA, Brajesh Mishra, who was doubling up as the Prime Minister's principal secretary, frantically called her for help. "I cannot contain the war lobby here without some help," he said.

This led US President George Bush to speak with Pakistani President General Pervez Musharraf to persuade him to make the statement that his soil would not be allowed to be used by terrorists; the fig leaf for India to not start war. Mishra had indicated that Musharraf was forced to make the statement because of India's successful coercive diplomacy. The then President, APJ Abdul Kalam told Parliament on 17 February 2003 that: "After the December 13 (2001) attack on our Parliament by Pakistan-based terrorists, we were constrained to deploy our troops along the international border. This decision achieved its purpose by showing both our firmness and our self-restraint in dealing with our hostile neighbour."

Put into perspective, mobilising the IA was a knee-jerk reaction of the Vajpayee government in the vain hope that Pakistan would get coerced. He did not consult its own army before ordering mobilisation. After the de-mobilisation, the army chief, General Padmanabhan said on 9 November 2002: "Whenever there is a situation calling for the army's help, the latter's role should be clearly defined to avoid confusion." Here was a government which instead of coercing got coerced, and the army chief who ordered his command to mobilise for war without knowing what he was supposed to do. If travesty of national security could not be imagined further, one had to only wait for 26/11 attacks in Mumbai to happen.

FORCE has the politico-military inside view of 26/11 from one of the three service chiefs at the time. For first three days as Pakistan-sent terrorists were creating mayhem in Mumbai, the government in New Delhi seemed in a tailspin; the political leadership did not contact the military leadership, and the three defence services did not deem it necessary to consult one another. After 72 hours, the National Security Advisor, M.K. Narayanan called the three chiefs for a meeting with Prime Minister Manmohan Singh, in which the intelligence agencies were not present. By then, it was clear that Pakistan was behind the dastardly act.

The mood in the room was tense and all agreed that Pakistan should not get away with its audacious move. When asked, the army chief, General Deepak Kapoor suggested artillery fire and raids by Special Forces across the Line of Control. The chief of air staff, Air Chief Marshal F.H. Major recommended punitive air strikes inside Pakistan Occupied Kashmir to hit terrorist camps and visible infrastructure, to which the army chief added that it would certainly lead to a full-scale war. There was disagreement over whether the Pakistan Army would escalate matters if the IAF conducted a few punitive sorties across the LC. The army chief felt that had the IAF crossed the LC during the 1999 Kargil conflict, the Pakistan military would have joined the conflict. The navy chief, Admiral Sureesh Mehta kept his counsel; he was neither asked much nor did he offer advice. Strangely, nuclear weapons were not discussed or even remotely mentioned especially when Pakistan has an undeclared nuclear weapons policy which has led to the speculation that it may use weapons early in a war. Maximum time was spent on debating the most inane issue meant for researchers: Pakistan's motives behind 26/11 attacks.

The overarching sense was to explore retaliatory options which would not lead to war. As none existed, the meeting broke with the Prime Minister telling the service chiefs to prepare for war. However, the army chief was unequivocally told by the NSA to not recall personnel from leave or move any formations forward till further orders as it would alert Pakistan. The next day, the defence minister A.K. Antony held his meeting attended by service chiefs and senior ministry bureaucrats. The single point agenda was the need to procure critical war equipment for the three services on fast-track basis.

The service chiefs heard nothing from the Prime Minister's Office for a week, after which NSA informed them that India would not go to war with Pakistan. The inevitable two conclusions of the single meeting between the Prime Minister and his service chiefs on 26/11 are: Neither wanted war and all hoped that the crisis blow over quickly, and none wanted to talk about nuclear weapons; probably there are too many unresolved issues. The services sought to utilise the crisis to make up for its critical equipment, something they never seem to do during peacetime. Few nations would have let 164 people die in vain as India did after 26/11 attacks without retribution for the aggressor. The killings which worried the world of a possible war were a non-event for India and its defence forces.

REPUBLIC OF CHINA AIR FORCE

The Republic of China Air Force is the aviation branch of the armed forces of the Republic of China (Taiwan). The ROCAF's primary mission is the defence of the airspace over and around Taiwan. Priorities of the ROCAF include the development of long range reconnaissance and surveillance networks, integrating C4ISTAR systems to increase battle effectiveness, procuring counterstrike weapons, next generation fighters, and hardening airfields and other facilities to survive a surprise attack.

In May 2005, the Ministry of National Defence indicated its intention to transfer command of all defensive missile systems to the ROCAF, while future offensive missiles would be placed under a newly formed missile command. As of 2006, all medium and long range SAM units were transferred from ROC Army's Missile Command to ROCAF, while ROCAF's airbase security units were transferred to ROC Army Military Police. But it's revealed in January 2011, 5 years of problems of integrating those long range ex-ROC Army SAM units into ROCAF has forced ROCAF high command to return those units back to ROC Army's Missile Command. Missile Command is now directly under Defence Ministry's GHQ control.

In July 2010, former United States Air Force deputy under secretary for international affairs, Bruce Lemkin said that Taiwan's ability to defend its airspace had degraded due to its aging fighters and that the sale of new fighter aircraft to Taiwan was an urgent priority. On 21 September 2011, it was announced that the US had agreed to a US$ 5 billion upgrade to the F-16s. In 2012 Rob Nabors wrote that the United States was considering the sale of fighter aircraft to the ROC.

Organization

Like most of the other branches of the ROC armed forces, much of the ROCAF's structure and organization is patterned after the United States Air Force. Like the USAF, the ROCAF used to have a wing '! group '! squadron structure. After November 2004, tactical fighter wing switch to wing '! Tactical Fighter Group, with some fighter squadrons stood down, with each tactical fighter group, still pretty much the same size as a squadron, now commanded by a full Colonel.

- Air Force General Headquarters Air Force GHQ is subordinate to the General Staff (military), the Minister of Defence (civilian), and the ROC President.
- Internal Units: Personnel, Combat Readiness & Training, Logistics, Planning, Communications, Electronics & Information, General Affairs, Comptroller, Inspector General, Political Warfare.
- Air Force Combatant Command
- Weather Wing: Tamsui, New Taipei City
- Communications, Air Traffic Control & Information Wing: Taipei City
- Air Tactical Control Wing
- Ground fixed and mobile long range air search radar sites, consist of various TPS-117, TPS-75V, FPS-117, GE-592 and HADR radars, plus 1 PAVE PAWS (Phased Array Warning System) early warning radar site in northern Taiwan, will enter service late 2012.
- Air Defence Artillery Command
- 4 Air Defence Missile & Artillery brigades, 951st (Taipei), 952nd (Taichung), 953rd (Kaoshung), 954th (Hualien)
- 4 Air Defence Missile I-HAWK battalions, 621st, 622nd, 662nd, and 664th battalions, with Phase III and 7 Phase I batteries.
- 1 TK-1/2 Air Defence Missile battalion, 951st Brigade, 611st battalion with 6 companies/batteries.

- 1 Patriot PAC-2+ GEM/PAC-3 Air Defence/Anti-Ballistic Missile battalion, with 3 mixed companies/batteries that are all upgrading to PAC-3 standard, with 7 more PAC 3 companies/batteries on order.
- 1 Skyguard Short Range Airbase Air Defence battalion, with 6 companies/batteries and radar sub units with OTO 35mm AAA, s
- 2 Antelope Short Range Airbase Air Defence battalions, with unknown companies/batteries.
- At least 2 AAA Air Defence Artillery battalions, with 40mm/L60 and 12.7mm AAA guns.
- Air Defence Artillery Training Centre: Pingtung
- Target Service Squadron
- Education Service Support Company
- First training company
- Second training company
- Third training company
- Education, Training & Doctrine Command
- Logistics Command
- Combat Wings
- 401st Tactical Fighter Wing : Hualien AB flying F-16A/B
- 17th Tactical Fighter Group "Thor"
- 26th Tactical Fighter Group "Witch"
- 27th Tactical Fighter Group "Black Dragon"
- 12th Tactical Reconnaissance Squadron "Tiger Gazer" (operates both RF-16 and 6 RF-5E)
- 427th Tactical Fighter Wing: Ching Chuan Kang/CCK AB flying F-CK-1A/B
- 7th Tactical Fighter Group "Wolf"
- Stood down: 8th Fighter Squadron "Flying Dragon"
- 28th Tactical Fighter Group "Baby Dragon"
- 439th Combined Wing : Pingtung AB flying C-130H,: E-2T/2000, and C-130HE
- 10th Tactical Airlift Group
- 101st Airlift Squadron
- 102nd Airlift Squadron
- 20th Electronic Warfare Group
- 6th Electronic Warfare Squadron
- 2nd Early Warning Squadron

- 443rd Tactical Fighter Wing : Tainan Air Base flying F-CK
- 1st Tactical Fighter Group
- 3rd Tactical Fighter Group
- 9th Tactical Fighter Group
- 455th Tactical Fighter Wing : Chiayi AB flying F-16 and S-70C
- Air Rescue Group
- 21st Tactical Fighter Group
- 22nd Tactical Fighter Group
- 23rd Tactical Fighter Group
- 499th Tactical Fighter Wing : Hsinchu AB flying Mirage 2000
- 41st Tactical Fighter Group "Holy Shield"
- 42nd Tactical Fighter Group "Cobra"
- 48th Training Group "Holy Eagle"
- 737th Fighter Training Wing : Taitung AB flying F-5E/F
- 44th Fighter Squadron
- 45th Fighter Squadron
- 46th Fighter Squadron
- Makung Air Base Command : Has one squadron of F-CK-1 from either CCK.
- Air Force Base Command
- Sungshan Base Command
- VIP Transport Squadron, with Boeing 737 (Air Force One), Fokker 50, and B-1900.
- Air Force Academy: Kangshan AB
- Basic Training Group, with T-34
- Advance Jet/Fighter Training Group, with AT-3
- Transport Training Group, with several of Sungshan air base's VIP Transport Squadron B-1900s.

Sources:

History

Formally established in 1920 as the Aviation Ministry, the ROCAF was active during the tenure of the ROC on Mainland China. In this period, various airplanes were purchased and deployed by warlords in their struggle for power until nominalChinese reunification in 1928. In February 1932, US Reserve Lt. Robert McCawley Short, who was transporting armed Chinese aircraft, shot down an IJN aircraft on February 19, 1932 and downed another on February 22 before he was killed (he was posthumously raised to the rank of Colonel in the Chinese Air Service).

During the Second Sino-Japanese War (1937–1945), the ROCAF participated in attacks on Japanese warships on the eastern front and along the Yangtze river including support for the Battle of Shanghai in 1937. The Chinese frontline fighter aircraft initially were mainly the Curtiss Hawk II and III and the Boeing P-26 model 281, and engaged Japanese fighters in many major air battles beginning on August 14, 1937, when Imperial Japanese Navy warplanes raided Chienchiao airbase; "814" has thus become known as "Air Force Day".

Chinese Boeing P-26/281 fighters engaged Japanese Mitsubishi A5M fighters in what is among the world's first aerial dogfighting between all-metal monoplane fighter aircraft. A unique mission in April 1938 saw two Chinese B-10 bombers fly a mission over Japan, but dropping only propaganda leaflets over the Japanese cities of Nagasaki and Saga. It was a war of attrition for the Chinese pilots, as many of their most experienced ace fighter pilots, such as Lieutenant Liu Tsui-Kang and Colonel Kao Chih-Hang were lost early in the war.

In the latter-half of the Sino-Japanese War, part of World War II, the ROCAF was augmented by a volunteer group of American pilots (theFlying Tigers) in 1941. Throughout the war, the ROCAF was involved in attacks on Japanese air and ground forces in the Chinese theatre.

ROCAF General HQ was established in June 1946. From 1946 to 1948, during the Chinese Civil War, the ROCAF participated in combat against the People's Liberation Army engaging in air to air combat on at least eleven occasions in the areas surrounding the Taiwan Strait.

The ROCAF reportedly enjoyed a 31:1 kill ratio against the PLA. GHQ was evacuated to Taiwan along with the rest of the ROC Government in April 1949 following the Communist victory in the Chinese Civil War. The ROCAF assisted in halting the PLA advance at the Battle of Kuningtou on Kinmen the same year.

The ROCAF regularly patrolled the Taiwan Straits and fought many engagements with its Communist counterpart (the PLAAF). The ROCAF received second hand equipment from the US at that time, such as the F-86 Sabrejets, F-100 and F-104.

During the Cold War, the ROCAF was involved in combat air patrols over the Taiwan Strait and engaged the PLAAF and PLAN-AF on several occasions. The ROCAF was also the testbed of American technology at this time. The first successful kill scored by an air-to-air missile was accomplished by an

ROCAF F-86 Sabrejet with then experimental AIM-9 Sidewinder. ROCAF pilots also flew U-2 recon overflights of the PRC during this time with assistance from the USAF.

Known as the Black Cat Squadron they flew a total of 220 missions, with 102 missions over mainland China, losing 5 planes. All five were shot down by SA-2 surface-to-air missiles, the same type of surface-to-air missile that shot down Gary Powers over the USSR in 1960. The 34th "Black Bat Squadron" flew low level missions into China as part of its mapping PRC growing air defence networks, conducting ESM and ECM missions, inserting agents behind enemy lines, and air drop resupply missions.

2

Indian Air Power

Airpower or air power comprises the application of military strategy and strategic theory to the realm of aerial warfare. Airpower began with the advent of mechanized flight early in the 20th century. Airpower represents a "complex operating environment that has been subjected to considerable debate". British doctrine defines airpower as "the ability to project power from the air and space to influence the behaviour of people or the course of events."

Airpower is a function of air supremacy and numbers. Roughly speaking, a combatant side that has 100% or near 100% control of the skies has air supremacy; an advantage of some 70–90% would indicate air superiority. A 50/50 split is air parity; lower than this, one side may be said to be air denied or air incapable.

Because airplanes generally take off from designed airfields on missions typically involving some hours of cruising, the precise state of air superiority is fluid and less defined vis-a-vis land or sea warfare. For example, a conteste dairspace directly above a battlespace bristling with anti-aircraft weapons may be denied to the airforces of both sides. Further, the completely different situations of a technologically advanced airforce with one flight of high-tech planes (air supremacy but low capacity) or a low-tech force of massive numbers of low-tech planes (e.g., An-2) resulting in high capacity but low long-term survivability demonstrate that 'air power' is multi-faceted and complex.

Significant contributors to theorizing about air power have been Giulio Douhet, Billy Mitchell, John Boyd and John A. Warden III.

Some early strategists/visionaries after World War I imagined that airpower alone would suffice to bring nations to their knees. TheBombing of Guernica was an early trial that revealed both capabilities and limitations. But yet another maxim, "no war was ever won solely by airpower" was challenged by the NATO victory in Kosovo. Airpower has been used to conduct lightning strategic strikes, to complement land offensives, to instill fear and lower morale similarly to a fleet in being, and to create broad-based destruction behind enemy lines. With airpower, supplies can be transported by cargo planes, providing a decisive edge in mobility.

Military and civilian aircraft interact in a number of complex ways, including shootdowns of civilian planes, whether mistaken or not; military escorts of civilian planes; civilian planes being used for military transport, espionage, or other purposes; and/or no-fly zones being enforced to punish or sanction a target nation. Airpower also relates to space power, although militarization of space remains regulated by international treaty.

Developed nations have enjoyed a consistent advantage in airpower since the beginning of mechanized flight. Airpower has been wielded mostly decisively in the last hundred years by Nazi Germany, the United Kingdom, the United States, the Soviet Union, Japan, Italy, and France, with many client nations using aircraft developed by one or more of these nations. A mass technological base is considered necessary for the development of airpower.

AIR POWER AT WORK

In recent weeks there have been numerous reports of outstanding victories by valiant Indian jawans who regained control of significant peaks in the Kargil sector from Pakistan Army infiltrators. There are also reports of the successes of the Indian Air Force (IAF), which is causing damage to the enemy's emplacements, infrastructure on the hills and stocks of food and ammunition, flying over difficult terrain and hostile heights.

Before discussing the IAF operations, it is important to understand the conditions in which the aircraft fly. As they move through air, the flow over the wings (of the planes) and over the rotor blades (of helicopters) provides a lifting force to support the craft in the sky. At high altitudes, the air density is lower than what it is at lower heights, for which the planes are designed. Consequently, in the rarefied atmosphere, for the same forward speed the corresponding lifting force is reduced.

The terrain in and around Kargil is between 4,572 metres and 5,486 m above sea level. The aircraft are, therefore, required to fly at altitudes of about 6,100 m. The density of the air at these heights is roughly 30 per cent less than that of the air at sea level. This causes a reduction in the weight that can be carried, and also the pilot's ability to manoeuvre as the radius of a turn is higher here than at lower levels. Also engine performance deteriorates with altitude, as for the same forward speed a smaller mass of air goes into the jet engine of the fighter or the engine of the helicopter, compared to low altitudes.

The airfields nearest to the targets in Kargil are the Srinagar air base and the neighbouring military airfield at Avantipur. Therefore, the IAF has to operate primarily from these two bases. According to media reports, the fixed-wing planes being used for ground attack are mainly the single-seat MiG-21s and MiG-27s. The MiG-21 is the older type of jet fighter, built mainly for air interception with a secondary role of ground attack. Its avionics and weapons are of 1970s vintage. However, this jet fighter can carry one tonne of bombs or four pods of rockets in addition to its 23-mm cannon. It is capable of operating in comparatively restricted spaces, which is of importance in the Kargil terrain.

The swing-wing MiG-27 is an airplane optimised for attacking targets on the ground. It can carry a load of roughly four tonnes, which could be a mix of various weapons, including a 23-mm cannon, rocket pods, multiple carriage free fall bombs of various weights and varieties (for example, the MiG-27 can carry 18 bombs each weighing 100 kg in addition to a 23-mm multiple-barrelled cannon), retarded bombs and smart weapons. It has a computerised bomb sight, which enables accurate weapon delivery. Its variable geometry wings are kept forward at 14o sweep for take-off and landing, and whenever required to fly at slow speeds. The other two sweep-back positions are for combat and for high-speed getaway. The MiG-27 is, therefore, ideal for the high altitude and mountainous terrain of Kargil.

The state-of-the-art Indian Mirage-2000 planes conduct electronic warfare, reconnaissance and a few sorties of ground attack, for which a great deal of accuracy is needed, using the 'smart' weapons that this plane can carry.

Because of the need to engage Pakistani targets in the valleys and on ridges, the slower helicopter gunship became a critically important requirement. The Mi-17 was hence modified to carry four rocket pods on external pylons. Each pod has a capacity of 16 or 32 air-to-ground rockets. This helicopter is proving very effective in engaging Pakistani bunkers and troops although one helicopter and its four crew members have been lost to a U.S.-made Stinger surface-to-air heat-seeking missile fired by Pakistani troops. It is understood that the Mi-17s being used in Kargil are also being fitted with additional safety features in order to protect the air crew. It is a pity that the infra-red flares, which the helicopter can carry and release to decoy heat-seeking missiles, were not imported.

The other helicopter in use is the Cheetah. The agile, light and small Cheetah is used to stay outside Pakistani gun range, locate enemy targets and direct artillery fire onto Pakistani targets. It is also used as an airborne Forward Air Controller (FAC) to guide Indian fighters to the targets.

In the high mountains, air crew face some difficulties in carrying out their operational missions. As aircraft performance is lowered in the rarefied atmosphere, pilots have to be very careful while flying in the valleys. The larger radius of turn reduces their ability to manoeuvre in the restricted width of the valley. It also increases the height lost in a pullout from a dive attack. Hence the pullout has to be initiated at a greater height. Therefore, the weapon release heights have to be raised correspondingly. This may cause inaccuracies in the aiming of weapons. The non-standard air density also affects the trajectory of weapons, which has been calculated for sea-level firing. The firing hence may not be accurate. In the mountains, be they in the valleys or on the ridges, the targets are relatively small, spread out and difficult to spot, particularly by high-speed fighter jets. This becomes worse in low visibility conditions or when there is clouding en route or over the target.

The operations restricted to just the Kargil area do not lend themselves to the classical use of air power. There is also the major constraint of the political requirement of not crossing the Line of Control (LoC). The IAF is, therefore, not at liberty to use large strike formations with an appropriate weight of attack to destroy the Pakistani supply lines and logistic bases and training camps. Such attacks are needed in order to reduce the pressure on the Indian Army and to obviate the use of these facilities in the near future too. Also, under conditions of large radius of turn because of the thin air and the small and spread-out nature of the targets in the mountains, it becomes difficult not to transgress the LoC unless the direction of attack is parallel to the LoC. The terrain configuration and the location of the target may not always make it possible.

These are some challenges faced by IAF planners and crews operating in Kargil. However, one learns to overcome these difficulties and find solutions with ingenuity, determination and practice. The IAF regularly exercises its fighter squadrons in high-altitude operations and has an air-to-ground firing range for practice in Ladakh. It needs to be noted that the IAF is the only air force in the world that carries out war operations in the mountains at such high altitudes and in such difficult terrain as in the Kargil area near the LoC. Crews of the IAF, the modern-day gladiators, are second to none in dedication, combat-worthiness, grit and professionalism.

On a typical day of operations, if the first few missions are to be on target at first light (20 minutes before sunrise), the pilots report to their fight offices about two hours before the Time On Target (TOT). After a short medical examination by the unit doctor and after changing into their combat flying kit, they are briefed on the weather at the base, at the alternative airfields and in the target area. They are told about the results of the previous sorties and given the latest intelligence reports. The Fight Commander then tells them about the specific target, the composition of the force, the weapons to be carried and the TOT. The Ground Liaison Officer (GLO), generally an Army officer, gives the latest Sitrep (Situation Report), details of the strike demand from the Army, radio call signs of the FAC in the target area and a detailed target description with photographs, if available. The pilots then pencil the route on their maps, calculate the transit time to the target, and thus the time of take-off. The take-off time is conveyed to the ATC and to the GLO. The ATC coordinates the mission with the rest of the expected air traffic and the GLO conveys the TOT to the Army formation and the FAC in the target area. The formation leader then briefs the other pilots in the strike mission with regard to the relative positions to be flown by each aircraft in the formation and the tactics to be adopted. The pilots have a quick cup of coffee and biscuits or sandwiches and proceed to the airplanes.

In the meantime, technicians carry out pre-night checks and inspections on the planes to be flown, refuel them and charge oxygen. The armourers load the ammunition, rockets, the infra-red decoy flares and any other ordnance that is required to get the aircraft ready for the mission. When the pilots arrive, the ground crew strap them up in the cockpit. In the technology-intensive world of military aviation there has to be close teamwork among the pilots, the technicians, the ATC controllers, the GLOs, the administrative and logistic personnel and so on. This close teamwork and interdependence creates a visible and strong camaraderie among them.

Regardless of how brave the pilots are, before a mission they tend to lose their appetite and sense of humour, and no amount of water quenches their thirst. However, once they get busy with the pre-night cockpit checks, the fear of the unknown is forgotten and professionalism and peer pride take over. The pilot is then busy and businesslike. On his return from a trip, the appetite and humour are back. On returning from a mission, pilots debrief each other. They are then debriefed by the GLO and the Fight Commander on what they had seen at and around the target area, about the damage inflicted on the enemy and if, in their view, there is further need for attacks on the same target. After each mission a new and a bigger picture about the enemy emerges. This is transmitted to the Army and the higher formations of the IAF. This new information also becomes part of the intelligence briefing for subsequent missions. In the meantime, the pilots of the next formation absorb all available information and stand by for their mission. The next team of gladiators is ready.

INDIA-THE QUEST FOR AIR POWER PROJECTION

India, along with China, is an emerging world power. For a long time India was more inward-looking and fixed on the conflict with Pakistan about Kashmir. As an emerging world power, India has its vital interests.

The protection of the supply flow of oil and gas from far away regions is one of India's most significant vital interests. Securing this supply is the aim and objective of political, diplomatic, economic and military actions. In the strategic triangle – China, India and the United States – hard power is an important currency in combination with elements of soft power. Concerning soft power India has a comparative advantage – e.g. its status as a democracy – in comparison to China. But India recognizes that it has to improve its hard power capabilities.

India's defence purchases should be seen as an essential part of the overall security environment that hinges on relations with Pakistan, China and America. The country is slated to spend US$100 billion in modernizing its defence forces over the next decade, with air power being a major component. Since 1999, India's military purchases have been worth US$25 billion; the country is likely to spend another $30 billion by 2012, making it one of the biggest military buyers amongst developing countries.

In the last couple of years India, as the new US strategic partner in Asia to dilute the growing influence of China has been sensitive to US urgings. One critical issue has been relations with Iran, with New Delhi taking a stand against Tehran at international forums. Awash with its new stature as "America's friend," New Delhi has been accused of deliberately delaying the US$7.5 billion, 1600 mile-long Iran-Pakistan-India (IPI) gas pipeline to keep Washington happy.

However, in the recent past the Congress Party-led New Delhi government headed by Prime Minister Manmohan Singh has stood up to the US on Iran, making an effort to emphasize an independent foreign policy not influenced by Washington's ideas.

Earlier this year in May, India hosted for a few hours President Mahmoud Ahmadinejad, the first Iranian head of state to visit India in five years. Although Ahmadinejad's Indian stopover was short on time, it was very high in its symbolic content and laid bare some of New Delhi's strategic thinking. While energy issues remained the main focus of the visit, attention was as much on perceptions of Washington, which has a major problem with Iran's independent nuclear program and has been urging nations, including India, not to deal with Tehran. Indeed, the reasons for India's new approach (standing up to America and appearing neutral in its foreign policy and strategic dealings) are many: Firstly, India desperately needs energy sources, with competitor China equally keen to tap Iran's rich hydrocarbon fields. China has expressed the willingness to join a truncated India-Pakistan-Iran (IPI) pipeline project should India keep away from it. Pakistan has been irked by Washington's pro-India tilt and would be happy to accommodate China. Pakistan's foreign office spokesperson has been quoted to have said that "If there are prospects of China joining the IPI project with or without India, we will welcome it. Pakistan is committed to the pipeline because of its desire to achieve energy security."

Keen to obtain new gas, India has formally joined the Asian Development Bank-sponsored and US-backed Turkmenistan-Afghanistan-Pakistan (TAP) pipeline project that has now been officially renamed as the Turkmenistan-Afghanistan-Pakistan-India (TAPI) gas pipeline.

Secondly, domestic Indian politics play a major role. Political parties will look to label New Delhi as a "US stooge" in the general elections due in the summer next year. There is fear of a backlash from Indian-Muslim voters who constitute a sizable constituency and despise America due to its attack on Iraq and the problems with Iran.

Indications are that whoever wins in the elections next year – be it the Congress Party, the main opposition Bharatiya Janata Party (BJP) or a Third Front formation – they will have to seek outside support from regional parties, many of which rely on Muslim backing. New Delhi's moves can also be seen as an attempt not to completely alienate the anti-US parties of the left, though the two have now fallen out over the Indo-US nuclear deal.

Thirdly, there is also a growing view that New Delhi has to learn how to deal and balance its various national interests in order to sustain a fast-growing Indian economy that is in need of new markets for both export and import. India's gross domestic product (GDP) has been growing at 8-9% per annum over the past few years. A tilt towards the US and an economy heading towards recession will not help matters when business is of concern. Such an approach can have its dividends and result in win-win situations.

INDIA'S BUSINESS IN AVIATION – CIVIL AND MILITARY

Aerospace, both civil and military, is an area of maximum activity in India that is an emerging destination for outsourcing development work and manufacturing aircrafts, including fighter jets. India's transition as a major hub for aviation-civil and defence-is a subject that has been talked about for a while.

Replicating the success in cars, with the south-Indian city Chennai referred to as the "Detroit of India," the country is looking to emerge as a production hub for aircraft as well. The combined reading of both civilian and defence aviation sectors is important as the global players, whether European Aeronautic Defence and Space (EADS), Boeing or Lockheed Martin, overlap.

According to the American Aerospace Industries Association, the bulk of US aerospace contractors are looking to shift business to India. "Apart from global requirements, the firms are keen to tap domestic Indian demand, given the rapidly rising civil aviation sector and air defence efforts." There is a growing base for manufacturing several aircraft components and software with firms such as Hindustan Aeronautics Limited, Tatas (tied to Boeing and Israel Aerospace Industries), Wipro (tied to Lockheed), already involved. Except for software, Boeing and EADS source various components, including aircraft doors, landing gears, window glass and cables for top plane-makers from India.

Domestic offset norms require that foreign defence contractors invest in India's defence industry. The bulk of the military hardware or software is going to be imported given the incipient status of India's indigenous defence industry.

AIR POWER

Chicago-based Boeing, Pentagon's number two defence supplier has said that it plans to bid for US$15 billion of military orders in India over the next 10 years. Boeing is negotiating for the $2 billion P-8i long-range maritime reconnaissance aircrafts for the Indian Navy. Meanwhile, competitor Lockheed Martin has broken into the Indian defence market with a billion dollar deal to sell six Super Hercules aircrafts, the biggest ever Indo-US defence contract.

Competition and lobbying is also going to be intense for the US$11 billion 126 multi-role combat aircraft (MRCA) deal, with a 50% offset clause that India is likely to sign a couple of years from now, for which both Boeing and Lockheed are bidding, apart from others.

Indeed, given the lethargy with which the Indian bureaucracy moves it is due to the almost obsolete state of India's arsenal and enormous pressure from the armed forces that matters are looking up. The Indian Air force (IAF) has begun replacing its Soviet-era MiGs, used for training pilots, with Hawk trainer jets from BAE Systems. In addition to the 66 Advanced Jet Trainers (US$1.45 billion deal signed in 2004), the IAF has sought 40 more.

New Delhi has invited global tenders for 312 light military helicopters to replace the vintage French and Russian fleet procured in the 1960s. Aviation firms in France, Italy, Russia and the US have been approached about the proposal. The IAF and Army have combined their respective orders, following the cancellation of the French Eurocopter deal. India has issued a request for global bids for a $1.5 billion upgrade for its 30 military airports; India and Russia have managed to clear the upgrade of 67 IAF MiG-29 fighter jets.

AVIATION SCENE

EADS

According to reliable media reports, New Delhi is seriously looking at offset options due to purchases from Boeing and EADS, the parent of Airbus and Eurocopter.

Government-run air carriers (Air India and Indian airlines that are now merged) have placed orders of around US$8 billion and more purchases are on the horizon. Indian Airlines had placed an order for 43 aircraft from Airbus (a division of EADS) worth US$2 billion, which carries an offset clause.

EADS has thus proposed Indian investments of 2 billion euros over 15 years. Offsets will also arise out of the $11 billion MRCA deal. One way to use up the investment requirement is to set up assembly units for medium-size civil transport aircraft. This could begin with 70-seater ATRs. According to reports, EADS is looking to closely engage with New Delhi and is open to a "mutually beneficial" arrangement that could also reassess a helicopter contract with Eurocopter for the defence forces. The deal was cancelled due to allegations of discrepancies in field trials, though pressure from the US to re-negotiate the contract played a role. A senior government official was recently quoted to have said that: "To begin with, we are looking to set up an assembly unit for turboprop aircraft with a capacity of 25 to 60 seats. Regional air-connectivity will grow to create adequate demand for any plane-maker to set up a unit."

High growth is expected in India's civil aviation sector despite the recent slow down and losses due to high crude oil prices. According to a recent survey by Airports Council International, the Indian civil aviation industry has grown twofold in the past four years and by 2010 the figures will double again. India's Federal Civil Aviation Minister Praful Patel said that India's air travel industry will need US$50 billion in investment in its infrastructure over the next decade. Patel said the sector, which has seen almost frenzied plane buying and airline launches in the past 4-5 years, would grow by 25-30 % in the near future. Indian aircraft carriers, both private and state owned, are expected to buy nearly 300 new planes by 2010, valued at US$15 billion, and spend another US$15 billion in the following decade.

Boeing

Boeing has said that India's Tata Group will supply parts for its 787 Dreamliner, which has been declared a "turning point" for the Indian aerospace business. A Boeing and Tata joint venture (JV) intends to produce defence-related aerospace components in India, with expected exports of US$500 million initially. In December last year, Boeing and state-owned Hindustan Aeronautics Limited (HAL) signed a deal to transfer more than US$1 billion of aerospace manufacturing work to India. There have also been discussions between the Tata Group and Microbiotics, a US aerospace company, to work out new opportunities in instrumentation and navigation systems. Not to be undone, US defence giant Lockheed has teamed up with top Indian software firm Wipro to produce electronic warfare systems, radars and flight simulators.

Tata Group

Recently, the Tata Group and European aerospace giant EADS agreed to jointly bid for a US$1-billion deal to supply tactical communication systems to the Indian Army. "The teaming arrangement would ensure that the solution proposed is cutting edge and meets all the requirements of the Army," said Tata Group chairman Ratan Tata.

The Tata Group has also signed an agreement with Israel Aerospace Industries for manufacturing a full swathe of defence products, including missiles, unmanned aerial vehicles, radars, electronic warfare and security systems.

Tata is also tying up with US helicopter producer Sikorsky to set up a manufacturing unit in India.

Others

US-based aerospace solutions provider Rockwell Collins (turnover close to US$4.5 billion) is setting up an engineering center at India's technology hub Hyderabad. This is the first such center outside Rockwell's headquarters. Rockwell supplies solutions to private Indian airline carriers, including IndiGo and Jetlite.

India's largest construction firm Larsen & Toubro (L&T) has also signed agreements with Boeing and EADS for joint exploration of businesses in India. Others such as BAE Systems, Bombardier and SAAB are planning forays.

MRCA Deal

Quite a bit of the interest of aviation majors in India has to do with the MRCA deal and the consequent offset norms that will require mandatory investments in India's defence sector of over US$5 billion.

The acquisition of the jet fighters is a crucial cog in India's defence modernization efforts. In April this year, the six contenders for this mega contract submitted their bids to the federal defence ministry, each offering "strategic and unequivocal partnerships" including joint production, government support and advanced jets at the cheapest cost. The request for proposal (RFP) for the deal was issued in August 2007 after delays that span over a decade and a half.

The fighters in the fray are the American Boeing's F/A-18 Super Hornet, Lockheed Martin's F-16 Falcon, Russian MiG-35, Swedish Saab's Gripen, French Dassault Rafale and the Eurofighter Typhoon by the consortium EADS. "We will now seriously examine all the bids and shortlist the companies in due course to two or three, before taking a final decision," a defence ministry spokesperson said. "Even if everything does work out smoothly, we don't expect the first batch of fighters in India before 2011."

Around 20 fighters will be bought off-the-shelf and the remaining ones will be produced in India under a Transfer-of-Technology (ToT) agreement. New Delhi has said in the past that it will ultimately settle for a single fighter jet platform instead of multiple sources. Many defence analysts say that Lockheed and Boeing are front runners to win the jet contract, but the race is far from over, given domestic Indian politics that oppose any US "hegemony" in any sphere, whether actual or apparent, apart from the technical considerations. The delayed Indo-US defence deal is one example.

"The protection of the supply flow of oil and gas from far away regions is one of India's most significant vital interests."

AIRPOWER AT 18,000′: THE INDIAN AIR FORCE IN THE KARGIL WAR

"Aviators have traditionally been a haughty breed. They are used to spending solitary hours with their machines, aloof, on top of the world, far removed from its mundane troubles. Everything that seemed important on terra firma becomes so much smaller. In the cockpit, few things can humble this pride. The mountains can. When you fly at the roof of the world and still have the impassive peaks of the mighty Himalayas look down on you at Flight Level 200, your perspective changes. The experience of air warfare in mountains teaches stern lessons. The aviator must respect the mountains."

An Indian Air Force Mirage 2000 pilot who flew in the Kargil War

The Indian Air Force (IAF) is the world's fourth-largest air service, operating more than 1,300 aircraft out of some 60 bases nationwide. It also is one of the world's oldest continuously functioning air forces, with roots going back to October 8, 1932, when it was established by Great Britain's Royal Air Force as an auxiliary of the Indian Empire during the time of the British Raj. Until the early 1990s, it was principally a support entity for the Indian Army.

Today, it has acquired independent strategic missions, most notably including those of nuclear deterrence and retaliation, and it is a diversified fighting force with manifest ambitions toward global reach and status. It also is a full-spectrum combat air arm with a precision conventional strike capability, fielding not only fourth-generation multirole fighters, but also force-extending tankers, a recently acquired airborne warning and control system capability, intertheater airlifters, unmanned aerial vehicles equipped with multispectral sensors for longdwell strategic and tactical reconnaissance, and the beginnings of a military space surveillance capability.

The field of strategic regard in which this maturing force most centrally figures now extends from the east coast of Africa to Sumatra and the entire Indian Ocean operating area. Like few other air arms around the world, the IAF operates over the most diverse range of geographic areas, from the Siachen glacier in the north to the deserts, jungles, and oceans that surround India's periphery. A former air officer commanding-in-chief (AOC-in-C) of the IAF's Western Air Command well captured the IAF leadership's now oft-expressed characterization of the steadily modernizing service when he wrote in 2009 of the IAF's "growing aspirations to transform itself from a mere subcontinental tactical force to an intercontinental strategic aerospace power in conformity with other leading air forces in the world."

India's principal external challengers—and hence the IAF's main objects of strategic and operational concern—are China and Pakistan, in that order.

China is generally regarded by the Indian defence community as posing a more downstream source of potential trouble, whereas Pakistan is deemed both a longer-term *and* a here-and-now threat to the country's security. Because both India and its two leading rivals all possess well-stocked inventories of readily available nuclear weapons, most planners in New Delhi assess the likelihood of an all-out war on the subcontinent as being quite low. The uppermost concern of the IAF leadership with respect to combat readiness today entails operating decisively at a conventional level against either rival when all sides in any conflict will be within immediate reach of a nuclear response option.

Given this omnipresent risk of escalation, most Indian threat assessors believe that any future combat engagement with either China or Pakistan will, in all likelihood, be sharp and intense but also brief and for limited stakes. In this regard, an official IAF publication released in 2007 frankly acknowledged the "likely short duration" of any war that India may have to contend with in the near-term future. The most probable prospect, according to retired IAF Air Commodore Jasjit Singh, is for "prolonged periods of peace with spurts of armed violence of great variety."

In a thoughtful enumeration of the diverse conflict possibilities that could confront Indian security planners in the next decade, a retired IAF air marshal in 2007 listed as being among the most plausible of those possibilities an extended border war with China, with little likelihood of nuclear weapons use; a shorter and more intense war with Pakistan entailing a very real chance of nuclear use—unlike India, Pakistan has never proclaimed a nuclear no-first-use policy; a simultaneous war with China and Pakistan operating in collusion; and a prolonged lower-intensity war in Kashmir against both Pakistani regular forces and indigenous Kashmiri insurgents.

An instructive preview of this last type of conflict scenario can be seen in the Kargil War that unfolded in the high mountains of Indian-controlled Kashmir in May, June, and July 1999. That intense border clash for limited but important stakes, which ensued for seventy-four days at a cost of more than a thousand casualties on each side, was overshadowed by NATO's higher-profile air war for Kosovo that occurred thousands of miles away in the Balkans at roughly the same time. In large part because of that more attention-getting distraction, the Kargil War remains only dimly appreciated by most Western defence experts—and barely at all by students and practitioners of airpower.

Western defence professionals have much to gain from a closer inquiry into this little-known chapter in the history of air warfare.

Nevertheless, it was a milestone event in Indian military history and one that represents a telling prototype of India's most likely type of future combat challenge in the immediate years ahead. No less important, it offers both an exemplary case study in the uses of airpower in joint warfare and a particularly revealing testament to the special difficulties of modern air employment in high mountain conditions. The Kargil experience is key to a proper understanding of India's emerging air posture because it constitutes the one instance of recent Indian exposure to high-intensity warfare that provides insights into the IAF's capabilities, limitations, relations with its sister services, and interactions with India's civilian leadership.

The conflict was also emblematic of one type of border skirmish between India and Pakistan, and perhaps also between India and China, that could recur in the next decade in light of the inhibiting effect of the nuclear overhang on more protracted and higher-stakes tests of strength. As retired Air Commodore Singh reflected on the experience six years after its successful conclusion for India, the conflict was "a typical example of a limited war in a nuclear weapons environment." For all these reasons, Western defence professionals have much to gain from a closer inquiry into this little-known chapter in the history of air warfare.

PRELUDE TO A SHOWDOWN

Flare-ups along the border between Pakistan and India have a long history, going back as far as 1947 when British rule of the subcontinent ended and the former British Indian Empire was subdivided into the newly independent Union of India and the Dominion of Pakistan. That development prompted Pakistan to launch a guerilla incursion into Kashmir in an attempt to establish control over the contested region. The Indian Army and the IAF countered in force by entering Kashmir and driving the Pakistani-sponsored irregulars out of all but a small portion of the high mountain state.

The seeds of the Kargil conflict were first planted in March and April 1999. Then, determined units of the Pakistan Army crossed the Line of Control (LoC) into the Indian portion of contested Kashmir in the remote and rugged Himalayan heights overlooking Kargil between the Kashmir Valley and the Ladakh plateau. The LoC running through Jammu and Kashmir that separates the Indian-held and Pakistani-controlled portions of the disputed territory is a long-standing product of the third Indo-Pakistani war that created Bangladesh. It bisects some of the most forbidding terrain to be found anywhere in the world, with most of the main ridgelines being offshoots of K2, the world's second-highest mountain.

While preparations were under way for an upcoming meeting of India's and Pakistan's prime ministers in Lahore, Pakistan, senior leaders in the Pakistan Army, led by the chief of the Army Staff, General Pervez Musharraf, and the chief of the General Staff, Lieutenant General Mohammed Aziz, were conducting initial reconnaissance and laying the logistical groundwork for the impending operation. The most likely aim of the planned gambit, apart from seeking to internationalize the Kashmir issue in Indo-Pakistani relations, was to take control of India's sole line of communication to troops on the Siachen glacier by obstructing the use of the key two-lane national highway NH1A in Ladakh running from Srinagar through Kargil to Leh. It provided access to the IAF's airfield at Thoise on the axis to Siachen.

The incursion's planners took full advantage of the relaxed atmosphere that had come to prevail in New Delhi after the visit of Prime Minister Atal Vajpayee to Pakistan to help promulgate the Lahore Declaration, which was signed by Vajpayee and his Pakistani counterpart, Nawaz Sharif, on February 21. With it, the governments of both countries swore their commitment to the vision of peace and stability embodied in the United Nations charter. The Pakistan Army leaders chose to exploit the nascent, and ultimately short-lived, feeling of goodwill that had emanated from that declaration in a way that might irreversibly change the status quo along the LoC to Pakistan's advantage.

Because of the capricious weather that predominates in the area, the Indian Army during the harshest winter months that immediately preceded the Kargil crisis vacated its most inhospitable forward outposts—typically at elevations of 14,000 to 18,000 feet—that were normally manned on India's side of the LoC throughout the remainder of the year. Since substantial gaps existed in India's defences in the segment of Kashmir that lay on both sides of the LoC, a segment featuring very few trails leading off from the main roadways, the Pakistani planners thought the vacated outposts made prime targets for seizure.

Adding further to the attractiveness of the planned gambit, the outposts were situated on easily defended high ground that Indian troops would have to attack from below in order to try to recapture them. A clever mix of regular combat troops and local civilian porters would infiltrate the area and present the Indian government with a fait accompli in Kashmir.

Pakistan's military leaders were all but surely emboldened by their country's acquisition of a nuclear weapons delivery capability within the preceding year. They may also have been encouraged by a derivative belief that the awareness of that capability in key leadership circles in New Delhi would more than offset any conventional military advantage India enjoyed in the region. And even if the operation were to be detected by India while it was still in progress, the incursion's planners likely judged that the Indian Army's reaction to it would be slow and limited at best. Most important, they probably took it as a foregone conclusion that were India to seek to conventionalize the ensuing conflict, pressure from the international community would quickly intervene and force the Vajpayee government to cease combat operations within a week, thus leaving Pakistan "comfortably in possession of gains it would make by infiltration," in the words of retired Indian Army Major General G. D. Bakshi.

Ultimately, in what turned out to be a phased infiltration in uniquely challenging mountain terrain, Pakistani troops moving by foot and helicopter occupied roughly 130 outposts on India's side of the LoC before the intruders were first detected by local shepherds on May 3. At least eighteen artillery batteries, most of them from across the LoC in Pakistani-controlled territory, were said to have supported the operation. Indian sources later reported that the occupying force numbered from 1,500 to 2,000 combatants, with perhaps four to five times that many troops mobilized to help supply the most forward elements on the Indian side of the LoC. The occupying troop contingent consisted mainly of elements of the local Pakistan Army Northern Light Infantry (NLI) and members of Pakistan's elite Special Services Group, with many outfitted in civilian garb so as to appear as indigenous Kashmiri mujahideen. The intruders were well armed, well trained in mountain warfare, and accustomed to operating at high elevations.

India's security principals and other informed experts have freely admitted that the Pakistan Army achieved "complete strategic and tactical surprise" in its execution of the incursion, owing to its having relied on inplace NLI formations rather than moving in a heavier troop contingent that would have generated a larger deployment signature. The incursion's organizers further sought plausible deniability of any culpability for their aggressive action through the use of a shrewd deception measure. They generated indigenous militant Islamist radio traffic within Pakistani-occupied Kashmir to convince Indian signals intelligence monitors that the incursion was insurgent activity over which Pakistan had no control. Finally, the intruders took special care to move only at times that would allow them to avoid detection by periodic Indian winter air surveillance operations.

As the Indian Army units that had manned the temporarily vacated outposts began returning to their stations during the first week of May, they slowly discovered the full extent of the occupation of those positions by Pakistani troops. The Indian Army's 121st Infantry Brigade assigned to monitor the LoC above Kargil launched a succession of probing patrols on May 5 that confirmed the infiltration. The full scale of the intrusions was validated on May 8 by IAF pilots in Cheetah light helicopters as they flew surveillance sorties along the Tololing ridge in the Dras subsector of the Kargil region.

It took more than a week in all for the Indian Army to take stock of its challenge at hand and to develop the beginnings of a course of action to drive the invaders out. Even then, the army's local commanders grossly underestimated and, accordingly, misreported the full magnitude of the situation they were facing. As late as May 19, Lieutenant General Krishan Pal, the commander of 15 Corps that represented the Indian Army's main fighting presence in Kashmir, was said to have been "blissfully oblivious [of] the deathly situation." At a key Unified Headquarters meeting in Srinagar to discuss next steps for addressing the situation, he predicted that in the coming showdown, the incursion "would be defeated locally." Other reporting up the line by the Indian Army offered soothing assurances that "the infiltration will be vacated in 48 hours." Clearly, local ground commanders in Kargil and Srinagar did not appreciate the full gravity of the Pakistani challenge at the start of the gathering crisis.

Once they understood more fully what had transpired along the LoC, the army's leaders finally responded by moving five infantry divisions, five independent brigades, and 44 battalions from the Kashmir Valley to the Kargil sector, ultimately mobilizing some 200,000 Indian troops in all. Most of this buildup occurred during the three weeks between the initial detection of the incursion and the eventual start on May 26 of a major joint counteroffensive codenamed Operation Vijay (meaning "victory" in Hindi). The avowed objectives were to drive out the intruding forces and to restore the LoC to its previous status. The response was almost certainly more determined than anything the Pakistan Army leaders had anticipated.

ENLISTING THE IAF'S INVOLVEMENT

After several early firefights with the entrenched Pakistanis that occasioned numerous Indian fatalities in an unsuccessful bid to recapture the closest of the occupied positions, the Indian Army approached the IAF on May 11 and asked it to help turn the tide through a commitment of armed helicopters to support the embattled ground troops. Conflicting views persist to this day regarding what happened over the ensuing two weeks after that initial army entreaty with respect to when and how the IAF should become involved in the conduct of India's looming counteroffensive.

One view maintains that the IAF initiated combat operations over Kargil only "reluctantly" and sought "to avoid involvement in the conflict altogether, claiming inexperience in mountain warfare and unfamiliarity with the terrain, as well as the risk associated with the heightened SAM [surface-to-air-missile] threat in the mountains." That view holds that the IAF committed itself to the fight only after an insistent demand for such involvement from the Indian Army leadership. This interpretation drew much of its claim to veracity from an assessment by an Indian civilian defence writer that appeared shortly after the war ended. The writer alleged that once the extent of the Pakistani intrusions was discovered, the IAF at first "sidestepped requests by the army to attack the infiltrators" and agreed to lend its support to the ongoing fighting only after its leadership "was presented with a *fait accompli* and pressed [presumably by higher government authority] into making attacks on May 26."

In truth, the IAF began conducting initial reconnaissance sorties over the Kargil heights as early as May 10, less than a week after the presence of the enemy incursion was first confirmed by Indian Army patrols. It also began deploying additional aircraft into the Kashmir Valley in enough numbers to support any likely combat tasking, established a rudimentary air defence control arrangement there because there were no groundbased radars in the area, and began extensive practice of air-to-ground weapons deliveries by both fighters and attack helicopters at Himalayan target elevations. On May 12, an IAF helicopter was fired upon near the most forward-based Pakistani positions overlooking Kargil and landed uneventfully with a damaged rotor. That hostile act prompted Air Headquarters to place Western Air Command, the IAF unit responsible for the Jammu and Kashmir sectors, on heightened alert and to establish quick-reaction aircraft launch facilities at the IAF's northernmost operating locations at Air Force Stations Srinagar and Avantipur.

The next day, IAF Jaguar fighters conducted tactical reconnaissance sorties in the Kargil area to gather prospective target information using their onboard long-range oblique photography systems, and a forward direction center for the tactical control of combat aircraft was established at the IAF's highest-elevation airfield at Air Force Station Leh.

Concurrently, Canberra PR57 and MiG25R reconnaissance aircraft were pressed into service over Kargil, and electronic intelligence missions began to be flown regularly by the IAF in the vicinity of the detected intrusion and beyond. Finally, on May 14, Air Headquarters activated the IAF's air operations center for Jammu and Kashmir and mobilized its fielded forces in that sector for a possible all-out air counteroffensive. At the same time, in close conjunction with their 15 Corps counterparts, Western Air Command planners developed a tailored concept of operations for kinetic air employment in the Kargil heights that included target-selection procedures, force deconfliction and other safety criteria, and an arrangement for conducting and communicating prompt battle damage assessment. From the very start, the IAF expected that it would be engaged in earnest against the intruders just as soon as it and the army leadership could agree on a final course of action. As the AOC-in-C of the IAF's Western Air Command at the time, Air Marshal Vinod Patney, later affirmed, "we were ready for a full-fledged war and had been for some days before May 25, 1999, when government clearance [to commit the IAF to combat] was received."

In an effort to set the record straight once and for all, since-retired Air Chief Marshal Anil Tipnis, who was chief of the Air Staff at the time of the incursion and who later oversaw the IAF's response, offered a detailed reconstruction in October 2006 of his own recollections regarding the sequence of events during the high command's initial deliberations about the Kargil crisis. As Tipnis recalled, on May 10, a full week after the incursion was first detected and the Indian Army had attempted an initial armed response on its own, his vice chief, Air Marshal Prithvi Singh Brar, informed him of a report passed up the line that morning by the IAF's assistant chief of staff for intelligence that the army "may be in some sort of difficulties in the Kargil area." Queried by Tipnis as to the nature of the rumoured difficulties, the vice chief replied that he was not sure but that "there reportedly was unusual artillery firing."

Tipnis learned later that day that the ground force organization responsible for the Kargil sector, Northern Army Command, had communicated nothing of its ongoing operations to its assigned provider of air support in case of hostilities along the LoC, the IAF's Western Air Command. The next day, Tipnis's vice chief told him that his army counterpart had indicated that the army "could handle the situation." Tipnis further learned that Northern Army Command had asked the local air officer commanding (AOC) for Jammu and Kashmir to provide immediate fire support by Mi-25 and Mi-35 helicopter gunships and armed Mi-17 helicopters to "evict a few 'intruders' who had stepped across the LoC in the Kargil sector." The AOC replied that the high terrain over which the requested support was to be provided lay above the effective operating envelope of the helicopters. He added that if the army genuinely needed significant air support for its operations, it would need to convey that requirement to higher headquarters for detailed consideration and approval.

In the meantime, Tipnis's vice chief again pulsed his army counterpart as to whether Northern Army Command really needed help from the IAF. As Tipnis recalled, the army vice "had expressed the army's ability to manage, but was upset that AOC Jammu and Kashmir had not acceded to Headquarters Northern Command's fire-support demand." At that, Tipnis recalled, "there was no doubt in my mind that the situation was desperate." Because committing airpower in close proximity to the LoC could dangerously escalate the conflict, Tipnis insisted that the army "needed political clearance" before the IAF could provide the requested fire support. He also ruled out any employment of IAF armed helicopters because they would be "sitting ducks" for enemy infrared surface-to-air-missile fire. Fixed-wing fighters, he said, would be essential for mission effectiveness, and the IAF "reserved the prerogative to give fire support in the manner it considered most suitable." To this, the army vice chief responded that "the army was capable of throwing back the intruders on its own" but, as Tipnis recalled, that doing so would take time and that air support from the IAF would hasten the process. The army vice continued to insist that such support be provided solely in the form of armed helicopters.

Facing this continued impasse in his dealing with the army, Tipnis called a meeting of his most senior subordinates at Air Headquarters on May 15 to review the known events as they had played out thus far. After being briefed on the situation, the air chief issued this assessment and direction:

I observed that the ground situation was grave. Army required air force help to evict the intruders. Army Headquarters was reluctant, possibly because it was embarrassed to have allowed the present situation to develop, to reveal the full gravity of the situation to the Ministry of Defence. Thus it was not amenable to Air Headquarters' position to seek government approval for use of airpower offensively.

Tipnis then reiterated his determination that despite the army's continued insistence on the use of helicopters in a fire-support role, such use would continue to be denied by the IAF because the helicopters "would be vulnerable in the extreme."

The following day, Tipnis met with the army vice chief at the latter's request (the army chief, General Ved Malik, was out of the country on official travel). The army vice chief once again pressed his request for immediate support by armed helicopters.

Air Marshal Patney proposed that Tipnis call a Chiefs of Staff Committee meeting to seek high-level closure once and for all on the IAF's involvement in the coming counteroffensive. In the meeting, Tipnis reiterated the need for prior government approval for any introduction of Indian airpower into the looming fight, since the chance that such a commitment could trigger a major escalation of the fighting was, in his view, very high.

As for the manner in which the army had responded to the crisis in its assessment and conduct up to that point, Tipnis recalled that there had been a *total lack of army-air force joint staff work. When the army found itself in difficulties, information/intelligence had not been communicated by Army Headquarters in any systematic manner to Air Headquarters. There had been no call for a joint briefing, leave alone joint planning, both at the service and command headquarters; just repeated requests for armed helicopter support.... There had been no joint deliberations at any level.*

On May 23, General Malik, having since returned to New Delhi, summoned Tipnis and the chief of the Naval Staff, Admiral Sushil Kumar, to his office. As Tipnis recalled,

His main thrust was that we needed to put up a united front to the CCS [Cabinet Committee on Security].... Ved said the air force had to join in as the army was in a difficult position. I told him that there was no doubt of that and the air force was very keen to join in, my only reservation being in respect of the use of helicopters—they would be too vulnerable.

After going back and forth with Tipnis on the helicopter issue, General Malik retorted, "If that's the way you want it, I will go it alone." Tipnis eventually gave in "against [his] better judgment" out of a desire "to save army-air force relations."

The next day, the Chiefs of Staff Committee met and adopted a unanimous stance regarding what should be done with respect to the intrusion. In the end, it took the incontrovertible evidence of the reconnaissance imagery provided by the IAF and by other sources for the army chief to realize the full extent of the problem and to agree to take the issue to the prime minister.

During a pivotal May 25 meeting of the Cabinet Committee on Security (whose members were the prime minister, defence minister, home minister, finance minister, and external affairs minister) chaired by Prime Minister Vajpayee, General Malik explained the seriousness of the situation in the Kargil sector and the need for the IAF "to step in without delay." At that, Vajpayee reportedly said: "OK, get started tomorrow at dawn." Tipnis then asked the prime minister for permission to cross the LoC while attacking enemy targets on India's side of the LoC. To that, Vajpayee responded adamantly: "No. No crossing the LoC." With that binding rule of engagement firmly stipulated by the civilian leadership, the die was finally cast for full-scale IAF involvement in the counteroffensive. Later the same day, Tipnis paid an incognito visit to the IAF's main operating base in Kashmir at Srinagar for an on-scene assessment of the situation. While there, he personally assured the commander of 15 Corps that his troops taking fire would receive all needed air support.

To be sure, Tipnis's seemingly conclusive firsthand recollection in no way closed the books on the interservice contretemps over the delay in getting the IAF engaged in the campaign. On the contrary, while not contesting the basic facts as outlined by the air chief, a former Indian Army vice chief lambasted Tipnis for, among other things, having refused to honour Northern Army Command's request for immediate on-call attack helicopter support, having voiced allegedly baseless concern over the chance that the introduction of airpower could result in escalation, and having delayed IAF involvement in the fighting until political approval by the Cabinet Committee on Security was first sought and granted. The former army vice chief went on to author an even more outspoken litany of similar complaints in 2009, which prompted, in close succession, a point-by-point rebuttal by a retired IAF air marshal; a riposte against that rebuttal from the former army vice chief; and a more authoritative rebuttal from another retired air marshal who had been the AOC for Jammu and Kashmir during the lead-up to and conduct of the Kargil operation. Despite the testy interservice back and forth both at the outset of planning for the campaign and later, the IAF was fully prepared for the looming conflict. It had been busy almost from the first day of the incursion's discovery marshaling its assets and positioning them to show how India's air arm might make an effective difference in the gathering confrontation.

INITIAL AIR OPERATIONS

Less than a week before the start of Operation Vijay, on May 21, the IAF had launched a Canberra PR57 from 106 Squadron to conduct a reconnaissance of the besieged area that overlooked highway NH1A and the adjacent town of Kargil. While descending to 22,000 feet just two miles from the LoC, which put the aircraft as low as 4,000 feet above the highest ridgelines, the Canberra sustained a direct hit in its right engine by what was later determined to have been a Chinese-made Anza infrared surface-to-air missile. From that moment onward, the IAF leadership knew without doubt that it was nearing the brink of a major combat involvement.

The initial attacks marked the first time that the IAF had expended ordnance in combat in Kashmir since its early-generation Vampire jet fighters destroyed Pakistani bunkers in the Kargil sector in December 1971.

Kinetic air operations began in earnest at 0630 on May 26 with six attacks in succession by two-ship elements of MiG-21, MiG-23, and MiG-27 fighters against intruder camps, material dumps, and supply routes in the general areas overlooking Dras, Kargil, and Batalik. These initial attacks marked the first time that the IAF had expended ordnance in combat in Kashmir since its early-generation Vampire jet fighters destroyed Pakistani bunkers in the Kargil sector in December 1971. The IAF fighters that were pressed into these first-day attacks conducted 57mm rocket attacks and strafing passes against enemy targets. A second wave of air attacks began that afternoon, followed by high-altitude reconnaissance overflights by Canberra PR57s and subsequent low passes by MiG-21Ms to conduct near-real-time battle damage assessment.

Nearly all of the targets selected for attack in those initial strikes were on or near jagged ridgelines at elevations ranging from 14,000 to 18,000 feet. The stark backdrop of rocks and snow made for uncommonly difficult visual target acquisition, complicated further by the small size of the enemy troop positions dispersed against a vast and undifferentiated snow background. Inspired by the unique view from the cockpit of a fighter flying high over the rugged terrain, the IAF codenamed its contribution to the campaign Operation Safed Sagar—Hindi for "white sea."

During the second day of surface attack operations, the IAF lost two fighters in close succession. The first, a MiG-27 from 9 Squadron, experienced an engine failure while coming off a target after its pilot had just conducted a successful two-pass attack with 80mm rockets and 30mm cannon fire on one of the enemy's main supply dumps. The ensuing in-flight emergency resulted in the pilot ejecting safely after several unsuccessful airstart attempts, only to be captured by the Pakistani intruders almost as soon as he hit the ground. Air Chief Marshal Tipnis later reported that the pilot had fired his rockets well outside the operating envelope stipulated for the weapon, causing the engine to flame out. The sudden loss of power in the thin Himalayan air could have resulted from rocket exhaust gas having been ingested through the engine's air inlets on either side of the aircraft. (The MiG-27 was flying at an altitude well above that at which the rockets had been cleared to be fired.)

The second fighter loss, a MiG-21 from 17 Squadron flying top cover for the strikers, sustained an infrared surface-to-air missile hit while its pilot was flying over the terrain at low level to assist in the search for the downed MiG-27 pilot. The pilot, Squadron Leader Ajay Ahuja, also succeeded in ejecting safely but was executed shortly after he was captured following his landing. His body was subsequently returned bearing fatal bullet wounds and clear signs of brutalization.

On the third day of air operations, an IAF Mi-17 helicopter was downed, again by an enemy shoulder-fired Stinger surface-to-air missile while conducting a low-level attack. The ill-fated helicopter had been the last in a four-ship flight of armed Mi-17s flying in trail formation and was the only aircraft in the flight that had not been configured with a self-protection flare dispenser to draw away any incoming heat-seeking missiles.

The stark backdrop of rocks and snow made for uncommonly difficult visual target acquisition, complicated further by the small size of the enemy troop positions dispersed against a vast and undifferentiated snow background.

The IAF's pilots quickly understood what the Israelis had learned at great cost during the Yom Kippur War of 1973, when Egyptian and Syrian surface-to-air missiles and antiaircraft artillery downed nearly a third of the Israeli Air Force's fighter inventory (102 aircraft) before the three-week war finally ended in victory for Israel. Demonstrating its adaptability, the IAF moved with dispatch to equip all of its participating fighters with flares in order to provide an active counter-measure against any enemy infrared-guided missiles. It also called a halt once and for all to any further use of slow-moving and vulnerable Mi-17 helicopters in an armed fire-support role and directed that all target attacks by IAF fighters be conducted from outside the lethal threat envelopes of enemy shoulder-fired surface-to-air missiles. In all, enemy forces fired more than 100 surface-to-air missiles at IAF aircraft throughout the conflict. After the service's first three days of combat operations, however, not a single one of its aircraft was downed or sustained battle damage.

Throughout the campaign, whenever IAF reconnaissance or ground attack operations were under way in the immediate combat zone, Western Air Command ensured that MiG-29s or other air-to-air fighters were also airborne on combat air patrol stations over the ground fighting on India's side of the LoC to provide top cover against any attempt by the Pakistan Air Force (PAF) to enter the fray in a ground attack role. PAF F-16s to the west typically maintained a safe distance of 10 to 20 miles on the Pakistani side of the LoC, although they occasionally approached as close as 8 miles away from the ongoing ground engagements. The PAF's director of operations during the Kargil War later reported that there had been isolated instances of IAF and PAF fighters locking on to each other with their onboard fire control radars, but that caution had prevailed on both sides and that "no close [air-to-air] encounters took place." IAF fighters never joined in aerial combat with the PAF F-16s due to the Vajpayee government's strict injunction that Indian forces not cross the LoC. Seven years later, however, Air Chief Marshal Tipnis recalled that he had personally authorized his escorting fighter pilots to chase any Pakistani aircraft back across the LoC in hot pursuit were those pilots to be engaged by enemy fighters in aerial combat.

In all, the IAF flew some 460 fighter sorties throughout the campaign dedicated exclusively to maintaining battlespace air defence. These medium- and high-altitude defensive combat air patrols and offensive fighter sweeps, typically entailing four-ship flights of MiG-29s, took place not only in the immediate area of ground fighting in the Kargil sector but throughout Western Air Command's area of responsibility. As Operation Vijay's air component commander later recalled, he was not just concerned about Kargil or the Kashmir region but had a potentially larger-scale war in mind: "I was working on a much bigger canvas.... I was fully conscious that as we hit and killed enemy soldiers, there was every possibility for escalation, possibly outside the immediate combat area, and it was my job to be ready with adequate remaining resources for that eventuality."

IAF strike aircraft operated primarily from three northern bases, Air Force Stations Srinagar, Avantipur, and Udhampur. The closest of those to the fighting, Srinagar, was more than 70 miles away from the war zone. Within just days after the full extent of the Pakistani incursion was confirmed and well before the formal start of Operation Safed Sagar, the MiG-21bis squadron permanently stationed at Srinagar was joined by additional MiG-21M, MiG-23BN, and MiG-27ML squadrons, while additional squadrons of MiG-21Ms and MiG-29s deployed northward to Avantipur.

By the time Operation Safed Sagar had reached its full stride, the IAF had deployed some 60 of its frontline aircraft to support the war effort, making for about a quarter of Western Air Command's combined fighter inventory. As they awaited mission tasking, those squadrons committed to the campaign initiated special training aimed at better acclimating their pilots to conducting night attacks under moonlit conditions. Such combat operations by fighters over high mountainous terrain at night had never before been attempted in the IAF's history.

Because of their rudimentary bomb sights, the inaccuracy of their unguided weapons, and the ruling against crossing the Line of Control, MiG-21, MiG-

23, and MiG-27 pilots typically achieved only limited effectiveness when attempting to provide close air support against enemy point targets.

Increasingly as the joint campaign unfolded, most Indian Army operations were preceded by preparatory air strikes, each of which was closely coordinated beforehand between 15 Corps planners and the AOC for Jammu and Kashmir. Because of their rudimentary bomb sights, the inaccuracy of their unguided weapons, and the ruling against crossing the LoC, MiG-21, MiG-23, and MiG-27 pilots typically achieved only limited effectiveness when attempting to provide close air support against enemy point targets.

Rapidly adapting to these constraints, on May 30, just four days after the start of Operation Safed Sagar, Air Chief Marshal Tipnis decided to take action to help correct the problem of inaccuracy. He chose to commit IAF Mirage 2000H fighters capable of delivering laser-guided bombs to ground attack operations in the Kargil sector. The fighters first had to be configured to deliver the bombs, so Air Headquarters launched an accelerated effort to do so at Air Force Station Gwalior, where the Mirage 2000Hs were principally based.

India's Aircraft System Testing Establishment (ASTE) in Bangalore was well along in a developmental program to integrate Israeli-made Litening electro-optical targeting pods onto the Mirage 2000H and Jaguar fighters. To support the accelerated effort at Gwalior, ASTE began a full-court press to prepare selected Mirage 2000Hs from 7 Squadron to be fitted with Litening pods for use over Kargil.

At the same time, ASTE helped modify the Mirage 2000H's centerline weapons station to carry 1,000-pound U.S.-made Paveway II laser-guided bombs instead of the IAF's French-produced Matra precision munitions, which were prohibitively expensive.

Concurrently, the IAF's elite Tactics and Air Combat Development Establishment located at Air Force Station Jamnagar took the lead in developing and validating best tactics, techniques, and procedures for delivering the Paveway II. By June 12, the upgraded Mirage 2000Hs were ready to commence precision strike operations in anger for the first time in IAF history.

In the meantime, air operations against identified intruder positions and support facilities continued in the Jubar and Mashkoh Valley sectors between May 28 and June 1. Throughout the first week of June, inclement weather hindered such operations and persisted to a point where a cloud deck below the ridgelines precluded air attacks entirely on June 10 and 11. Fortunately, 15 Corps had no urgent target servicing requirements for the IAF during those two days.

THE IMPACT OF AIR POWER

The basic characteristics of air power are speed, reach, flexibility, mobility and lethality. Presently, even when India's land forces possess far greater combat capability than they ever did, the IAF is still viewed as the principal rapid response component of Indian military power. In the prevailing scenario the possibility of limited war under the nuclear shadow being more likely, the role of the IAF has become even more critical.

In numerical terms, the IAF has to confront two adversaries, Pakistan and China, who routinely maintain close to 700 combat aircraft equivalent to the IAFs own strength...

Indian air power therefore, must be potent enough to achieve air superiority to permit the three services to successfully carry out their assigned missions. For such a strategy to be successful, requires the IAF to maintain significant quantitative and qualitative superiority against Pakistan and sufficiently dissuasive power against China. India successfully managed to maintain superiority in force levels throughout the 1980s with a 2.9:1 advantage in combat aircraft over Pakistan. The current shortfall in combat potential has cut deeply into the comprehensive air superiority essential to India's military strategy.

The PAF

Pakistan has managed to maintain its combat aircraft inventories, thanks to the support from the US and China. The PAF has 22 combat squadrons against the IAF's 29. The IAF has around 630 combat aircraft, which, in comparison with Pakistan's 380-odd fighters, constitutes a ratio of 1.6:1, clearly a far cry from the 2.9:1 superiority that the IAF enjoyed in the 1980s. The PAF is also in the process of acquiring Beyond Visual Range Air-to-Air Missile (BVR AAM) capability for its fighter fleet, a lethal weapon system she did not possess earlier. These are the American AIM 120-C Advanced Medium Air-to Air Missile (AMRAAM) to arm the F-16C. The Chinese PL-12 (BVR AAM) for the new JF-17 Chinese jets, will allow the PAF to contest the Russian R-77 BVR AAMs, on board the Indian MiG-21 BISON and Su-30 MKI fighters. The PAF is also acquiring Airborne Early Warning (AEW) platforms, composed of four Swedish SAAB-2000 aircraft equipped with the ERIEYE phased array radar and four additional Y-8 AEW platforms from China. These acquisitions will enhance PAF's air surveillance envelope, improve survivability of ground-based air defence network and enable combat aircraft to operate more effectively in both defensive and offensive missions against India.

This force structure reveals that the PLAAF will have more fourth generation aircraft a decade from now than the total number of aircraft in the

IAF inventory. The IAF still enjoys significant advantages over the PAF. It has a larger contingent of high performance aircraft; operates more BVR capable platforms; its airplanes deploy better on-board sensors and electronic warfare systems; its pilots are more proficient in advanced air combat tactics including operations in a BVR environment. The IAF possesses superior combat support aircraft, better infrastructure and a continually improving integrated air defence network. However, India's falling numbers of front-line combat aircraft will enhance risks and curtail flexibility. While these limitations will be less significant if the scale of conflict remains limited, they will become critical in the event of a large-scale war.

The PLAAF

The PLAAF has traditionally outnumbered the IAF by an order of magnitude. In the early 1990s, the Chinese air force inventory was huge, consisting of around 5,000 airplanes. From the IAF's perspective, this threat was manageable because the backbone of its combat capability consisted of about 3,000 obsolete second-generation fighters such as the J-6/MiG-19. Third-generation fighters particularly the J-7 E/G and the J-8, were few. The J-7 fleet included roughly 500 aircraft in varying configurations and the J-8s probably never exceeded 100 airplanes in the PLAAF inventory.

Along with the J-7s and J-8s, a smaller but rapidly growing fleet of advanced combat aircraft—over 350-odd fighters presently—the most prominent of which are, the Russian Su-27/30 and the indigenous F-10 which incorporates Israeli technology. The strength of the PLAAF will probably be around 1,700 aircraft in 2020, the proportion of advanced systems will keep increasing. It would be reasonable to expect PLAAF to have close to 500 Su-27/30s and 500 F-10s, as well as a small number of fifth-generation stealth fighters. The rest of the fleet would c consist of 300 F-7 and F-8 aircraft along with lightweight fighters –FC-1/JF-17 aircraft.

This force structure reveals that the PLAAF will have more fourth generation aircraft a decade from now than the total number of aircraft in the IAF inventory. This fleet would be armed with advanced AAMs like the PL-12 BVR AAM and would be supplemented with superior air-to-ground weapons, advanced EW systems, tanker support aircraft and advanced UAVs.

The up gradation is certain to result in a very capable air defence system, comprising comprehensive sensors, secure communication and data links, a robust command and control system and advanced SAMs. The large investments in intelligence, surveillance and reconnaissance (ISR) systems, space capabilities and cyber warfare have already attracted widespread attention. China is well on its way to becoming a genuine aerospace power rather than being merely an air force with high performance aircraft. The situation is now clearer with the IAF needing to augment force levels initially by 126 MMRCA subsequently increasing to 200, and restoring the authorised level of 39.5 squadrons.

These improvements are also steadily becoming manifest in Southwestern China, which borders India. This region deploys 300 combat aircraft. The quality of this force has steadily improved with the deployment of fourth-generation aircraft such as the Su-27 and the F-10. Chinese capabilities in the Tibetan plateau has seen improvements in roads, railways, airfield infrastructure and fuel supply. The high elevation of the Tibetan plateau will entail reduced take-off weight restricting weapon load. This handicap can be partially offset through in-flight refueling. Unless India acts to stem the reduction in force levels of its fighter fleet, the IAF will face critical challenges.

In numerical terms, the IAF has to confront two adversaries, Pakistan and China, who routinely maintain close to 700 combat aircraft—equivalent to the IAF's own strength—in the territorial regions contiguous to the Indian border. Although Indian superiority over Pakistani air power will continue in the foreseeable future. However, superiority of the IAF will diminish as the capability of the PAF improves. China poses a greater challenge. Not only is the IAF poised to lose forever its traditional numerical superiority where advanced combat aircraft are concerned, this segment of the PLAAF alone is likely to exceed the size of the entire IAF by 2020. When the larger transformation of the Chinese military is taken into account, the situation becomes serious indeed.

In terms of pure numbers, by 2020, the IAF will have to confront around 1,500 fourth-generation Pakistani and Chinese fighters not to mention cruise missiles, UAVs, ballistic missiles, electronic warfare, cyber and space warfare.

THE INDIAN AIR FORCE AND 24 X 7 CAPABILITIES

A nation of the size, power, responsibilities and stature of India cannot ignore global happenings. Indeed we must anticipate and if possible shape them or risk being overtaken by events. It is a decided advantage to be proactive but we have been far from it. This requires the backing of analysis, determination of national interests and long-term policies. A smaller nation could get away without it but not India in the contemporary world.

Apart from having a volatile neighbourhood and the associated threats and influences, India is faced with the full spectrum of threats. The spectrum itself is increasing in complexity and technological sophistication. With the changing spectrum, its unpredictability, and India being looked upon to play a bigger role in global affairs, we have no choice but to ensure that we have full-spectrum dominance. The Armed Forces are an important component of national power and can help generate options for the Govt. The application of Air Power is intrinsic to the gamut of National Power and we will have to focus in the same direction.

If we have to tread the path of full spectrum dominance, it is prudent that we move away from a threatbased assessment to a capabilitybased approach. A capability can always be tailored or applied to meet the emerging challenge. Capability will also allow us to apply the right force in any form of conflict. Transformation for us will be a continued series of fundamental changes each leading to a better capability. Keeping all this in mind, we need to understand what we need for our capability build-up.

Pillars of Capability

Our National zone of interest and influence stretches from the Gulf of Hormuz in the West, to the Malacca Straits in the East and beyond. Just like other capabilities, strong and comprehensive aerospace capability is required in today's scenario to meet our country's aspirations. I envisage that the capability build up of our aerospace power will be based on four pillars.

Very simply put, these are SEE, REACH, HIT and PROTECT. We need to SEE farthest and first. This involves utilisation of space based assets, long range radars, aerostats, AWACS and other ISR sensors. We need to collect and process relevant information in real time. Having SEEN, we need to REACH our area of interest. Trans-oceanic reach by long range combat and transport aircraft, along with air to air refuellers, is the next pillar of our capability. Once we reach, we need to HIT the target. Hit the target with precision; hit it hard. And so, modern weapons are required. While doing all this, we need to PROTECT our assets both in war and peace. This involves all aspects of Air Defence, EW (Electronic Warfare), Cyberspace and Information Warfare.

Effect on IAF and its Preparedness

Aerospace power is going to play a major role in all operations in the future. Technologically, aerospace power will definitely seek to enhance its fundamentals. Reach, Accuracy, Lethality, Situational awareness as well as command and control are going to improve manifold. Aerospace power will find increasing application in homeland security as well as in tackling asymmetric forces with faint footprints. The path that we have to tread is influenced by emerging technologies and I can state with confidence that aerospace power's applicability will only increase in times ahead. Aerospace power will proliferate and find utility with many agencies. In addition to the

Armed Forces, the Paramilitary and now the Home Ministry want their integral aircraft and Air Wings. This will raise a host of fundamental questions on organisational structures, management and ownership issues. Undoubtedly, aerospace power will be the 'preferred tool' for all conveniences and contingencies, but we need to manage it properly.

In the future, there are many challenges but also opportunities. Some are evolutionary and some are truly revolutionary. On one end, we have 5th generation fighters like F-35 and F-22, PAK-FA or T-50, while on the other end, increasingly capable RPAs (Remotely Piloted Aircraft) are also stealing limelight. Since these RPAs are offering new horizons for air and space operations, they have started playing critical roles in war and conflict zones. From surveillance to delivering ordnance with precision, RPAs will undoubtedly continue to make revolutionary advances. Similarly, precision munitions are getting smaller, more precise and more autonomous while on the other side, weapons using directed energy are beginning to emerge.

There will be a need for specialisation, greater networking and assimilation of space, for any air force that has a reckonable area of interest. Transportability of national power by airlift will be more essential than ever before.

IAF'S Future Roadmap

If this be the future of air power then, then the vision and long term perspective of IAF is clear. The underlying objective of the Air Force during the coming 10 to 15 years is to build itself into a credible aerospace power. Always keeping in mind that there is a compelling need to keep the technological level of our equipment at such a pitch, that it is viable for precise and effective force application in all possible types of threat scenarios.

IAF envisions itself to be a networkcentric force. The Aim being to have a common operating picture, reduce the sensor to shooter time and enable successful time critical operations. In fact all this will shortly become "bread and butter" stuff. Capabilities like the Integrated Air Command and Control System (IACCS), AWACS and Operational Data Link (ODL) are different aspects of an emerging network-centric environment. Space would be very vital, though largely an invisible component in this mosaic of Network-Centric operations.

Contemporary capabilities like AWACS and some others in the pipeline are already changing and transforming the way we are likely to fly and fight. The demands on the aerospace leadership of the future are also going to change. Leaders will also have to transform themselves. A change of mindset is mandatory to meet the challenges of the future.

Technological advances will continue to revolutionise military affairs in future too. Despite the unpredictabilities, it is certain that the need for application and transportability of national power – hard and soft – and thus for aerospace power, with enhanced fundamentals, would remain. We expect aerospace power to permeate the fabric of national security more completely, including homeland security. IAF foresees greater specialisation; tailored capabilities for each occasion; an increased dependence on Remotely Piloted Vehicles and a greater accent on force enhancers; particularly the intangible ones, such as quality of people and their skills. Hardware is important but it is converted into capabilities by people. Aerospace power requires highly-skilled and trained personnel. Attracting quality youth, training and retaining them is another of IAF's challenges. Inculcating qualities of leadership and innovativeness will be vital on IAF's agenda.

Networking and assimilation of space, both interdependent, are already the way forward and can tilt the balance considerably. Perhaps more than others, it is air power that is most significantly enhanced by the integration of space-enabled capabilities. Evolving into a potent aerospace force is thus a logical progression in the scheme of things. But then, the vulnerability of satellites to anti-satellite weapons becomes an issue, due to risk of attack from adversaries. Development of ASAT technologies is taking place in our neighbourhood. In order to ensure that our increased dependence on space does not become our vulnerability, defending space based assets would assume vital importance within the 21st Century.

MODERNISATION OF IAF

With all this in mind the Indian Air Force also has a major transformation plan in place. This is three-pronged. The first is to preserve and maintain what they have. This is achieved with a well-conceived product and maintenance support plan.

Secondly, they plan to selectively upgrade and improve the lethality of their assets that have adequate residual life left. Some of the fleets and assets that are being upgraded are:

a. Upgrade of the MiG-29 series by 2014. Upgraded aircraft will be available by 2017.

b. Technical upgrades of Mi-17 upgrade.

c. In fact, upgrades of Su-30 are already in the pipeline and in various phases.

d. In parallel, MAFI (Modernisation of Air Fields Infrastructure) programme for upgradation of airfield and maintenance infrastructure is also being progressed.

The third prong of the transformation is to progress the acquisitions and replacements where no residual life is left:

a. The final round of the procurement of 126 Medium Multi-Role Combat aircraft is on with Rafale.

b. Procurement of additional Su-30 is under progress. Our total numbers are going to be in excess of 270 Su-30s.

c. The LCA (Light Combat Aircraft) IOC certification was done in Jan 2011. There are delays. Induction is expected in this year, by which time all teething issues should hopefully be sorted out.

d. RFP for six additional Flight Refuelling aircraft was re-issued in Sep 10. FETs (Field Evaluation Trials) have been completed.

e. 10 C-17 Globemaster III Heavy Lift Aircraft.

f. Induction of new Medium Lift Helicopters (Mi-17 V5) has already commenced.

g. Induction of Combat helicopters and Heavy Lift Helicopters is being progressed.

h. Contract for Spyder LLQRMs has been signed and the first squadron is expected soon.

i. All the three AWACS aircraft have been delivered. Contract for Medium Power Radars, Low Level Transportable Radars and Low Level Light Weight Radars has been signed and delivery has commenced.

j. MTA (Multirole Transport Aircraft) and FGFA (Fifth Generation Fighter Aircraft) programmes are being progressed with Russia. FGFAs will be available around or just after 2017. The requirement is for about 200 to 250 aircraft.

INDIAN ARTILLERY

Upgradation of the weapon system is a continuous process based on threat perception and technological development. Accordingly, upgradation of the existing stock of artillery and procurement of advanced guns based on modern technology for the modernisation of Indian Artillery are being planned. In written reply to a question on the acquisition of different types of Guns for the Indian Artillery, the Ministry of Defence have furnished the details as given below : Wheeled SP Gun-Request for Proposals (RFP) for procurement of 155 mm/52 Calibre Wheeled Self Propelled (SP) Guns was issued to 11 vendors. Only 5 vendors responded. Of these, 4 were rejected in Technical Evaluation as they did not meet the required parameters. Since only one SP Gun met all the qualitative requirements, it has since been decided to explore if there are any additional vendors currently producing Wheeled SP Guns so that a competitive situation can be developed. Tracked SP Gun-Tracked SP Gun is a project developed by Defence Research and Development Organization (DRDO). It involves mating a suitable imported 155 mm /52 Calibre turret with indigenously developed BHIM chassis.

Process of identification of a suitable turret was completed after global tendering and successful trial evaluation. Commercial negotiations were completed in December, 2003. The case is being processed for approval of the competent authority.

Towed Guns-Global RFP was in December, 2001. Three vendors responded. Trial evaluation of all three guns was carried out in May/July, 2002 and June/ July, 2003. Validation firing of all three guns were held in November, 2004. Currently, environmental tests are in progress.

About the upgradation plan of Guns in Indian Artillery a representative of the Ministry of Defence stated as under: "We are upgrading 130-mm guns to 155-mm guns, 45 calibre. Ten regiments are being done with imported kits, and the ordnance factories would do for another 14 regiments.

We are planning to introduce 155 mm 52 calibre guns, which are presently at trial stage as propelled guns.

For self propelled guns, we are determined that Bhim T 6 gun will cater for the requirements of target as propelled guns, and in future, we will continue to look for wheeled self propelled guns. The upgradation of existing 155-mm guns, that is, Bofors Guns is also on the anvil. We are planning to introduce a long-range rocket artillery, the Pinaka System, which is an effort of DRDO.

For this system, two major firms, L & T and Tata, have collaborated. For a multi-barrel launcher system, capable of sending rockets up to a depth of 90 kms., negotiations are currently under way. We hope that they will be contracted some time in the current year." In regard to the acquisition programmes of guns the representative further stated: "We have 155 mm SP Guns for the artillery. We were to acquire in two versions. One was wheeled version and the other was tracked version.

Track is like a tank and it was mounted on tracked chassis and you have got a turreted gun on top. Both planned to be the same. One between the wheels and one would be on tracks. What we have now sent up to the CCS or will be sending for the CCS for approval will be high breed gun as was mentioned, used the Arjun chassis, which is a heavy chassis and used the South African gun to be mounted on top of it.

That has been on trial and evaluated and it is found to be in order. South African gun mounted on Arjun chassis. This will not impede production of

Arjun tanks because they will be manufactured by Bharat Earth Movers Limited, an alternative production line for the chassis.

As far as wheeled guns are concerned, we are not yet ready for it. We are going to have or invite vendors and check out with out trials and identify the suitable wheeled gun. So, that is the present situation.

As far as Towed Guns are concerned we had carried out trials earlier.

zNow we want fresh trials and more competitors to come in. Hopefully, in the next year, we will be going for GSQR evaluation. It will be ready for contracting.

There were three vendors in this trial evaluation as a user trial has been carried out. Three rounds of trials have been carried out and now maintenance and evaluation and other aspects are going on. All three will be processed for all stages of the trials. User trial is just one stage of the trials. Then, there are maintenance and environmental trials and DGQA trials".

The Committee note that the Indian Army is facing critical shortage of wheeled Self Propelled (SP) guns of the required standard. The Ministry have informed that though the request for proposals for its procurement was issued to 11 vendors in response to which 5 bids were received and one gun has been finally found to be matching the qualitative requirements.

The Committee are, however, surprised to note that no fields trials were held to decide the suitability or otherwise of the bids received which is the normal procedure. The Committee also note that trials are still continuing for the procurement of tracked SP Guns and towed Guns.

The delay in the procurement of such crucial weaponry has adversely affected the modernisation of schemes of the defence sources resulting in wastage of a lot of time. The Committee feel that global RFP should have been issued in the first instance to avoid the single vendor situation. The Committee now want immediate decision to be taken to procure the guns at the earliest. The Committee further recommend that R & D efforts for their indigenous production should go simultaneously with the acquisition programme of the Ministry so that Artillery is not made to face the shortage of critical components of the weapons system. 501-1-

Phasing out of Cheetah /Chetak Helicopters

Presently, Indian Army depends on Cheetah and Chetak helicopters for surveillance system in the high altitude regions. The design of these helicopters is 40 to 45 years old due to which the emerging requirements of the Army in the high altitude terrains are inadequately addressed. In reply to a question on the replacement of ageing Cheetah/Chetak Helicopters the Ministry have stated in a written reply that the Army is looking for alternative options for replacement of Cheetah with the state-of-the-art technology helicopters available in the global market. Salient technical specifications of the replacement helicopter of Cheetah are as under:-

a) Integrated Doppler Global Positioning System (GPS) Navigation System;
b) Auto Pilot in all three axis;
c) Service ceiling not below 6500 m (desirable 7000m) pressure altitude;
d) The helicopter must be cleared for full night and inclement weather operations; and
e) The helicopter must be capable of being fitted with :-
    - Suitable Sighting System comprising of Forward Looking Infra Red Radar, Laser Range Finder and a designator.
    - Data Link System
    - Flare / Chaff dispenser with suitable defence mechanism.

The Advanced Light Helicopter (ALH) Dhruv, is in the category of 5.5 Ton class. It can operate in high altitude, but due to its larger class than that of the Cheetah, it requires bigger landing ground/helipads.

A representative of the Ministry of Defence, during oral evidence stated: "As far as Army Aviation is concerned, what we are looking at is superior reliability and endurance in high altitude areas; rapid response to emerging situations in combating terrorism; enhancement of capabilities in the utility role and armed helicopter capability.

This being the benchmark requirements, the present acquisitions which are planned are that we are planning to upgrade our existing Cheetah / Chetak fleets. Two squadrons we have already inducted and in a couple of months it will be finished and the third squadron the order for which has already been placed.

We are also going ahead with weaponising the Dhruv helicopters for six squadrons of them eventually and we are also planning a replacement of the Cheetah and Chetak fleet for which the trials are presently on. Utility Helicopters in the 10-12 class to enable the Army to move at core and divisional level, a certain body of men to quickly and rapidly react to report about infiltration being undertaken by the terrorists as also for various other operations in conventional wars and helicopters mounted surveillance systems".

The Committee note that the Army is looking for alternative options for replacement of Cheetah Helicopters with state-of-the-art helicopters available in the global market.

The Committee, keeping in view the requirement of superior reliability and endurance in high altitude areas, rapid response to emerging situations in combating terrorism, desire that the Ministry should also examine the feasibility to upgrade existing Cheetah/ Chetak fleets before inducting the new helicopters. The Committee also desire that efforts should be made to modify the configuration of Dhruv Helicopters so as to make it operate at high altitude regions.

The Committee also desire that a time bound road map for indigenous manufacturing of helicopters should also be drown up at the earliest. The Committee hope and trust that sufficient financial allocations are made available to make the new purchases in a time-bound manner.

3

Air Warfare Weapons and Equipment

Air warfare weapons and equipment in the 21st century mainly will be smart ammunition, thinking operational platforms and integrated automatic C3I systems.

Smart Munitions

In the course of its development, air force munitions went through three stages unable-to-control after launching, able-to-control after launching, and, finally, unnecessary-to-control after launching. The first state of air force munitions was in the decades after aircraft came into being until World War II, when all airborne weapons were aimed by sight, which has a low-kill probability. Along with the rapid development of information technology and control technology after WWII, airborne sight weapons developed into guided target-seeking weapons, and the development of air munitions progressed to the second stage and then to the third. Before early air-to-air missiles, air-to-ground missiles, and precision-guided bombs were launched, information about targets was transmitted to their control section by pilots. In order to control the missiles, pilots continually transmitted information about targets to the control section after launching the missiles or bombs, in order to insure that they flew precisely toward targets. As information technology further develops and is applied to air munitions, active and passive information devices can automatically acquire information about targets after air munitions have left their platforms. Thus the munition is able to change its own flight and destroy targets precisely. "Unnecessary to control after launching" has therefore been largely achieved. According to calculations, if the kill probability remains unchanged, while precision increases by 1, 2, or 3 times, the efficiency equals, respectively, that of 4, 9, or 16 times that of warheads, or that of 8, 27, or 63 times that of ammunition equivalent. Increased ammunition performance enables air warfare to develop toward "one warhead, one target." According to relevant data, to destroy a strong underground fortification in World War II, 9,000 bombs were needed; in the Vietnam War, 600 bombs; in the Gulf War, only 1 or 2 bombs. Thus, "unnecessary to control after launching" air munitions for the 21st century are already under research, and the amount of this kind of munition is increasing rapidly. It is predicted that, with its high precision, this kind of ammunition will play a dominant role in the air battlefield of the 21st century.

Informationized Platforms

An early aircraft was only a machine able to fly in the sky. Only after it was used in war did it become an operational platform. Aircraft have undergone a development course from a mechanical platform to an informationized operational platform and finally to an intellectualized operation platform. The first generation aircraft were jet-propelled and pursued supersonic speed; the second generation could reach bi-sonic speed and a height of over 20,000 meters. On this basis, information equipment on board second generation aircraft began to hold an important position. Fire-control radars were generally used in second generation aircraft. Information equipment in third-generation aircraft holds a more important position. What are generally used on board include pulse Doppler radar, forward-looking infrared devices, night vision devices, low-light TV, navigational and digital headsup displays, etc.

Equaling 50 to 60 percent of the total cost of common aircraft (or over 60 percent of the total cost of stealth planes), information equipment aboard fourth-generation aircraft holds a far more outstanding position. For example, there are more than 700 computers on a B-2 bomber. For this reason fourth-generation aircraft have become intellectualized operational platforms, which have three apparent advantages: they can extensively collect information; they can deal with all kinds of information; and they can carry all kinds of ammunition. With the help of the fire-control system, they can automatically distribute targets and control a number of warheads to attack simultaneously. Their electronic warfare system can authoritatively judge the threatening sources and provide the pilot with conduct methods for him to select. Additionally, their operations assisting system can help drive the aircraft. Nowadays, modern aircraft has become an information-dominated weapon. Compared with that of WWII, the efficiency of the battle aircraft of the 21st century will increase more than 100 times.

Integrated and Automated C3I Systems

Radar is an information-collecting device which was designed to adapt to aerial warfare weapon's characteristics. Its emergence made it possible to control air warfare and brought to an end the epoch when air warfare equaled blind men touching an elephant. However, in the long period ever since, because of low-level of information technology, the command system was restricted to the realm of manual operation, thus the operation or capability of air power was heavily limited. Since the 1950s, when collecting, transmitting, processing and using information were fused, the command system of air warfare has witnessed such a rapid development process "manual operation command became semi-automatic command, which became automated command," resulting in the eventual appearance of integrated and automated C3I systems.

EMPLOYMENT CONCEPTS OF AIR POWER

In the multipolar international framework of the 21st century, a focus of national attention will be on how to cope with local wars and regional crises. In multilevel military operations, in peacetime or in times of neither-war-nor-peace, air power will play a more important role. The employment concepts of air power will become more diversified.

Air Deterrence

Compared with actual combat, deterrence has some limitations. However, because its functions are broad, one may both launch an attack and make peace, achieving goals without sacrifice. So deterrence can be used separately or as the precursor of actual combat. In the 21st century, air deterrence will become the first-choice mode of employing air power.

High-tech conventional deterrence is a new mode of deterrence developed after nuclear deterrence. Although the effect of nuclear deterrence is very strong, its actual value has decreased because of the height of the "nuclear threshold." High-tech warfare requires deterrence strength capable not only of maneuvering rapidly in vast battle space, but also of moving about freely and quickly within hostile borders. It further requires the deterrent force to be able to attack and withdraw quickly after destroying the enemy's strategic targets. Air power happens to possess these characteristics. Air deterrence has three advantages:

- It is highly effective for a fixed period with wide coverage. Modern air forces are capable of carrying out supersonic maneuvers and intercontinental missions and can cover any target in any part of the world.

- There is low political risk. Modern air forces can attack strategic targets with precision of less than 1 meter. On the one hand, this ability can ensure target destruction and, on the other, avoid unfavorable political effects, which is the inevitable result of killing or wounding civilians or destroying civilian facilities.
- It can operate under a range of conditions. It can function both separately or jointly with the Army and the Navy, and it can also function both in conventional conditions and nuclear conditions.

Therefore, air deterrence will become the basic employment mode of future deterrence.

No-Fly Zones

A "no fly" zone is a forbidden airspace set up in a conflicted area, using air power as its main force. In the no-fly zone, none of the opponent's air actions is permitted, nor can any opponent install ground-to-air weapons that may threaten one's own air actions. No-fly zones are a new application mode of air power in the last decade of the 20th century. For example, the United States, Britain and France set up a no-fly zone in Iraq to protect the Kurds, and the U.N. Security Council passed a resolution to set up a no-fly zone in Bosnia-Herzegovina.

A CRITICAL LOOK AT THE 1965 OPERATIONS

Early in 1965, Pakistan attacked us in Kutch, in Western India. The attack caught the armed forces unawares. The Army took the field without any prior planning or preparation. Its reaction was fast but there was no joint Army-Air Force plan, and all that the Air Force could do was to provide logistic support with light aircraft. The possibility of tactical support was considered after the fighting began. It was then realised that our bases were so far from the battle zone that our aircraft would have to operate at extreme range with reduced weapon loads while Pakistani aircraft could dominate the entire combat area from bases close by. Given time, we could also have improvised an airfield or two In or near Kutch, but the fighting ended before that. The incident was soon defused but, apparently, not before It had encouraged Pakistan in the belief that the time had come to settle the Kashmir dispute by force of arms.

Then In August and September 1965 came the second Kashmir War..It began with skirmishes in the valley by so-called freedom fighters, in reality agents of Pakistan. These were followed, towards the end of August, by an all-out attack by Pakistani armour in the Chamb area of Jammu province, with the obvious objective of cutting the Jammu-Srinagar highway. Our Army, working under the restrictions of the Cease Fire agreement, was lightly equipped in that sector and though it fought valiantly, its AMX tanks were no match for the more.powerful Pakistani Pattons. While there was some hope of the Army holding the Pakistani attack on its own, there was no talk of bringing the Air Force Into the conflict. But on 1st September, with the Pakistanis pressing forward from Jaurian, General Chaudhuri, the Army Chief, was compelled to ask for air support.

There had been no prior joint planning for such an eventuality. Air Marshal Arjan Singh, the Air Chief, had on his own alerted the air bases in the Punjab. When the call came, a force of fighter bombers from Pathankot mounted a strike on the Pakistanis within minutes of being ordered to do so. It was a touch-and-go affair, because the demand for air support came late in the afternoon and the strike had to be mounted in an area with which our pilots were not familiar. With only a few minutes of daylight left, they could have missed the battle zone or attacked the wrong targets. Fortunately they did neither and so helped to bring the Pakistani force to a halt.

At this point, it is interesting to consider in somewhat greater detail why there was no prior planning of Army-Air operations even though, as General Chaudhari said In his 1971 National Security Lecture, he expected the Pakistanis to attack In Kashmir after the Kutch Incident. Basically, I think. It was because he and his commanders were wedded to the idea that military operations were principally an Army affair and that the other services could only operate on the fringe, as it were, with an occasional bonus from the Air Force. This was compounded by a big-brother attitude towards the Air Force which led to its being treated with a certain amount of indulgence but prevented it being accepted as a vital and equal partner in war. Matters were further complicated by the belief that If the Indian Air Force took part In the fighting then the Pakistani Air Force would do likewise, thus Increasing the likelihood of a general war between the two countries instead of a localised conflict in J & K. There was a good deal of truth in this, of course, but this was a possibility from which there was no escape. Indeed, this was a possibility that could not be ignored for Pakistan had already been warned that any attack on Jammu and Kashmir would be treated as an attack on India. With a political direction as clear as that on the record, it was incumbent on the Chiefs of Staff to have their plans ready for such a contingency. The fact that they did not is indicative of the thinking at the time.

The events In the Chamb-Jaurlan sector leading to the call for air support took matters out of the Army's hands. At that stage the Government had to decide whether to enlarge the area of conflict, and it did so without hesitation. That, indeed, appeared to be the only way to divert Pakistani forces from the vulnerable Jammu-Srinagar highway, the loss of which would have jeopardised the defence of the Valley. With the decision to fight Pakistan outside J & K, the Army had to move up forces from peace time stations, some from the Deccan and further south, and formulate an operational plan at short notice.

During the five days that elapsed between the Government decision and the date set for Implementing it, there was some discussion of how the Army and the Air Force should operate. On the Army side, the notion persisted that it would fight on its own, with the Air Force providing an occasional bonus; and in the Air Force, where I was Vice-Chief, we thought of fighting mainly an air war against the PAF and what we considered to be strategic targets, assigning relatively low priority to support the Army. Separate plans were hastily drawn up by each Service with no Joint consultation worth the name. And again, no tasks were envisaged for the Navy.

In 1965, the higher defence organisation was functioning and the Chiefs of Staff Committee met regularly under the chairmanship of General Chaudhuri. Officers In positions of authority had read and studied and taught the procedures for inter-service co-operation. It was not realised, however, that even when the general drill is known, each particular task still requires a great deal of preparatory work, that the persons taking part need to be trained for It, that supporting facilities have to be arranged for In advance, and this has to be done for every contingency that can be envisaged. Flexibility in battle Is gained only through long and arduous preparation.

That we discovered when we entered Pakistan. Soon the Army found that it could not fight entirely on its own, for the PAF was constantly harassing It. The Army needed air defence and tactical support but no detailed arrangements-had been made for either. The Air Force was willing to help and it did all it could but in the absence of joint plans, large gaps remained in the air cover in the combat zone. Neither did the air operations, through which we hoped to immobilize the PAF and reduce Pakistan's ability to make war, achieve much for we had no well thought out target system for the purpose. Having had some responsibility for all this, I must confess that the air war became a somewhat hit-and-miss affair, that depended heavily on finding targets of opportunity for its success. The aircrew performed magnificently, doing all that was expected of them and more; had there been a coherent joint war plan, we would have derived much fuller benefit from their courage and sacrifice.

Our advance Into Pakistan caught the Pakistani forces by surprise. I Imagine they had not thought the Indian Government and Armed Forces capable of swift decisions and speedy action. The initial successes of our Army were soon checked by stiff resistance, a notable feature of which was the close co-operation between the Pakistani Army and Air Force. The two of them had obviously done their homework well for our jawans reported that the PAF were quick to appear whenever the Pakistani ground forces were In difficulties, and gave them most effective support. This was the more remarkable because unlike our set-up. In which all three Service Chiefs and their Headquarters were based at Delhi, the Pakistani Air Chief was located at Peshawar, the Army Chief at Islamabad, near Rawalpindi, and the Naval Chief at Karachi. The fact that their forces managed to work well together speaks well for their mutual understanding, which is more Important than physical proximity. Furthermore, since Pakistan had been the one to start the fighting In J & K, it Is to be presumed that Its Service Chiefs had given some thought to the possibility of a more widespread conflict and prepared for It accordingly.

Despite Its preparations, however, Pakistan failed to make any inroads In J & K and just about held its own elsewhere. We advanced up to the Ichhogil canal. West Pakistan's first line of defence, and towards Slalkot. Pakistani forces came into Indian territory around Gadra Road in Rajasthan. Except for a single PAF attack on an Indian Air Force base near Calcutta, there was no fighting In the east. Our Navy had no operational tasks but suffered a sea-borne attack at Dwarka In the west. The fighting was brought to a halt by 22nd September, the Army having been engaged In combat for nearly a month and a half and the Air Force for 22 days. At the turn of the year came the Tashkent agreement, negotiated by our then Prime Minister, the late Mr Lal Bahadur Shastri.

In retrospect, it is clear that the 1965 war was successful as a defensive action, for it managed to preserve the status quo In Kashmir, but the operations In the Punjab and Rajasthan were Inconclusive. We failed to make a real dent In Pakistan's forces, both on the ground and in the air. The Navy being far removed from Kashmir took no part In the fighting.

With the benefit of hindsight, we can now see what part the higher defence organisation played in the 1965 war. Frankly, I do not think It made any significant contribution. I say this after careful thought, knowing that one of our distinguished Army Chiefs, General J N Chaudhuri, was then Chairman of the Chiefs of Staff Committee. Even at the risk of his displeasure, I must say that he failed to get the organisation working as It should have done. The General himself admits as much, without meaning to. In the published version of the National Security lectures that he delivered in this institution In 1971. He said In those lectures that he saw the Kutch incident as a prelude to an attack by Pakistan in Jammu and Kashmir, and he therefore began the Army's preparations well in advance. He omits to mention that the Air Force and the Navy were kept in the dark about this. He goes on to say that he often discussed the threat with the Defence Minister and the Prime Minister and that, once in a while, he took the Air Chief along with him. The impression conveyed Is that he looked upon the Impending conflict as an Army affair, in which the use of the Air Force would be Incidental. To my mind, this reflects an attitude long prevalent in the Army, and only recently dissipated, to the effect that Its larger size and greater age gave It a commanding superiority over the other services and Invested It with the sole right to decide how wars should be fought. I may be reading too much Into a single statement, but to me It is axiomatic that effective co-operation between the Services can grow only out of mutual trust and full understanding of each others capabilities and limitations. I think that was lacking In 1965.

In any case, the Air Force and Navy, not having been alerted about the possibility of another war over Kashmir, no inter-service contingency plans were drawn up, nor was any course of action agreed upon with the Air Force in the event of Its being called out to support the Army. This mental block against consultation and joint planning continued right through the phase of guerrilla activity and was only partly removed when Pakistani armour threatened to cut the Jammu-Srinagar highway. It was at that critical stage, on 1st September 1965, that the Air Force was asked for air support, which It gave at short notice. Complaints from our forward troops about the limited extent of air cover in the war that followed were well-founded, for in the absence of precise plans the Air Force had simply maintained Its normal forces at its bases in the Punjab and In (Jammu and Kashmir. To do Its job properly, some redeployment of squadrons and of logistic and communication facilities should have been effected before the commencement of hostilities. Had the joint planners been able to do their work In advance, I am certain more positive results would have been achieved In 1965. However, apart from preserving the status quo in Kashmir, the 1965 war was valuable for the many practical lessons it taught us In the conduct of operations from the highest level to combat in the field. In the years that followed these lessons were absorbed and applied.

INDO-PAKISTANI AIR WAR OF 1965

The Indo-Pakistani War of 1965 saw the Indian and Pakistani Air Forces engaged in large-scale aerial combat against each other for the first time since the Partition in 1947. The war took place during the course of September 1965 and saw both air forces conduct defensive and offensive operations over Indian and Pakistani airspace. Both countries made contradictory claims regarding the number of losses that they suffered and the number of planes that they claimed to have shot down. Indian losses have been placed at between 59 and 110, while Pakistani losses were between 18 and 43.

Background

The war began in early August 1965 and initially the fighting was confined mainly to the ground. Later, however, as the war progressed, the war took on another dimension as the two sides began air operations against each other. Although the two forces had previously taken part in the First Kashmir War which had occurred shortly after Partition, that engagement had been limited in scale compared to the 1965 conflict and the air operations that both sides had undertaken were limited and largely confined to interdiction and other strategic purposes such as re-supply and troop transport operations. Although there had been one incident where Indian fighter aircraft intercepted a Pakistani transport, there had been no significant air-to-air combat. During the 1965 conflict, however, the PAF flew a total 2,364 sorties while the IAF flew 3,937 sorties.

All out War erupted between India and Pakistan, and during the vicious 17 day conflict PAF flew defensive CAPs over its own bases, offensive counter air missions against Indian airfields, and close-support and interdiction sorties, causing significant damage.

Main Battle

The aerial phase of the war began on 1 September 1965 when the Indian Air Force (IAF) responded to an urgent call for air strikes against the Pakistani Army, which had launched an attack known as Operation Grand Slam. The IAF's 45 Sqn was tasked to carry out Close air Support missions in support of Indian troops. The squadron had recently been moved from Pune to Pathankot, after a merger of No 220 Sqn into it, under the command of Sqn. Ldr. S.K. "Marshal" Dhar. Three missions of four aircraft each were tasked, with the first wave taking off at 1719 hours. These strafed Pakistani positions and attacked Pakistani tanks and ground targets, though a lot of damage from "friendly fire" was also reported later on. The Indian aircraft were intercepted by two Pakistan Air Force (PAF) F-86 Sabres, flown by S/L Sarfraz Rafiqui of No 5 Sqn and F/L Imtiaz Bhatti of No 15 Sqn. In the ensuing dogfight four IAF Vampires were lost, one from the first wave and three from the second. After this, the IAF immediately withdrew about 130 Vampires, together with over 50 Ouragons, from front-line service.

On 2 September, both sides flew in support of their ground forces, however no major aerial engagement was observed.

The next day witnessed an aerial combat of two Sabres of No 11 Squadron and four Gnats of No 27 Sqn from Akhnur. The Sabres were augmented by an F-104. In the course of action, one Sabre was severely damaged, though its pilot managed to land safely. Later on, one of the Gnats landed at Pasrur Airfield, resulting in the capture of the aircraft.

On 4 September, an F-86 Sabre was lost. The PAF claimed the cause to be friendly ground fire while the IAF claimed to have shot it down.

Rafiqui was shot down over Halwara on 6 September, while Bhatti ended the war with 34 combat missions to his credit, the maximum combat missions flown by any pilot during the war.

During the conflict, the Pakistani F-86 Sabre Flying Ace, Muhammad Mahmood Alam shot down seven Indian aircraft including claims of two as 'probable'. Five Hawker Hunter aircraft were shot down in one minute, of which four were brought down in 30 seconds.

On September 6, the Indian Army crossed the border at Lahore to relieve pressure on the Chamb Jaurian sector. On the evening of the same day, the PAF responded with attacks on Indian airfields at Pathankot, Adampur and Halwara. The attack on Pathankot was successful, while the attacks on Adampur and Halwara were failures. The IAF lost almost ten aircraft on the ground at Pathankot. The Adampur strike turned back before even reaching Adampur while at Halwara two of the three attacking raiders were shot down for the loss of two Indian Hunters in air combat. Both the Indian pilots survived as they ejected over their base, whereas the intruding Pakistani pilots were killed in action. This included the ace Squadron Leader Sarfaraz Rafiqui who had shot down two Vampires on 1 September. Before being shot down, Rafiqui is credited with shooting down the first of the Hunters. He was later posthumously awarded the Sitara-e-Jurat for the Chamb action and the Hilal-i-Jurat for the Halwara action.

On 7 September 1965 the PAF parachuted 135 Special Services Group (SSG) para commandos at three Indian airfields (Halwara, Pathankot and Adampur). The daring attempt proved to be an "unmitigated disaster". Only ten commandos were able to return to Pakistan, the rest were taken as prisoners of war (including one of the Commanders of the operations, Major Khalid Butt). At Halwara and Adampur these troops landed in residential areas where the villagers caught and handed them over to police.

Also on 7 September the IAF mounted 33 sorties against the heavily guarded PAF airfield complex at Sargodha. The IAF lost two Mysteres and three Hunters due to the defence mounted by the PAF's local squadrons. One of the Indian Hunter pilots, who ejected near Sargodha, was made POW and released after the war. One of the crippled Mysteres flying solo got involved in a dogfight with an F-104 Starfighter and each somehow shot the other down; the Pakistani pilot safely ejected, while the Indian pilot, Squadron Leader Ajamada B. Devayya, was killed. Squadron Leader Devayya was awarded the Maha Vir Chakra for his bravery 23 years later, after his feat was revealed by an author appointed by the PAF to write its official history of the 1965 war.

The seventh of September also marked the day when the PAF attacked IAF airfields in the Eastern Sector. During the PAF's raid on Kalaikunda, Indian pilot Flight Lieutenant A T Cooke engaged four Pakistani Sabres, shooting down one while flying at tree-top height and making another a write off in the process.

The war lessened in intensity after 8 September, with occasional clashes between the IAF and the PAF. Both air forces now changed their doctrine from air interdictions to ground attack and concentrated their efforts on knocking out soft skin targets and supply lines, such as wagons carrying ammunition; and armoured vehicles. During the conflict IAFEnglish Electric Canberras raided a few of the Pakistani bases. On 10 September one Mystere was downed by anti-aircraft fire in Pakistan but the pilot ejected safely.

On September 13 one PAF F-86 Sabre was downed while attacking a train near Gurdaspur and the pilot was killed. In another encounter the same day between PAF Sabres from Sargodha and IAF Gnats from No. 2 Squadron, an Indian Gnat was shot down by a PAF F-86 Sabre flown by Flt Lt Yusaf Ali Khan although the Indian pilot managed to eject safely. The other Gnat was engaged and damaged in air combat by Flt Lt Imtiaz Bhatti. The experienced pilot somehow managed to return to base, where according to All India Radio the Gnat's pilot later died of wounds sustained during the combat. He was said to have brought his damaged aircraft back to base and to have died during landing. His funeral was attended by the Indian President. Yusaf Ali Khan was credited with a kill whereas, Imtiaz Bhatti was credited with damaging the IAF Gnat despite the later confirmation that the pilot died of wounds and the Gnat crashed during its landing attempt. Later in the night of 13/14 September, Indian Canberras undertook the deepest penetration of Pakistani airspace of the war, attacking Pakistani bases around Peshawar and Kohat. Rather than bombing the Peshawer runway, however, IAF bombers mistook the mall road in Peshawer as the runway and dropped their bombs there instead. The PAF admits that the IAF came very close to annihilating its entire fleet of B-57 bombers. The Canberras were intercepted by a Pakistani F-104 near Lahore but they managed to evade the Starfighter and return home safely. They also had an encounter with F-86 Sabres, one of which fired at the Canberras, which sustained some damage. A Pakistani F-86 Sabre also crashed while conducting an evasive maneuvere in an attempt to escape pursuit, from an escorting Gnat as it tried to defend the Canberra bombers; the PAF pilot was killed. The Gnat pilot, W/C Singh, was later credited with an aerial victory for this incident near Amritsar. Later, one Pakistani B-57 was shot down by anti-aircraft fire over Adampur, although both of its crew managed to eject safely and remained POWs.

On 15 September the PAF employed a number of its Lockheed C-130 Hercules transport aircraft as bombers, which proved unsuccessful; two of them were shot down by the IAF. The following day, one IAF Hunter and a PAF F-86 Sabre were shot down over Halwara. The IAF pilot was killed in the encounter, although the Pakistani pilot ejected and spent the rest of the war as a POW. A Pakistani Cessna was also shot down that day, as well as an Auster observation aircraft. On 18 September a Sabre was shot down by a Gnat over Amritsar; the matter was reported by the Collector, who had witnessed the entire dogfight. The same day a Pakistani Sabre shot down a civilian Indian aircraft even after the civilian plane indicated its identity, the PAF pilot assuming it to be a reconnaissance mission. Years later, the PAF pilot wrote a letter to the Indian pilot's daughter to apologize for shooting down the aircraft. The aircraft had been carrying the then Gujarat Chief Minister Balwant Rai and his family.

On 19 September a Gnat and two Sabres were downed over Chawinda. One of the Sabres that were shot down was credited to Squadron Leader Denzil Keelor, the brother of Trevor Keelor, who was credited with the first Indian aerial victory of the war. The following day, another two Hunters and an F-86 Sabre were lost over Kasur, Pakistan.

At one stage the IAF was operating 200 air missions simultaneously. IAF Folland Gnats of Nos 9 and 23 squadrons played a significant role in major air battles.

On 21 September IAF Canberras carried out a daring daylight strike into Pakistan against the radar complex in Badin. The raid proved to be successful. Under the command of Wing Commander Peter Wilson, six Canberras from No. 16 Squadron took off from Agra, over 1,000 km from Bladin and proceeded towards the radar complex at low level. About 80 miles (130 km) short of the target, one Canberra climbed to an altitude of 10,000 feet in order to act as a decoy, before returning to base. The other five Canberras continued on towards the target. The flight then separated and four of the aircraft approached the target in two sections, each two minutes apart, at low level; before climbing to 7,000 feet from where they carried out bombing runs, dropping approximately 10,000 lbs of explosives. Wilson then approached from the south at an altitude of just 30 feet firing a salvo of 68mm rockets at the radar dome.

On the same day a PAF F-104 intercepted a Canberra bomber on its way back from Sargodha and shot it down, while one Hunter pilot who was the son of Chief of the Indian Army was shot down by anti-aircraft fire; he ejected and was taken POW. The ceasefire was declared on the night of September 22, 1965.

Outcome

There are conflicting claims by either side on this issue. Pakistani sources suggest that Indian losses were in the range of 59–110 and Pakistani losses were around 18–43. Recent works have, however, attempted to move beyond the raw statistics of the number of losses each side incurred, arguing that in terms of aircraft lost to sorties flown, the Indian Air Force's attrition rate (1.5%) was lower than the Pakistani attrition rate (1.82%). Arguably this indicates that had the war continued, the PAF would have found it increasingly difficult to sustain operations at the same level. Nevertheless, a similar argument can be made about the IAF also, although it did have a significant size advantage that might have proved telling if the war had been prolonged.

Another factor which makes it difficult to determine the outcome of the 1965 air war is the issue of aircraft lost in the air in air-to-air combat or to ground fire as opposed to aircraft lost on the ground due to bombing. Indian sources claimed that a large number of Indian aircraft losses occurred on the ground during the attacks on Kalaikkunda and Pathankot—up to 60 per cent by some accounts

Learning the Lessons

Much of the lessons of the 1965 war lead India to refine tactics which proved decisive in the 1971 war. Pakistani forces failed to take account of the extent to which they had relied on two factors which the IAF could not take for granted-complete ground based defensive radar coverage and an adequate supply of air-to-air missiles. Much effort was expended in India to remedy these deficiencies before 1971.

With Soviet aid, India established a modern early warning radar system, including the recently introduced 'Fansong-E' low-level radar, linked with SA-2 'Guideline' surface-to-air missiles and a large number of AA guns. By December 1971 the IAF comprised a total of 36 squadrons (of which 10 were deployed in the Bengal sector) with some 650 combat aircraft.

Moreover, the 1965 war resulted in the USA imposing a 10 year arms embargo on both sides. This had no effect, on India, which had always looked to Britain, France and even Russia for arms, but was disastrous for Pakistan, which was forced to acquire 90 obsolete second hand Sabre via Iran, a mere

28 Mirage IIIs from France and 74 maintenance intensive Shenyang F-6s. It was unable to replace losses among its (already weak) force of B-57s, or to acquire a modern interceptor in realistic numbers.

THE MILITARY REVOLUTION IN AIR POWER

The new military revolution has brought about changes to the entire military sphere, particularly to the reforms in the air force. To study the impact of the revolution on contemporary air power is of momentous significance to China's defense modernization and air force development.

Air Force Development and New Military Revolution

The fundamental cause of the current military revolution is the extensive application of modern technologies, within which information technology is the core. A modern air force is equipped by information technology, whose use in modern local war reveals the great changes in air power and its bright future. The development of air power is the most direct catalyst of such a revolution.

Since the 1950s, information technology has been developed worldwide. Automatic control and artificial intelligence technology have advanced quickly. Modern information technology was first applied in air weapons. Because of computers, automatic equipment and artificial intelligence, weapons have been invented, such as precision-guided weapons, telemetry and remote-sensing systems, electronic confrontation technology, and automatic C I systems. Air weapons have become the epitome of contemporary information technology. The special requirements of developing air weapons are the incentive for developing information technology. The mutual acceleration and simultaneous development of air weapons and information technology have resulted in the following accom-plishments:

- The transition from nonguided weapons to precision-guided weapons. Ground-to-air missiles have been developed in four modes high-altitude long range, medium-altitude medium range, and low-altitude and ultra-low altitude short range. Air-to-air missiles come in long, medium, and short range. Air-to-ground missiles come in two types strategic and campaign tactical . It is predicted that by the end of the 1990s, more guided weapons will be produced with higher intelligence that can identify the enemy force, avoid interference, and attack targets selectively. Such weapons will become the most important conventional equipment.
- The transition from "hard-kill" weapons to "soft and hard kill" weapons. Radio and eletro-optical equipment has become the core of modern

air weapons. The electronic equipment is 33 percent of the cost of planes, 45 percent of missile costs, and 66 percent of the cost of unmanned aircraft. The comprehensive aerospace electronic warfare system under development will even bring acoustic frequency into the weapon system, which can function to defeat radar, telecommunication, navigation and guided weapons.

- The transition from manual command to automatic command. The C I system has become the "nerve center" of modern air combat. The U.S. Air Force established the Strategic Air Command, the North America Air Defense Command, the ballistic missile long-range warning system, and the space monitoring systems. In addition, it possesses tactical air command centers, an air surveillance center, and AWACs. The future aerospace automatic command system will retain high reliability, confidentiality, confrontation, and information processing capacity.
- The combination of air defense, aviation and space defense and weapons. Since the end of the 1950s, the United States and the Soviet Union have developed ground-base anti-missile weapons and established layer antimissile systems. In the 1980s, military satellites, space aircraft, airships and space stations were developed. It is expected that by the end of the century, military utilization of flying machines can protect ground and air forces operations. By the early 21st century, attacks on space, air, ground and sea targets will have materialized. Air defense and space weapons will be able to fly both in the outer space and in the atmospheric layer.

The above changes illustrate that space-weapon development is in a transitional period of integrating information technology with weapon production. Space weapon systems have possessed some quasi-human functions (such as observation, memory, analysis and synthesis). Missiles have become "shells with eyes." Future air force C I systems and various weapons will be controlled by intelligence machines, and will have dialogue with human beings through connection with information processing and displaying working stations. The systems will not only change the air combat information process and transmission modes but also integrate humans, combat theory, and computers into a whole. Through the systems, human intelligence can be immediately released in the form of energy to obtain unprecedented combat effectiveness. Since World War II, the conventional destructive capacity of aircraft has increased by 70 percent. Specifically, modern air weapons have developed in seven aspects:

- Higher precision. Precision-guided weapon technology helps to produce space weapons that can attack various objects thousand kilometers away around the clock. The deviation of cruise missiles is only around a dozen meters, and that of various tactical missiles is 1 meter. The percentage of hits can amount to 98 percent. High-speed, antiradiation missiles can automatically shun radar inference and strike the target. Short-range missiles can fly at a speed three times faster than sonic speed. The range of precision glide bombs reaches 80 km. The highest speed of long-range air-to-air missiles is 43 Mach and the range is 110 to 165 km. Laser-guided missiles are able to go through the vents of fortifications, windows, or doors and explode inside the building. Antitank missiles, after being launched from aircraft, can search for a target automatically at an altitude of several thousand meters.

- Increased stealth. The development of stealth aircraft reduces radar determining range from a few hundred kilometers to a bit more than a dozen kilometers. Further advances in stealth aerospace weapons will make sudden attacks realistic and disable the air-defense warning system and entire air-defense systems.
- Improved night vision. The infrared observation system installed in aircraft makes it possible that a pilot can position at night, discover and destroy targets. The wide application of new technical night vision equipment will bring an end to airmen's "night shift."
- Increased long-range attack ability. Advanced aviation power, impetus technology, and new materials have greatly improved the mobility of aircraft. Accompanied with in-flight refueling and space technology, an air force can realize the legend of combat at the global range.
- Increased destruction power. High-tech equipped weapons have more power to attack and destroy targets. Ordinary aircraft, when equipped with new weapon systems, are doubled and redoubled in combat ability. An operational assignment that needed 230 B-17 bombers during World War II can now be accomplished by eight F-16 fighters.
- Increased command and control capacity. Infrared, laser, telemetry, and remote-sensing technologies have greatly improved the function of air and space reconnaissance systems. The side with technical advantages will take the initiative of the war by controlling information, and use the highly automatic C I to control air operations effectively. The prewarning command aircraft can improve the combat effectiveness by a few dozen times.
- Increased electromagnetic confrontation capacity. Electron confrontation technology provides air electromagnetic combat with high efficiency, complete coverage, and strong power.

The development and application of air information weapon systems immediately resulted in revolutionary changes in the war field. A lot of concepts only imagined or developed a few years ago became reality in Operation Desert Storm. To a great extent, information combat has been enlightened by the Gulf War, in which multinational troops captured all the high-frequency and ultrahigh frequency radio signals of the Iraqi army and stored the numerous amounts of information gathered by the 34 reconnaissance satellites, 260 electronic reconnaissance planes, and 40 prewarning aircraft. Then, the multinational troops used various information systems and high-tech weapons to destroy the Iraqi communication system and take control of the war. The Iraqi command system, radar, and command systems of missiles, aircraft, and artillery were at a standstill. This demonstrates that information is the key to victory. The side that controls information can give full play to the materials and energy possessed, and thereby increase combat power.

After the Gulf War, the U.S. military gradually increased research centered on information combat. U.S. Defense Secretary Perry put forward the proposal of "military revolution" in early 1994, which officially confirmed the existence of the revolution. A special group was organized to conduct research on how the Pentagon can obtain and maintain decisive military superiority within the next two and three decades. Therefore, modern high technology, the key to the new military revolution, has caused the development of contemporary air power. The application of air power in Desert Storm, on the other hand, is the "trigger" of the new military revolution. It is predicated that future air strength will have much greater development under the influence and acceleration of the revolution.

THE BUILDUP OF AIR STRENGTH

The Gulf War displayed not only the embryonic form of information combat but also the advantages of air power and revealed the importance of air power in bringing about satisfactory operational effectiveness in information combat. Therefore, each nation has prioritized the development of air strength under the principle of upgrading the entire defense system and developing all forces:

- Acknowledge that air power is the dominant force in contemporary local war.
- Maintain a stable or increasingly growing air force.
- Keep a relatively higher input of military expenditure in the air force. Emphasize the role of the air force as the nucleus in the theory of war as a breakthrough of reforming the contemporary military.
- Strengthen the buildup of ground forces and naval air forces.

The reasons why each nation lays stress on the buildup of the air force are:

- The demands of the information age. The Gulf War revealed the power of information combat. Western countries, particularly the United States, are keen in their preparing for information combat to consolidate their military positions through highly efficient military construction during the new military revolution. Although various military forces will play different roles in future information war, air strength will possess a unique superiority that is more adapted to modern war.

In battlefield command, gaining the upper hand in information confrontation can help commanders make decisions and work out strategies. Hence, information superiority is becoming a tremendous combat strength. The C I system is important to winning information superiority in battle and to improve the flexibility of the army and navy. Under the influence of modern high technology, the ability to obtain battlefield information from air and space has witnessed fundamental changes. Outer space itself becomes a battlefield of monitoring to provide reliable information with the assistance of reconnaissance, communication, navigation, and orientation systems and early-warning systems. Information gathered can be used for strategic command, for campaign and combat command and even by single vessels, vehicles, and soldiers. From the viewpoint of electromagnetic combat, armed strength in ground and marine battlefields will be greatly heightened by electromagnetic domination obtained through integrated electronic combat. Air and space are the major fields of electromagnetic confrontation in modern war. Air electronic confrontation equipment, compared to that on the ground, can cover a wider space and have a higher fighting efficiency. The U.S. Army has developed more than 600 electronic combat devices, of which 70 percent is installed in aircraft. Electronic combat in air raids can use electronic devices to reconnaissance, interfere, search, position and monitor an opponent's targets, as well as to cope with enemy electronic mechanisms, in combination with automatic command system and electronic suppression and deceiving devices. Thus, enemy communication will be cut off and radar and guided weapons disabled. Losses on one's own side will be reduced to minimum.

As for firepower, the destruction power has seen great improvement because of the combination of space electronic measures, firepower, and application of weapons with high precision and coverage. One prominent change is the growing proportion of air firepower in modern war. According to statistics, the U.S. Army's air munitions have increased dramatically. Today's stockpile is four times that of WWII, three times that of the total ammunition used in the Korean war, twice that of the Vietnam War, and a fifth more than that used in the Gulf War. In addition, 70 percent of casualties and injuries to enemy troops in the Vietnam War was caused by U.S. air firepower. Half the Arab tanks damaged during the fourth Middle East War was destroyed by the Israeli Air Force. During the Falkland Islands war between Britain and Argentina, 90 percent of the 29 vessels that were lost was due to air strikes. All the above indicates that with the rapid development of air weapons, the focus of modern war is gradually shifting to the air. Air firepower is becoming the backbone of joint military forces.

An important feature of information combat is the speed. Strategic air transport serves as the key to releasing and expanding the operational potential of strategic mobility. Speed and strength are the two core elements of measuring the combat effectiveness of strategic mobile force. In contemporary conditions, the contrast of strategic strength is not determined by the military force in a certain area but by the strength of strategic mobility. In modern times, partial wars break out quickly in a vast space, which allows very limited time to carry out an effective reaction. Only through speedy delivery of combat forces to favorable positions can decisive impact be exerted. Among various delivery measures, air transport is the most effective action because of its strong mobility, fast speed, and less restrictive geographic conditions. Air transport in modern times has a greater effect because of its capability of delivering force in large freight size, over a long distance, and at a fast speed between continents. To a certain extent, air transport is the amplifier of the combat strength of the strategic mobile forces of military powers and is an important condition in winning an information war.

- New and higher demands for air force are needed with the change of war format in the information era. Strategically, the focus of international military struggle in the information era has been changed from actual combat to menace. To be able to threaten other nations, one should possess a powerful attacking force. Currently, each country has some kind of means to threaten others. However, air threat takes a predominant position owing to its features of high technology, large capacity, multifunctions, all levels, and speed. Air intimidation shortens the distance between the antagonistic parties, although physically they might be thousand miles apart. Each action will arouse the opponent's vigilance. An air force can facilitate speedy and effective attacks on the enemy. Modern strategy enhances the need of air combat capacity and its function of achieving the strategic goal. This is inevitably a great impetus to develop air force.

On the other hand, military combat strength in the information era is relatively reduced. Coping with local war and controlling crises becomes the strategic concern. Local war, which restricts operational goals, time, and space, puts forward new requirements for air combat ability. To achieve the strategic goal, ground operational measures are greatly restrained and air operations enhanced. Air operations often become the major or even the only force to be used. On the other hand, the air force, which can avoid direct contact with the opponent and quickly deliver strategic proposal, can start and stop operations easily so they will not result in territorial disputes and a cease-fire agreement. This is definitely what military decisionmakers want to apply in today's conflicts, in which no one wants to escalate the conflicts but everyone is eager to restrain the other. The standard of winning and losing is changed to a great extent. The ultimate goal of the parties involved is not to occupy the other's territory but to check the enemy country and take initiative at the negotiation table. Because an air force can achieve such a goal without escalating the conflict, it has more opportunities to be employed. In addition, the attacking side places more importance on reducing human casualties by increasing material loss. As a former U.S. Air Force Chief of Staff said before the Gulf War, the only way to avoid excessive bloodshed by the army was to use the air force.

- The limitation on use of nuclear weapons in the information era also provides opportunity to develop air force. Since the 1970s, the United States and the former Soviet Union have made fundamental changes in designing future operational conditions. This is because the quantity and quality of the strategic nuclear weapons of both sides was increased quickly, and both parties have had the nuclear capacity to destroy the other. Therefore, they believe that using nuclear weapons surpasses the purpose of war. In nuclear war, there is no winner. On the other hand, the conventional operational ability of air force has been greatly improved with the materialization of information technology. The number of weapons with comparable strength to small nuclear weapons has been increased. Currently, a heavy bomber's fatal efficiency index can reach 207 million, compared to 170 million of a 1,000-ton equivalent nuclear warhead. This means that informationized air weapons not only can replace nuclear weapons to a certain extent, but also have larger application in war. As individual weapons, most aircraft cannot compete with nuclear weapons in terms of power. However, the gap between the added effect of multiple use of air weapons and small nuclear weapons is narrowing.

Because of the strict restriction on use of nuclear weapons and the air force's replacement of nuclear force, nuclear-possessing countries have started to shift their attention from preparing for nuclear war to conventional war.

The production of nuclear weapons is slowed down. The principle of using nuclear weapons has been changed from "using in the first place" to "using at the last stage." Strategic rockets are in a declining position and the air force enjoys a rising importance. Both the United States and the former Soviet Union have re-emphasized the role of air force to make up the gap in fire structure caused by restrictions on the use of nuclear weapons.

This analysis shows that strengthening the air force is an inevitable outcome of the development of the new military revolution, and the changes in war format and the world nuclear situation. Further development of the air force will eventually increase the struggle among nations in fighting for air superiority. Future information war will rely more and more on air superiority. The air force will no longer be an important independent strategic force but an effective conventional campaign force that all services will depend upon. Each service will own a troop of airmen. Such a trend will further spur the conventionalization of high-tech equipment, development of information war and nonlinear operation of combat modes, therefore, strengthening the polar position of air force in modern military strategy.

Quality Restructuring of the Air Force

After the Gulf War, each key country adjusted its military strategy and the structure of its armed forces to adapt to the transformed military threat and to ease the tension between demand and possibility of armed force establishment. The core of the adjustment is to promote quality military establishment. As a high-tech-equipped service, the air force will be given these considerations:

- Consensus on a small but high-quality army. To adapt to new military strategy and tasks, large countries have adopted the policy of reducing the size of their air forces. The U.S. Air Force has taken a large step in this regard. Within 5 years, the U.S. Air Force has reduced its service staff from 600,000 to 400,000 and the number of aircraft in service has been cut from 7,000 to 5,000. The Russian Air Force has been cut by half because of the collapse of the former Soviet Union and the downsizing of troops (its military force was cut to 250,000). Both the British and German Air Forces have been reduced by one-fourth and their aircraft by 20 to 50 percent.

LIMITED AIR STRIKES FOR PEACEKEEPING MISSIONS

According to relevant resolutions of international organizations and at the request of peacekeeping forces, limited air strikes may be carried out by authorized countries or a group of countries against military targets that violate relevant rules; these are called limited aim air strikes. For example, in November 1994, in accordance with U.N. resolution 958, NATO's air forces bombed Udbey airport in Bosnia-Herzegovinia, which was controlled by Serbs. Soon after, Serbian military targets, such as ground-to-air missile positions and groups of tanks, were attacked by air.

Air Blockades at Sea

The sea-air blockade is one of the basic application modes of air power. It is a military action blockading a certain section of the sea, a certain coastal area, or a certain country by way of aerial mining in order to blockade seaports and sea lanes as well as attack targets trying to break the blockade. Naval blockades against Japan in World War II and against important ports of northern Vietnam in the Vietnam War were enforced mainly by aerial mining. In air battles of the 21st century, air blockades will still be important.

Strategic Air Lift

Strategic airlift is a large-scale operation to transport troops to warring regions by air. With the improvement of air transport, strategic airlift has demonstrated some incomparable advantages which other transport modes do not possess:

- It is high speed. Modern air transports are able to cover a distance of 800 to 900 km per hour while cruising, which is 10 times that of land transports. Because air transporters commonly take a direct route, air transport is the most rapid means of transport.
- Air transporters can cover a long distance. Modern strategic transports can travel thousands of miles. With air refueling, they are able to carry out global lift.
- Air transport is highly maneuverable and seldom restricted by geographic conditions. It can transport troops and military equipment to any airport in the world.
- Air transport has large freight volume. For example, an An-124 can carry 150 tons per sortie; the An-225, over 200 tons; the U.S. C-5, 120 tons. Modern air power is capable of transporting strategic troops. During Desert Shield in the Gulf War, the U.S. Army used 90 percent of its strategic transport and commandeered part of the civil aircraft fleet to air lift more than 500,000 personnel, equaling 99 percent of the total, and over 500,000 tons of material.

Precision/ Surgical Operation Air Strikes

Surgical air strikes are a growing aspect of air power employment in high-tech local wars. Its strategic objective is obtained by precisely attacking the enemy's sensitive strategic targets. Typical examples include the Israeli air force bombing both the Iraqi nuclear reactor in 1981 and the PLO headquarters in Tunisia in 1985, and the United States striking Libya in 1986. In this kind of operation, air power is the main strength, and sudden attack is the main operational principle.

Large-Scale Air Offensives

By studying the regional wars after World War II, especially recent regional wars, we can conclude that air offensives begin with massive air strikes in rather long and relatively separate phases.

Characteristics.

- It is large scale. In the Gulf War, the multinational forces used more than 2,700 planes, and 2,600 sorties were dispatched each day.
- It lasts a rather long time. The Gulf War can be divided into four stages strategic air strikes, seizing local air dominance, battlefield preparation, and ground operations. Missions in the first three stages were done in 38 days, equaling 90 percent of the total time of the war.
- In large-scale air offensives, there is a direct confrontation for victory and domination. In the Gulf War, air operations reduced the Iraqi troops' operating capability by 50 percent, which ensured that the U.S.-led multinational forces would win the ultimate victory.

Joint Operation of Various Services

Joint operation of various services means air power joins in an equal partnership with the army and navy. This symbolizes a qualitative change from previous history. In the past, the air force assisted the army or the navy to carry out missions. In past large-scale wars, the air force's operational role was subordinate to that of the army and navy and could only share the victory of the army and navy. When air operations became decisive, a great breakthrough was made in applying air power.

Characteristics.

- Air power is in an equal partnership with the army and the navy. Air power is mainly used in strategic depth and campaign depth.
- Air power is able to function in more special fields, such as reconnaissance, warning, electronic warfare, aerial mining, artillery and anti-aircraft strike tasks, road blockades, feints, protection of supplies and communications, etc.

BASIC OPERATIONAL METHODS

Before the Vietnam War, when air strikes were carried out by the same type of aircraft, visual coordination was the main type of strike. Air operation methods qualitatively changed during the Vietnam War, when several joint operational methods with various types of aircrafts taking part came into use. In order to cope with the integrated air-defense systems comprising fighters, surface-to-air missiles, anti-aircraft guns and air-defense C3I systems, an operation took shape to include formations such as airborne early warning and command formations, escort and protective formations, strike formations, air defense suppression formations, reconnaissance formations, electronic warfare formations, air refueling formations, air-rescue formations, etc. Among these the strike formations are the main force, with the rest supporting, protecting and assisting.

Along with the further development of the operational mode, joint air strikes were invented. In the Gulf War, a typical daytime strike group of aircraft of the multinational forces comprised 60 aircraft, in addition to the stealth aircraft. The daytime strike formations included 24 F16-A/Cs, "Tornados," and A-10s, escort formations of 12 F15Cs and Mirage-2000s, accompanying jamming formations of EA-6Bs, EF-111As and one EC-130H, and finally hard-target electronic warfare formations of F-4Gs and A-6Fs equipped with antiradiation missiles. There were also some airborne early warning aircraft and air refueling aircraft participating in actions. Joint air strikes became the main operational mode the multinational forces used in the Gulf War.

As the basic operational mode, joint air strikes completely alter the operational state of air battle space. Thus, joint air strikes have the typical characteristics of nonlinear operations. What may be pointed out is that the way air battlefields were dominated by air power completely changed in the Gulf War. Participants in air operations also included army helicopters, navy Tomahawk cruise missiles, reconnaissance satellites, communication satellites, and global positioning systems comprising over 30 satellites. This change lifts the joint air operation to a new height, unlike previous small joint operations. While a great number of digitized troops are going to be established and a large number of digitized battlefields are taking shape, the three-dimensional air strikes that developed in the Gulf War will become a basic mode of air operations in the future.

Global Strike and Global Reach

When the operational mode of global strike and global reach is applied, the battle space is enlarged, and traditional theories and ideas about the battlefield are broken. Any target in any part of the world is within striking range of air power. After the Gulf War, the main military powers in the world decided to enhance their air power's ability to carry out global strike and all-depth operations. In May 1993, the Russian Air Force organized a large-scale intercontinental maneuver operational exercise from its European region to the Far East. According to the military strategy of "forward presence plus troop transport," the U.S. Air Force established an operational doctrine of "global reach and global operations."

Over-the-Horizon Air Combat

Air combat is the main means of air power used to annihilate the enemy air force. According to distance, it is divided into visual air combat and beyond-the-horizon air combat. The main concept of air combat has been to attack from behind at a distance of hundreds to thousands of meters. The precondition of attacking is the occupation the advantageous position at the rear of the opponent, called short-range air combat.

In the Gulf War, most planes of the multinational forces belonged to the third generation. These planes are of advanced performance, their airborne fire-control radars are capable of surveilling a distance of more than 100 km, simultaneously tracking quite a number of targets from scores of kilometers away, and carrying out attacks over a wide range of altitudes. These capabilities provide a reliable launching platform to make beyond-the-horizon attacks. According to materials the U.S. Defense Department released after the Gulf War, 38 Iraqi aircraft were destroyed in air combat, among which 28 were destroyed by Sparrow AIM-7M mi-range missiles; 10 were shot down by Sidewinder AIM-9L short-range missiles; and the rest were ruined by aircraft guns. The Gulf War was the first rather large-scale regional war in which the number of aircraft destroyed in beyond-the-horizon air combat exceeded those destroyed in visual air combat. It indicates that beyond-the-horizon air combat technology is maturing.

Deep-Strike and Stand-Off Munitions

Ever since air weapons came into being, the way to attack ground targets was to bomb right over the targets after penetrating the ground-to-air defense. In the past 10 years, this method has been used less frequently. Instead, a method that has been used more and more often is to stand off and launch munitions from a long range. This tendency is bringing great changes to air-to-ground operations. Primarily because of stand-off air-to-ground missiles, air power is capable of launching attacks from a long distance, out of range of the defense.

Stealth Penetration

In the first air raid in the Gulf War, 30 U.S. Air Force F-117A stealth fighters directly attacked Baghdad after flying beyond Iraqi air-defense troops, instead of attacking air-defense radars and neutralizing airports and air-defense ground positions to open a penetrating corridor for followup units. This new operational method is characteristic of nonlinear operations. It stops the enemy from organizing effective defenses by harassing the enemy's air-defense rhythm. Relying on stealth fighters' being difficult to be detect, stealth penetration neutralizes the enemy's old formula of air-defense operations, which can be described thusly: find incoming targets; judge the nature of the targets and degree of threat; assign targets; order air defense troops to annihilate the targets. With stealth, the enemy is attacked before they detect the incoming targets. Because it is the crucial positions of the enemy's air-defense system that are first attacked by stealth planes, the enemy's air-defense troops have been paralyzed before they are put into action, so it is impossible for them to arrange organized resistance against the air -raid. Therefore, the air raid attacks predetermined targets without facing resistance. Using this method in the Gulf War, the U.S. Army reduced the ratio of assault troops to service troops to 1:1, and kept the loss rate at 0.03 percent. More and more stealth planes will be rushing into the air battlefields of the 21st century, and stealth penetration bombing will be more commonly applied.

All-Weather and Round-the-Clock Air Strikes

The performance of airborne fire-control-radar is being improved, and night-vision devices such as infrared and low-light devices and space-based precision guidance systems are being added. Many midrange air-to-air missiles, air-to-ground missiles, infrared-guided bombs and laser-guided bombs are being used. Air power has greatly enhanced its ability to attack air and ground targets at night and in any meteorological conditions. Meanwhile, air power can perform all-weather and round-the-clock attacks. This was the case in the Gulf War. Throughout the Gulf War, all-weather and round-the-clock continuous operations were carried out by the multinational forces, in which sorties dispatched at night equaled 70 percent of the total. Characteristics. Because all-weather and round-the-clock operations are widely used, the better equipped side benefits from the night and bad weather, which previously favored the less well equipped side. Because of high-technology, night battlefields become transparent. Bad weather is no longer an obstacle to the better equipped side. Meanwhile, the poorly equipped side can no longer utilize the night and bad weather to change its unfavorable situation. This operational mode greatly intensifies operations and speeds up the rhythm of war. Attacking Joints and Ripping Fabric The third generation of precision-guided bombs has an accuracy of less than 1 meter. Modern air strikes tend to be "one bomb, one target." Air power's ability in precision strike is increasing and the mode of long-range precision strike is used. It is possible through joint strikes to achieve fabric ripping.

According to systematic opinions, modern military strength is entirely composed of various services and various weapon systems with different functions. Joining various weapons is decisive in the operational system. We call this striking the seams and ripping the fabric in order to "take down" the enemy's operational system, to weaken or even to paralyze it by way of precisely attacking the system or its crucial positions with a certain number of weapons.

It was by way of attacking the seams of the Iraqi air-defense system that the multinational forces ripped the fabric of the Iraqi air-defense system in the Gulf War. The multinational forces took the Iraqi C3I system as the main target to assault. Twenty hours before the first air raid, electronic warfare began to jam and neutralize the Iraqi C3I system. In the first air raid, Iraqi targets such as command and communication centers were heavily attacked by Tomahawk cruise missiles and F-117 stealth fighters of the multinational forces. Because Iraq's C3I system had been violated, even though it had preserved a great deal of weapons and equipment with the help of advanced defense systems, its anti-aircraft guns could merely fire separately, its ground-to-air missiles could only be launched without aim, and its operational aircraft could not take off. It is predicted that the operational concept of assault on the seams and fabric violation will be commonly used in the air battlefields of the 21st century.

EQUIPMENT AND PROCUREMENT OF CHINA

Current ROCAF inventory includes over 400 combat aircraft, the mainstays being the F-CK-1 IDF and F-16 while the Mirage 2000-5 provides the most formidable air-defence capabilities. Older F-5 fighters are gradually being phased out but remain in service.

The United States serves as the ROCAF's main supplier of equipment and also provides training for German Air Force (Luftwaffe) and German Naval Aviation (Marineflieger)pilots at Luke AFB in Arizona.

Domestic Development

Prior to 1984, ROCAF fighters were almost exclusively American-made aircraft sold under terms of a mutual defence treaty between the Republic of China and the United States. Development of the F-CK-1 "Ching-kuo" Indigenous Defence Fighter (IDF) began in 1984 due to U.S. refusal to sell F-16s to the ROCAF as a result of changes in national policy between the U.S. and the People's Republic of China. After a successful maiden flight in 1989, the domestically produced fighter entered service in 1994. However, the ROCAF was subsequently able to obtain F-16s from the United States as well as Mirage 2000-5 fighters from France, resulting in delays to later IDF development that had been anticipated.

In response to American refusals to supply "smart bombs", Taiwan is developing their own equivalent of the Joint Direct Attack Munition for attacks against the PRC mainland in case of invasion preparations.

Foreign Procurement

In January 2006, the ROCAF announced interest in procuring planes with VSTOLcapability, especially the F-35. The ROCAF also sought next-generation upgrades to its current F-16s and Mirage 2000-5s and, in mid-2006, announced plans to buy 66 F-16 C/D Block 52 aircraft from the US for $3.1 billion USD. Later that year, however, the U.S. delayed the purchase; according to sources cited by National Defence Minister Lee Jye, the American stance was that, until a long-stalled arms purchase package consisting of six Patriot Missile Batteries, 12 P-3C Orion anti-submarine aircraft and 8 conventional submarines cleared the legislature, it did not see the ROC as having a consistent military procurement plan.

On February 28, 2007, the US Defence Department approved an order made by the ROC for 218 AIM-120C-7 AMRAAM missiles, as well as 235 AGM-65G2 Maverick missiles, associated launchers and other equipment. The total value of this order was revealed to be $421 million USD.

In June 2007, the Legislative Yuan also approved the upgrade of the existing PAC-2 batteries to PAC-3 standard, and, in November, the Pentagon notified the U.S. Congress of the Patriot upgrade order. On August 10, 2007, a shipment of Harpoon anti-ship missiles, valued at an estimated $125 million, was also authorised by the U.S. Defence Department, including 60 AGM-84L Block II missiles and 50 upgrade kits to bring the ROCAF's existing Harpoons up to Block II, Mark L standard.

On October 3, 2008, arms notifications were sent to Congress concerning, amongst other things, the sale of 330 PAC III missiles, 4 missile batteries, radar sets, ground stations and other equipment valued up to $3.1 billion USD, the upgrade of 4 E-2T aircraft to the Hawkeye 2000 standard and $334 million USD worth of spare parts for the ROCAF's F-16s, IDFs, F-5E/Fs and C-130s. Late in January 2010, ROCAF received the first batch of new TC-2(V) BVR missiles ordered from CSIST, believed to have new radar seeker and improved performance from the original missile which entered service over 10 years ago. The U.S. government also announced 5 notifications to Congress for additional arms sales totaling some $6.39 Billion USD, under which the ROCAF will receive 3 PAC-3 batteries with 26 launchers and 114 PAC-3 missiles. On February 3, 2010, ROCAF also announced at a Singapore Airshow that it had signed a new contract for 3 EC-225 SAR (Search-And-Rescue) helicopters that was awarded to Eurocopter back in December 2009 for $111 million USD, along with options for 17 more EC-225s.

On November 26, 2011, the 3 EC-225 C-SAR helicopters were loaded on board an An-124 cargo plane and delivered to Chai-yi AB in Taiwan, and should enter service on July 1, 2012.

On August 31, 2010, it was announced for next year's defence budget, ROCAF's "Medium Transport aircraft" plan to replace 12 B-1900 VIP/transport training aircraft, believed to be 6-8+ Lockheed C-27J, has been put on hold and might be axed, due to lack of budget, but will allocate 20+ million US dollars over next 4 years for quick runway repair. Other items mentioned including increases in runways from 3 to 6 at Eastern Taiwan's 3 airbases, moving 2 I-HAWK batteries to Eastern Taiwan to protect those airbases, which will double to 4 batteries, and others.

On November 8, 2011, a second pair of E-2T Hawkeye AEW(s/n 2501 and 2502) were loaded on ship and sent to US for upgrade to E-2C 2000. The first pair of E-2T (s/n 2503 and 2504) were sent to US in June 2010 and returned to Taiwan December 18, 2011, and will be return to service by end of the year.

On August 15, 2011, the United States again deferred the ROCAF request to purchase 66 new F-16C/Ds but offered a retrofit package for older F-16A/B's. A $5.3 billion upgrade package for ROCAF's existing F-16A/B fighters was announced on 21 September 2011.

The upgrade budget was to be spread over 12 years, though the Ministry of Defence indicated that it would try to reduce the period. In November 2011, the United States-China Economic and Security Review Commission recommended that new fighters be sold to the ROCAF. Nonetheless, as of 2012, the MND was still haggling with the Pentagon over cost and local industry participation on the upgrade.

After denying the RoC Air Force the funds needed to upgrade their jet engines, President Ma Ying-jeou said that he hoped that the upgraded fighters would have on par performance. Taiwan is also balking at the cost of the radar upgrade, as it does not want to be the lead customer who pays to develop the upgrade and also because they will be unable to afford both the upgrade and the new fighters, should these be offered.

In response to a U.S. vote in the House of Representatives to force the sale of the C/D models, the ROC MND said that the upgrade package offered some superior capabilities over the C/D model aircraft and some defence officials have said that in light of the PRC's increasing capabilities, only the F-35 would be sufficient.

In July 2012, Taiwan's Aerospace Industrial Development Corp. and Lockheed Martin announced plans to establish a maintenance and overhaul centre to upgrade and maintain the F-16s in place without having to ship them back to the United States.

In 2012 a letter of acceptance was agreed on for a US$3.8 billion deal that included the radars, electronic warfare, structural improvements and new weapons. The high cost of the fighter upgrade is causing other modernization priorities such as tanks to be pushed back. A Pentagon report has corroborated that claim, asserting that the PRC would probably seek to destroy ROCAF airfields in the first stages of any attack, making a STOVL fighter such as the F-35B vital for effective defence.

4

Development of Airpower of China

QUEST FOR IMPROVED AEROSPACE POWER

China's quest for improved aerospace power is based on the Chinese Communist Party's (CCP) evolving strategic needs. The CCP's claim to legitimacy has tradi-tionally been based on the championship of national pride and the delivery of economic success. Challenges to these claims appear to have driven the CCP to resort to the exploitation of territorial sovereignty claims in the East China Sea and South China Sea. This is indicated by China's recent increasing presence and assertiveness in its near seas, which leads to regional tensions and potential confrontations with the US and its allies (in particular Japan).

The PLA has been prepared for a range of missions beyond China's immediate periphery for more than two decades. The current modernization plan is designed to improve the PLA's capacity to fight and win short, highly-intense regional contingencies, with a focus on deterring or defeating third-party intervention. It includes the development of capabilities to attack, at very long ranges, adversary forces that might deploy or operate within the Western Pacific in the air, maritime, space, electromagnetic, and information domains. To this purpose, China has been constantly increasing military spending with an emphasis on developing key Anti-Access / Area Denial (A2/AD) capabilities in the Asia-Pacific region, for which modern aerospace power and an 'informationized military' (see paragraph on Infor-mation Warfare) play a decisive role. Although the PRC has never publicly acknowledged an A2/AD strategy, it is widely regarded as obvious that China is developing A2/

AD in response to US dominance of the air and sea in the Pacific. China is, therefore, significantly upgrading its naval and naval aviation capabilities (notably, the first Chinese aircraft carrier 'Liaoning' was put into service in 2012). How-ever, the primary modernization focus has been to update the People's Liberation Army Air Force (PLAAF) along with the long-range strike and missile defence capabilities of the Second Artillery Forces.

Advanced Combat Aircraft

China began to acquire the Russian 4th generation -Su-27 Flanker-family fighters in the 1990s and later produced its own variants. Meanwhile, China has gone beyond cloning Russian aircraft and is now designing and building modified or new military aircraft and systems with limited or no foreign assistance, including their own 4th generation designs.

The PLAAF currently possesses more than 2,800 (manned) aircraft in total. Approximately 2,100 of these are combat aircraft, 600 of which are modern. The PLAAF's 4th generation aircraft include the FLANKER family with the J-11, J-15 (designed for carrier oper-ations), and J-16, as well as at least three versions of the J-10 FIREBIRD family, which is frequently compared to the F-16. More than 50

% of the fighter inventory is expected to be 4th generation by end of 2016.

Furthermore, China is continuing to design, upgrade and produce the JH-7 and JH-7B FLOUNDER fighter-bomber, the JF-17/FC-1 light fighter, and the L-15 advanced trainer. An upgraded version of the H-6 bomber aircraft (Chinese version of Tu-16 Badger) will have the ability to launch the CJ-10 cruise missile.

Indigenous 5th generation fighter / bomber aircraft -development is underway, with stealth capabilities, super-cruise capable turbofan engines, modern phased array radar technology, and internal weapons carriage. The J-20 will probably become operational in 2017 – 18. A second stealth fighter, the J-31, is also being tested. Finally, China is conceivably working on a new bomber concept, a large delta wing bomber with stealthy bomb bays.

Aircraft Weaponry

The PLAAF has a considerable number of tactical air-to-surface missiles (ASMs) as well as precision-guided munitions (PGMs), including all-weather, satellite-guided bombs, anti-radiation missiles and laser-guided bombs. China is developing smaller-sized ASMs such as the AR-1, KD-2, HJ-10 (anti-tank) and Blue Arrow 7 (laser-guided) in conjunction with its increasing development of Remotely Piloted Aerial Systems (RPAS). China is also adapting PGMs similar to the US Joint Direct Attack Munitions (JDAM) such as the FT-5 and LS-6 for RPAS.

Integrated Air and Missile Defence and Air C2

Within 300 nm of its coast, China has credible Integrated Air and Missile Defence (IADS) that relies on robust early warning, fighter aircraft, and a variety of SAM systems designed to counter adversary long-range airborne strike platforms. China is the main buyer of advanced Russian long-range SAMs SA-20 -(S-300) and the SA-21 (S-400) 'Triumf'. It is also scaling up the production of at least four indigenous advanced medium-range SAMs: HQ-9 (Chinese-built SA-10), HHQ-9 (naval version of the HQ-9), HQ-15 (upgraded SA-10), and HQ-18 (Chinese-built SA-12).

China has developed and fielded advanced modern passive radar systems and active, phased array, over-the-horizon (OTH) radars. Other indigenous radars, the JL-1A and the JY-27A, provide the basis for a considerable Ballistic Missile Defence (BMD) capability, supported by the development of an intercept cap-ability at exo-atmospheric altitudes (kinetic energy) as well as within the upper atmosphere.

Finally, two indigenous Airborne Warning and Control System (AWACS) programmes, known as KJ-2000 and KJ-500, improve detection ranges well beyond China's borders. After initial testing and operating in several -larger aircraft such as the IL-76, Y-8W, as well as the Israeli type Beriev A-50, the development of the Y-20 multirole transport aircraft will likely solve China's problems regarding the appropriate air frame for their AWACS.

Long Range Precision Strike

The development of China's conventionally armed missile capability has been extraordinarily rapid.

Improved accuracy has made China more capable against adversary air bases, ports and ships, logistic facilities, communications and other critical infrastructure. China's 'Second Artillery' Force fields a large array of conventionally armed ballistic missiles (currently at least 1,200).

Ground- and air-launched Land-Attack Cruise Missiles (LACM), as well as ground-, air-, ship- and submarine-launched Anti-Ship Cruise Missiles (ASCM), can hold targets at risk throughout the Asia-Pacific region. US and allied bases in Japan are in range of a growing number of Medium Range Ballistic Missiles (MRBM) as well as a variety of -LACMs. The US territory of Guam could be targeted by air-launched LACMs as well as by a new Intermediate Range Ballistic Missiles (IRBM) whose development is reaching close to maturity. Anti-ship variants of those IRBM, in combination with seaborne detection radars and precision guidance, might be used for -engaging adversary naval assets in distances up to 900 nm from the Chinese coast.

Remotely Piloted Aerial Systems

In order to increase the ability to conduct long-range reconnaissance and strike operations, China is pursuing a major RPAS development and employment -effort with impressive technological awareness and financial resources involved. The main High Altitude Long-Endurance (HALE) RPAS is the Xianglong, which can be compared with the US RQ-4 'Global Hawk'. The most important Medium Altitude Long Endurance (MALE) RPAS are the Yilong, Sky Saber, and the stealthy Lijian, all of which are designed to carry precision-strike weapons.

Space and Counterspace Capabilites

China boasts the most dynamic space programme in the world today, supported by a robust capacity for space lift. Over the last five years, China has launched 15 – 20 Space Lift Vehicles (SLV) and placed 17 – 25 satellites annually. For military purposes, China increased the number of on-orbit assets including intelligence surveillance reconnaissance (ISR), meteorological, communications, and navigation satellite constellations, which are capable of supporting targeting and theatre missile operations. These include electro-optical / infrared (EO / IR) or synthetic aperture radar (SAR) imagery satellites and electronic intelligence (ELINT) satellites. China is also improving the current constellation of -Beidou navigation satellites (NAVSATs), including the production of ground receivers. A global NAVSAT constellation is expected to be completed by 2020. This would provide the Chinese with a proprietary national satellite navigation capability independent of the US-governed Global Positioning System (GPS).

The PRC has successfully produced SLVs, called the 'Long March (LM)', in different payload classes (heavy, medium, and light). These LM SLVs are usually based on ballistic missile platforms and designed to launch small satellites into a low-Earth orbit with little effort and at low cost. In September 2015, China successfully launched the LM-6, its first liquid-fuelled SLV, which is intended to provide new flexibility for civil and military space missions. The LM-6 reportedly has a seven-day launch cycle which allows the PLA to rapidly replace satellite capabilities lost in the event of attack.

In terms of counterspace capabilities, the PLA is acquiring a range of technologies such as directed energy weapons and satellite jammers. In January 2007, China demonstrated a direct-ascent kinetic kill cap-ability against satellites in low Earth orbit by destroying one of its own defunct weather satellites.

Information Warfare

China has established imperatives for the PLAAF's modernization in a way that allows an 'informationized' force to win an 'informationized' war.

The concept of 'informationization' permeates the PLA's doctrine, which emphasizes the holistic integration of digitally linked information, sensors, weapons, and an automated command and control system operating via common networks. PLAAF military writings furthermore describe informationized warfare as an asymmetric means to defeat a technologically superior, information-dependent adversary through dominating the battlefield's information space, weakening its ability to acquire, transmit, process, and use information, and thereby forcing the adversary to capitulate perhaps even before the onset of conflict. The PLA therefore conducts military exercises simulating operations in complex electromagnetic environment, viewing Electronic Warfare (EW) and cyber operations as a means of information dominance.

Outlook

The PRC appears to have undertaken a comprehensive development programme of aerospace capabilities and is clearly pursuing methodical and rapid modernization of its offensive air, air defence, missile defence, space, counterspace, ISR, EW and cyber cap-abilities. Given its will and resources, the PRC is likely to continue its military advancement programmes with increasing speed and ambitions. The material and technological disadvantages which the PLA has historically faced are therefore likely to decrease rapidly. Conversely, NATO and its allies cannot single-mindedly rely on superior technology. The PRC's parallel advancements in ground and naval capabilities reveal that the PLA has significantly matured in all three pillars of a successful A2/AD strategy: modern technology, dominance of the maritime, air and space domains, as well as information superiority.

As General Frank Gorenc, Director of the JAPCC, stated in a September 2014 interview, NATO needs to come to the realization that it does not have complete air dominance. It might have to either suppress or destroy enemy air defences. 'We tend to take some things for granted, like air superiority', Gorenc asserted. 'But in an A2/AD environment – the kind of layered long-range defense being built by Russia, China, and to a lesser extent Iran – we would have to earn air superiority.' In other words, NATO would have to fight for it. Readers who are employed in the current series of NATO exercises should therefore not be surprised: the 'SOROTAN' scenario confronts them with an enemy air order of battle that is designed to challenge NATO oper-ators with a realistic A2/AD scenario.

AIR FORCES AND COMBAT AIRCRAFT

The People's Liberation Army Air Force, PLAAF, currently possesses about 4,350 aircraft, of which the majority are combat aircraft. IDDS estimates that the inventory of Chinese combat aircraft on 1 January 2000 includes the following: 1900 J-6/MiG-19 (all roles and models: fighter, reconnaissance, trainer); 720 J-7/MiG-21 (all roles and models: fighter, reconnaissance, trainer); 222 J-8I/II/III; 55 J-11/Su-27SK; 440 Q-5 (modified MiG-19); 307 H-5/Il-28; and 142 H-6/Tu-16. Small numbers of JH-7s (fewer than 12) and K-8s (10-15) may also be in service. Of these aircraft, the great majority (J-6 and J-7) are of types which began to be deployed before 1972. With the exception of 10 Il-76s, the airlift capabilities of the Chinese Airforce are limited to old Soviet tactical airlift planes built under license or reversed-engineered in China, such as the Y-5/An-2, Y-7/An-24, and Y-8/An-12.

Much confusion exists as to the direction China will take in the future regarding combat aircraft acquisition. The Chinese government has made a priority of the development of a local aerospace industry capable of producing technologically advanced aircraft. However, the results produced by the Chinese aircraft industry to date have not been promising. Despite decades of work, the only original combat aircraft to be designed and produced in China are the J-8 and JH-7, both of which took so long to develop that by the time they entered service, they were already obsolete by Western standards. The newer J-10, which has been in development for twenty years, probably won't enter service for another five years.

China is by no means unique in this respect. Except for the five largest industrial arms producers (the USA, Russia, Britain, France, and Germany), other countries that have attempted to produce indigenously designed combat aircraft, such as Israel, South Africa, India, Taiwan, and South Korea, have abandoned these efforts and returned to importing systems from one of the five main producers. The basic reason is that the economies of scale required to finance research, development, and production of all the systems and sub-systems that make up today's frontline combat aircraft are not available to smaller industrial countries nor to large developing countries with smaller GNPs and smaller industrial bases. (In fact, for this reason, Russia is lagging increasingly behind the West in most areas of military technology.)

As a result of the inability of the Chinese aircraft industry to produce indigenously designed, technologically advanced combat aircraft, the Chinese government has partially reversed its policy of relying on domestic arms production and has renewed imports of combat aircraft from Russia—specifically, Su-27s and Su-30s—in small numbers. Over the next decade, China will produce Su-27s, with the Chinese designation J-11, under license from Russia. Up to 200 Su-27s may be built, but the total may be curtailed if China obtains licensing rights to the Su-30, which offers several technological advances over the Su-27. China currently plans to buy 30–60 Su-30MKs. In addition, China will continue to pursue its own aviation projects. Production of the latest model of the J-8 will continue in small batches. The JH-7 may also be produced in greater numbers, if PLAAF or PLAN can find a role for the aircraft in their inventories. The J-10 is scheduled to enter service around 2005 with initial reports of expected production up to 300 aircraft (depending in part on the progress of the Su-27 program). In any case, the J-10 and the J-11/Su-27 are expected to form the mainstay of the Chinese Air Force in the early 21st century.

Of great significance is China's plan to buy one-to-four AWAC aircraft from Israel. 11 If China purchases just one copy of the aircraft, which is an insufficient number for operational use, it will still provide an opportunity for the PLAAF to experience the use of airborne command and control. China is also making progress in in-flight refueling, and several H-6/Tu-16 bombers and Y-8/An-12 transports have been converted to tankers. As is the case for AWAC aircraft, more acquisitions of tankers will be needed if China seeks to obtain the capability to conduct combat aircraft operations at any distance from its own territory.

CHINESE ARMY MODERNIZATION: AN OVERVIEW

The Chinese People's Liberation Army (PLA) is in the third decade of a comprehensive program of modernization and transformation that began in 1979 after the PLA's last major campaign against a foreign enemy, its "self-defensive counterattack" against Vietnam. The program continues with renewed vigor into the new century.

Chinese military modernization encompasses all four services with priority of effort directed toward the PLA Navy (PLAN), the PLA Air Force (PLAAF), and the strategic missile force (known as the Second Artillery). The ground army, which previously had been the centre of gravity of the Chinese Armed Forces, remains the largest service and still provides the bulk of senior leadership for the military, but it has felt the brunt of force reductions as the PLA's mission emphasis has shifted. U.S. Army personnel who served in the post-Vietnam and post-Gulf War military should be able to appreciate the scope of what the Chinese are attempting and understand the time period required to achieve their goals.

The strategic underpinning for a long-term military modernization process was set in 1985 when China's supreme military command, the Central Military Commission (CMC), headed by paramount leader Deng Xiaoping, declared the most likely military contingency China faced to be "local, limited war" (replacing the threat of the "early, major, and nuclear war" foreseen by Mao Tse-tung).

Because the threat of major war was deemed low, senior Chinese leaders made the critical strategic decision to subordinate military modernization to other aspects of national economic development, such as agriculture, industry, and science and technology. Thus, in the 1980s and early 1990s, the Chinese Government did not spend vast sums of money and national resources to rapidly modernize the PLA. The "bloated" PLA could take its time to reform, focusing first on downsizing its 4-million-plus force.

For the first 10 years of modernization, China perceived its major potential foe to be the Soviet Union. Using force to reunify Taiwan with the mainland was low on the list of China's military priorities. By the mid-1990s, the situation between the mainland and Taiwan had changed considerably.

A multiparty democratic form of government was taking hold on the island, and voices for independence had risen. After the 1995-1996 crisis in the Taiwan Strait, China's leaders decided they needed to develop military capabilities more rapidly to prevent what Beijing perceived as further steps toward Taiwanese independence.

Although Chinese leaders preferred peaceful reunification of the island with the mainland, they knew Taiwan and its supporters in the United States had to see China's military power as credible. As a result, after 1999 the intensity of the PLA's modernization process increased, focusing principally on the goal of deterring Taiwan's independence and, if necessary, on imposing the will of Chinese leaders by force. Although the Taiwanese scenario became the top planning priority, training for a variety of military missions continued throughout the country and in all PLA units.

The acceleration of PLA modernization after 1999 became possible to a large extent because of the confluence of a more specifically defined mission, the availability of increased resources, a smaller force, and 20 years of previous effort that had laid the groundwork for what was to follow. In particular, many advances in the PLA since 1999 have taken advantage of the Nation's impressive economic growth during the 1990s, especially developments in the Chinese electronics industry. The end of the Soviet threat, along with the availability of advanced military weapons from a cash-strapped Russian Government, also contributed to changes in China's strategic posture in the late 1990s. Still, despite some marked improvements in China's military capabilities, the effectiveness of PLA modernization has yet to be proven in battle against a hostile force.

Elements of Modernization

By the turn of the 21st century, several distinct but interrelated elements have been seen in the PLA's modernization program. The following components of modernization were directly linked to developments of the previous two decades and enhanced by increased resources available since 1995:

* Reduction in force size.
* Changes in force structure.
* Reform of the structure and missions of the reserves and militia.
* Changes in the personnel system.
* An influx of new equipment.
* Doctrinal revision to prepare the PLA to fight and win Local Wars Under Modern High-Technology Conditions or Local Wars Under Informationalization Conditions.
* Improvements in the frequency, content, and methods of military training, with emphasis on joint operations.
* Transformation of the PLA logistics system.
* Enhancement of all soldiers' standard of living, pay, and lifestyle.
* Modification of the professional military education system.

Members of the U.S. Army will appreciate the complexity of the PLA's transformation, its long-term nature, and the difficulty of the tasks Chinese military leaders face. The PLA is also pursuing modernization with a much smaller resource and combat experience base than did the U.S. Army in the 1970s and 1990s. On the positive side, the PLA's modernization goals are more manageable because, unlike the U.S. Army, the PLA does not seek to project force across oceans, and it limits its scope of operations to what it considers protection of Chinese sovereignty (which, by definition, includes Taiwan and much of the South China Sea). The PLA does not have to man foreign bases and respond to a web of defence commitments throughout the world. Moreover, unlike the U.S. Army, the PLA remains a party-army bonded by loyalty to the Chinese Communist Party.

Security apparatus. The PLA is one of three elements of the Chinese Armed Forces, each of which is a separate, distinct organization, although all are closely related. According to China's National Defence Law of March 1997, Chinese Armed Forces are composed of the—

* PLA, both active and reserve units.
* People's Armed Police (PAP) Force.
* People's militia (ordinary and primary units).

The PLA is primarily responsible for defending China from external threats, with the secondary mission of domestic security in accordance with the law; that is, when requested by local authorities and approved by the central leadership. The ultimate command authority for the PLA is the CMC, with command running through four general headquarters departments in Beijing to the forces deployed in seven military regions throughout the country. The PLA, PAP, and militia wear similar but distinct uniforms, have similar organizational and rank structures, and undergo similar basic training, but they have separate systems for command and control, funding, promotion, education, and training. All three support national economic development with labour and service projects and can be mobilized to provide rescue and relief support in the event of floods, earthquakes, and other natural disasters. The PAP and militia are paramilitary organizations. By law and in practice, the PAP is not part of the PLA, although it is sometimes mistakenly called military police by Chinese and foreign sources alike. The PAP's primary mission, worked in conjunction with the Ministry of Public Security police force, is internal security. The PAP has a dual command structure that includes the CMC and the State Council through the Ministry of Public Security. Its secondary mission is to help the PLA in local defence against external enemies.

The militia supports the PLA in time of war and also helps maintain public order when necessary. The PLA chain of command and local civilian governments are in the militia's command structure. They cooperate through established joint civilian-military organizational mechanisms.

The 1.7-million-person civilian Ministry of Public Security police force is primarily responsible for law enforcement and domestic security. It and the Ministry of State Security, with the missions of counterespionage and domestic and foreign intelligence, respond to the State Council and are not part of the Chinese Armed Forces. However, in its annual human fights reports, the U.S. Department of State (DOS) includes the Ministry of Public Safety with the PLA, the PAP, the Ministry of State Security, and "the state judicial, procuratorial, and penal systems" as part of the Chinese Government's security apparatus.

According to a recent DOS report, "[c]ivilian authorities generally maintained effective control of the security forces." What kind of control they exercised is not altogether clear because "[s]ecurity policy and personnel were responsible for numerous human rights abuses.... At times, police used excessive force against demonstrators." There is no recent confirmed evidence of the PLA being used routinely to control domestic demonstrations or dots, although that could change if the civilian police force and PAP fail in their missions.

The PLA is also distinct from the civilian-run (but mostly government-owned) defence industrial sector composed of some 2 million workers and thousands of enterprises that produce and sell military equipment and civilian goods and services.

Reductions in force. The PLA has undergone two large reductions in force in the past decade, starting with about 3 million people in 1995 and losing 500,000 people from 1997 to 2000 and another 200,000 from 2003 to 2005. By the end of 2005 the PLA have about 2.3 million people on its active duty roster. As the largest component of the PLA with the lowest priority in modernization, army ground forces suffered the largest proportion of cuts. Current estimates put the number at 1.6 million—town about 500,000 from 1995. Reserve personnel, most of whom are in reserve army units, number about 800,000. The PAP might have up to 1.5 million in its ranks. The primary militia, according to a 2004 defence white paper, has 10 million members, but the number of ordinary militia, presumably a larger force, was not announced.

While PLA active duty forces have been cut by approximately 23 percent over the past 10 years, the officially announced defence budget has nearly quadrupled from about 64 billion yuan in 1995 to 248 billion yuan in 2005. Yet these figures do not account for the total funds available to the PLA from extra-budgetary sources, such as support from local governments and special budgets for the purchase of foreign weapons. The PLA-watching community has debated exactly what should be included in estimates of actual Chinese defence expenditures and what factor should be applied to announced budget numbers to arrive at true defence spending. Estimates range from about 1.5 to 3 times (or greater) the announced figure. Whatever the true amount of funds available, such a large force is still relatively resource-constrained; thus, PLA leaders constantly look for ways to save money as new equipment enters the force and training opportunities increase. Future personnel reductions with increased defence budgets would not be surprising.

PLA AIR FORCE

The People's Liberation Army Air Force is organized into seven Military Region Air Forces (MRAF) and 24 Air Divisions. The largest operational units within the Aviation Corps is the air division, which has 2 to 3 aviation regiments, each with 20 to 36 aircraft. The surface-to-air missile (SAM) Corps is organized into SAM divisions and brigades. There are also three airborne divisions manned by the PLAAF.

Second Artillery Corps

The Second Artillery Corps (SAC) is the strategic missile forces of the PLA. It controls China's nuclear and conventional strategic missiles. China's total nuclear arsenal size is estimated to be between 100 and 400 nuclear weapons. The SAC has approximately 90,000-120,000 personnel and six ballistic missile divisions (missile corps bases). The six divisions are independently deployed in different military regionsand have a total of 15 to 20 missile brigades.

People's Liberation Army Air Force (PLAAF)

The Chinese Air Force comprises approximately 250,000 personnel. Conscripts make up approximately 37% of the total force, although in line with the PLA's overall policies on conscription that proportion is being steadily reduced.

From an equipment perspective, the PLAAF has approximately 1,762 combat capable aircraft in its inventory. Of those aircraft, 1,179 are fighter/ interceptor aircraft, largely variants of the J-7 and J-8 aircraft which entered service in the 1970s and 1980s, although the most recent variant of the J-7, the J-7G only entered service with the PLAAF in 2003; and the Su-27 SK/J-11B. Since 2004 the PLAAF has also augmented its fleet with the introduction of the J-10, a multi-role fighter with sophisticated avionics and more advanced weaponry which has been considered the first Chinese-developed fighter aircraft to meet the performance and capabilities benchmark provided by Western fighter aircraft. The third regiment to have received the J-10 was identified in 2007 under the 2nd Air Division in Guangdong Province. Some analysts have suggested that the PLAAF will have acquired 300 J-10 aircraft by 2010, although US Defence Intelligence has reportedly estimated the PLAAF's overall J-10 requirement to be up to 1,200 aircraft.

At present it is unclear whether the PLAAF will acquire the JF-17/FC-1 multi-role fighter that China is currently developing in conjunction with Pakistan and which entered serial production in 2007. The aircraft is considered a less capable, albeit less expensive aircraft compared to some of the aircraft that China is currently procuring, including the J-10. China has also reportedly begun development on its fourth-generation fighter, the J-X (or J-XX/J-14). China's fighter/interceptor aircraft are equipped with AA-12, P-27/AA-10, P-37/AA-11, PL-2B, PL-5B and PL-8 air-to-air missiles, in addition to the new PL-12 beyond-visual-range-air-to-air-missile (BVRAAM) which is deployed on the J-10 and J-11B aircraft.

In addition to its interceptor aircraft, the PLAAF also has 551 ground attack (FGA) aircraft. The FGA fleet consists primarily of the Q5-C and Q5-D aircraft, although since the 1990s significant capability improvements to the fleet have been made with the addition of the JH-7, the improved JH-7A variant which entered service in late 2004, and the Su-30 MKK. Aircraft are equipped with AS-14, AS-17 and AS-18 air-to-surface missiles. The Q5 is also believed to be nuclear capable. The PLAAF's bomber divisions consist of approximately 82 aircraft comprising the H-6 and more recent upgraded variants of that aircraft including the H-6E/ F and H. The newest variants of the H-6 have recently been equipped with the YJ-63 which is the air force's first air-launched land-attack cruise missile (LACM). Up to 20 H-6 bomber aircraft are believed to be nuclear-ready.

Supplementing the PLAAF's fast jet and bomber aircraft are 183 reconnaissance (the ageing MiG-19 and MiG-21 and the JZ-6 and JZ-8) and airborne early warning aircraft; an unspecified number of UAV; 314 tanker and transport aircraft and in excess of 522 training aircraft. The PLAAF also has a small support and utility helicopter fleet. In order to supplement and modernise its airborne early warning fleet, the PLAAF is currently developing a number of AEW platforms including the KJ-200 which is based on the Y-8 transport aircraft and is being configured for an AEW role as well as intelligence and maritime surveillance; and the KJ-2000 airborne warning and control system which is based on the Russian A-50 AWACS aircraft.

Overall these forces are organised into 32 air divisions (22 fighter, 3 bomber, 5 attack and 2 transport divisions) and are deployed among the PLA's seven military commands. The majority of forces are, however, located in the eastern part of the country, a reflection of the priority given to any potential offensive against Taiwan.

The exact nature of the infrastructure supporting PLAAF operations is, however, the subject of debate. According to the Federation of American Scientists those 32 divisions are located across 37 military air bases and four airfields which may be capable of supporting both civilian and military operations. Six of those airbases are considered to be within short range of Taiwan (<400km); whilst 11 are within medium range (400-600km). The organisation Global Security has suggested, however, that the number of Chinese air bases or airfields/airports capable of supporting military operations is in the region of 150.

The PLAAF also has a dedicated air defence force equipped over 1,578 surface-to-air missiles. The manufacture of most of China's combat aircraft has been undertaken domestically. However, China's aviation industry has its limitations, particularly its ability to successfully manufacture Turbofan engines for its combat and heavy aircraft. Like most of China's naval vessels, therefore, China's air forces have benefited significantly from the incorporation of foreign technology and other assistance, particularly from the Soviet Union/Russia.

A significant number of Soviet and Russian fighter aircraft have, for example been reverse engineered by Chinese industry over the years (with varying degrees of success) and then upgraded into second and third generation variants.

The J-7 was, for example, initially copied from the Soviet MiG-21 and then upgraded domestically. More recently China has also indicated that it will attempt to reverse engineer the Russian turbofan engine which has been incorporated into its J-10 for use in future variants of the aircraft. China's H-6 bomber is also a domestic copy of the Russian Tupolev Tu-16, while its HY-6 tanker aircraft is a copy of a converted Tu-16. The majority of China's transport aircraft are also based on the Antonov AN-2 (Y-5), the AN-12 (Y-8), the AN-24 (Y-7) and the AN-26 (Y-7H).

China has also established a number of licensed production agreements with Russia including an agreement for the domestic production of the Su-27Sk/J-11B aircraft. On occasion China has also directly purchased aircraft from overseas in order to supplement its fleet. The PLAAF operates, for example, several variants of the Il-76 transport aircraft purchased from the Soviet Union and Russia in the 1990s. In 2005 China ordered a further 38 Il-76MD long-range transport aircraft and Il-78 tanker-transport aircraft from Russia in a deal reportedly worth $1bn.

China has also taken a similar procurement approach to some, although not all of the PLAAF's missile capabilities. The PL-2B and PL-5B missiles, for example, are upgraded versions of the PL-2 which was produced under licence in China and based on the Soviet K-13 air-to-air missile. China also acquired a number of its missile technologies from Israel during the 1980s, including the PL-8 which is produced under licence and based upon the Israeli Python-3 air-to-air missile. Israel has also been an important source of unmanned aerial vehicle (UAV) and unmanned combat aerial vehicle (UCAV) technologies. Despite improvements in China's aviation industry it has been pointed out that even with the potential indigenous production of a fourth generation fighter aircraft, China will still be a generation behind the technological capabilities of the US.

People's Armed Police (Paramilitary Forces)

The People's Armed Police, in its current configuration, was established in the 1980s following a decision by the Chinese government to re-establish a dedicated force for internal security and law enforcement purposes. The force comprises 1.5 million active personnel broken down into 45 divisions and deployed across China's 22 provinces and four autonomous regions. During peacetime, the PAP is responsible for guarding key targets, including personnel and key economic and industrial installations; dealing with emergency crises including riots, insurgency and other mass incidents; anti-terrorism, including anti-hijacking and bomb disposal; and assisting in the economic development of the country, including mining and taking part in large transportation and energy construction projects. In a situation of conflict the PAP could also be used for the purposes of territorial defence and in support of regular ground forces.

CHINA GROWTH STEALTH FIGHTER MILITARY TECHNOLOGY

The aircraft in the above photo looks at first sight as a complete prototype, but it actually is a very detailed full-scale engineering mock-up. It can be speculated that, after having been used to study the aircraft's internal installations, the mock-up has also received an external finish for presentation purposes. Its real function at this point, however, is probably to buttist in the definition of the required logistic support (i.e., access to the various avionics boxes and on-board systems, ground support equipment like the various ladders and the external power source units, air conditioning units and so on) as well as to study the engines' removal-installation procedures.

Since some time now it has been known that the rapidly-developing Chinese aeronautical industry is studying a new and technologically very advanced combat aircraft, also boasting significant low signature characteristics. This programme is a logical step in China's "Long March" towards full independence in designing, developing and producing combat airplanes of a technological level in line with China's status as the "other" world superpower, on an equal footing as Russia and eventually even the USA.

The scarce information available about this new advanced combat aircraft indicates that two, possibly competing, study groups (both part of the AVIC I Group of aeronautical industries) are or have been working on the subject. One of these groups (601 Insbreastute) originates from Shenyang Airplane Corporation (SAC) which is in charge of the large, twin-engine J-8 fighters in service with the PLAAF (People's Liberation Army Air Force) as well as of licence production of the Su-27SK under the local designation of J-11. The overall configuration of SAC's preliminary design, apparently designated J-13, owes significantly to the American F-A-22, being a tailed delta but with wing and horizontal tailplanes more in line with those of the F-16. The other study group (611 Insbreastute) from Chengdu Airplane Corporation (CAC), has developed the J-12, a concept which follows the less conventional canard layout used with success in the company's J-10.

While previous information (albeit admittedly unconfirmed), gave to the SAC concept the edge, perhaps as a result of the company's experience in large twin-engine fighters, this seems to have since been reversed in favour of the Chengdu design. It is however still not clear whether the designation of J-14 is intended to suggest a successor design to both the J-12 and the J-13, and whether the existence of the J-14 engineering mock-up (clearly based on the

J-12) indicates that the type has been selected for development, or the compebreastion is still going on with parallel activities underway on another such mock-up based on the J-13.

While no data is available about the J-14, some speculation can be done in the attempt to extrapolate the aircraft's characteristics and thus the roles it is called to perform. The following considerations are based on what can be seen in the photo, but also involve making some buttumptions on the basis of what is known of the Chinese armed forces' perceived priorities in operational requirements, the domestic industry's approach to combat aircraft design and, finally, the well-know Chinese weaknesses in some technological fields. In addition, the well-developed cooperation with Russian companies, particularly in areas such as powerplant, avionics and possibly computer-based fly-by-wire flight control systems is also taken into consideration.

General Configuration

The J-14 will surely be fitted with a fly-by-wire flight control system and be designed for artificial stability. The Chinese should by now have matured an adequate experience in this field through a number of experimental programmes and application to actual in-service types.

The general configuration of the aircraft is clearly born out from CAC's experience in developing the J-10, with its canard layout and ventral air intake. But while the J-10 is known to be related to the Israeli LAVI, this new and much more ambitious design rather appears to have a definite relationship with the ill-fated Russian 5th generation fighter studied a few years ago, the MiG 1.44 MFI and in fact it shares a number of elements which can doubtless be traced back to the Russian demonstrator. It is thus very probable not to say certain that an agreement has been reached between the Russian and Chinese governments allowing for the transfer of information and technological data as well as consultancy services being provided by RSK MiG and Russian research centres (arguably including the TsAGI aerodynamic research insbreastute) to develop the new Chinese fighter. The J-14's planform closely matches that of the MiG 1.44, i.e. a canard layout (the canard surface are fully movable) with mid-positioned wing and widely separated twin-vertical surfaces canted outward, which continue under the wing in twin ventral fins, these too being canted outward à la J-10.

While not visible in the photo, wind tunnel models show that the 1.44 configuration has been maintained also in the booms protruding from the wing and contributing to support the vertical tailplanes and ventral fins.

These booms probably end with radomes covering electronic warfare antennas and possibly also a rearward facing radar, similar to the installation experimented in the Su-37 a few years ago. In the MiG 1.44, the portion of wing between the fuselage-engine pods and the booms is extended rearward past the wing trailing edge and includes a couple of moving surfaces contributing, together with the all-moving canard surfaces, to the longitudinal control of the airplane. It is not yet possible to buttess whether this solution, too has been maintained for the J-14.

But while the overall aerodynamic configuration of the J-14 follows that of the MiG 1.44 demonstrator, a radical redesign has been implemented in the pursuit of a significant reduction in the radar cross-section value.

In particular, the aircraft incorporates a pronounced wing-body blending, which was totally lacking in the original Russian design. Further, the air intake, while in the same ventral position under the forward fuselage, has a completely new shape, and by the same token the upper part of the airplane is also completely different and shows towards the rear the protuberances of the engine "pods" which blend with the fuselage and wing roots in a curious reminiscence of the Northrop YF-23. Also, the front fuselage merges down into the upper wing, blending with the separated engine bay bulges while maintaining some relation with the "clbuttical" Su-27 forward fuselage shape. The search for enhanced stealth performance is also apparent in the "flattened" profile of the entire front fuselage section (nearly identical to the Su-32), as well as in the generalised use of serrated doors to cover the landing gear and missile bays.

On the other hand, it remains clear that a canard configuration is hardly the ideal solution from the point of view of a reduced radar signature. Summing up, it would thus seem safe to buttume that the J-14 is a "stealth-optimised" aircraft rather than un uncompromising stealth design à la F-A-22 or (in a different clbutt) the F-35 JSF.

Above the raised front fuselage is located the single-seat pilot chickenpit. This is closed by a single-piece frameless bubble-type transparent canopy which appears technological very demanding under various aspects such as manufacturing process, adequate optical qualities and bird-impact resistance, yet allowing through-ejection.

On the other hand, the pilot is provided with superb all-around visibility also due to the position of the chickenpit above the forward fuselage "hump", again a reminiscence of the Su-27.

After Chinese visit Ships, U.S. Officials Hope for Reciprocation

After Chinese visit ships, U.S. officials hope for reciprocation {EXCERPT}, by Allison Batdorff, Stars and Stripes Pacific edition, Friday, June 23, 2006 ANDERSEN AIR FORCE BASE, Guam ˜...

The main landing gear, with single wheels mounted on telescopic legs, retracts outward, with the legs being accommodated in the fuselage side blending into the wing bottom and the wheels into the wing (a similar geometry has been selected for the F-A-22). In order to minimise the volume of the bay occupied by the gear in the retracted position, the telescopic main gear legs are shortened via a pulling bar acting on a lever, similarly to what has been introduced in the Eurofighter TYPHOON. While not clear in the photo, it is possible that the same landing gear leg shortening design has also been selected for the nose twin-wheel element.

Powerplant Installation

In view of the twin-engine layout of the J-14 and its estimated TO weight in air combat configuration (some 25-28 tons with full internal fuel, gun ammunition, 2 x SRAAM and 4 x MRAAM), its engines should give a thrust in the range of 13-14 tons in afterburning mode, so achieving a thrust-to-weight ratio in the order of 1:1.

Now it seems difficult to envisage a stateof-the-art Chinese engine, particularly in this thrust clbutt, achieving full production status by the mid of the next decade when the J-14 could reasonably be expected to enter service. Even for the J-10 a Russian engine has been at last preferred.

It can thus be buttumed that a Russian engine has been selected for the J-14 as well, and indeed the model which can be seen in the picture to the rear of the right wing of the mock-up has the accessory gearbox mounted above the engine in the traditional Russian style. If, as it is highly probable, this engine is a member of the Saturn-Lyulka AL-31-41 family (but it could also be a prototype of the Chinese Liming LM WS10A in the same thrust clbutt), this would make the type not fully interchangeable with the version selected for the J-10, which has the accessory gearbox located on the engine bottom, Western-style. It is also possible to speculate that the idea is to have the prototypes powered by the lower-thrust AL-31 as used in the J-11-Su-27SK-Su-30MKK, with either an evolved higher-thrust version of AL-31 or a series-production version of the AL-41 being then adopted for the series aircraft.

Coming to the engine-airframe installation, the air intake located in the bottom part of the front fuselage is of the fixed geometry type with no moving ramp, unlike the case with the J-10. This solution has made it possible to eliminate the sharp angles and slots between the moving ramp and in general to provide smooth shapes which reduce radar reflectivity. The pronounced bulging up of the air intake inner duct helps avoid a direct presentation of the critically reflective engine fan-compressor face to enemy illuminating radar from the forward emisphere. In addition, the bulge is needed to make room for the nose landing gear bay and, even more, for the bottom fuselage weapons bay.

Notwithstanding its fixed geometry, the air intake shows elements which should generate a couple of oblique shock waves before the normal one, thus guaranteeing an adequately efficient dynamic pressure recovery in the supersonic flight regime. The well-shaped bulge along the bottom of the centre fuselage entering the air intake, which forms the upper part of the air intake duct, seems reminiscent of the latest Lockheed Martin's vaunted design for a fixed-ramp, multi-shock air intake planned for use on the production F-35 and already experimented on an F-16.

This peculiar layout, together with the forward-raked air intake lip (already seen in the late 1950s on the F8U-3 CRUSADER III) is clearly intended to generate the oblique shock waves mentioned above.

The location of the air intake under the fuselage is well suited to provide a smooth distortion-free airflow to the engines. From this particular point of view, the hinged bottom lip present in the TYPHOON works even better at extreme angles of attack, but it implies the penalty of a higher radar signature. In more general terms, the choice of a single air intake configuration in a twin-engine airplane may be open to some criticism, in that it is less than ideal to maintain correct working conditions (i.e., smooth undistorted airflow to the remaining engine) in the event of an engine flaming out for whatever reason. The air intake thus establishes a potential single point failure in an otherwise completely redundant twin-engine installation.

It can be expected that Thrust Vector Control (TVC) nozzles, probably of the axisymmetric type (despite their not insignificant contribution to overall nuclear signature), will be a standard feature of the J-14 to both enhance manoeuvrability and reduce trim drag in cruise flight.

Armament

Chinese design derived from a Russian model such as the GSh-6-23 23mm installed in the MiG-31 and the Su-24. The gun is installed in the upper right fuselage side, just above the canard surface. The firing port, unlike the F-A-22 is left permanently open, hence generating a not so negligible radar reflection.

The main armament is carried in three weapons bays, whose arrangement looks like virtually a clone of the F-A-22. Two smaller bays are located on the fuselage sides and appear to be tailored to each accommodate a single short-range air-to-air missile, while the large underfuselage bay, closed by twin doors, will probably accept at least four medium-range AAMs. It may be speculated that the J-14 is intended to carry "compressed carriage" clipped-wing versions of the AAMs already in use with the PLAAF, i.e. the PL-8 and the Russian R-73 for short-range dogfights and the R-77 and the indigenous PL-12 for medium-range work. The R-77 is already suitable for carriage in an internal bay in its standard version, being equipped with very small span wings while the lattice tail control fins can be fold forward flush with the missile body.

Underwing store stations are surely foreseen to carry additional weapons and fuel tanks, when there is no need to maintain a high level of stealthness.

Combat Avionics

J-14 is already in full-scale development, the main choices related to the avionics systems should have already been made, at least at the conceptual level. However, the Chinese domestic industry is almost certainly not in a position to supply the advanced avionics required in a sophisticated aircraft like the J-14, and contributions from abroad will be required-from Russia, Israel and arguably even Europe.

The J-14 being intended to enter service in around 2012-2015, it may be expected that the Chinese are aiming at equipping it with a radar with electronically scanning (ASEA) antenna, capable of multiple targets engagements-provided that a source for such a radar could be identified. In the Russian tradition, a pbuttive search and track system based on optronic devices (FLIR with integrated laser rangefinder) is expected to be also installed in a retractable or faired turret. As already mentioned, the dual rear booms could carry, in addition to various pbuttive and-or active defensive systems also a rear-facing radar.

Finally, it can be expected that the chickenpit instrumentation for the production version will be based on an Helmet Mounted Display-Sight (HMD-S) totally replacing the HUD, although the latter instrument is clearly visible in the photo. The head-down displays would probably include three or four large Multi Function Displays (MFD), which should have the possibility to present a digital map and a complete tactical situation. A real-time data link is also an expected addition to the fully integrated avionics system to enhance the situation awareness of the pilot, particularly when operating in multiships combat groups to make the most use of the commonly available information from the various platforms.

CHINESE NUCLEAR WEAPONS

After its first test of a nuclear weapon in 1964, China advanced fairly rapidly in nuclear weapons technology. In January 1969, Secretary of Defence

Clark Clifford informed the Congress that: From October 1964 through December 1967 they [the PRC] detonated seven nuclear devices, including three thermonuclear and one low yield device delivered by a missile. (On December 27, 1968, the Chinese communists detonated their eighth nuclear device.) This test was similar to the sixth, conducted in June 1967. Both were apparently thermonuclear devices with yields of about 3 MT which were air dropped. According to China expert Brad Roberts, through 1982 there was "a steady accretion of deployed weapons systems such that China was able to threaten to attack by nuclear weapons all of its potential adversaries – and, in addition, to threaten U.S. military bases in the Western Pacific and the allies that hosted them." China's nuclear weapons complex has reflected this buildup.

Warhead Development and Deployment

The principal nuclear weapons organization, the Chinese Academy of Engineering's Institute of Physics, employs 8,500 professional technical staff members. Yu Min, described by *Xinhua* as the "architect of the country's first H-bomb" claims that China's key nuclear capabilities are "on a par with the United States and the former Soviet Union." Xue Bencheng, one of the most important scientists involved in the development of China's neutron bomb, stated that the July 1996 Chinese nuclear test was "a great spanning leap" because it solved the problem of nuclear weapons miniaturization. According to a report in the Hong Kong press, China's Central Military Commission Vice Chairman Zhan Wannian told the Commission that there will be "further upgrading, and further development [of Chinese nuclear weapons] from 2001 to 2009."

China is today heavily invested in the process of modernizing its strategic forces. Viktor Mikhaylov, while he was Russia's first Deputy Minister for Atomic Energy, stated that, "China is very closed in its weapons work and the scope of its nuclear efforts can be judged from a number of indirect signs. But one needs have no doubt that such efforts are significant and dynamic." Retired Russian Major General Valdimir Belous in July 2006 wrote that, "China is transforming itself into one of the 21st Century's most influence centres of power, something that is to a considerable degree facilitated by the reequipping of its Armed Forces and the buildup of its nuclear missile potential, which in terms of total quantity of warheads has surpassed the equivalent indicators of France and Great Britain." According to Vyacheslav Baskakov and Aleksandr Gorshkov, Russian military journalists: Specifically, it [China] will succeed in making the shift from its current megaton-class nuclear ordinance to a level of hundreds and tens of kilotons, thereby increasing the effectiveness of available forces and weapons, flexibility of use in various circumstances and combat situations on both a strategic and tactical level. For example, it is believed that the yield of the strategic nuclear warheads with which Chinese ICBM's are now equipped will decrease from 1-4 megatons to 250-650 kilotons each. The yield of tactical and operational-tactical nuclear warheads, according to expert assessments, will total from 90-100 kilotons each.

There are convincing reports that this recent progress has not been entirely indigenous. For example, the House Select Committee on U.S. National Security and Military Commercial Concerns with the People's Republic of China, generally known as the Cox Committee, concluded that: The People's Republic of China (PRC) has stolen classified information on all of the United States' most advanced thermonuclear warheads, and several of the associated reentry vehicles. These thefts are the result of an intelligence collection program spanning two decades, and continuing to the present. The PRC intelligence collection program included espionage, review of unclassified publications, and extensive interactions with scientists from the Department of Energy's national weapons laboratories.

The stolen U.S. secrets have helped the PRC fabricate and successfully test modern strategic thermonuclear weapons. The stolen information includes classified information on seven U.S. thermonuclear warheads, including every currently deployed thermonuclear warhead in the U.S. intercontinental ballistic missile arsenal. Together, these include the W-88 Trident D-5 thermonuclear warhead, and the W-56 Minuteman II, the W-62 Minuteman III, the W-70 Lance, the W-76 Trident C-4, the W-78 Minuteman III Mark 12A, and the W-87 Peacekeeper thermonuclear warheads. The stolen information also includes classified design information for an enhanced radiation weapon (commonly known as the 'neutron bomb').... The Cox report continued that there was additional PRC espionage in the mid-1990s that included information about "the W-70 warhead [that] contains elements that may be used either as a strategic thermonuclear weapon, or as an enhanced radiation weapon ('neutron bomb'). The PRC subsequently tested the neutron bomb...."

The Central Intelligence Agency released the following assessment of Chinese nuclear espionage: China obtained by espionage classified US nuclear weapons information that probably accelerated its program to develop future nuclear weapons. This collection program allowed China to focus successfully down critical paths and avoid less promising approaches to nuclear weapon designs.

China obtained at least basic design information on several modern US nuclear reentry vehicles, including the Trident II (W88). China also obtained information on a variety of US weapon design concepts and weaponization features, including those of the neutron bomb. We cannot determine the full extent of weapon information obtained. For example, we do not know whether any weapon design documentation or blueprints were acquired.

We believe it is more likely that the Chinese used US design information to inform their own program than to replicate US weapon designs. China reacted very strongly to the Cox report, claiming, inaccurately, that the nuclear weapons design information had been declassified by the United States and also stating that the PRC had tested an enhanced radiation weapon in the 1980s. In an interview in June 2001, Xue Bencheng, chief engineer of the PRC neutron bomb, also claimed that the July 1996 Chinese nuclear test resulted in "a great spanning leap," a significant breakthrough in nuclear weapons technology which solved the problem of miniaturization and reached the same level of technology as the advanced nuclear nations.

Whatever the source, miniaturization has enabled China to develop a number of warhead options. China is reported to have "tactical nuclear warheads, theater nuclear warheads, and nuclear mines." Hong Kong military commentator Ma Ting-sheng has even suggested on Hong Kong television that China would transport nuclear bombs into the United States "before a war breaks out." A number of heavily-redacted CIA intelligence reports on China's nuclear weapons testing have been declassified.

They include details which suggest a broad interest in developing nuclear weapons for tactical platforms, modernizing and replacing older warhead technologies, and building up a body of test data to continue the process in the context of a Comprehensive Test Ban Treaty (CTBT). What Chinese testing has occurred since the announced end of China's nuclear testing in 1996 is not certain. The Cox reported concluded that "nuclear tests related to development of the PRC's next generation of thermonuclear warheads may be continuing at the PRC test site at Lop Non Nor." In May 2006 *Chinese Defence Today* also reported possible "low yield nuclear tests" after the declared end of testing.

The Stockpile Size

The precise number of Chinese nuclear weapons is a closely guarded state secret. The assertion that China has 200 warheads is actually an invention of the Western press and academia based on inference from a 2004 claim by the PRC that it had conduct the fewest nuclear tests and had the smallest arsenal among the nuclear powers.

Other estimates of China's nuclear stockpile dramatically differ. According to Lieutenant General Michael Maples, Director of the Defence Intelligence Agency, "China currently has more than 100 nuclear warheads." Maple's statement was in 2006, however, a declassified 1984 DIA estimate of the Chinese nuclear weapons stockpile put it, "Between 150 and 160 warheads." Many estimates are much higher. A November 1997 Congressional Research Service report by Jonathan Medalia, citing a report by the National Resources Defence Council, concluded that "....China has perhaps 300 deployed nuclear weapons and 150 tactical nuclear weapons that are available but not deployed, and that the stockpile could actually be two or three times larger." A study by the Carnegie Institute estimated that China had 450 nuclear weapons. Other estimates span the range from 200 to 2000.

In evaluating the wide range of estimates of the number of Chinese nuclear weapons Dr. You Ji observed in 1999: "The lower end of the estimates, 200, is certainly too low.... A *Rand* report also claims that by 2003 China will possess between 600 and 1500 nuclear warheads. This higher end of the estimates may be as unrealistic as the lower end, especially if one thinks in terms of warheads deliverable after a first strike." DIA estimated that China had 150-160 nuclear weapons as far back as 1984 and "the number of warheads is not restricted by Chinese materials production, but on what the Chinese perceive their needs to be."

AEROSPACE OPPORTUNITIES IN CHINA

The aerospace market in China potentially presents huge, long-term opportunities for UK companies, but with serious challenges and difficulties in achieving success. A|D|S and the CEO's of all the UK's Regional Trade Associations have recently completed a trade mission to China, supported by UKTI and the British Embassy, to understand better the opportunities and challenges for the sector. Senior level discussions were held with Chinese government officials, senior management from COMAC and AVIC companies, as well as UK companies that are successfully operating in China today. Following this visit, it is intended to define a UK national strategy to support UK industry in achieving success in the Chinese Aerospace market. To ensure that this strategy puts in place the correct support mechanisms, we are very keen to hear views direct from companies with respect to their current activity and future aspirations in the Chinese aerospace market. To begin this process, we would be grateful for your initial, brief views, through a very short questionnaire.

Aerospace Sector Mission to China

An immediate opportunity is available to FAC members to participate in a trade mission to China in June, coinciding with the Shanghai Expo. This mission is subsidised to keep prices as low as possible and for eligible companies, flights can be heavily subsidised. UK Trade & Investment (UKTI) is organising an aerospace sector mission to China to enable UK companies to meet with the key aerospace manufacturing organisations and to get a better understanding of the market opportunities for new business. The mission will be timed to coincide with a major UK advanced Engineering Showcase event that UKTI is organising in Shanghai.

AIRCRAFT CARRIERS

In late April 2009 the incomplete former Soviet/Ukrainian aircraft carrier Varyag made its first voyage in Chinese waters. From its berth in Dalian harbor, where the PLA has kept it since 2002, the Varyag moved about two miles to a drydock in a nearly complete new large ship construction facility that did not exist in 2007. This new shipyard, and the Varyag's placement in it, demonstrates that China is now mobilizing resources to fulfil its longstanding ambition to build an aircraft carrier navy.

Long a matter of debate, at times complicated by Chinese disinformation, doubts about China's ambition to build a carrier navy have been laid to rest by series of public and semi-public Chinese disclosures. In mid-November 2008 Major General Qian Lihua, Director of the Foreign Affairs Office of the Chinese Ministry of Defence, told the Financial Times, "The navy of any great power...has the dream to have one or more aircraft carriers..." From late December 2008 through January 2009 Chinese military and shipyard sources made a rare series of press leaks to Japan's Asahi Shimbun and Hong Kong's South China Morning Post, previewing plans to build up to four new aircraft carriers by 2020.

The first two would be 50,000 to 65,000 ton conventionally powered carriers similar to the Varyag, while the later two would be nuclear powered and similar to the uncompleted Soviet carrier Ulyanovsk. Then at the early March 2009 National People's Congress session, PLA Navy (PLAN) East Sea Fleet Commander Admiral Xu Hongmeng stated, "China really needs a carrier. Both technologically and economically, China already has the capacity to build a carrier...China will very soon have its own aircraft carrier." Then in late March 2009 Defence Minister General Liang Guanglie told visiting Japanese Defence Minister Hamada Yasukazu, "We need to develop an aircraft carrier."

Provided requisite funding and political support continue, the PLA will have to simultaneously advance at least four interrelated tasks to realize its carrier ambition. First the PLA will have to assemble the necessary design, construction, logistic support and combat support capabilities to sustain a carrier navy. Second, it will have to refurbish the Varyag to mission capable status and commence construction of indigenously designed carriers. Then it will have to expand the PLA Navy Air Force to include a range of carrier-capable aircraft for training, combat and combat support missions. Fourth, the PLA will have to train requisite personnel for their carriers and air wings.

In his 2004 memoirs Liu Huaqing (now 92) noted that he began investigating the construction of aircraft carriers for China in 1970. But he was not able to place a top priority on carriers, and as noted in his memoirs, instead pursued an intensive intelligence gathering campaign. This included the purchase of retired carriers from Australia, Russia, and a reported attempt to purchase the Clemenceau from France, culminating in the 1998 purchase of the Varyag for $20 million. Scores of PLA personnel have visited U.S., Russian, British, French and Brazilian carriers, to even include interrogating docents on the U.S.S. Midway carrier museum in San Diego. There has been extensive PLA contact with Russian carrier related companies, who stand to play a significant role in China's carrier development.

Starting in the 10th Five Year Plan of 2001-2005, the PLA started in earnest to build the infrastructure to support a future carrier fleet, as well as start to build the first generation of large warships which could serve as future carrier escorts. In early 2001 an Asian military source told Jane's that the PLA had started building a major new naval base on Hainan Island. Starting in 2002 the PLAN launched two Type 093 second-generation nuclear attack submarines, plus two Type 052B and two Type 052C air defence destroyers, which could serve as initial carrier battle group escorts.

China's carriers: Soon after the Varyag arrived at its new location it is increasingly apparent that this ship has entered a new more active phase in its eventual refurbishment as China's first aircraft carrier. DigitalGlobe images obtained by Jane's show the Varyag is now surrounded by four large construction cranes and Internet-source imagery shows that three new material and personnel elevators have been built around the carrier. The normally 58,500 ton (full load) Varyag was reported to be about 70 percent complete when it arrived in Dalian, and much speculation has centred on the condition of its steam-turbine engines. A possible end-goal for the Varyag or perhaps a PLA version of this design was potentially revealed by the Harbin Institute of Technology, a major PLA research subcontractor, when students and faculty built a large scale model of this ship for the university's 50th anniversary in 2003.

This model showed a near copy of the Varyag equipped with at least 48 HQ-9 SAM launchers, 24 YJ-62 size cruise missiles, two Type 730 CIWS systems, all mounted the ship's periphery, and a phased array radar system—

the same weapons and systems that equip the new Type 052C Luyang II destroyer. The possible lack of deck-hull mounted vertical launch anti-ship cruise missiles on a PLAN version of the Varyag may mean it can carry more than the usual 18 Sukhoi Su-33 size fighters.

Less is known about the PLA's nuclear-powered aircraft carrier plans, save that reports in January noted it would be larger, displacing as much as 65,000 tons. China has no previous experience with nuclear powered surface ships. However, inasmuch as Russia has announced the intention to build three to four new nuclear powered 50,000 to 60,000 ton aircraft carriers, it is possible that Russia stands to make a substantial contribution to China's nuclear carrier plans. Reports that China has acquired plans for the 80,000 ton Project 1143.7 (Ulyanovsk) class nuclear powered carrier are another indicator that China may seek Russian assistance.

Carrier Air Wing: Since 2005 Russian industry sources have told the author of China's interest in acquiring an initial group of Sukhoi Su-33 jet fighters for carrier operations. Since then negotiations between the PLA and Russia have waxed and waned, with reports ranging from China insisting on acquiring a small number that would not justify reviving production, to China's interest in purchasing up to 100 new Su-33s upgraded with more powerful radar, engines and weapons.

Russian reluctance to sell the Su-33 is prompted by its concerns over China's Shenyang Aircraft Corporation having copied previously co-produced models of the Su-27SK/J-11, to include the new J-11B with Chinese radar and avionics, and soon engines, and the twin-seat J-11BS. In the late 1990s China also acquired an early T-10K/Su-33 prototype from the Ukraine, fueling speculation that China is developing its own carrier capable J-11, despite doubts that it can master the complex modifications necessary for carrier operations. More recently Chinese sources indicate that Shenyang may be developing a separate twin-engine 4th generation combat aircraft called the J-13 or J-15, which may be closer in size to the Boeing F/A-18C and slated for early development into a carrier capable version.

Should the PLA opt for upgraded Su-33s, they would quickly obtain a carrier combat aircraft that would have greater unrefueled range, greater maneuverability and options for longer range weapons than possessed by the current U.S. Navy Boeing F/A-18E/F fighter. During the recent April 2009 60th Anniversary celebration of the PLA Navy, Commander Wu Shengli publically called for the development of a "supersonic cruise" capable fighter for the PLAN, an indication of interest in 5th generation fighters that could eventually equip Chinese aircraft carriers.

Both the Shenyang and Chengdu Aircraft Corporations are known to be developing 5th generation fighters. They may also be developing lightweight 5th generation fighters, inasmuch as a Chinese source disclosed to the author in 2005 that Chengdu was considering the development of a Lockheed-Martin F-35 class 5th generation fighter. The PLA has had a longstanding interest in acquiring vertical take-off fighters, having considered the British Harrier and the Russian Yakovlev Yak-141 at different times.

The PLA is also known to be developing carrier combat support aircraft, that initially could focus on airborne early warning (AEW) and anti-submarine versions of the Changhe Z-8 helicopter. A 2005 Chinese magazine photo of politician visiting an unknown design bureau revealed a possible model of an AWACs aircraft similar in size to the U.S. Navy E-1 Tracer.

More recently China's Northwestern University, another major centre for PLA-funded aerospace research, conducted wind tunnel analysis of the twin-engine Sukhoi Su-80 cargo/passenger aircraft with saucer-shaped and "rail" shaped radar arrays. All of these designs could be configured for anti-submarine or cargo missions. In addition, the PLA can be expected to modify future unmanned combat and support aircraft for carrier operation. Shenyang's Warrior Eagle UCAV concept revealed at the 2008 Zhuhai Airshow could form the basis for a future carrier-based UCAV similar in size to the Northrop-Grumman X-47B.

Less is known about the PLA's personnel and training programs to sustain its carrier fleet. The Varyag, once it enters service, possibly between 2012 and 2015, will serve initially as a platform for training and doctrine development. The PLANAF's existing regiment of Su-30MK2 fighters could also provide experienced pilots carrier training. Recent reports indicate that the PLAN may have access to the Saki carrier training facility at Saki in the Ukraine, and may pursue a training relationship with Brazil, who's Sao Paulo is the former French carrier Foch.

Future issues: If early 2009 reports from Chinese sources prove correct the PLAN would have a four-carrier force by the 2020s. Two smaller "Varyag" size carriers might prove best suited for regional and pro-SSBN missions, while the two larger nuclear powered carriers would be available for global political image projection or military projection missions. Again, provided the PLA retains its political power into the coming decades, a number of variables, ranging from a precipitous decline of U.S. global leadership to the emergence of hostile relationships with Russia, India, Japan or other powerful neighbors, could lead the PLA to build a larger number of carriers. It is likely that China's future 5th generation combat aircraft will have carrier capable variants. The potential emergence of a 5th generation short take-off and vertical landing (STOVL) 5th generation fighter could also lead the PLA to consider smaller pro-SSBN carriers or enable larger landing helicopter dock (LHD) amphibious assault ships that could fulfil secondary SSBN support missions.

GROWING AMPHIBIOUS CAPABILITIES

The PLA has long maintained a capability for short-range amphibious projection, with the PLA Army providing the majority of amphibious equipped and trained divisions, and the nominally PLAN-controlled PLA Marines fielding two brigades. Having long used former U.S. World War 2 landing ship tanks (LSTs), the PLA began designing its own LSTs in the 1970s, maintaining a small force of 17-20 until earlier this decade, when these were effectively doubled by the construction of 10 Yuting-II and 10 Yubei class LSTs between 2003 and 2005. PLAN LSTs are credited with a capacity of either 10 tanks or about 250 troops. In addition the PLAN maintains a much larger number of smaller LSM and LCU size amphibious transports. Recent reports indicating PLA interest in the large Russian Zubr assault hovercraft have yet to lead to a sale.

In 2006 the Taiwan Ministry of Defence estimated that the PLA could also mobilize 800 "civilian" ships to assist an invasion. China has about 150 or so fast ferries that could carry 100-500 troops each. The PLA could also mobilize fishing ships, regular ferries and Roll-on/Roll-off (Ro-Ro) cargo ships to pour troops, armor and material into captured ports. However, the use of such a "Dunkirk" collection of an invasion force would require substantial surprise plus flawless planning and weather, difficult variables on the Taiwan Strait.

Starting in the 10th Five Year Plan it is apparent that the PLA commenced the building of larger amphibious assault ships capable of distant projection missions. This represents a stark change from previous PLAN practice and even exceeds the Soviet experience, whose largest Rogov class amphibious assault ship was intended for tactical operations, not strategic. During the later six months of 2006 the PLA built and launched its first 20,000ton Type 071 landing platform dock (LPD). With an estimated capacity for about 800 troops the Type 071 has a helicopter landing deck that can accommodate two Z-8 size assault helicopters. In 2005 there were reports that the PLAN was interested in purchasing Russian Kamov Ka-29 specialized naval assault helicopters, but such has not happened. The PLAN can be expected to eventually place versions of the Z-10 or lighter Z-11 attack helicopters on its larger amphibious assault ships. The Type 071 also has a well deck designed to carry the new Yuyi class hovercraft, similar to but smaller than the U.S.

Landing Craft-Air Cushion (LCAC). This will allow the deployment of heavy armor and equipment from beyond the horizon.

In 2007 a Chinese source at the Singapore IMDEX naval show confirmed to the author that China was developing the Type 081 landing helicopter dock (LHD). Subsequent Chinese-source concept illustrations indicate this 20,000 ton ship differs from the Type 071 by having a full length aircraft deck and provision for SAMs and a phased-array radar. Some sources report that the PLA intends eventually to build a force of 6 Type 081s and 3 Type 071s. If realized, this would enable the PLA to mount an amphibious projection force of several thousand troops plus their associated armor and equipment, as far as logistic support ships or port access would allow.

In addition the PLA has invested considerable effort to develop new and more effective amphibious assault equipment and armor. The PLA has developed its version of the "Funnies," specialized beach assault equipment which the Allies perfected during World War 2, to include mine-clearing rockets and trucks that lay aprons to assist trucks getting over beaches.

In the late 1990s the PLA revealed that it had developed the Type-63C amphibious tank, equipped with a Russian-designed 105mm gun-launched anti-tank missile that out-ranges Taiwan's 105mm tank guns. These are now being supplemented by a new family of amphibious assault vehicles that began appearing in 2005.

The ZBD2000 utilizes a powerful pumpjet and a planning hull to achieve high speeds over water, and has a version armed with a 105mm gun, an infantry fighter vehicle version with a 30mm cannon, plus command and logistic support variants. This new assault vehicle family is now entering PLA Army and Marine units. It has succeeded in part due to its smaller size, compared to the similar but larger and troubled/over budget U.S. Marines Expeditionary Fighting Vehicle (EFV), which has recently had its planned procurement halved and is in danger of cancellation altogether.

Future issues: The Type 071 and 081 represent the PLA's first generation of large amphibious projection ships. It is reasonable to expect that the PLA may develop larger successors to both classes nearer to the 2020s. The PLA would have more cause to develop larger LHDs if the Chengdu Co. were to develop a short take-off vertical landing (STOVL) capable 5th generation fighter. The PLA's apparent success in developing a family of fast planning amphibious assault vehicles serves to enable PLAN amphibious ships to strike from beyond the horizon, the long objective of the U.S. Marines. It is just as possible that in the future U.S. Marines will be cooperating with their PLA counterparts in distant humanitarian or other missions, as it is also possible that the U.S. Navy and the PLAN could race to dominate a distant critical beachhead. In the near future, if a U.S. Navy and PLAN LPD arrived simultaneously at the same assault point, it is possible that the PLAN would succeed first in placing dominant armoured forces ashore.

Destroyers and Frigates

Modern PLAN surface warships are quickly emerging to fulfil air defence, escort, and perhaps in the future, anti-missile and anti-submarine missions. The PLAN is slowly retiring its long-serving Luda class destroyers, of which 17 built during the 1970s and 1980s. About 14 remain in service, equipped mainly with anti-ship missile and gun armament, intended mainly to extend further out to sea previous PLAN doctrines of sea denial. As it acquired four Russian-built 1980s technology Sovremenniy class destroyers, from 2000 to 2006, the PLAN was developing three new classes of air defence destroyers that used purchased and co-developed sensor and weapon systems. Starting in 2003 the PLAN launched its new stealthy Type 054 Jiankai frigate, and a second class of stealthy frigate is expected before the end of the decade.

It appears that in building two ships each of three classes of air defence destroyers, filling a long-standing gap in capability, among the PLAN's possible goals were to build different capability levels and to test different technologies and weapon-sensor combinations.

The Type 051C, based on the transitional Type 051 Luhai class hull, features the high performance Russian Fort vertical-launched SAM system, which could deal with some tactical ballistic missile threats and high-speed cruise missiles. Then the Type 052B Luyang I featured the medium range Russian Shtil rail-launched SAM, and medium-range ASMs, perhaps also offering a more cost effective design. The Type 052C Luyang II was more ambitious, featuring an Aegis-like phased array radar and the HHQ-9 vertical-launched SAM co-developed with Russia's Almaz-Antey SAM company.

This SAM may have some ATBM capability, a feature that the PLAN will likely further develop for future destroyers. The next class of PLAN destroyer is the subject of constant speculation by Chinese military magazines and websites, but there is little indication from open sources what capabilities it will stress.

A recent issue of Shipborne Weapons, which seems to specialize in such speculation, posited a future PLAN destroyer class that apparently utilizes a smaller more capable version of the phased array radar of the Type 052C, and the new vertical launched SAM that equips the new Type 054A Jiankai II frigate. It would appear to be quite similar to the later versions of the U.S. Burke class air defence destroyer. It also features a larger bow sonar dome, indicating it may have a much improved anti-submarine capability. Such a ship would appear to be designed for carrier escort missions among others, but again, this is just speculation from one popular Chinese military magazine.

The PLAN frigate force now includes over 25 1970s vintage Jianghu class ships and 14 Jiangwei I and Jiangwei 2 ships, built from the late 1980s up until 2004. Both classes are ill equipped for modern naval warfare but could help enforce blockades if covered by land-based airpower. Some Jiangweis have been seen undergoing refurbishment while some Jianghu's have been converted to carry 122mm multiple artillery rocket systems to perform amphibious fire support missions.

The 2003 arrival of the Type 054 signaled the PLAN's intention not to ignore this warship class. Having a similar stealthy shape to Taiwan/French LaFayette class frigate, the Type 054 and especially the later Type 054A with a new vertical launched SAM, they are a more capable though less expensive compliment to the PLAN's new destroyers. The PLAN is expected to build up to 12 Type 054A frigates. In 2007 a European source told the author that Germany's MTU maritime engine concern had won the competition to provide co-produced diesel engines for the next class of PLAN frigate, also expected to number 12 when completed.

Future issues: The PLAN follows closely global naval development trends and Chinese academic and popular military literature reflects an interest in how foreign navies are applying new technologies to produce more combat and cost effective solutions to naval challenges. It should be expected that future PLAN warships will make greater use of stealth, advanced electronics, automation to reduce crew size and Chinese-developed gas turbine engines. Future PLAN warships could also feature much longer range SAMs, new supersonic anti-ship and land-attack missiles, new laser or railgun weapons, and make greater use of UAVs and UUVs.

Small Combatants

In the 1960s and 1970s the PLAN build hundreds of fast attack craft (FAC) based on Soviet Komar and Osa class FACs armed with HY-1 copies of the Soviet Styx early anti-ship missile. Tied to coastal defence "People's War" doctrines these FACs were intended to operate in large numbers in conjunction with mines, submarines and air forces to thwart invasion from the sea. The decline of this threat from the 1980s onward also saw a decline in PLAN FAC numbers.

However, the PLAN has revived interest in this class of warship during the 10th and 11th five year plan. In 2004 the PLAN launched its first Type 022 stealthy wave-piercing catamaran FAC and in early 2009 Jane's Fighting

Ships estimated that about 60 had been built, out of a potential requirement for 100. Based on a fast-ferry design developed by the Australian AMD Corporation, the 220 ton Type 022's wave-piecing catamaran configuration gives it a high 36 kt speed and offers such smaller ships better sea keeping ability in higher sea states. The Type 022 also uses stealth shaping, stealth coatings and disruptive camouflage to reduce its radar and optical signature. It is armed with up to eight YJ-82 anti-ship cruise missiles though it only has very light defensive armament consisting of one 25mm gun turret and MANPADS. This means that Type 022s can be used to add scores of ASMs to surface action groups for operations within the First Island Chain. In November 2007 Type 022s did join a surface action group consisting of larger destroyers and frigates for naval exercises in the South China Sea. However, the large missile bays could be configured for other types of missile ordinance, such as 300mm artillery rockets to assist amphibious operations. With adequate external cuing the Type 022 could also carry longer range land attack cruise missiles.

Future issues: Of some importance the Type 022 points the possibility of the PLAN building larger wave-piercing catamaran ships for more diverse missions. Starting in 2005 China has built a rescue ship and a fast ferry using a wave piercing catamaran hull, both roughly in the 300-400 ton range. The first fast ferry may have been launched on June 2, 2009. It appears to be able to carry 200-300 passengers. This is not as large as the 950 ton Joint High Speed Surface Vessel (JHSV) wave-piercing catamaran to be built for the U.S. Navy, but it does indicate the PLA could opt to build larger similar warships to enable high speed troop and material movement for amphibious operations. In early 2008 the popular Chinese military magazine Shipborne Weapons printed a speculative article exploring future versions of the Type 022, to include a larger "corvette" version which could carry unmanned helicopters or small manned helicopters, to perhaps serve as a command ship.

Auxiliaries

A rapid buildup of logistic supply and other auxillary support ships would be a key indicator of the PLA's intension to assemble a navy increasingly capable of regional and extra-regional power projection. But so far into this decade, it would appear that the PLAN is not yet ready for a significant expansion of its logistic support fleet, though it has demonstrated a clear capability to do so should it make that decision. From 2002 to 2003 the PLAN built two 23,000 ton Fuchi class modern underway replenishment ships (AORs). Based on an earlier design produced for Thailand, the Fuchi is a modern AOR capable of underway transfer of fuel and solid stores. These ships have supported PLAN naval diplomatic deployments to Europe and Asia, and also supported the first anti-piracy deployment in December 2008. Prior to this the PLAN built two 21,000 ton Fuqing class underway replenishment ships in the 1970s, and acquired the Ukraine-built 37,000 ton Nanyun underway refueling tanker in 1993.

Smaller versions of the Fuchi hull appear to forms the basis of two other new auxiliaries. In 2006 the 14,000+ ton Danyao class was launched. While its primary mission was not readily apparent, Chinese sources have pointed to its being designed to replenish Paracel and Spratly Island outposts. It can lower smaller cargo landing craft into the water to move supplies to the shallow water islets in the Spratly group, or use a helicopter. This ship would also seem suited to for potential future missions to deploy or tend underwater sensors in the South China Sea. Then in 2007 the PLAN launched its first purpose-built 14,000+ ton Type 920 Anwei class hospital ship. While its medical support capabilities have not been reported, this ships gives the PLAN a hefty tool play a major role in future humanitarian relief operations. It can also serve to raise combat morale by offering a greater assurance of medical support for military personnel deployed for Taiwan, regional or extra-regional military operations.

TACTICAL NUCLEAR WEAPONS AND ELECTROMAGNETIC PULSE (EMP)

There is a tendency in some Western literature on Chinese nuclear capability to downplay the PRC's development of tactical nuclear weapons, particularly low yield tactical weapons. Yet, according to David Shambaugh, Chinese military doctrine "envisions use of tactical nuclear weapons in a battlefield environment – either airbursts or fired for artillery. Since the mid-1980s, PLA forces training in north China (Hua Bei) have simulated such conditions."

He also notes that tactical nuclear weapons are important because China "envisions offensive limited nuclear war-fighting….at a regional, intermediate-range, theater level." There are Chinese generals who openly extol the military utility of tactical nuclear weapons. One of them, Lt. General Mi Zhenyu, wrote that a: First strike has always been the combat phase that militarists attach greatest importance to…. Field tactical nuclear weapons are an effective antipersonnel weapon….This weapon not only has the superior tactical technical capabilities of long range, fast firing rate, high accuracy, and great destructive power, but it could also be used as a surprise weapon in major field operations to strive for and grasp the field initiative.

In its tactical use, in an offensive situation it could directly break up the effective fire power of the enemy and destroy the defence points of the enemy from a distance, or it could attack the depth defences of the enemy and cut off the enemy's retreat. In a defensive situation it could attack the enemy rear echelon troops, stop the continuous assault of the enemy, and defend against the enemy making a direct deep push.

Coordinated and complementary field tactical nuclear missiles used with various other conventional weapons systems could give the military greater military benefits and battlefield power. In a situation where, temporarily, no global wars are being fought, localized wars will be the major forms of combat for a period of time. In localized wars, the possible use of field tactical nuclear weapons by the enemy cannot be dismissed. Thus, China appropriately and within reason must develop field tactical nuclear weapons in order to further break down the various kind of nuclear threats of the hegemonists and restrain the use of field tactical nuclear weapons by the enemy.

The Chinese arsenal of tactical nuclear weapons may be very large—400—according to a 2002 estimate by Russian analyst Dr. Nikolai Sokov. There are also reports of Chinese development of low yield nuclear weapons or advanced types of tactical nuclear weapons. Writing in 1999 in a Hong Kong publication, Tsao Kuo-chung reported that a "Chinese military source" disclosed that China had developed "miniaturized nuclear warheads [for] 'non-strategic nuclear weapons'."

According to the source, by the late 1980s China could deliver "'miniature and super-miniature nuclear warheads,' which are mainly atom bombs....The destructive power of the miniature and super-miniature atom bomb is about that of 10 to 100 tons of TNT....Beijing can deliver 'fixed-point attacks' on any military target and minimize damage to non-military objects."

In the year 2000, Chinese Major General Wu Jianguo, a former Associate Professor and Dean of the Chinese Antichemical Warfare Academy, gave "several proposals for new kinds of Chinese nuclear weapons, including a ground-penetrating nuclear weapons with an equivalent of 10 tons of TNT, an antimissile nuclear weapon with an equivalent of 100 tons of TNT, and a ground-to-ground and air-to-ground nuclear weapon with an equivalent of 1,000 tons of TNT." Qing Tong, writing in 2002 in a Hong Kong journal which reportedly has close ties to the PRC military, stated that, "China has achieved progress by leaps and bounds in its tactical nuclear weapons, making nuclear weapons practical and facilitating their use in future high-tech, local wars." The Chinese DF-15 missile reportedly carries a neutron bomb.

China has officially announced that it has tested a neutron bomb and the declassified CIA report, Chinese development of gun type nuclear artillery shell. Apparently, the Russian military also believes that "the possible makeup of the nuclear reserve [of China] consists of tactical missile warheads and artillery rounds."

Another Russian analyst, Colonel Viktor V. Stefashin, a professor at the Academy of Military Sciences, linked the 1988 Chinese test of an enhanced radiation weapon to the development "of a very low yield neutron weapon and about creation (or work on creation) of nuclear artillery." Stefashin reported that the 1988 Chinese test of a neutron warhead had a yield of 1-5 kilotons. Additionally, one senior U.S. intelligence official, Lt. General Michael Maples, has raised concern about the ASAT capability of China's nuclear ballistic missiles.

There is also concern about Chinese preparations for a nuclear electromagnetic pulse attack on Taiwan, the United States and Japan as part of its strategy to facilitate the conquest of Taiwan. The Congressional Commission on the Threat to the United States from Electromagnetic Pulse reported that, "China and Russia have considered limited nuclear attack options that, unlike Cold War plans, employ EMP as the primary or sole means of attack." The 2005 Pentagon report on Chinese military power observed that, "Some PLA theorists are aware of the electromagnetic effect of using a high-altitude electromagnetic pulse (HEMP), and might consider using HEMP in an unconventional attack, believing that the United States and other nations would not consider it as a use of force and a crossing of the nuclear threshold." A Congressional Research Service report by Ronald O'Rourke concluded that a U.S. naval force coming to the aid of Taiwan against a Chinese attack would have to be prepared for use of nuclear weapons and EMP because, "China could also use a nuclear-armed ballistic missile to detonate a nuclear warhead in the atmosphere to create a high-altitude electromagnetic pulse (EMP) intended to temporarily or permanently disable the electronic circuits of U.S. or other civilian and military electronic systems."

These concerns are shared by foreign analysts. A Taiwanese defence publication, *Ch'uan-ch'iu Fang-wei Tsa-chic*, pointed out the risk of Chinese nuclear EMP attack against Taiwan's aircraft early warning system. Chung Chien, writing in the *Taiwan Defence Review*, outlines the threat posed by EMP attack using very low yield nuclear devices:

The PLA now possesses a matured vehicle carrying low-yield nuclear weapon to detonate at the appropriate height, that is the battle-tested, combat-ready Dong Feng-15 (M-9 for export version) short range ballistic missile (SRBM)....The nuclear EMP attack creates an extremely high electric field of 10,000 volts per meter, covering up to 100 km from ground zero.

The sudden onset of electric field can cause permanent damage on electronic devices containing micro memory chip, logic circuit, integrated circuit, diode, transistor, and amplifier as well, virtually shut down all C4ISR [command, control, computers, communications, intelligence, surveillance, and reconnaissance] equipment used by both military and civilian communities.... A tandem nuclear EMP attack over Taiwan, one in north and one in south, could knock out...[the critical electronic systems] system island wide.

An October 2003 report on *China Military Strength* by Taiwan's Democratic Progressive Party goes further asserting that China is "engaged in quantitative production and deployment of electro-magnetic pulse (EMP) [proceeding three words in English] micro...nuclear warheads." According to an official at the Taiwanese Defence Ministry, the Chinese M-11 missile "can fire a variety of warheads ranging from nuclear and chemical warheads to electromagnetic pulse warheads." In May 2001 Lin Chong, Vice Chairman of Taiwan's Mainland Affairs Council, warned the public to "pay special attention to the so-called EMP (electronic magnetic pulse) tactics."

He pointed out that, "In an English language article published in 1992, Lin pointed out that Beijing is seeking to develop small nuclear warheads that can be detonated in the skies above Taiwan." Wang Chuo-chung writing in November 2003 stated that China would have military superiority over Taiwan in 2007 and that sources, presumably in the Taiwanese government, "claimed that by then, the [PRC] military will have the capacity to launch electromagnetic pulse attacks against Taiwan.

It was said that pulse attacks are sufficient to paralyze 65 percent of Taiwan's forces." A report published on a Hong Kong website owned by China's official news agency quoted an unidentified Chinese official as saying that China might not only stage two EMP attacks against Taiwan but also might "conduct an announced nuclear EMP 'test' 1,200 km east of Taiwan to keep US forces at bay." Reportedly the Taiwanese military takes the threat of EMP attack so seriously that it has EMP hardened its military electronics.

China expert Dr. Michael Pillsbury has linked nuclear EMP attack to the Chinese "assassin's mace" concept of defeating the superior with the inferior. He stated before the U.S.-China Security Review Commission in August 2001 that the Chinese "write a lot about EMP effects that could be achieved in an assassin's mace weapon on U.S. forces because the U.S. depends so heavily on, not vacuum tubes, which tend to be less affected, but on circuit boards."

According to Dr. Pillsbury, high altitude EMP weapons are seen "as a natural enemy of more technological advanced militaries and an 'electronic

Assassin's Mace'." Pillsbury has elsewhere noted that the March 2000 issue of China's *Military Digest* featured an article by Xian Fengli, Lu Young and Ming Xiang which argued that "EMP warheads will make it much easier to cross the nuclear threshold." The designers of the Chinese DF-11 SRBM "have demonstrated the most interest in HEMP [high altitude nuclear EMP] weapons." Pillsbury observed that Chinese military writings on EMP are often ignored in the West because of the technical nature Chinese language on EMP and the fact that the technical language does normally appear in English-Chinese dictionaries. However, the Chinese may have decided to advertise their capabilities. According to the *Wall Street Journal*, "China and Russia have the capability to launch EMP weapons – and have let us know it. China recently published an article on EMP in a Chinese-language technical journal. To make sure the U.S. got the message, the article appeared in English."

FUTURE LOGISTICS MODERNIZATION

Deng Xiaoping attaches great importance to the logistics modernization of our armed forces, considering the question of logistics construction in the context of the overall strategic situation. He has made many important statements on logistics in accordance with the new requirements of modern warfare and the new situation that our logistics construction faces in the new era. He has emphasized the importance of the modern logistics to the modern army and modern war. He asks us be subordinate to the overall situation of national economic construction, making full use of the limited defence budget. We should race against time and prepare for anti-aggression war. We should pay special attention to the study of the new situation and the new problems facing our logistics. We should improve the standard of management in our logistics, and learn to do more work with less spending. Things should be straightened out in our logistics, and the good tradition of hard and honest work should be carried on. His instructions have become important parts of the theories on defence building in the new era, and have given guidance to the revolutionizing modernization, and regularization of our logistics.

A Clear Understanding of Logistics

As the modernization of the armed forces progresses, the role and function of logistics become more important. The fourth Middle East war in the 1970s, the war over Malvinas in the 1980s, and the Gulf War in the early 1990s have all attested to this. In the early days of our Republic, Mao Zedong pointed out, "To the modern army, it is of extreme great importance to organize good logistics in the rear area." Deng Xiaoping said in 1978, "As military science and technology develops, and our military equipment gradually improves, we have to come up with new situations in our logistics. In the past, ours was an army of millet and rifles, and our dependence on logistics was not great. Now that the situation has changed, our military supplies, arms and ammunition, and military equipment are all dependent on the supply from a strong rear." President Jiang Zemin also pointed out, "There would be no high combat effectiveness without a strong logistics supply. Fighting under the condition of modern technology, there is the problem of a big consumption of materials, the complexity of the technical aspect, and the demands of time requirements. The dependance on logistics and technology is much greater. We should fully recognize the role and function of logistics supply, and continuously strengthen our logistics construction."

Faced with this new situation, we should not only make sure that the army is well prepared for military struggle, but also make sure that the army maintains a good standard of living, that army cohesiveness is strengthened, and that combat effectiveness is improved. Our logistics department staff should clearly understand the responsibilities they bear and be firmly committed to servicing the army. Catering to the needs of the grass-roots units and servicing the army wholeheartedly should be the point of departure for our logistics. We should strive to ensure good service and efficient supply; our motto should be "we serve." We should make sure that our logistics serve the army, our department offices serve the grass-roots units, and higher levels of authority serve the lower levels. Warehouses, hospitals, recreation centres, supply stations, and army service stations are windows on the spirit of logistics. We should improve the quality of our service through promoting good service activities, and create good images. Good service for the armed forces in the remote and hardship areas should be our priority. The investment of expenditures and materials should favour the grass-roots units and the remote and hardship areas. We should continuously improve the level of logistics service to facilitate overall army modernization.

Modernize Logistics Within National Economic Construction

Military modernization being subordinated to the overall situation of economic construction is a scientific policy that will ensure a prosperous country and a strong army. Military power in the final analysis is based on economic power. The scale, speed, and quality of army building are all conditioned by the country's economy. On a weak economic foundation, military maintenance is constrained by economic conditions; thus it is difficult to develop and strengthen the military. Only when the economy is developed and the economic power strengthened will it be possible to build a strong and solid national defence. Deng Xiaoping has therefore emphasized, "The four modernizations can be summed up as economic construction. There would not be the modernization of national defence without the necessary economic foundation.... The modernization of national defence can only be based on the development of the whole sector of industry as well as agriculture." Therefore, we must exercise restraint and adhere to the central task of economic construction.

We should strive to develop our national economy, because without the development of our national economy there will be no military modernization. Stressing military reconstruction but ignoring the national economic construction will certainly affect the speed of economic development and fundamentally constrain the speed of military modernization. To gain the initiative in the next century, many countries in the world now choose the road of giving priority to the development of the economy, science, and technology. Deng Xiaoping's idea that military modernization be subordinated to the overall goal of national economic construction is suitable for the conditions of our country and of our military and is absolutely correct.

An important principle of logistics in the new period is to serve and be subordinated to the overall situation of national economic construction. We should attach importance to the overall situation, starting out from the overall interests of the nation and the military. We should give up individual or local interests for the sake of the whole, and immediate interests for the sake of long-term interests. We should firmly establish the concept of the overall situation, and overcome and prevent selfish departmentalism and decentralism. We should conscientiously put the interests of our unit or department under the interests of our nation and the military. Just as military modernization is subordinated to the overall situation of economic construction, logistics construction should be subordinated to overall military modernization. The fact that we show consideration for the overall situation does not mean that we are passively exercising restraint, attempting nothing and accomplishing nothing. We should be eager to make progress in the context of "subordination and restraint." We should liberate our minds, renew ideas, and use our brains to find our way toward reform. New ideas and new ways should be tried in our efforts to strive for the continuous development of logistics modernization.

Improve Logistics Supply Capability

In the field of logistics, doing an excellent job for combat readiness is an important aspect of being prepared for an anti-aggression war. Modern wars, especially high-tech local wars, have raised new and higher requirements for combat readiness in the field of logistics. We should carefully study and seek new ways to deal with the question of combat readiness in the field of logistics. We should closely follow military strategic policy in this new era, to ensure that the entire armed forces are well prepared for military struggle, and at the same time greatly improve the combat readiness of the logistics itself. We should pay close attention to the building of emergency support forces for logistics, and make serious adjustments in the structure of combat material stockpiling. The portion of high-technology materials should be increased. Materials stockpiling should be combined with that of production capability, and stockpiling by the military should be combined with that of civilians. The logistics mobilization structure should be improved and we should study and formulate rules and regulations concerning mobilization during wartime. The building of a logistics reserve force should be strengthened, and preparation work for logistics mobilization should be carried out. In light of the characteristics of a high-tech war, we should stress the study of theories, principles, and methods of wartime supply.

Equipment for logistics is an important component part of military equipment and an important factor in fighting capability. Acceleration of the modernization of logistics is a key way to improve the capabilities of logistics supply. In future wars, without an advanced logistics supply, costs will increase and the time it takes to win a war will be prolonged. We should have a sense of urgency about updating our logistics. There should be a unified plan for overall logistics and for combat equipment, as well as a coordinated development between the two. Priority goals should be set with an obvious focal point. Currently, we should first of all increase the mobility of logistics supply and improve the capability of emergency supply. Human beings are the decisive factor in war, including the area of logistics supply. It would be impossible to improve wartime capability of logistics supply without high-quality personnel suited to high-technology war.

Therefore, the training and education in the field of logistics should be strengthened and be seen as a basic project in the improvement of logistics supply capability. In order to strengthen training and education in the field of logistics, training and education reforms should be implemented. We are in a time of rapid development in science and technology. High-technology arms have come into the combat field, with many features of modern warfare. Training in and education of logistics should incorporate the realities of modern war, quickly changing from coping with general warfare to dealing with the problems of logistics supply on a high-technology battlefield. We should pay attention to the needs of supply under high-technology conditions.

The intensity and degree of difficulty of training should be raised, and the contents and methods be reformed. We should try to find different ways to train various logistics forces. Training on new equipment, with new technology, to gain new knowledge, should be increased. Training in the areas of mobility, supply, rescue operation, repair work, and protection under different conditions should be stressed. Real combat situation training should be increased. Methods of training in the field for night warfare and for expedient materiel supply should be studied. Training and real combat situations should be closely related. Modern science and technology are the most important factors of logistics capability. Research in logistics will generate great cost effectiveness not only for the military but for the economy as well. Therefore, strengthening research in logistics will be of great significance to logistics modernization and improvement of logistics supply capability. In order to do this, our leaders at various levels should strengthen their awareness of science and technology. The idea of building a strong army by relying on science and technology and improving logistics through science and technology should be genuinely fostered. Scientific research work should be put on the agenda, and an atmosphere should be created so that the entire logistics forces attach importance to science and technology. Scientific research should focus on logistics modernization and on logistics supply under high-technology conditions. President Jiang Zemin stated, "In the field of defence science and technology, we should focus on researching and developing some key technologies," and we should concentrate our manpower, material, and budget on a number of high-technology items that influence overall logistics work. We should give full play to our scientific research department's skills and knowledge and tap their potential. On the basis of high-quality research and achievements, we should promote popularizing and utilizing the results of scientific research by organizing the transfer of research results, offering technical service and consultation, and signing technical contracts. Our logistics department has a lot of intellectuals and technical professionals and is a department with a high concentration of skills and knowledge. We should uphold Deng Xiaoping's policy of "respect knowledge, respect talents," and create an environment in which people's talents will emerge and be fully utilized. We should give full play to our scientific research workers' talents and creativity.

Reform the Logistics Field

As the country has set up its socialist market economy system, the environment of military logistics reconstruction has seen great changes. For a long time, logistics reconstruction was been carried out under the planned economy system. The various aspects of the logistics construction are all suited to the planned economy system. As the economic system changes, logistics construction faces new situations. We should keep in mind Deng

Xiaoping's instruction: "Pay attention to the study of the new situations and new problems of logistics work under new historical conditions." We should raise our reform consciousness, follow the development of the situation, and make sure that the guiding ideology, our goals, supply system and logistics methods in this new era are in step with the establishment of the socialist market economy system. Logistics reconstruction should be pushed to a new phase.

In the defence industry we should adhere to the method of "linking peacetime and wartime production, and having compatible utility for both the military and civilians." In the last few years, we have made some progress and had some pleasing results. The defence industry has been connected with the civilian industry. After ensuring that the military has all of its needed supplies, the defence industry has entered the market place, and reform has been carried out in all production areas. We have organized the transfer of defence industry technology to commercial use.

The portion of commercial products made by the defence industry has increased year by year, thus creating wealth for the country and greatly invigorating the industry itself. Furthermore, logistics department units have made improvements in the long-time problem of single-product and low-efficiency manufacturing, by tapping potential markets and expanding plant functions. On the basis of accomplishing various logistics tasks, they have provided services to society, which both facilitated their own development and also brought about greater economic and social cost effectiveness. Social forces to improve logistics supply have also greatly promoted military logistics reconstruction. We have trained a great many people, providing them with skills suitable for defence and commercial sectors, thus providing a source of talents for both military reconstruction and civilian economic development. Practice has shown that, under the conditions of a socialist market economy, it is correct and practical that the logistics industry adhere to the principle of linking peacetime and wartime production that has both defence and commercial applications.

According to the principle of linking unified supply with separate supply, it will be a long-term task to carry out adjustmenta and reform in the logistics supply system. Currently, the materials and services that various military forces use should be procured according to the principle of proximity and convenience, and we shall further improve the supply system by allocating supplies, medical services, and repair work according to region. This will meet the needs of the army to strengthen combined forces and raise efficiency and will also be in accord with the market economy trend of to strengthening cross sectorial ties and raising efficiency.

The essential criterion is to improve the capability of logistics supply and to improve the combat effectiveness of the armed forces. We should deepen the reform of the logistics supply system and gradually establish a centralized, unified, flexible and highly efficient logistics supply system suited both to the military strategic policy of the new period as well as to the development of the socialist market economy.

We should actively carry out reform in a way that will allow us to raise money, stockpile and provide supplies. At present, the logistics department should work with the main channels of government. We should take the initiative in reporting to the relevant government departments our military supply needs and gaining support of the country. We should work through legislation to ensure there is a large stockpile of necessary military materials for the armed forces. In addition, we should study new channels, methods, and measures for increasing military materials and stockpiles, by actively exploring the market. With regard to stockpiling military materials, Deng Xiaoping pointed out that the army "should not store too much, otherwise there will be waste.... What is the use of storing too much. We should not store too much because the service life of materials is limited, and things become useless after storing them for too long."

In the future, apart from storing combat-use materials according to regulations, materials and equipment that have both defence and commercial applications should be ordered by contract according to market conditions. We should use specially designated civilian enterprises to supply the set amount of materials at agreed upon times, and let society shoulder more responsibility. We should have various and useful ties with the large and medium-size commercial enterprises and establish stable channels of supply. Army supply stations should be connected, exchange and redistribution of supplies should be strengthened, and unified supply should be organized. When logistics has really adapted to the new track of the market economy, when it can better use the market mechanisms and work according to market prices, we will be able to closely follow the steps of the national economic reform, and the reform of logistics will continuously progress.

Strengthen Logistics Management

The shortage of defence funds has always been a bottleneck constraining the modernization of our military, and the tension between supply and demand is not likely to ease. Under the conditions of scarce funds and big demands of reforms, we should strengthen logistics management and use the limited amount of funds efficiently. We shall use less money, accomplish more, and do a better job, for this is the only option for us in the strengthening of our army's logistics construction in the new era. To strengthen logistics management, we should above all manage according to rules and regulations.

Deng Xiaoping pointed out, "In the past, we did not have much property. But we have more things now. It is a new problem for us to manage the logistics work well. We need to have a whole series of rules and regulations that are suited to the new situation and can solve the problems. We should fight against those who have no regard for the financial rules and regulations, and oppose extravagance and waste." Rules and regulations governing logistics work should be perfected and be strictly followed in order to regulate the various activities of logistics work. We should prevent wilful use of funds, materials, and equipment, and conduct technical operations. Logistics work should gradually become systematized, standardized, and regularized. All those actions that violate financial regulations should be seriously dealt with, and the maintenance of a system of standards and financial disciplines should be taken seriously.

Financial administration is the key to strengthening of logistics management. Military logistics is, in a certain sense, financial administration. On the premise that the defence budget cannot increase much, the rate of defence modernization is, to a large degree, determined by the management of logistics and especially the management of the defence budget. Deng Xiaoping said, "Those who do the logistics work should learn how to manage things well, and should learn to use less money and do more chores....The defence budget as a portion of the government budget can not be increased now, and it is the job of the army to use the money effectively. It takes a lot of knowledge to know how best to spend money, and we need to study carefully... strict budgeting.

The policy should be correct, and the method right." We should examine the annual budget and its implementation, to make sure the money is correctly spent and the amount is appropriate. Because the defence budget is tight, we should concentrate our financial resources and focus on key projects.

Taking into consideration the need to continually improve the living standard of the troops, the military expenditure should be tilted toward equipment, key forces, and key direction. That is to say, to ensure stability of the armed forces, we must modernize the armed forces. At the same time, we should closely follow and assess the results of the actual spending after the funds have been distributed. Auditing and supervision by the broad masses should be perfected, in order to meet the requirement put forward by Deng Xiaoping that "the money should be put to better, rational use, and should be used genuinely to improve combat effectiveness."

The foundation of logistics management lies at the grass-roots level, and when the performance of logistics management at the grass-roots unit is good, the whole logistics management system will be excellent. Therefore, leaders at different levels should attach importance to logistics management at the grass-roots level. "Regulations on Logistics Management at the Grass-roots Level," issued by the Central Military Committee, lists important regulations for grass-roots level reconstruction of the whole military. These are regulations for the standardized management of logistics at the grass-roots level.

Each level should work according to headquarters requirements and consider the implementation of the regulations to be part of its day-to-day management. Emphasis should be laid on improving the quality of the managers and raising the standard of management. The self-managing capability at the grass-roots level should also be strengthened. We should rely on the masses to do a good job in logistics management at the grass-roots level in order to ensure that everyone cares about management, everyone takes part in it, and everyone encourages its development.

Logistics management is a scientific matter, and the strength of the members of the logistics department determines the results of the management. Deng Xiaoping has repeatedly emphasized the importance of training logistics personnel. We must use various ways and means to strengthen the training of logistics personnel to increase the number of good managers. Better software for logistics management is the essential solution to the improvement of the logistics management.

Strengthen Improvement of the Logistics Department

Logistics personnel, especially the leaders, should set good examples, and not take advantage of being in a favored position. They should be honest in performing official duties and be good managers.

According to the plan of the Party and Central Military Commission, we should further carry out our anticorruption policy and advocate honesty. Army logistics is in charge of money and materials and is vulnerable to the corrupting influences of pleasure seeking, money worshipping, and extreme individualism that exist in a developing socialist market economy. To carry on the excellent tradition of hard work and thrift in the new era, anticorruption and pro-honesty activities should be seriously carried out and not conducted perfunctorily or superficially. We should reform our production and management, and maintain the distinctive character of the people's army. The army is basically dependent on public revenue, but it is necessary to undertake some production in order to make up for the deficiency of public funds. But the army should not attempt to completely support itself. It would be extremely dangerous to put all its energy into business and making money. The level of corps must not engage in business activities, but instead engage in agricultural and side-line production. Production and business activities should be grouped together and be under the unified management of a larger unit. The financial affairs of production and business activities should be strictly managed and earnings from production should be distributed in a unified way. It should be stressed that illegal acts will not be tolerated in production and business activities.

This is an important policy for the military in the new era, and should be resolutely, earnestly, and fully implemented. We should fully understand the significance of rectification and reform in our production and management. Through rectification and reform, we can carry on the fine tradition of hard work and thrift, strengthen the development of honest administration and Communist Party style in the army, and better perform the essential duties and functions of our army.

5

Air Power in the 21st Century

Air power has completed a century of its existence and impact on military power and its application in a vast range of situations varying from the delivery of nuclear weapons to casualty evacuation and disaster relief.1 When trying to assess the role and scope of air power in the next century, or at least in its early decades, it would be useful to start by devoting some thought to at least some of the key elements and consequences of air power so far. Such an evaluation in a paper of this nature by definition has to be selective rather than exhaustive.

A CENTURY OF AIR POWER: INTENSIFIED ASYMMETRY IN WAR

Few will argue that air power came to play a crucial if not dominant role in 20th century warfare. There is little doubt today that many of the early prophets were ahead of time and technology. But there is little doubt that while air power may not be able to win a war by itself, no war can be won without it, and would certainly be lost without its appropriate application. It is amusing to watch many proponents of land and sea power argue that air power still only plays a support role to their primary role, and some air power practitioners in the developing world accepting such formulations unquestioningly.

To start with, there is the question of asymmetry. Perhaps the most telling lesson of the 20th century is that warfare, in essence, is the generation and successful application of favourable asymmetry of force whether in time or space. Air power has come to provide the most significant of capabilities that, if employed correctly, contribute almost dramatically to the generation and employment of asymmetry. This central role of air power is likely to grow in the coming decades.

Historically, successful exploitation of asymmetry has almost inevitably led to victory in warfare. In fact, starting from deterrence through combatant force structures to employment of military power, it is essentially asymmetry (and its exploitation) which holds the key to success. A closer scrutiny of some of the widely accepted cardinal principles of war (surprise, concentration of force, etc) would reveal that they primarily seek to establish a situation of favourable asymmetry. The classical doctrines of warfighting, whether based on attrition, manoeuvre, or the theory of the indirect approach, all seek ways and means of creating a favourable asymmetry through the state of the human mind, morale and will. The classical concept of numerical superiority in certain force ratios as an essential prerequisite for success in offensive action is predicated on similar values.

In earlier wars, the primary means of achieving decisive asymmetries were essentially based on human courage (and skill) of the fighting man, and operational (tactical and strategic) surprise. In warfare involving well trained military forces, tactical surprise to achieve asymmetry became an almost prime factor of success; and hence the importance and value of the "art" of Generalship. However, the industrial and scientific revolution has had a profound impact on the prime means of achieving asymmetry. Starting with the grooved rifle and connoidal bullet in the mid-19th century, technological growth has been accelerating the pace of war. But even more important are the basic changes that have taken place in the means of achieving asymmetry. Air power in this century has represented the essence of the capabilities that have provided the means and methods, if applied correctly, of achieving a favourable asymmetry.

Air power operates at a technological level normally higher than that obtaining in other components of military power leave alone civil sectors. Superior technology has been a major factor in providing battlefield dominance. And this does not operate on a linear paradigm. For example, a 10 percent greater lethal range of weapon does not imply a mere 10 percent superiority, but provides 100 percent superiority over the adversary. Experience of warfare in the 20th century has proved again and again that technological superiority is a tremendous force multiplier. The 1991 Gulf War demonstrated the importance of high technology and most countries have sought to prepare themselves for the future based on a search for high technology weapon systems.

But the experience of war in this century has also shown that it is not enough to merely possess higher technology systems. It is also the way technology has been employed (and the asymmetry created by the way the adversary employs it) that has, more often than not, provided the crucial and deciding edge. Iraq's weapon systems were not of the type that would normally be classified as low technology. It is also not correct to assume that the US-led coalition employed military power in a way that was dramatically different from earlier wars. In fact, for anyone who had cared to watch (and the defence establishment should be doing so as a priority occupation), the 1982 Beq'a Valley operations by Israel provided the essence of how dominance in the air, and hence on the ground could be achieved. The 1991 Gulf War, for all that the "CNN factor" produced, was still an expanded version of the 1982 war.2 The synergy created by the interface of doctrine and technology, therefore, holds the key to success in modern warfare.

Given the nature of changes taking place in technology, technological, more than tactical surprise will increasingly hold the key to achieving asymmetry of military capabilities and operational results. The ingredients of technological surprise must, of course, be applied and exploited tactically to achieve the end result. But technological capabilities have the intrinsic potential to help neutralise tactical surprises. Nowhere is this more pronounced than in the information-decision-action cycle of war and air power which accelerates this as well as incorporates technological asymmetries in its capabilities. Information of hostile capabilities, moves and even intentions can be available to much greater extent and scope than was ever possible before and air power capabilities provide significant assets for this purpose. And this single factor alone would have far-reaching effects on the paradigms of asymmetry and conventional traditional approach to assessing military balances and employment of force. The autonomous momentum of technological growth promises to increase the importance of technological asymmetries in future. The impact of higher technology of weapons systems in an operational environment otherwise involving lower levels of military technology can be crucial; at times, leading to results totally disproportionate to the absolute quality of such weapon systems. The most vivid example perhaps is the dropping of the nuclear bomb from an aircraft in 1945. At the extreme level, the application of combat air power against an adversary that has no such capabilities provides unprecedented advantage to the side that is able to do so. And the effect is symbolised by the use of the airborne early warning and control system (AWACS) by one side only which creates an asymmetry similar to a man with all possible tools fighting another who is blind.

Warfare during the 20th century clearly moved toward increasing degree of mobility and mechanisation. The factor of momentum was also added to the traditional elements of mass and firepower. Air power, by its very nature has a greater impact on manoeuvre warfare as compared to static wars. Air power is relatively far more inefficient in bombing out foot soldiers than it is in knocking out mechanised elements. Mechanisation of warfare made it far more vulnerable to air attacks since mobility could be adversely affected by both the level of destruction that could be brought down on such forces, as well as the disruption of the momentum of move that could be caused. Mechanised forces are heavily dependent on extensive logistics support which itself starts to get vulnerable to destruction and disruption from the air, raising the requirement of logistic support further. Increasing reliance on manoeuvre warfare and mechanisation of the battlefield, therefore, has further enhanced the impact of air power, in both offence and defence.

The key element determining the success or failure of application of military power has always been the ability to disengage and the degree of control that can be exercised on this process. More often than not, this ability also determines the costs and benefits of applying military force. Throughout the century, air power has offered a range of policy choices for application of force for political purposes.

This is because air power, by its very nature, offers tremendous capabilities for offensive strike. Technology had advanced sufficiently by World War II to take air power to the level of all weather operations in air-to-air warfare. But air-to-surface warfare essentially remained limited to line of sight operations because of the need to visually acquire and engage the target. Nearly (five decades would elapse before air power could be applied in poor visibility and night conditions in air- to-surface operations. As we approach the end of this century, we also stand witness to the phenomenon of increasing ability to acquire, engage and destroy surface targets from the air, beyond visual range and visibility conditions.

CHINA'S AEROSPACE INDUSTRY

China has become the world's second largest national air travel market trailing only the United States. The civil aviation transportation growth has advanced at an average annual rate of 17.6% since 1978.

In 2011, the volume of passenger traffic was 0.293 billion passengers and cargo throughput totaled 5.58 million tons, carried by fleets of 1,764 transport aircraft and 1,124 general aviation airplanes. According to The China's 12th Five-Year Plan, the volume of passenger and freight traffic were projected to be 0.45 billion and 9 million tons respectively in 2015 with an annual growth rate of over 10%. Accordingly, there will be 2,750 transport aircraft and over 2,000 general aviation airplanes, and the airports may be increased from 180 to more than 230.

PIM's market research division has concluded that the potential growth may provide foreign aviation related component manufacturers and service providers with new opportunities

Market Size

Based on *The Assessment of China ' s Civil Aircraft Market 2010-2029* issued by Commercial Aircraft Corporation of China (COMAC).China's air transportation market was projected to require a new demand of 4,400 civil aircraft with the value of 456.8 billion USD from 2010 to 2029, in which the number of single-aisle jet airliners would account for 75%. This represented approximately one-eighth of the total global demand. The global proportion of Chinese airline fleet will be increased from the current 8% to 14% accordingly.

Although China's general aviation sector was still in an early stage of development at the formation of China's 12th Five-Year Plan, China was projected to require 10,000 to 12,000 general aviation aircraft in operation from 2011 to 2015. During the next 5 to 10 years, the number was expected to increase by an average of 30% annually with the value of 159 billion USD (exchange rate: 1USD=6.3RMB).

According to PIM's analysis, the primary factors contributing to this growth encompassed the following items:

- The continuous and stable development of China's economy
- The rapid urbanization development
- The overwhelming development of the domestic and international tourist industry
- Government policy initiatives.

Current Commercial Aircraft Production

Essentially, all aircraft manufactured in China were produced by the Aviation Industry Corporation of China (AVIC) and COMAC and their subsidiaries, however, some major components, such as engines, hydraulic systems and other critical parts are mainly either being produced abroad or by foreign OEM's in China . There are two domestically designed commercial passenger aircrafts in the market China produced: the MA60-series turboprop and the ARJ21 regional jet. The MA60 is a 60-seat turboprop airliner manufactured by the Xi'an Aircraft Corporation (XAC), an AVIC subsidiary. The ARJ21, manufactured by COMAC, is a 90-seat regional jet that has been in testing since November 2008, and was project to delivery in 2013. COMAC is also developing a 190-seats passenger aircraft named C919 with the goal of initial production in 2014, and by the end of February 2012, the order has reached 235 aircrafts. It aims to be customers' another competitive choice besides Boeing 737 and Airbus A320. China also performs final assembly on Airbus A320-series narrow-body airliners and produces the Embraer ERJ-145 regional jet under license. All wide-body aircraft will be imported at least through 2020.

Competitive Landscape

Although most of the aircraft related companies are SOEs, the government has issued policies to encourage Chinese private capital or foreign investment to invest this industry. Up until now, foreign involvement in China's civil aerospace sector has unquestionably contributed to its development. Several foreign companies, such as Honeywell Suzhou Aero-engine Co., Ltd, GE, Pratt & Whitney, Boeing Tianjin Composites Co., Ltd, Harbin Embraer Aircraft Industry Co.ÿLtd, SAM (Suzhou) Co., Ltd, have already been active in China.

CURRENT STATUS OF CHINA'S COMMERCIAL JET ENGINE PROGRAM

Aviation Industry Corporation of China (AVIC) Commercial Aircraft Engine (ACAE) is investing heavily in the new engine and says that it wants to increase its commercial turbofan design and development staff to 500 people by the end of 2011. This would represent a more than 60% increase in staffing for the company's commercial turbofan division and the company would like to see 40% of the new hires come from abroad, according to *People's Daily*. ACAE is hiring substantially from abroad already and has held a recruitment event in the UK, and is planning one in the U.S.

ACAE plans further expansion, with the company website saying the company plans to add 3,000 staff over the next 5-8 years. To put ACAE's staffing increase plans into context, an industry expert tells us that to develop a truly indigenous commercial jet engine could require on the order of 5,000 to 10,000 or more workers. For instance, GE and SNECMA may have used a staff of as many as 2,000 engineers and as many as 5,000 or more technicians to develop the CFM56 engine, if all sub-suppliers are counted. Even with this staffing level, electronics, sub-modules, fasteners, and other components came from outside vendors. In light of this, the staffing levels that ACAE currently plans mean that: (1) the engine is unlikely to be fully indigenous and (2) that it is likely to receive substantial "off the books" funding.

In late June 2011, COMAC displayed a 1:2 scale model of the engine, which it calls the CJ-1000A (Exhibit 1). The company also says that it has already conducted trials of prototype engine components and that it intends to release an overall design plan for the CJ-1000A by the end of 2011. The C919 passenger jet is scheduled to enter service in 2016.

It is set to be powered, at least initially, by the CFM International (CFMI) Leap-X1C high-bypass turbofan engine. One of the world's premier commercial jet engine makers, CFMI is a 50-50 joint venture company between GE Aviation (U.S.) and Snecma (France) formed expressly to produce the CFM56 engine family. Based on the CFM56-5B and CFM56-7B, the Leap-X1C will reportedly offer enhanced composite materials use, a blisk fan in the compressor, a second-generation Twin Annular Pre Swirl (TAPS II) combustor, a ~10-11:1 bypass ratio, and fuel consumption reduced by 16% compared to the CFM56 Tech Insertion engines used in the Airbus A320 and next generation Boeing 737s.

This will give the C919 a world-class state-of-the art engine; the Leap-X will be employed simultaneously on the Airbus A320neo (new engine option) and reportedly also on the Boeing 737 MAX. If this all proceeds as planned, aeroengine hardware per se will be one area in which the C919's competitors cannot add value to justify higher prices—though there may well be many others, including engine maintenance and global after-service support.

Commercial Aircraft Corporation of China, hopes to produce up to 2,000 C919s and it appears that while the first aircraft will likely be powered by foreign engines, China aspires to fly later versions of the plane with indigenous power plants, as reflected by an April 2011 *Global Times* article stating that China's domestically made large jet engine would enter service "around 2020."

Scale Model of COMAC's Indigenous Large Jet Engine

To us, this suggests that the company feels the commercial jet engine human capital base in China remains inadequate and that it will be more effective to simply try to poach experienced personnel from global commercial engine leaders like Rolls Royce (RR), GE, and Pratt & Whitney (P&W), the "Big Three," as opposed to developing them in China. Coming years will be interesting in terms of seeing how China's domestic universities can turn out graduates capable of designing and building competitive commercial turbofans, and in terms of how many "technical *haigui*" will return to China with critical skills.

ACAE plans to spend an average of US$300 million per year on jet engine R&D during the next five years, according to *People's Daily*. For comparison, the current jet engine market leaders (RR, GE, and P&W) spent between US$1.4 and US$2.0 billion each on R&D in 2010 (8.3% to just under 13% of their respective sales revenue). Viewed in this light, ACAE's investment level may not enable it to catch up and develop a competitive commercial (and military) jet engine construction capability.

An industry expert tells us that possible explanations include: (1) ACAE may in fact have a less advanced goal (either in engine performance or in the degree of integration/indigenization), (2) it enjoys significant off-budget subsidies, (3) its projections are quite over-optimistic, or (4) some combination of these factors. By design or necessity, then, it is always possible that ACAE will focus on assembly and continue to rely on imported components. In any case, since competition in the commercial jet engine sector is an iterated game, and ACAE would likely have the power of the Chinese state behind it, Big Three engine manufacturers would likely only challenge such illegal non-market subsidies (as defined in the World Trade Organization/WTO agreement on Subsidies and Countervailing Measures) if Chinese aeroengines became competitive on the global marketplace.

Global Jet Engine maker R&D Investment Comparison

Amount in million USD (left vertical axis), % of sales (right vertical axis), 2010

Requirements for Successful Commercial Aeroengine Development

China will need to develop a general product development strategy. Options include stand-alone engines for each aircraft type, or a family concept like P&W's Geared Turbofan (GTF) or RR's Trent; as well as focusing on certain aircraft types/sizes or serving as an across-the-board supplier.

A general architecture strategy necessiates important choices. Among Big Three aeroengine manufactueres, one of the most important choices has involved three shafts vs. two shafts. RR's Trent employs a relatively complex three-shaft-design, which it advertises as offering sufficiently enhanced engine rigidity and reduced performance degradation in service to justify a price premium. P&W's GTF, its new-generation engine for the Airbus 320Neo and the Mitsubishi Regional Jet (MRJ), is advertised to have impressive fuel efficiency.

From a functional perspective, challenges fall into several categories. First, there is the engineering itself. This involves exhaust gas temperature (EGT) margin stability; acceleration/deceleration properties; cold/hot start properties; high and hot (H&H) performance; general performance; foreign object damage (FOD) resistance; volcanic ash resistance; high angle of attack (AOA) performance to avoid airflow disruption; vibration resistance of the entire engine, including the engine control unit (ECU); fuel lines; and emissions/noise trade-offs (carbon dioxide vs. nitrogen oxide vs. dirt vs. noise). Emissions/noise trade-offs are particularly complex, as the relevant regulations can vary by time and market. It is fairly easy to reduce CO_2 emissions, but only at the expense of increasing noise and particulate emissions; how to optimize these parameters against eachother and maintain the balance over time is challenging.

Even basic areas that might appear ripe for outsourcing to subcontractors can produce serious systemic problems. Typical "low-tech weak points" include the gear box, starter, and variable stator vane (VSV) system. The tradeoffs assumed in developing and integrating these systems typically impose significant design implications and path dependency.

The technological and systemic challenge of integrating an aeroengine with an aircraft as a whole is significant. Effective coordination of objectives and activities by COMAC and ACAE will be essential; otherwise, significant problems and suboptimal outcomes could manifest themselves. Even in a best-case scenario, decisions regarding such as hydraulic and electrical systems can lead to major unintended consequences. Optimization of integration and maintainability among such key components as the engine, nacelles, cowlings, pylon, and thrust-reversers, is another important factor. Engine efficiency despends to a large degree on efficient air inflow; the aerodynamic configuration of the inlet cowling alone can make a meaningful difference in efficiency (e.g., as measured in fuel burn).

Other Principal requirements include:

- Performance guarantees (regarding thrust; on-wing-life; reliability/ plannability—mean time between failures/MTBF, i.e., how long an engine lasts; and mean time before overhaul/MTBO, i.e., how often an engine must be serviced fully) impose non-fungible requirements.
- Design/total lifecycle management tools (including computational fluid dynamics capabilities).
- U.S. Federal Aviation Administration (FAA)-European Aviation Safety Agency (EASA) certification. This requires transparency regarding design processes and intellectual property (IP), making IP theft difficult to conceal.
- Extended Twin Operations (ETOPS) certification. This FAA/EASA-Japan Aviation Administration (JAA) global rule allows twin-engined airliners to fly long-distance routes, thereby increasing reliability demands on aeroengines.
- Maintainability, including ease of engine change, ease of replacing submodules (e.g., swapping access panels without dissassembly), ease of correcting for vibrations, transportability of engines (i.e., some GE90 variants must be split to fit into B747 freighter) is a major consideration of potential purchaser airlines.

- Global spare parts and special tooling (e.g., installation slings, engine change kits) support (in-house vs. outsourced after-service function).
- Parts manufacturing authority (PMA) parts policies/management/lock-out.
- Global spare engine availability. A global engine population is far more costly to maintain than the ~200 engines that might be needed to support China's domestic market.
- Global 24/7 "Aircraft on Ground" (AOG) support.
- Global 24/7 engineering support.
- Credible Airworthiness Directive (AD)/ Service Bulletin (SB) management to address mandatory inspections and modifications.
- Functional and customer-friendly training—service culture matters in a competitive market.
- Residual value guarantees for first (many) launch customer(s) that front-loads cost and liability for aeroengine producers.
- Financing is an important factor in attracting customers.
- Pricing (in US$ or RMB)? Implications of US$ pricing given likely long term changes in USD-RMB exchange rates.

These factors will be explored in the context of China's specific conditions in subsequent sections.

China Tries to Build a Commercial Jet Engine

Prospective Chinese jet engine makers are driven by a range of strategic and economic motivations. On the commercial side, the vast engine sales and service market in China will create a wealth of opportunities for Chinese engine makers to exploit. Citibank has estimated that some jet engine makers may derive seven times the revenue from aftermarket service and parts sales for their engines that they do from the sale of the powerplants themselves.

For example, in 2010, GE Aviation obtained 36% of its $17.6 billion in total revenues from servicing commercial engines, 25% from selling commercial engines, and 23% from selling and servicing military engines. Also, servicing jet engines tends to be much more profitable than selling the engines themselves, leading some analysts to say that many engines makers "sell the hot air moving out of engines" as opposed to the engines themselves (*Economist*).

Buyers in China are expected to purchase 5,000 commercial aircraft and more than 2,300 business jets in the next 20 years, a number of aircraft that could require nearly 16,000 commercial turbofan engines to be purchased in the base scenario and 13,000 engines in the pessimistic growth scenario (Exhibit 3). Either way, the likely engine needs of China's commercial aviation sector are going to be huge in the coming two decades. Atop this, major large aircraft buys by China's military could easily add another 500-1,000 engines to these totals.

Potential Chinese Demand

Engine demand comes from a base assumption of 2 engines in each aircraft, plus an inventory of one spare engine for each 10 engines in operation. Of the engines needed, at least half are likely to need to produce 20,000 or more pounds of thrust, enabling them to power civilian airliners as well as a range of military transport and tanker aircraft.

In addition, if Chinese firms can master commercial jet engine production, they may be able to also eventually enter the export market by packaging Chinese engines with Chinese-made passenger aircraft. AVIC could order that Chinese-made aeroengines be included on aircraft sold by the company. A key question is how the resulting aircraft would sell in a competitive market. Foreign buyers could simply decline to purchase them, but Chinese airlines would confront a more complex situation. Faced with official indigenous engine use requirements, Chinese airlines could not refuse outright, but could nevertheless marginalize/minimalize/sideline said aircraft in practice.

Chinese commercial jet engine exports are at a minimum many years away, but given China's record of becoming a serious export competitor once it masters domestic production of a product, is one that deserves consideration. Emerging markets in which China is building an increasing economic presence are among the largest growth markets for commercial aircraft over the next 20 years.

On the strategic side, government and company officials may also seek to reduce China's dependence on P&W, GE, and RR for its jet engines. This would be driven primarily by a desire to be able to power future Chinese military tanker, transport, and airborne early warning (AEW) aircraft with domestically-made engines that would never be hostage to embargoes or disputes over prices and other issues with foreign suppliers (this strategy only works if *all* critical subcomponents and parts are produced indigenously).

A country can build a robust commercial aircraft industry with a global supply chain, as Embraer has done in Brazil, but reducing reliance on foreign vendors offers strategic advantages for military aircraft production. Eliminating reliance, by contrast, is typically unrealistic: at present even the U.S. uses foreign engine technology for some of its military aircraft; for example, many U.S. non-combat military aircraft are powered by CFM engines, from a U.S.-French joint venture, and even the content of combat aircraft engines is not 100% U.S. domestically designed/produced. For China to even approach this level of limited reliance would be a very tall order indeed.

Prestige and Development of Other Industries

China's desire to build commercial jet engines is also likely driven by national industrial pride and the desire to develop other industries. For example, aero-derivative gas turbines can be used as "stand-alone" powerplants to generate electricity. Jet engine derivatives can be used to power ships, especially those for which speed is an issue; a "low performing" jet engine can still make a potent propulsion system for frigates, destroyers, and cruisers.

Jet engine production involves exceedingly complex supply chains and ACAE will face significant challenges in creating a sufficiently large and flexible supplier base when it becomes capable of producing its own commercial engines. The company's status as an aspiring producer of commercial and military engines both means that it is likely to try and obtain as many components as possible domestically. NPO Saturn currently sources more than 90% of its components locally and we believe that ACAE is more likely to take this route than it is to emulate a global supply chain approach such as that used by RR, for example.

ACAE might achieve such a local sourcing goal as a second or third step; going indigenous for *all* subassemblies and parts would take a very long time and make for "non-disaggregated" learning curve(s). It would be much easier to design one or a few components domestically and see how they hold up in otherwise "reliable" imported systems and next higher assemblies (NHAs) rather than having the NHA fail in its entirety and not knowing where to start the root cause analysis. In terms of industrial clustering of manufacturers and suppliers, the Xi'an, Chengdu, Shenyang, and Shanghai areas will be the primary zones of importance.

Joint Ventures and Subcontractors

To reduce NHA failure risk, ACAE may emulate the Big Three engine makers' production model. This involves identifying the 5-10 most critical sub-modules, thereby narrowing down areas of potential problems. It entails roughly 80% indigenous and 20% foreign content. China's reported allocation of people and resources to date appears inconsistent with an all-indigenous aeroengine approach. Indeed, even the Big Three themselves do not pursue such an approach—to do so would be too expensive and too risky technologically.

That is where joint ventures (JVs) play a useful role. Aviation is a low-quantity business, making economies of scale and learning curves tremendously important. As a leading aeroengine producer, GE makes only several thousand engines *per year*. By comparison, auto plants of major manufacturers such as Honda often have the capacity to produce 250,000 or more vehicles per year and in the U.S. typically run at capacity utilization rates of between 60% and 90%, depending on economic conditions.

It is thus no accident that CFM engines are produced by a JV involving GE and SNECMA: this distributes risk, matches complementary expertise, and enhances financing and market access. GE, for instance, lacks technological knowledge in certain specialized areas, especially in low-level assemblies, e.g., with specialized clamps. It would be tremendously inefficient for GE to develop such expertise.

Chinese engine makers are likely to make even greater use of JVs, but likely have different motives, incentives, and constraints because of their government connections and subsidies. Their pursuit of dual-use civilian and military technology and expertise is likely to be much better coordinated and targeted to further military programs that cannot obtain such advances directly. With respect to indigenization and production, their approach will likely be to identify which subcomponents, assemblies, and parts are lacking in China, and have JVs focus on the most important ones. Prioritized items will likely include those that (1) cannot be purchased freely on the world market, because of export controls or monopolistic supplier structures; and (2) offer critical knowledge for military programs.

Examples include high-pressure turbine technology and airflow computational software. A counterexample would be clamps and big fan cases for which there are several global suppliers, and for which supply is not restricted. In practice, where parts are localized will likely hinge on both production logic and path dependence in China's industrial base. If a certain facility has historically produced a certain type of component or system, and retains the requisite bureaucratic support, it is likely to retain ownership of those areas to protect "rice bowls."

IP and Tech Transfer Challenges

In public statements, foreign companies express confidence that Chinese firms will not be able to obtain and reverse engineer, or improve on their engine technology. For example, in June 2011 Chaker Charour of CFMI told the *Wall Street Journal* that the company does not see an indigenous Chinese jet engine as a near-term threat. "We're not really concerned with intellectual property in China," he adds. "We know how to integrate with them without transferring technology. We know how to play that game and protect our property." Such statements are in fact made to maintain good relations with Chinese decision-makers and to avoid looking weak vis-à-vis competitors; in fact, we are told that all foreign companies are extremely worried, as none has found an effective way of protecting IP.

CFMI tells us it has signed a memorandum of understanding (MOU) with AVIC "*to discuss the potential of establishing a final assembly line in Shanghai, as well as an engine test facility, but nothing has been finalized. The working team noted the in that release is still developing a viable business model. There are many factors to be considered and, at this point, we have not yet determined where LEAP final assembly will take place. We do source extensively in China for our current product line, so I am certain that will remain the case for LEAP, however, we are also still in the process of selecting our suppliers overall, so it is too early to say what parts will be produced in China.*"

We suspect one of the reasons the process is taking so long is because the engine makers want to use the "maquiladora model" in China whereby they fabricate the most critical components (such as turbine blades) in places where they know their intellectual property will be protected, and then ship them to China for final assembly. Airbus's state-of-the-art Tianjin assembly line, the most modern foreign airliner assembly facility in China today, is a case in point. Airbus fabricates the parts at its Hamburg, Germany plant, and then ships all of the components to Tianjin for final assembly. In this case, China-based assembly does not even seem to be driven by cost concerns. Rather, it is driven by the importance of having a figurehead manufacturing element on Chinese soil in order to secure product sales in that market, as well as the creation of production capacity needed above and beyond the Toulouse (TLS) and Hamburg (HAM) final assembly lines (FALs).

China's auto industry has had similar experiences with JVs with foreign partners that in reality either transferred little technology overall or only transferred technologies that were basically obsolete in developed markets. This issue is likely to remain a sticking point between ACAE and potential foreign engine manufacturing partners because China will work hard to avoid being a secondary market into which outmoded technologies can be transferred to wring out a bit more profit. Automotive components, for instance, offer a great example of how IP protection did *not* work. Today, following years of assiduous technology transfer effort by multiple means, many Chinese JV partners are serious competitors in the domestic automotive component industry, threatening foreign suppliers, including in the area of R&D.

Military Jet Engines and Commercial Engines

There is a reason why there are only a handful of globally trusted aeroengine producers in the world at this time—it is a very difficult business indeed, and there is no tolerance for error. China is making progress in both fields, but there are substantial differences. Military engines represent primarily an engineering challenge, a key Chinese strength.

Civilian engines, by contrast, require engineering (R&D); design-to-cost; global support (e.g., parts, cosignment inventory, engineering, aircraft on ground/AOG status, training, spare engines, airworthiness directive/AD and service bulletin/SB management, parts manufacturing authority /PMA parts policies/management/lock-out); residual value guarantees; FAA/EASA certifiability; global management; cooperation; as well as IP coordination and guarantees that whatever IP is used in the first place was obtained licitly.

After-market service comes with very strong expectations per global industry standards. AOG status means that an aircraft has been grounded, entitling it to priority service from suppliers, albeit at a price premium. Servicing within 24 hours is typically expected, with only 12 hours allowable in some cases. This norm must be upheld or clients will hesitate to procure products; establishing a large warehouse in the Seattle, WA area dramatically enhanced Airbus's spare parts supply in the U.S., and hence greatly facilitated its market entry there.

Safety must be ensured on a 24-7-365 basis or international standards bodies will rescind certifications. For instance, ADs are internationally standardized means by which commercial regulatory authorities can communicate urgent action requests to aviation operators, i.e., concerning a specific aircraft type or component, regarding mandatory actions to be taken (e.g., grounding, inspection, and replacement). SBs are global standards communications means between an original equipment manufacturer (OEM, e.g. a Chinese aeroengine manufacturer) and an operator (e.g., a foreign airline).

Meeting such requirements demands both performance and service delivery, with little room for learning on-the-job. This requires a responsive managerial setup and a global resource and service network, including technically-qualified English speakers to ensure real-time global product service and thereby ensure consumer safety and confidence. A fully indigenous engine might require 500-1,000 people for ongoing customer support alone. The range of technology on sub-modules requires a range of experts on all areas to issue SBs at any time. For this, good coordination with subcontractors in real time is imperative. Here, unauthorized technical shortcuts to speed development and production could prove extremely costly in the long run. Airline requirements can include borrowing special tools per prior customer service agreement. Service is the key to profits, and keeping initial engine prices low to attract customers.

In contrast to OEM parts, PMA parts are generic. Like a printer and its ink cartridges, an aeroengine itself is relatively cheap compared to the costs of parts and servicing over time. PMA parts offer airlines a key way to control costs, since OEM parts typically carry a hefty markup. PMA versions are typically only available for lower-performance, less-sensitive parts, e.g., screws, washers, clamps, and less-demanding fan blades. At a mere 20-30% of OEM part costs, they offer the same properties, and sometimes better performance. Compatibility can be an issue, and what PMA usage aeroengine manufacturers will accept grudgingly from what customers (e.g., tolerating PMA parts for lower-performance spares) is the subject of constant negotiation. Some companies do not allow PMA parts on leased aircraft. Litigation and counter-litigation concerning technical prominence and performance of parts, especially PMA parts, occurs constantly.

Residual value guarantees represent commitments by manufacturers to make up the difference between expected and actual market value after a fixed period of time (e.g., for resale after 5 years). They can be critical to securing a sale, are required by aeroengine buyers in many cases, and would likely be demanded for all Chinese aeroengines, at least initially. This is on top of a warranty, typically lasting 2-5 years, negotiated individually, and documented in a detailed multi-paged contract stipulating specific provisions. To ensure confidence in its products, a Chinese aeroengine manufacturer would have to go far beyond providing the generous warranties that eased Korean manufacturer Hyundai's automobiles into the U.S. market despite concerns about their reliability.

One area in which Chinese aeroengine suppliers may actually already enjoy an advantage is in financing. Chinese government organizations and SOEs can draw on substantial resources when authorized, and have significant experience in tailoring financing to a client's needs. A complicating factor is pricing currency, as thus far the U.S. dollar remains the global transaction standard. To the extent that China attempts to indigenize aeroengine inputs, it will lack a natural hedge against the exchange rate. With the RMB likely to appreciate further, this creates an unfavourable dynamic for an exporter. This is likely surmountable given policy prioritization of aeroengine development, but will impose additional costs. Designing engines based on tight operating and ownership cost parameters and providing reliable global technical and maintenance support represent key weaknesses and gaps in capability that may hinder China's ability to enter and compete successfully in the global market. For military applications, performance is more important than cost. For civilian applications, the total cost of ownership (TCO)—over the entire life cycle of the engine—is far more important than marginal increases in performance, once a sufficient level is reached.

The initial purchase price of a civil aeroengine pales in importance compared to the on-wing time and maintenance costs over the total operational lifecycle. The aviation industry, in which a major airline consumes several billion dollars of fuel per year, is extremely sensitive to total operating costs. Here Chinese products would face a very different calculus than in other markets; Chinese aeroengines, if they were to be sold at low prices but could not demonstrate high reliability and low total operating and ownership costs, could be viewed widely as a source of false economy.

It is unclear exactly how much ACAE's leadership truly understands how difficult complying with global certifications and efficiency benchmarks can be in practice. Their bureaucratic-corporate positions may make them far more attuned to technical manufacturing standards than to international after-market service demands. This is a problem of both culture and resource allocation.

Chinese firms have yet to prove themselves in the critical areas of design, certification, sales, servicing, and other after-market support; these remain *terra incognita* for them in virtually all respects for commercial aviation inasmuch as Chinese aircraft/engine OEMs have not yet placed products with leading operators outside China. In addition, widely available service infrastructure makes engines for large commercial jets more attractive for military applications. With respect to the CFM56 (military designation F108) engine that powers the KC-135 Stratotanker, Snecma notes that "*The use of a Commercial Off the Shelf (COTS) product has allowed the USAF to leverage commercial experience and hardware improvements into its fleet. The worldwide base of commercial repair facilities also provides the USAF with a significant level of "warm base" support.*"

Another vital difference is that for China's military jet engine programs to have a major positive impact on the country's ability to produce fighters that can attain 5th-generation aerodynamic performance with indigenous components, it only needs to reach 1990s-level technology standards (meaning engines analogous to the P&W F119 that powers the F-22 Raptor). With the bar slightly lower, even just attaining the ability to reliably mass produce engines with performance equivalent to the 1980s-era P&W F100 or GE F110, which power the F-15 and F-16, would enable China to build its J-10, J-11, and J-15 fighters entirely from domestically-made parts, a major strategic improvement.

For "hare-like" military engines, peak performance is the key variable. This necessitates such specific efforts as squeezing the last bit of performance out of a given alloy. Other factors may be compensated for as the user sees fit; for example, engine maintenance and life limitations may be addressed to some extent by purchasing additional engines. This calls to mind country western singer Toby Keith's lyric "I'm not all that I once was, but for once I'm all that I ever was." This makes for a good song and a tolerable military turbofan in a developing country—but not a civilian engine in a competitive developed market. "Tortoise-like" civilian turbofans, in contrast, support commercial activity and are judged on long-term profitability. This makes them arguably more technologically challenging overall. Commercial engines need to be at or very near the global state of the art in terms of fuel efficiency; durability (on-wing life); reliability; exhaust gas temperature (EGT) margin stability; emissions; noise; weight; maintainability; optimization of fit between the engine, cowls, nacelles, thrust reversers (TRs), etc.; and safety to be competitive in the market. EGT monitoring and management is essential to maximizing fuel burning efficiency and avoiding metal fatigue. It is easy to design for increased thrust; keeping it stable over time on-wing even with gradually deteriorating subcomponents is the real challenge.

Beijing could conceivably create a protected market space for less advanced Chinese-built commercial jet engines by using indigenous content rules that mandate the use of domestically-made engines in aircraft sold to operators based in China.

That said, it is unlikely that Chinese airline executives will be content with lower profits caused by having to fly their aircraft with inferior, less efficient domestic engines.

They would also face customer defection on routes served by foreign airlines with more efficient, safer engines. Furthermore, Chinese carriers—and any non-Chinese user, for that matter—might fear that in case of serious quality/reliability/safety issues putting pressure on Chinese engine OEMs could be much more difficult than on foreign engine OEMs due to the nature of ownership of the former and the prevalence of the user base of the latter.

Given such perceptions, China's own airline CEOs could remain a very powerful base of support for using foreign-made engines if Chinese-made commercial engines cannot rapidly attain the performance and efficiency parameters of the CFM56 or newer Leap-X engines.

As a harbinger of Chinese airlines putting their interests in customer preferences and quarterly profits before those of long-term national development goals, we note that state-controlled airlines in China have already pushed back against the government because they do not want to make substantial promises to purchase the domestically-made ARJ21 and C919 airliners, despite Beijing's desire to see COMAC grow into one of the world's key producers of regional jets and larger airliners.

Moreover, other "non-commercial/-profit" factors such as the aforementioned, especially the ability—or lack thereof—to put pressure on a state owned enterprise (SOE) like AVIC in case of problems, may exert influence.

WAR IN THE 21ST CENTURY

The nature of war has been undergoing some basic changes during recent decades, and this provides the pointer to the nature of war in the 21st century. Territorial wars in the past were fought for resources (human and mineral) where the industrially superior states (mostly of Europe) controlled military technology and this also helped them to control populations.

The decolonisation process starting in the middle of the 20th century also ensured that populations could no longer be kept under control against their will. Advances in technology also made the earlier necessity of human and natural resources less critical since the locus of power shifted in favour of trade, technology and financial control. The only resource base which might trigger armed conflict at the level of an inter-state war is that of oil and gas. In fact, this was the central reason for the territorial war in 1990-91, which may well be the last regular inter-state war for a long time.

Nuclear weapons have limited the aim, scope and extent of war among states that possess such capabilities because of the tremendously destructive potential of such weapons.* As Martin Creveld writes, "From Central Europe to Kashmir, and from the Middle East to Korea, nuclear weapons are making it impossible for large sovereign territorial units, or states, to fight each other in earnest without running the risk of mutual suicide."3 Total and unlimited conventional war has been relegated to the backyard of history because the age of imperial colonies which was a major factor making war a global phenomenon has long passed away. States simply do not have the means to conduct a total war, unless they use nuclear weapons. And this would result in mutual assured destruction, nullifying any possible political goal for which it might have been started.

But modern states are also increasingly vulnerable even to conventional war. Conventional weapons' attack on nuclear power stations, for example, could result in a hundred Chernobyls in Europe. It may be recalled that the accident in the Union Carbide plant in Bhopal (which resulted in 3,000 dead and over 5,000 injured in December 1984) could be replicated by a 500-kg conventional high explosive warhead. The potential damage of conventional war may be judged from the fact that nearly two million tons of chemicals are abroad in transit or storage at any one time in Europe. While fire-bombing caused much of the damage during bombing of cities in World War II, asphyxiation is likely to be the major cause of casualties of the conventional attacks of tomorrow in a society that relies so extensively on synthetics.

Modern precision guided weapons make it possible to execute damage of the scale carried out during the strategic bombing campaign in World War II with a fraction of the earlier air effort. It is not merely that the highly organised industrially developed states would be so vulnerable to conventional warfare. The developing states are even more vulnerable because of the few high value assets they possess which have been acquired through investment of scarce resources. The case of Iraq, where development has been set back perhaps more than three decades first, by Iranian air attacks and, later, by the US-led coalition air campaign is a prime example.

If nuclear war and total global war are no longer viable propositions as an extension of politics by other means, the only choice available to states to use destructive force for political purposes is through limited conventional war, sub-conventional war with military type weapons, and the use of coercive military force without necessarily resulting in war. The overall result has been a reducing potential of war down to limited wars, and from that point, an expansion of opportunities for limited wars, sub-conventional wars and use of force without war as shown in Fig. 1.

Some Trends in Military Power

The end of the Cold War has marked a new era where the dimensions of conventional thinking on military power and its application are undergoing some profound changes because of many objective factors, partially due to the fundamentally altered global strategic environment. Global defence spending has come down by more than one-third from the peak of $1,285 billion in 1988. India cut back its defence spending by 37 percent to a level of 2.4 percent of GDP in 1997, Pakistan reduced its defence spending by over 15 percent since 1993, and Japan, has maintained its spending level. But almost all other countries of Asia have recorded significant increase in the allocation of national resources to military capability. Going by its official data, China, which is the largest military power in Asia, tripled its defence spending since 1988 in spite of a 30 percent cut back in force levels. East Asia's defence (in current US dollars) increased by 62 per cent during the five years since 1990. While some of the rise in defence spending is due to modernisation (as indeed was that of India in the mid-1980s), this is already generating images of a new armaments race in Asia. It is sobering to recall that the military build up that started with Iran's arms acquisitions in the early 1970s led to a chain reaction and finally wars in the Persian Gulf region.

The important issue is not merely the levels of defence spending and arms acquisition, but the politico-strategic doctrines for the employment of military power. The countries of Asia, as a general trend, are not formally articulating their strategic doctrines. This generates its own dynamics of uncertainty and problems of assessments. The shift toward higher-technology weapons and equipment, especially reliance on long range strikes as the preferred option of their efficient utilisation, would tend to push strategic doctrines toward an offensive orientation. Concurrently with the global reduction in defence spending, military power has also witnessed retrenchment worldwide. From a total military manpower of nearly 29 million troops in the militaries of the world in 1988, by 1997 the figure had come down to less than 23 million. Further reductions may be expected in the coming years. The smaller size of military forces also has its own implications on the use and usability of military power.

The reduction in global defence spending and force levels has led to procurement budgets being reduced, and dramatically in some cases like Russia which has seen reduction by 90 percent with little prospect of restoration to earlier figures. Retrenchment of defence industry has led to increasing cost of weapon systems (the effect somewhat reduced temporarily due to upgrade programmes) and collaborations/mergers (the latter amounting to $53 billion worth last year alone). The defence industry has entered an invigorated phase of interdependency.

As it is, the increasing sophistication, complexities, costs, budgetary deficits and stagnation of developed economies, and drastically reducing production runs have been leading the global defence industry since World War II to increasing mergers and collaborative programmes. Compared to 42 major arms producers in West Europe and North America in 1950, which had come down through mergers to 21 in the early 1980s, the number dropped sharply to 11 in 1996. US arms manufacturers were reportedly operating at 35 to 45 percent of their capacity; and more mergers/closures are on the cards. The industry has had to lay off hundreds of thousands of workers. These industries will need to collaborate further in future, especially in regions like Asia where the basic costs of manpower, infrastructure, and production are lower.

The Soviet Union was the only country (besides China) to maintain a costly self-sufficient defence industrial system with consequent high costs which had been kept down by the larger production runs and an incremental approach to design and development. From the early 1980s, a qualitative jump in military technology commenced, imposing a similar dynamics on the industry as applicable in the West. By 1992, Russia employed nearly 4 million people in 200 production and 600 research/design centres. With the drastic drop (of over 90 per cent) in procurement funding and arms exports (which came down from an estimated $23 billion in 1987 to a mere $1.6 billion in 1992, and stayed at $1.8 billion even in 1994 and 1995), the Russian defence industry simply cannot sustain itself as an autonomous self-contained industry dealing with all its weapon needs. The Russian defence industry, in fact, is at the crossroads of collapse or revival.

Russia will find it increasingly difficult to sustain its defence industry without collaborative programmes and co-production arrangements with industries abroad. It made a few arrangements with West European defence industry, but these have already reached a saturation level. The only real choices for Russia lie in collaboration with China or India (or both) which have extensive infrastructure, where the costs will be low, and where there is a significant domestic demand and substantive compatibility with Russian design philosophy and industrial capabilities. India lacks the capital, but China has a favourable trade balance from which to fund acquisition of Russian military technology. The agreement for licensed manufacture of Su-27 multi-role combat aircraft in China is symptomatic. Russia and China have been moving toward increasing levels of cooperation which, as the recent Sino-Russian agreements indicate, is described as a "strategic partnership", a framework not very different from that of the early 1950s. The growth of Chinese military capabilities has its own dynamics for peace and stability in Asia; and the rapid progress in its strategic partnership adds another dimension. In addition, modernisation of the Chinese military will enhance the attractiveness of Chinese produced military systems to developing countries and also have a corresponding effect in diffusion of higher technology systems to recipients of Chinese arms. China's economic strength will increasingly allow it to offer attractive terms for arms transfers. Already, the arc of countries stretching from Syria to Myanmar (with the exception of India) is substantively equipped with weapons supplied by China.

Military forces worldwide are shifting toward greater professionalism, which are also high technology, high-cost (for creating, sustaining and replacement of capabilities), and significantly less usable. National support for carrying the costs of military power, therefore, is eroding, especially as society experiences extending periods of peace and concerns of conflict casualties expand. Paradoxically, prolonged periods without war have resulted in trends toward the search for alternative roles for the military forces, mostly for peace-keeping and internal security. Technological advances promise greater effectiveness of military power. Force multipliers offer attractive solutions to many problems. However, force divides also exist along with force multipliers. In a continuing contest of arms between two military forces (unlike that in cases of long range coercive use of force without war), quantity and numbers are likely to continue playing a crucial role; and force multipliers are not a substitute for force.

It may be hypothesised, therefore, that regular inter-state war, in the classical Clausewitzian concept, is unlikely to remain a viable instrument of politics in the 21st century. On the other hand, because of the increasing vulnerability of modern states, the effectiveness of modern military technology, and due to the higher stakes inherent in smaller but more effective professional military forces in future, if and when a regular war at the higher levels of intensity takes place, its impact will be far greater than a similar war in the past.

Use of military power for political purposes, however, is likely to remain an important tool in the hands of states. But use of force for political goals is more likely in circumstances that do not necessarily result in wars (defined here as continuing armed conflict). Long range strike capabilities of certain components of military power are particularly suited for such coercive use of force for political purposes.

Given this scenario, not only is the prospect of war reducing, but the ability of countries to cope with sudden and surprise attack will also reduce in spite of significantly enhanced surveillance capabilities. Defence, therefore, will need to be able to respond more rapidly and with great flexibility. Only air power has the basic attributes to be able to perform this function with a degree of efficiency. At the same time, it needs to be noted that surveillance itself depends heavily on air power systems and capabilities, as do most of the force multiplication capabilities. Reliance on air power, therefore, will increase in the coming decades.

FUTURE WARS AND AIR POWER

Given the increasing vulnerabilities of modern states, whether developed or developing, to even conventional war and the limitations intrinsic to small professional high-cost forces, it is inevitable that states will seek to adopt doctrines and strategies for prevention of war rather than seek war as an instrument of politics. Deterrence, therefore, is likely to assume greater importance in the coming decades.

War in the traditional and classical sense will be less viable in the 21st century as an instrument of politics since states are increasingly vulnerable to the effects of even conventional wars. Combined with technological and cost imperatives, this is shifting the locus of armed conflict from traditional regular war to the use of military power on the pattern of modern "gunboat" coercive diplomacy. Long-range strike capabilities, reinforced as they have been by advances in sensor technologies and precision guided munitions, now make it possible to attack targets across long distances which earlier would have required close combat.

The era of wars of occupation has long passed into history. Even traditional territorial wars are already a phenomenon of the past, except possibly armed clashes where energy resource base still makes control of territory important. This does not necessarily mean that regular wars have become obsolete. What it implies is that highly professionalised high-cost militaries, serious difficulties of re-supply and replenishment, deepening vulnerabilities of modern states and society (to even conventional war), and the fear of losing parts or the whole of precious military capability combine to reduce the probability of conventional war. But if and when it does take place, war will be sharp and swift, and rely much more on superior technology, while the impact of its outcome will be far more crucial than what is generally believed.

In essence, countries will increasingly seek to avoid war as we have seen it; and rely even more than before on deterrence. The most significant characteristic of the changing nature of war is the growing accuracy of weapon systems and the ability to strike at long range with great precision almost independent of weather. Increase in accuracy and range has historically increased the risk of pre-emption. Surprise may appear an even more attractive option because of the smaller size of military forces. Land forces have inherent friction in war that operates limits on their flexibility especially to surprise attacks. Air power, on the other hand, possesses intrinsic attributes to respond rapidly across a vast range of contingencies spanning large distances. The quantum of firepower per unit of air power assets has been increasing. Air power is also at its best in achieving effective results when faced with mobile forces—a scenario almost inevitable in a hostile surprise attack seeking a breakthrough.

Warfare since World War II has been increasingly shifting towards greater mobility and firepower. Air power, by its nature, is more effective in a manoeuvre warfare situation rather than in situations of static warfare. This is largely due to its ability to disrupt and destabilise the momentum of manoeuvre besides its ability to impose kinetic shock. Mechanised warfare creates the conditions for air power to maximise its effect, and mechanised warfare is also the form of fighting most vulnerable to air power. Reduction in the size of military forces will tend to shift force structures more toward mechanisation in the coming decades. Mechanised warfare is also heavily dependent on mobile and large logistic assets without which mobility is deeply affected, nullifying the very utility of mechanisation. This opens up additional areas of opportunities for air power to influence the course of warfare on the ground.

The time-space dimension of warfare has been undergoing some marked shifts during the 20th century. Earlier, wars were compressed in space and spread out in time. Technology has been reversing this equation. Increasingly, future wars are likely to be expanded in space and compressed in time.

This fundamental change in the time-space paradigm of warfare places a heavy premium on the information-action cycle. Increasing pace of warfare in the years ahead implies a greater rate of change in the military situation (in air and sea warfare), and, consequently, greater challenges arising therefrom, thus, demanding an accelerating speed in response. It has been argued that the real revolution in military affairs now taking place is not so much a revolution in information warfare as conventional wisdom would have us believe, but that in the control and management of time.4 Air power is the only component of military force that is capable of meeting the challenge of accelerating speed of response needed if destructive power has to be applied effectively on the inside of the enemy's information-decision-action cycle.

The future of deterrence and successful warfighting rests heavily on accurate long-range strike capabilities, whether conventional and/or nuclear armed. At the same time, the preferred method of employing military power for political purposes will centre on the use of force that does not lead to continued armed conflict. This, coincidentally, requires similar capabilities: high-technology long-range, "surgical" accurate strikes, which are best undertaken by (and in many cases, only by) air power. The very nature of these capabilities is such that defence against them will need to rely on similar capabilities for deterrence in future. Strategically, air power will assume increasing importance in the coming years. During the Cold War, air power was the primary vehicle for strategic nuclear deterrence to avert war. In the years ahead, air (and missile) power will be the central tool for conventional deterrence, as well as controlled punitive strikes for coercive diplomacy.5 Naval power in this regard, would come a close second.

It is, therefore, not surprising that Asian countries from Israel to Japan are already placing greater emphasis on stronger air forces (including missile capabilities) and naval forces. China's military modernisation and arms acquisition programme relies heavily on upgrading its air and naval capabilities, besides long-range nuclear delivery systems. In spite of a substantive cut back in defence posture worldwide, the US decided to create a new naval fleet (whose primary role would be to apply its powerful integral combat air power) after the end of the Cold War.

In the process, power projection dynamics are changing from the traditional means and goals related to territorial wars to functional power projection with capabilities that can strike accurately at long distances; even if staying power remains limited. Sensor technologies provide an important additional dimension in enhancing reconnaissance surveillance, and target acquisition capabilities while precision guidance of striking power adds greater accuracy and lethality at long ranges.

Air Power and Coercive Diplomacy

Recorded history of the use of armed forces as a political instrument without actually engaging in armed conflict goes back to the days of the Roman Empire.

In an earlier era, Sun Tzu had eulogised it: "For to win one hundred victories in one hundred battles is not the acme of skill. To subdue the enemy without fighting is the acme of skill"6 However, in earlier times, coercive politics had remained closer to deterrence in the threat of use of force. Few means were available till this century to project power and force beyond the national frontiers without getting engaged in war.

The main instrument of force has primarily been the land forces. For a state to apply direct pressure on the centre of power of another state with the use of Armies, it first had to contend with and even defeat the Armies of the target state. As long as sovereigns and states maintained Armies, they could be interposed between themselves and those applying force to impose their will. Thus, a military victory, in fact, became important in the conduct of war because it became the prelude in most cases to the imposition of the victor's will on the vanquished.

Naval forces offered greater flexibility and options. The industrial powers which managed to establish extensive colonial empires were inevitably strong maritime powers, perhaps because sea power gave them flexibility and freedom of action. They could select the points of application of force in a geo-strategic framework to exploit local vulnerabilities and weaknesses while applying pressure in a manner and place where the maritime power was strongest. Sea power also provided the capacity for disengagement where the situation turned unfavourable. Continental powers like Russia were unable to expand their empires beyond the limits of their land conquests; and the intrinsic vulnerability of such powers to maritime powers is still noticeable in their security perceptions. India's neglect of its maritime security was largely responsible for the intrusive establishment and expansion of European powers to establish their colonial rule on the subcontinent. This is why, in fact, sea power assumed special importance; and the earlier phenomenon of use of force without war accordingly was termed "gunboat diplomacy". Till the advent of air power changed the dimensions of application of force, only sea power, (especially after the invention of the steamship because of the speed and freedom of action it gave to sea power), permitted discrete application of force via the high seas and on the shores of the target country.

This was possible for two reasons: firstly, sea power could be applied without necessarily having to first defeat the military forces of the target country. Thus, it was not inevitable for the use of force in pursuance of perceived national interests to result in war, as was (and still is) the case with land forces. Secondly, sea power provided the discretion of an option to select disengagement at will. Thus, surgical and discrete application of force could be resorted to without running into the problems normally associated with war termination.

World War II saw the emergence of a combination of naval and air power in the shape of the aircraft carrier. This provided the two complementary capabilities: great freedom of action and offensive power to naval forces, and greater staying power to air forces at long distances from the homeland. And advances in science and technology have finally resulted in the aircraft carrier battle groups becoming the symbol of one complete military system deriving its heightened value from the strength of each of the three major elements of military power: land, sea and air. It is, therefore, not surprising that naval-air military forces, especially those centred on aircraft carriers, have constituted the preferred option in the use of force without war.

Employment of naval-air (especially air) forces for coercive politics reduces the risks of war because escalation can be better controlled, and provides superior disengagement control. For, while war serves as an instrument of policy in international politics, its failure to achieve its poitical objectives is mostly created by the lack of favourable control on war termination. The interminable Iran-Iraq War seems to be a typical example. The use by the People's Republic of China of war as an instrument of policy has been mostly successful (after the initial partial failure in the Korean War) largely because of the excellent control China has retained on war termination. Use of force without war, especially with naval air forces, provides the capabilities of application of force while retaining control over disengagement. And better escalation control is assured because the onus of retaliation lies with the target country.

The Coming Revolution

There is a growing belief since the 1991 Gulf War that a Revolution in Military Affairs (RMA) is sweeping across the world although it is affecting different countries differently. The issues related to RMA and its implications for warfare will be debated for a long time to come. Much of this revolution will rely extensively on air and space power capabilities. But there are also specific technological developments that promise to create a revolution in aerospace power.

Space-based systems are becoming a critical factor in the evolution of warfare on land and an even greater factor in warfare at sea. Previously, controlling the oceans required the ability to defeat the enemy's Navy at sea or control the sea-lanes of communication. This can be carried out increasingly more effectively by stand-off weaponry, especially like the anti-ship cruise missile. Sea-based or air-launched land-attack missiles of the type repeatedly used against Iraq and more recently against Afghanistan and Sudan also require exploitation of space. As the range of such cruise missiles increases, these must rely increasingly on space-based assets. Control of patterns of trade is also consequently likely to be increasingly dependent on space capabilities.7

The operational environment in future, therefore, would be air power critical and characterised by a central role for air power which would have a predominant influence on the environment and the course of battles at sea and on land. Air operations, however, will need to be deeply integrated with land and sea operations. The vital issue which defence establishments throughout the world will need to resolve relates to the means and method of this integration: the resolution, in fact, of the essential conflict and contradiction between increasing specialisation (and its concomitant costs and benefits) on the one hand, and the needs of integration between diverse and disparate military systems (with intrinsic risk of duplication and diffusion of expertise) on the other. Control and exploitation of space assumes importance in this respect.

Historically, there is a height band above the surface of the earth ranging between about 25-125 km altitude that has not been exploited fully except for transit. Aircraft like the SR-71 and MiG-25 did touch the edges of this envelope although experimental aircraft went up higher. Space launch vehicles and satellites have used altitudes higher than this band for practical operational manoeuvres. However, we seem to be now approaching an era where exploitation of this critical altitude band will be possible. This is likely with trans-atmospheric hyper-velocity vehicles which could be launched from normal airfields and thus even evade the space-based early-warning system put in place over the decades by the industrially advanced countries.

The National Aeronautics and Space Agency (NASA) expects to launch a practical vehicle by the end of 1999. What such a capability implies is that the operating envelope of air power will finally merge with that of the lower end of outer space.

At the same time, unmanned aerial vehicles technology is reaching practical shape to provide a high altitude (lower space) solar powered flight that will reduce the necessity for satellite launch and use for a variety of tasks. The range of potential capabilities of future space planes and unmanned aerial vehicles, both trans-atmospheric and upper atmospheric will fill the gap in aerospace power that has existed through the 20th century.

At some not too distant future, it is not difficult to visualise trans-atmospheric vehicles able to fly at great speeds and perform combat in ways which the present day air defence systems (with the possible exception of ballistic missile defence systems) are totally incapable of dealing with. The important point is that except for ballistic missile defence technologies, existing air defence capabilities will become almost redundant against such capabilities. The net result will be an expansion of the third dimension which will generate substantive asymmetry of military power.

Air power, by its ability to operate in the third dimension, transcending national frontiers and natural obstacles, has an attribute wherein there is application of force in a manner more selective, surgical and discrete than was possible with sea power.

However, unlike the other two components of military force, air power cannot hold territory and thus may be seen to lack staying power unless it is through repeated application. Notwithstanding this limitation, which is more important in the case of war, air power has great utility for application of force without war in pursuance of coercive politics. With the development of the trans-atmospheric vehicles or hypersonic cruise missiles, the options and capabilities of air (and aerospace) power for its employment in support of coercive politics will increase tremendously.

In conclusion, it is clear that in the early decades of the 21st century, military power will become smaller in size, technologically more advanced, more costly, and less usable for frontal war except for applications for political purposes without necessarily leading to war. Above all, it is likely to become more dependent on air and space power. Exploitation of the boundaries of the upper atmosphere and lower space will have special significance symbolising the nature of the new revolution in the making. Aerospace power will continue to be central to the use of nuclear weapons. Its impact in conventional wars will increase because of the increasing sensitivity of modern surface warfare to influence and interference from the air. Sub-conventional wars, which already appear to be the dominant trend, may be less amenable to influence from the air in spite of some dramatic results achieved by Israel.

The real shift in the application of force is toward the long-range strike, mostly of the "surgical" type, which does not lead to full scale war. This is likely to be the primary 21st century version of the 19th century "gunboat diplomacy" to achieve political results. It is here that air power provides a range of options, especially of engagement and escalation control which other forms of military power do not. And this is why air power will assume greater importance in the coming decades.

6

Pakistan's Air Force

The history of the Pakistan Air Force (PAF) began when it was established in 1947 following the independence of Pakistan.

BRITISH ERA

In 1933, the British colonial government established the first Air Force station in the Indian subcontinent near Drigh Road, now called PAF Base Faisal in Karachi. In 1934, this element of the Royal Indian Air Force (RIAF) was extended to the north for operations in NWFP. The RIAF had also contributed to the defeat of Japanese invasion during World War II.

PAKISTAN'S NUCLEAR TRAJECTORY

Pakistan's nuclear program has been at the center of attention for nonproliferation pundits for several decades for a variety of reasons. For them, the acquisition of nuclear technology, even for non-NPT states, both for peaceful and military applications (self-defense), is the divine right of the chosen few who are either unable or unwilling to recognize the legitimate security concerns of states in regions mired in a perpetual cycle of hostility. Faced with the traumatizing separation of its Eastern Wing in 1971, Pakistan resolved never to witness such an event at the hands of India again, and was forced to respond to India's nuclear challenge only three years later in the wake of Pokhran-1.

Pakistan had taken the lead in calling for nuclear restraint in South Asia even before India's 1974 test when it first proposed a Nuclear Weapon Free Zone in 1972. This call was repeated twice, once after Pokhran-1 and again in 1978 when Pakistan proposed that both countries simultaneously renounce the acquisition or manufacture of nuclear weapons.

The following year, Pakistan again offered India mutual inspection of each other's nuclear facilities and also proposed a simultaneous accession of India and Pakistan to the NPT and full-scope IAEA safeguards. In 1987, it expressed willingness to enter into a bilateral nuclear test-ban treaty with India and proposed a missile free zone in South Asia in 1994.

None of these proposals were given any serious consideration. Since 2007, India has consistently rejected six nuclear-related Confidence Building Measures proposed by Pakistan on one pretext or another. Regrettably, India has rejected each one of these proposals in the past four decades even though there have been a few successful CBM's which have stood the test of time such as the agreement of non-attack on each other's nuclear facilities and the agreement of pre-notification of flight tests of ballistic missiles.

However, proposals for a strategic restraint regime that would include a commitment not to build missile defences and include prior notification of cruise missiles were not accepted by India.

Therefore, when in the backdrop of a deep history of mistrust Pakistan resorts to indigenous efforts to build its nuclear deterrent, based on its own force goals and resources, it stands accused of following a "mistaken trajectory" and is seen as "punching above its weight." A dispassionate assessment of Pakistan's nuclear trajectory vis-à-vis India and the size of its nuclear fuel cycle in terms of the production capacities of various plants and facilities shows that while it has consistently built up its nuclear capabilities over time, there has been no abrupt or exponential increase in fissile material production comparable to India (for both existing or projected capacities).

It is also a fact that Pakistan has reached this stage in its nuclear capability only after four decades of sustained effort and progressive indigenization in its nuclear and missile programs. It has learnt to brace sanctions, find solutions and improvise, and mastered all aspects of the fuel cycle at a fraction of the cost of producing any nuclear plant or facility of the same type or size anywhere else in the world (such as plutonium production facilities).

A closer look at Pakistan's nuclear trajectory demonstrates that while India has been producing plutonium from CIRUS since 1963 and from Dhruva-I since 1988 and has a much larger infrastructure outside safeguards to produce more plutonium in addition to its considerable advantages in existing stockpiles of plutonium.

Pakistan is using infrastructure to produce plutonium from 1998 onwards which PAEC was able to build over a period of 25 years (1973 to 1998), save for second, third and fourth 50 MWt production reactors at Khushab (the fourth one nearing completion), all of which were initiated during the fifteen years after the 1998 tests.

Thus, Pakistan's pre-1998 plutonium infrastructure comprises a fuel fabrication plant at Kundian (completed 1976-80); the New Labs reprocessing plant at PINSTECH (1973-1981); the 50 MWt Khushab-1 reactor, heavy water and tritium production plants (1985-1997); and the partially completed Chashma reprocessing plant (1978) which has recently been retrofitted and reportedly commissioned.

After Khushab-1 was commissioned in 1998, Pakistan was able to add three additional reactors of the same type and size only because it was developing indigenous design and manufacturing facilities in parallel with work at Khushab Nuclear Complex in the 1980s and 1990s.

For comparison's sake, it would be useful to recall that Pakistan has built only two unsafeguarded reprocessing plants since the 1970s; one pilot-scale plant (New Labs) with 20-40 (completed in 1981-82) and the other commercial-scale plant (Chashma) with 40-100 tHM/yr capacity which the French had abandoned in 1978. At the same time, India has built five commercial-scale reprocessing plants (all outside safeguards); one at Trombay (50 tHM/yr) two at Tarapur (100 tHM/yr) and two (100 tHM/yr) at Kalpakkam (the second one nearing completion in 2014).

But Pakistan has no Fast Breeder Reactor and no unsafeguarded heavy water power reactors on its soil. India already has 100 MWt Dhruva-I in operation coupled with 125 MWt Dhruva-II nearing completion along with another 30 MWt reactor being planned. Its 40 MWt CIRUS reactor had already produced 500 kg of weapon-grade plutonium up to 2006 (IPFM 2006) and an additional 45 kg before it was shut down in 2010. Dhruva-I continues to produce 20-25 kg of weapon-grade plutonium every year. India's 8 heavy water power reactors kept outside safeguards under the Indo-US nuclear deal can produce 1250 kg of weapon-grade plutonium each year, even though India claims that the unsafeguarded reactor-grade plutonium produced by them during normal operations would be used as fuel (MOX) for its breeder reactor program (also unsafeguarded). India's 500 MWe EFBR can produce 145 kg of weapon-grade plutonium each year.

Comparisons in highly enriched uranium capabilities and stockpiles show a similar trend. Pakistan has not increased or expanded its uranium enrichment capacity in the past 20 years, where as India is doubling its existing enrichment potential (floor space) at its Rare Materials Plant (Rattehali) in Mysore.

In fact, Pakistan's HEU stocks might be less than the known estimates since it is difficult to determine the precise SWU capacity of an enrichment plant and its UF6 feed production. That Pakistan is not engaged in, nor aims at entering into a fissile race with India, is exemplified by the following comparison of unsafeguarded fissile material stockpiles and production capabilities (existing and projected).

Curiously enough, Pakistan's plutonium quest has been at the heart of western non-proliferation efforts since the 1970s when the country was striving to complete the nuclear fuel cycle.

It is intriguing that towards the late 1970s when Pakistan was completing research and development work on various plants and facilities for the enriched uranium route (uranium processing, conversion and enrichment) as part of the fuel cycle, and was also quietly building other unsafeguarded facilities for the plutonium route, the United States had used its full diplomatic pressure to secure a major non-proliferation objective in order to force France to cancel the deal for the safeguarded commercial-scale reprocessing plant in August, 1978 (which was never intended for Pakistan's weapons program anyway).

Only a year later, a June 6, 1979, a de-classified US State Department cable stated that Pakistan might be "allowed" to complete its gas-centrifuge program while the United States (in its misplaced opinion) had succeeded in stopping Pakistan's plutonium program in its tracks.

This might have been so as the United States was probably not sure that Pakistan could build uranium processing, hexafluoride gas (UF6) production, and gas-centrifuge plants for the enriched uranium route anytime soon, but more significantly because plutonium was and still is the major non-proliferation concern for Pakistan since it provides the capability to develop miniaturized, boosted fission, tactical and thermo-nuclear warheads—the basis of a first-class operational nuclear deterrent. Thermonuclear weapons is yet another area where Pakistan has shown restraint and has been punching below its weight, even though the capability exists to build these weapons, but perhaps boosted-fission warheads might suffice for existing force goals.

Pakistan's ballistic missile program was largely driven by the effects of the Pressler Amendment. Yet its missile development and testing trajectory does not reflect any arms racing with India in this field with both countries pursuing divergent pathways in the field.

For instance, Pakistan's missile development and testing is solely geared towards the consolidation of its existing capabilities designed to achieve greater accuracy, reliability against increasing Indian ballistic and planned cruise missile defences and survivability of its strategic forces. This has been explained in a recent Carnegie study, which states that "*An analysis of aggregated missile test data since 1998 reveals that the armament dynamic is far more complex.*

The Indian and Pakistani nuclear programs are largely decoupled. The data show little correlation between the adversaries' testing behaviour contrary to what would be expected in a classic arms race. In fact, the types and ranges of missiles under development provide concrete evidence of the divergence in their nuclear objectives and security strategies. Pakistan is building weapons systems to deter India from conventional military operations below the nuclear threshold. India is developing systems primarily to strengthen its strategic deterrent against China...."

This fact was reiterated when Pakistan did not respond to India's 5000-7000 km-range Agni-V ICBM. in kind, but conducted tests of improved versions of its 1000-1300 km-range Shaheen-1A ballistic missile as a potential substitute to the liquid-fuelled Ghauri.

Pakistan also has no ballistic or cruise missile defense programs; no ICBM projects like *Agni*-V which is being armed with MIRVs and no SSBNs like India's *Arihant* armed with the 700 km-range *Sagarika* SLBMs. Pakistan's defense budget has largely remained static at around 2-3% of GDP ($5-7 billion) in the past decade compared to India's which has increased to around $ 40 billion. Similarly, a growing imbalance in conventional forces (which Pakistan can never bridge) is exacerbating with India becoming the world's largest net importer of conventional arms for several years in a row in the past few years.

This then brings forth the logic of Pakistan's recent development of battlefield or tactical nuclear weapons designed to deter limited conventional war below its nuclear threshold. TNWs would be used only as weapon of last resort in case of deterrence failure and collapse of conventional forces or the crossing of its perceived nuclear thresholds, whichever comes first. In case of deterrence failure, there would be no escalation control would become impossible and ineffective resulting in the employment of every means available to Pakistan to defend itself against aggression. Pakistan opted to build TNWs (presumably in limited numbers for deterrence only and not for war fighting) as means to supplement conventional defences.

Nonetheless, when Pakistan tested a 60-km range nuclear capable battlefield missile (Hatf-IX) *Nasr* in 2011, it caused considerable consternation in India and elsewhere. However, when India tested the 50-150 km-range *Prahaar* shortly thereafter,, and dubbed it a "tactical surface to surface missile capable of carrying *different types of warheads*, which operates as battle field support system to the Indian Army" or has recently added another 60-170 km tactical missile *Pragati,* to its missile arsenal, no one raises a finger.

That is mainly because India has stopped short of declaring these systems nuclear capable and have declared them to carry conventional warheads only. But if India can develop unconventional warheads for the nuclear capable *Prithvi*-I and II, then it is only a matter of time before nuclear warheads for *Prahaar* and*Pragati* are developed, especially given their deployments against Pakistan and China.

So how many warheads would then suffice for credible minimum deterrence? Pakistan is being placed ahead of India in warhead count by a number of international publications and experts. What is astonishing is the basis of such estimates unless they have had the privilege of having done a warhead count themselves or been able to determine the exact amount of fissile material and the corresponding non-nuclear components developed to produce warheads. Warhead count and the amount of fissile material weaponized would invariable depend on various weapon designs (boosted fission, composite core, two-stage etc.) This in any case would be any nation's most classified information and neither India, nor Pakistan have declared their respective inventories of fissile stocks or warheads.

Since some of India's leading strategic analysts such as K. Subrahmanyam have called for the development of a strategic triad comprising a 400-warheads, Pakistan should settle for at least a triad consisting of a 200-250 warhead force that might include different types warheads required to maintain a credible minimum deterrent, designed to absorb an Indian first strike and respond—a capability needed for any country to maintain strategic stability with a nuclear armed neighbor.

However, any such force goals would depend on the availability of fissile material (especially plutonium and tritium for miniaturized warheads) whose production would be limited by the finite domestic reserves of natural uranium, unlike that of India who is being lavishly furnished by the NSG countries with the means of making the most optimum use of all its natural uranium stocks for weaponization.

When Pakistan attempts to consolidate its strategic forces and ramp up plutonium production—which has enabled it to operationalize its nuclear deterrent—it is accused of punching above its weight. It knows what it is doing within its capabilities and resources. Its force goals have been quantified and its fissile material production will continue till those targets are achieved so as to develop a triad-based assured second strike capability that can withstand massive retaliation and prevent the exploitation of strategic space at the tactical level.

Pakistan is in no way competing with India in pursuing regional and global ambitions through ballistic missile nuclear submarines, ICBMs or space weaponization or retaining huge stocks and production capacity of fissile material outside safeguards—a fact accepted by the NSG countries which accorded India the unique distinction of being the beneficiary of an NPT signatory state without any obligations and allowed it to retain a substantial part of its fuel cycle outside safeguards for producing more fissile material in the future.

Given these realities, if India today were to ask to sign the FMCT and the CTBT, it is most likely that it won't agree to be a part of either of these treaty arrangements and is conveniently taking cover behind Pakistan's stance on the FMCT at the CD.

Some Indian scientists doubt whether all the Pokhran-II tests were successful, while many others question Pakistan's claims of having built a miniaturized nuclear warhead for*Nasr* without hot tests. So should both India and Pakistan jointly announce a second round of tests purely for technical reasons in addition to ensuring the reliability and "one-point safety" of their respective warheads and then unilaterally or jointly sign the CTBT, depending on their respective security calculus?

Finally, Pakistan is accused of abetting terrorists and non-state actors when it has been fighting a war on terror on its soil for over a decade and has suffered more than 40000 casualties (including high-ranking civil and military officers) and incurred financial and economic lossesamounting to tens of billions of dollars. Such insinuations are used to justify India's appetite for limited conventional war in the region. So should the recent admission by India's former army chief, that it has been involved in sponsoring and abetting terrorist activities in Baluchistan be used by Pakistan to warrant its own version of Cold Start or proactive operations across the border?

Nonetheless, the silver lining is that a certain degree strategic stability in South Asia might be achieved in the foreseeable future when both India and Pakistan acquire assured second-strike capabilities. In fact, they are steadily moving on the path of technological maturation and once Pakistan is able to deploy a highly survivable triad-based credible minimum deterrent, then it would be irrelevant whether India adds to its capabilities for global reach and power projection beyond South Asia that might one day have the potential to target Europe, North America or Australia.

1947–1950: THE FORMATIVE YEARS

The Royal Pakistan Air Force (RPAF) was established on 14 August 1947 with the independence of Pakistan from British India. The RPAF began with 2,332 personnel, a fleet of 24 Tempest II fighter-bombers, 16 Hawker Typhoon fighters, two H.P.57 Halifax bombers, 2 Austeraircraft, twelve North American Harvard trainers and ten de Havilland Tiger Moth biplanes. It also got eight C-47 Dakota cargo planes which it used to transport supplies to soldiers fighting in the 1947 War in Kashmir against India. However, it never received all the planes it was allotted at the time of independence of South Asia. It started with 7 operational airbases scattered all over the provinces.

Operating these inherited aircraft was far from ideal in Pakistan's diverse terrains, deserts and mountains; frequent attrition and injuries did not make the situation any better. However, by 1948 the air force acquired better aircraft such as the Hawker Sea Fury fighter-bomber and the Bristol Freighter. These new aircraft gave a much-needed boost to the morale and combat capability of the Royal Pakistan Air Force; 93 Hawker Fury and roughly 50-70 Bristol Freighter aircraft were inducted into the RPAF by 1950.

1950–1958: ENTERING THE JET AGE

Although the Royal Pakistan Air Force had little funds to use and markets to choose from, it entered the jet age quite early. Initially it had planned to acquire US-built F-94Cs, F-86s, or F-84s and produce its order in Pakistan. However, lack of funds and strong British pressure persuaded the PAF to acquire the British Supermarine Attacker. The first squadron equipped with these aircraft was the Number-11 "Arrow". The Supermarine Attacker had a rather unsatisfactory service in the Royal Pakistan Air Force with frequent attrition and maintenance problems. The prefix Royal was removed when Pakistan became a republic on 23 March 1956. It has since simply been called the *Pakistan Air Force* (PAF).

In 1957 the Pakistan Air Force received 100 American-built F-86 Sabres under the U.S. aid programme. Squadron after squadron in the PAF retired its Hawker Furys and Supermarine Attackers, and replaced them with F-86 jet fighters. In 1957 thirty-six-year-old Air MarshalAsghar Khan became the Pakistan Air Force's first commander-in-chief.

1959–1964: PAF DRAWS 'FIRST BLOOD'

On 10 April 1959, on the occasion of the Islamic Eid ul-Fitr festival holiday in Pakistan, an Indian Air Force (IAF) English Electric Canberra (Photo Reconnaissance Variant: PR Mk.57) intruded into Pakistani airspace on a photo reconnaissance mission. Two PAF F-86F Sabres from No. 15 Squadron on Air Defence Alert (ADA) were scrambled from Peshawar Air Base to intercept the IAF intruder. The Sabre pilots were Flt. Lt. M. N. Butt (leader) and Flt. Lt. M. Yunus (wingman)(Later Air Vice Marshal) whereas Pilot Officer Rab Nawaz was the on-duty Air Defence Controller for this mission. Nawaz successfully vectored both Sabres to the location of the high-flying Canberra. Butt attempted to bring down the Canberra by firing his Sabre's machine guns but the Canberra was flying at an altitude of more than 50,000 feet - beyond the operational ceiling of the F-86F. When Yunus took over from his leader, the Canberra suddenly lost height while executing a turn over Rawalpindi. Yunus grabbed this opportunity and fired a burst from his 12.7 mm guns that struck the Canberra at an altitude of 47,500 feet and brought it down over Rawat, near Rawalpindi.

Thus, PAF drew 'first blood' against the IAF. '55-5005' was the serial number of the F-86F Sabre that was flown by Flt. Lt. Yunus that day. Both the occupants of the IAF Canberra, namely Sqn. Ldr. J.C. Sen Gupta (pilot) and Flt. Lt. S.N. Rampal (navigator) from the IAF's No. 106 Sqn., ejected and were taken prisoner by Pakistani authorities and were subsequently released after remaining in detention for some time.

1965 INDO-PAKISTAN WAR

Rann of Kutch Border Skirmish

In June 1965, prior to the outbreak of the 1965 India-Pakistan War, India and Pakistan had a border skirmish in the Rann of Kutch region near the south-eastern coastline of Pakistan. The PAF was tasked with providing point-defence to the Rann of Kutch region to prevent the Indian Air Force (IAF) from intruding into Pakistani airspace and attacking Pakistan Army positions. On 24 June 1965, an IAF Ouragan fighter (Serial No. IC 698), flown by Flt. Lt. Rana Lal Chand Sikka of No. 51 Auxiliary Squadron from the IAF's Jamnagar Air Station intruded into Pakistani airspace. A PAF F-104A Starfighter from No. 9 Squadron intercepted the IAF fighter near Badin in Sindh, Pakistan. Just as the PAF pilot locked on to the Indian fighter and was about to release his AIM-9B Sidewinder Air-to-Air Missile (AAM), the Indian pilot lowered his aircraft's landing gear (an internationally recognized sign of aerial surrender). The IAF pilot landed at an open field near Jangshahi village near Badin. The IAF pilot was taken prisoner and released on 14 August 1965 - as a goodwill gesture on the 18th Anniversary of Pakistan's Independence Day - minus the IAF Ouragan fighter, which was retained by the PAF as a trophy and flown by a PAF pilot to an airbase in Karachi. (NOTE: This event is not to be confused with the surrender of an InAF Gnat on 4 September 1965 during the 1965 India-Pakistan War, which is on display at the PAF Museum Karachi)

Outbreak of War

The PAF fleet at the time consisted of 12 F-104 Starfighters, some 120 F-86 Sabres and around 20 B-57 Canberra bombers. The PAF claims to have had complete air superiority over the battle area from the second day of operations. It is believed that the Indian Armywould agree. Close air support to the Pakistan Army was unexpectedly effective and the PAF is widely considered to have single-handedly neutralised the large difference in military strength of India and Pakistan.

Many publications have credited the PAF's successes to U.S. equipment, claiming it to be superior to the aircraft operated by the IAF and giving the PAF a "qualitative advantage". However some people refute this argument.

As per them, the IAF's MiG-21, Hawker Hunter andFolland Gnat aircraft had better performance than the PAF's F-86 fighters. According to Air Cdre (retired) Sajad Haider, the F-86 Sabre was inferior in both power and speed to the IAF's Hawker Hunter.

According to Air Commodore (retired) Sajjad Haider who flew with No. 19 squadron, the F-104 Starfighter did not deserve its reputation as "the pride of the PAF" because it "was unsuited to the tactical environment of the region. It was a high-level interceptor designed to neutralise Soviet strategic bombers in altitudes above 40,000 feet." Nevertheless the IAF is believed to have feared the Starfighter although, according to some, it was not as effective as the IAF's Folland Gnat. The F-86F performed reasonably well over IAF's Hawker Hunters but had trouble in dealing with the Gnats, which earned the nickname *Sabre Slayers*.

Post War Sanctions and Acquisitions

After the 1965 war the U.S. placed an arms embargo on Pakistan and the PAF was badly affected. Its entire fleet was of U.S. origin and spare parts could not be sourced from the United States.

The PAF began searching for new combat aircraft. China was approached and agreed to supply an initial 72 Shenyang F-6 fighters and it was inducted on 30 December 1965. China also supplied a squadron of Harbin B-5 bombers which the PAF was not satisfied with due to their lack of a modern bomb aiming system. These were later returned to China in exchange for more Shenyang F-6.

In 1968 the PAF's No. 5 Squadron started converting to the Dassault Mirage IIIEP. As the F-6 was a short range air defence fighter, the Mirage III was the PAF's main offensive weapon. Even still, the Mirage was not equipped with modern munitions such as anti-runway bombs for attacking airbases, cluster bombs for attacking armoured formations or anti-ship weapons because such weapons could not be sourced from the U.S. or Europe. The Mirage was also restricted by lack of equipment such as bomb pylons and missile launchers, which meant the Mirage III fleet was limited in terms of weapon configurations.

1971 INDO-PAKISTAN WAR

Build-up to War

In the late 1960s, many East Pakistanis believed that their wing of the country was being exploited economically by West Pakistan. They also saw that the military in East Pakistanwas very low in numbers and had seemingly left East Pakistan defence less. An election in 1970 resulted in a win for the Awami League, a popular East Pakistani party. However the governing Pakistan People's Party (PPP) refused to allow the Awami League to take over governance of Pakistan. At the time Pakistan was ruled by a military President who did not move to resolve the political conflict, resulting in uprisings springing up in East Pakistan. In March 1971 the government in West Pakistan decided to use military force to quell the uprisings, resulting in a civil war in East Pakistan. India claimed that 10 million refugees had entered its territory, using this as an excuse to assist the East Pakistani rebels and later invade the country to ensure its secession and independence from Pakistan. India's alliance with the Soviet Union ensured full backing of the superpower.

Disparity in Equipment and Numbers

In December 1971, India and Pakistan went to war over East Pakistan. At the start of the war, the PAF inventory contained around 270 combat aircraft while the IAF had over 1,200 - outnumbering the PAF 4:1 in West Pakistan and 10:1 in East Pakistan.

At the end of the war, the Indian Air Force claimed it had shot down 94 PAF aircraft, including 54 F-86 Sabres. According to some sources, the overall attrition rate (losses per 100 sorties) was 0.48 for the IAF and 1.42 for the PAF, the PAF flying 2914 combat sorties while the IAF flew 7,346 combat sorties during the conflict.

1972–1979

In 1979, the PAF's Chief of Air Staff, Air Chief Marshal Anwar Shamim, was told by then President, and Chief of Army Staff General Zia ul Haq that Pakistan had reliable information of Indian plans to attack and destroy the Pakistani nuclear research facilities at Kahuta. ACM Shamim told General Zia that Indian aircraft could reach the area in 3 minutes whereas the PAF would take 8 minutes, allowing the Indians to attack the facility and return before the PAF could defend it. Because Kahuta was too close to the Indian border to be effectively defended it was decided that the best way to deter an Indian attack would be to procure new advanced fighters and weaponry. These would be used to mount a retaliatory attack on India's nuclear research facilities at Trombay in the event of an Indian attack on Kahuta. It was decided the most suitable aircraft would be the F-16, which the United States eventually agreed to supply after the PAF refused to buy the F-5E and F-5G. In 1983, when the first batch of F-16s reached Pakistan, ACM Shamim informed Zia of the PAF's capability to respond to an attack on the nuclear research facilities at Kahuta.

1979–1988: SOVIET-AFGHAN WAR

The Soviet invasion of Afghanistan in 1979 in support of the pro-Soviet government in Kabul, which was being hard-pressed by Mujahadeen rebel forces, marked the start of a decade-long occupation. Mujahadeen rebels continued to harass the occupying Soviet military force as well as the forces of the Afghan regime that it was supporting. The war soon spilled over into neighbouring Pakistan, with a horde of refugees fleeing to camps across the border in an attempt to escape the conflict. In addition, many of the rebels used Pakistan as a sanctuary from which to carry out forays into Afghanistan, and a steady flow of US-supplied arms was carried into Afghanistan from staging areas in Pakistan near the border. This inevitably resulted in border violations by Soviet and Afghan aircraft attempting to interdict these operations.

The PAF is believed to have evaluated the Dassault Mirage 2000 in early 1981 and was planning to evaluate the General Dynamics F-16 Fighting Falcon afterwards.

A letter of agreement for up to 28 F-16A and 12 F-16B was signed December 1981. The contracts, *Peace Gate I* and *Peace Gate II,* were for 6 and 34 Block 15 models respectively which would be powered by the F100-PW-200 engine. The fist *Peace Gate I* aircraft was accepted at Fort Worth in October 1982. Two F-16A and four F-16B were delivered to Pakistan in 1983, the first F-16 arriving at PAF Base Sargodha (now known as PAF Base Mushaf) on 15 January 1983 flown by Squadron Leader Shahid Javed. The 34 remaining *Peace Gate II* aircraft were delivered between 1983 and 1987. Six F-16A and four F-16B Block 15 OCU models were ordered as attrition replacements in December 1988 under the *Peace Gate III* contract. Another 60 F-16A/B were ordered in September 1989 under *Peace Gate IV*. These were later embargoed.

Between May 1986 and November 1988, PAF F-16s have shot down at least eight intruders from Afghanistan. The first three of these (one Su-22, one probable Su-22, and one An-26) were shot down by two pilots from No. 9 Squadron. Pilots of No. 14 Squadron destroyed the remaining five intruders (two Su-22s, two MiG-23s, and one Su-25). Most of these kills were by the AIM-9 Sidewinder, but at least one (a Su-22) was destroyed by cannon fire. Flight Lieutenant Khalid Mahmood is credited with three of these kills. One F-16 was lost in these battles during an encounter between two F-16s and six Afghan Air Force aircraft on 29 April 1987, stated by the PAF to have been an "own-goal" because it was hit by an AIM-9 Sidewinder fired from the other F-16. The pilot, Flight Lieutenant Shahid Sikandar Khan, ejected safely. Most of these air kills were achieved within Pakistani borders. No.9 Sqn was credited with 3 kills, where as No.14 Sqn was credited with 5 kills.

Project Sabre II was initiated by the PAF in 1987 and was aimed at developing a replacement for the ageing Shenyang F-6 fleet. After a design study by Grumman Aerospace determined it would be to financially risky, it was abandoned by PAF and the Chengdu F-7P was introduced in 1988 to replace the F-6.

1989–2001: SANCTIONS AND THE 'LOST DECADE'

After the Pressler Amendment was passed, the U.S. placed sanctions and an arms embargo on Pakistan on 6 October 1990 due to the country's continued nuclear weapons programme. All eleven *Peace Gate III* F-16s, along with 7 F-16A and 10 F-16B of the 60 *Peace Gate IV* F-16s, which had been built by the end of 1994 were embargoed and put into storage in the United States.

Desperate for a new high-tech combat aircraft, between late 1990 and 1993 the PAF evaluated the European Panavia Tornado MRCA (multi-role combat aircraft) and rejected it. The Mirage 2000E and an offer from Poland for the supply of MiG-29 and Su-27 were also considered but nothing materialised. In 1992 the PAF again looked at the Mirage 2000, reviving a proposal from the early 1980s to procure around 20-40 aircraft, but again a sale did not occur because France did not want to sell a fully capable version due to political reasons. In August 1994 the PAF was offered the Saab JAS-39 Gripen by Sweden, but again the sale did not occur because 20% of the Gripen's components were from the U.S. and Pakistan was still under U.S. sanctions.

In mid-1992 Pakistan was close to signing a contract for the supply of 40 Dassault Mirage 2000, equipped with Thomson-CSF RDM/7 radars, from France but the deal was never signed. In mid-1994 it was reported that the Russian manufacturers Sukhoi and Mikoyan were offering the Su-27 and MiG-29. But Pakistan was later reported to be negotiating for supply of the Dassault Mirage 2000-5. French and Russian teams visited Pakistan on 27 November 1994 and it was speculated that interest in the Russian aircraft was to pressure France into reducing the price of the Mirage 2000. Stated requirement was for up to 40 aircraft.

In 1996 it was reported that Pakistan was negotiating a $160 million contract for missiles with South Africa, believed to be for the Kentron (now Denel) U-darter imaging-infra-red short range air-to-air missile.

1999 Kargil Conflict

The Pakistan Air Force (PAF) did not see active combat during the low-intensity Kargil Conflict between India and Pakistan during the summer of 1999 but remained on high air defence alert (ADA) and performed F-16 and

F-7MP combat air patrols (CAPs) near the eastern border with India. The PAF closely monitored and tracked the IAF's movements near the Line of Control in Kashmir as well as the India-Pakistan international border.

2001–2011: WAR ON TERROR HERALDS A 'NEW DAWN'

Counter-insurgency Operations

The Pakistan Army faced several problems during its 2009 offensive against the Taliban in northwest Pakistan. Hundreds of thousands of Pakistanis fled the area when the offensive was announced and, eventually, over 2 million had to be accommodated in refugee camps. The offensive was to be completed as quickly as possible to allow the refugees to return to their homes but the army's fleet attack helicopters were not sufficient to provide adequate support to the infantry. The PAF was sent into action against the Taliban to make up for the lack of helicopter gunships. Because the PAF was trained and equipped to fight a conventional war, a new "counter-terrorist doctrine" had to be improvised.

The PAF's *Saffron Bandit 2009/2010* exercise focused on extensive training of combat personnel to undertake COIN operations. New equipment was inducted to improve the PAF's joint intelligence, surveillance and reconnaissance (ISR) capabilities. A C-130 transport aircraft was indigenously modified for day/night ISR operations.

The PAF had initially been forced to use Google Earth for reconnaissance imagery until high resolution infra-red sensors were provided by the U.S. prior to the army's 2009 campaign in the Swat valley. These were installed on around 10 of the PAF's F-16 fighters and used to gather detailed reconnaissance imagery of the entire valley. Use of laser-guided bombs was increased to 80% of munitions used, as compared to 40% in the previous 2008 Bajaur campaign. A small corps of ground spotters were trained and used by the PAF, in addition to PA spotters, to identify high value targets.

Prior to the PA's offensive into South Waziristan the PAF attacked militant infrastructure with 500 lb and 2000 lb bombs.

After the Mumbai attacks and threats made by India PAF was put on high alert. Pakistani press reported an outstanding order to launch a counterattack in case of an air attack from India after Indian Foreign Minister Pranab Mukharjee threatened Pakistani President in rough tone.

On the morning of 14 December Indian aircraft started moving towards Pakistan,PAF moved swiftly and intercepted them before they entered international borders. Two of the aircraft did cross the border but Indian aircraft managed to turn back. PAF was ordered to carry on the defensive combat patrols but avoid hostile action unless further hostile action was to take place.

A number of civilian deaths occurred during PAF air strikes on 10 April 2010 in the Khyber tribal region. According to a Pakistani military source, the first bombing was targeted at a gathering of militants in a compound. Local people, who had quickly moved onto the scene to recover the dead and wounded, were then killed during a second air strike.

There was no confirmed death toll but at least 30 civilian deaths had occurred according to the military source, whereas a local official stated at least 73 locals, including women and children, were killed. A six-member committee of tribal elders from the area, tasked with finding the exact number of civilian casualties, reported that 61 civilians were killed and 21 wounded. This was not confirmed by military or political leaders but Pakistan's Chief of Army Staff, General Ashfaq Kayani, gave a public apology on 17 April. It is reported that BBC news and several other media correspondences were not allowed to take interviews from injured which makes the whole episode more mysterious.

On 22 May 2011 it was reported that the PAF had retaliated against attacks by Afghan mortar and machine gun positions on the Pakistani posts at Miskinai and Sangpura in theBajaur area. It was stated that since 19 May, around 1000 Afghan Askaris had entered the Bajaur area at Sahi as well as Miskinai and Sankpura. The Afghan forces had been firing at the posts during night and, after reconnaissance sorties, PAF aircraft destroyed the Afghan positions.

Modernisation and Acquisitions

In light of Pakistan's significant contribution to the War on Terror, the United States and Western European countries, namely Germany and France, lifted their defense related sanctions on Pakistan; enabling the country to once again seek advanced Western military hardware. Since the lifting of sanctions, the Pakistan Air Force (PAF) became heavily active in evaluating potential military hardware such as new fighter aircraft, radars and land based air-defense systems. However the urgent relief needed in Kashmir after the2005 Kashmir earthquake forced the Pakistani military to stall its modernisation programme so it could divert its resources for fuel and operations during the rescue efforts.

The modernisation stall would end in April 2006 when the Pakistani cabinet approved the PAF's proposals to procure new aircraft and systems from several sources, including modern combat aircraft from the U.S. and China. The AFFDP 2019 (Armed Forces Development Programme 2019) would oversee the modernisation of the Pakistan Air Force from 2006 to 2019. The Bush administration on 24 July 2008 informed the US Congress it plans to shift nearly $230 million of $300 million in aid from counterterrorism programs to upgrading Pakistan's aging F-16s. The Bush administration previously announced on 27 June 2008 it was proposing to sell Pakistan ITT Corporation's electronic warfare gear valued at up to $75 million to enhance Islamabad's existing F-16s. Pakistan has asked about buying as many as 21 AN/ALQ-211(V)9 Advanced Integrated Defensive Electronic Warfare Suite pods, or AIDEWS, and related equipment. The proposed sale will ensure that the existing fleet is "compatible" with new F-16 Block 50/52 fighters being purchased by Islamabad.After 9/11 the U.S. and Pakistan began discussing the release of the embargoed F-16s and a purchase of new aircraft. Of the 28 F-16A/B built under the *Peace Gate III/IV*contracts and embargoed in 1990, 14 delivered as EDA (Excess Defense Articles) from 2005 to 2008., two of which were delivered on 10 July 2007.

Between 2005 and 2008, 14 F-16A/B Block 15 OCU fighters were delivered to the PAF under renewed post-9/11 ties between the U.S. and Pakistan. These had originally been built for Pakistan under the Peace Gate III/IV contracts but were never delivered due to the U.S. arms embargo imposed in 1990.

To upgrade the F-16A/B fleet, 32 Falcon STAR kits were purchased for the original *Peace Gate I* aircraft and 35 Mid-Life Update (MLU) kits were ordered, with 11 more MLU kits optional, in. 4 F-16A/B being upgraded in the U.S. to F-16AM/BM, delivery expected December 2011. F-16A/B in PAF service to be upgraded starting October 2010 byTurkish Aerospace Industries, 1 per month.

The *Peace Drive I* contract for 12 F-16C and 6 F-16D Block 52+ (Advanced Block 52) aircraft, powered by F100-PW-229 engines was signed on 30 September 2006. The first F-16 to be completed, an F-16D, was rolled out on 13 October 2009 and began flight testing. The first batch of F-16C/D Block 52+, two F-16D and one F-16C, landed at PAF Base Shahbaz, Jacobabad, on 26 June 2010 and one more F-16C was received by 5 July 2010.

On 19 May 2006 the PAF inaugurated a refurbished Sector Operations Centre at PAF Base Mushaf (Sargodha) which had been installed with a Pakistani-developed air defence automation system for command and control.

An old air defence system installed in the 1980s was replaced. The TPS-77 radar was introduced into service in April 2008.

During talks with a delegation from the French Senate on Monday 28 September 2009, Prime Minister Yousuf Raza Gilani stated that the PAF had used most of its stockpile of laser-guided munitions against militants in the

Malakand and FATA regions and that replacements for such types of equipment were urgently required.

December 2009 saw the delivery of the PAF's first Saab 2000 Erieye AEW&C from Sweden and Il-78MP Midas aerial refuelling tanker/military transport aircraft fromUkraine.

The PAF is reported to be considering purchasing the Hongdu L-15 advanced jet trainer to train pilots for high-tech fighters such as the FC-20. Extensive evaluations of the aircraft took place in Pakistan during December 2009.

On 26 June 2010 the first batch of 3 F-16C/D Block 52+ fighters were delivered to PAF Base Shahbaz, Jacobabad.

According to Air Chief Marshal Rao Qamar Suleman the new fighters would eliminate the PAF's limitations in precision night-time strike operations, the existing capability being based on around 34 Dassault Mirage 5 fighters upgraded with new avionics for night-time precision strike missions under the Retrofit Of Strike Element (ROSE) programme during 1999-2004.

It was reported in 2010 that the R-Darter, an active radar homing beyond visual range air-to-air missile, is being operated by the Pakistan Air Force.

2008 Air Alert

On 13 December 2008, the Government of Pakistan stated that two Indian Air Force aircraft were intercepted by the PAF kilometres within Pakistani airspace. This charge was denied by the Indian government.

Introduction of Female Engineers and Pilots

Previously, women had been employed by Pakistan's armed forces in non-combat roles only, such as the medical corps, and the PAF had remained all-male throughout its history. However, in 2003 women were allowed to enroll in the aerospace engineering and other programs of PAF Academy Risalpur, including fighter pilot training programmes. It was stated that standards would not be compromised for women and those who did not achieve the same performance as their male counterparts would be dropped from the course. A level of segregation between the genders is maintained. For example, early-morning parades are performed together but some parts of training, mainly physical exercises, are done with males and females separated. According to Squadron Leader Shazia Ahmed, the officer in charge of the first female cadets and a psychologist, this also improves confidence of the women.

In 2005 it was reported that two batches in the Air Force Academy's flying wing contained 10 women, with many more in the engineering and aerospace wings. Cadet Saba Khan, from Quetta in Balochistan, applied after reading a newspaper advertisement seeking female cadets. She was one of the first four women to pass the first stages of flying training on propeller-driven light aircraft and move onto faster jet-powered training aircraft.

In March 2006, the PAF inducted a batch of 34 fighter pilots which included the organisation's first four female fighter pilots. Three years of training had been completed by the pilots at PAF Academy Risalpur before they graduated and were awarded their Flying Badges during the ceremony. Certificates of honour were handed to the successful cadets by a "delighted" General Ahsan Saleem Hayat, vice chief of the Pakistan Army, who acknowledged that the PAF was the first of the Pakistani armed forces to introduce women to its combat units. One of the women, Flying Officer Nadia Gul, was awarded a trophy for best academic achievement. The other female graduates were Mariam Khalil, Saira Batool and the above-mentioned Saba Khan. A second batch of pilots, including 3 female pilots, graduated from the 117th GD(P) course at PAF Academy Risalpur in September 2006. The Sword of Honour for best all-round performance was awarded to Aviation Cadet Saira Amin, the first female pilot to win the award. Aviation Cadet Saira Amin won the Asghar Hussain Trophy for best performance in academics. In September 2009 it was reported that seven women had qualified as operational fighter pilots on the Chengdu F-7, the first female combat pilots in the PAF's history, one of them being Ambreen Gull. Commanding Officer Tanvir Piracha emphasised that if the female pilots "are not good enough as per their male counterparts, we don't let them fly." It was noted that some of the female pilots wear the hijab while others do not.

STATUS OF COMBAT ARMS

The Pakistani army is organized into nine Corps and Force Command Northern Area. These contain 22 divisions, 15 independent brigades (6 armoured and 9 infantry), 9 Corps artillery brigades, 7 engineering brigades and 15 army aviation squadrons - including two of attack helicopters.

In addition, the Pakistani army has 8 air defence brigades. It must be pointed out, however, that Pakistani brigades and divisions are somewhat smaller than their Indian counterparts. Again, this order of battle differs to a certain extent from that normally quoted. The order of battle is as follows:

Pakistan's two principal fighting formations are Army Reserve North (ARN) and Army Reserve South (ARS). These are an approximate equivalent to the Indian Strike Corps in terms of size and composition. These have, as in the case of their Indian counterparts, a nucleus of a single armoured division and up to two infantry divisions with numerous brigades:

3Armour

As in the case of the Indian army, the Pakistani army possesses three armoured division and a number of armoured brigades. These operate almost 2,500 Main Battle Tanks of a bewildering variety and from various generations.

The most recent acquisitions are 320 T-80 UD MBTs from the Ukraine. This deal has been mired in controversy because of Russia's refusal to supply spares, including gun barrels, and doubts over Ukraine's ability to provide spares and support.

The T-80UD is a major improvement over the existing Pakistani tank fleet. The most modern units, until the arrival of the T-80UDs, were license made Chinese T-85 II tanks. An indigenous MBT - the Al-Khalid - has failed to materialise. The rest of the fleet consists of over a thousand T-69/-59 tanks of Chinese origin, which have been upgraded with 105mm guns. The rest of the fleet is a mixture of 1950s & 1960s vintage M-47/-48A5 tanks. These, while serviceable, are not really a match for even older Indian armour. The Pakistani tank fleet lacks modern fire control equipment and advanced night-fighting capabilities. It can be expected that Pakistan will attempt to rectify this in the near future.

Artillery

As in the case of its Indian counterpart, Pakistan's Regiment of Artillery has undergone a tremendous re-organization and modernization programme. While substantial quantities of new equipment have been inducted, large numbers of completely obsolete artillery pieces - long since relegated to reserve/storage status in the Indian army - remain in service.

Pakistan created the subcontinent's first artillery division using a core component of two artillery brigades and an air defence unit. While Pakistan has far fewer artillery tubes than the massive Indian artillery park, it is interesting to note that it was responsible for this major organizational innovation.

The most noteworthy feature of Pakistan's artillery is the number of 155 and 203mm self-propelled guns. This gives Pakistani armour an integral artillery capability that is currently lacking in Indian armoured units. Moreover, these guns are more easily operated in an NBC environment than towed guns.

Pakistan's artillery also comprises an assortment of older pieces, including some Second World War vintage 25 pounders. As in the case of the Indian artillery, considerable progress has been made in the introduction of fire control computers and other surveillance and target acquisition equipment. This, of course, dramatically enhances the efficacy of artillery - no matter how old the guns are.

Infantry

There is not much difference between Pakistani and Indian army infantry formations. Pakistan has not developed an organization equivalent to the Indian RAPIDS and has not attempted the massive modernization programme - in terms of modern night vision, target finding and anti-tank weaponry - that the Indian army has recently undertaken. The only really noteworthy aspect of the Pakistani infantry is the fact that it was the first to introduce mechanized units to the subcontinent. These mechanized infantry units are provided with over eight hundred M-113 armoured personnel carriers. While not as capable as India's BMP-2 units, these older APCs provide Pakistan's infantry with a reasonable degree of battlefield mobility. However, as far as NBC warfare is concerned, these older APCs offer somewhat less protection than the BMPs.

Air Defense

Unlike the Indian army, Pakistan lacks any medium self-propelled surface-to-air missiles and modern self-propelled air-defence guns. Pakistan's six air defence brigades are equipped with a wide variety of shoulder-launched SAMs and thousands of towed air defence guns. These are used with both Western and Chinese fire-control radar. It is not known if Pakistan intends to obtain any more advanced radar and target acquisition equipment. The Pakistani army air defence units remain constrained in their ability to obtain advanced self-propelled air-defence assets since Russia, the principal producer of these items, will not sell these items to Pakistan. Strangely enough, Pakistan does not seem to be making particularly vigorous efforts to rectify this shortcoming in their army air defences.

NBC Warfare

Both the Indian and Pakistani armies are extremely well trained. This is especially true up to brigade level. Both armies possess a high degree of tactical skill and pride themselves on their ability to perform their assigned tasks. Using a mixture of traditional methods and modern techniques and equipment, both armies are extremely capable. In the area of NBC warfare, however, a rather confusing picture emerges. Both countries frequently made mention of their ability to fight in NBC conditions, but little hard information is available on the degree of NBC readiness.

In the 1980s, the Indian army began some tentative preparations for NBC warfare. In the early part of that decade, a limited quantity of S6 respirators and No.1Mk.3 NBC suits - both of British origin - was purchased. A quantity of NBC equipment was imported from the USSR, but proved to be useless in Indian environmental conditions. Moreover, India's defence research organization, in 1987, produced prototypes of NBC suits, decontamination suits, facelets, overboots and NBC tents. This equipment has entered production and service with the Indian armed forces.

As regards training, from 1987 onwards, the Indian army, through its College of Military Engineering, began running familiarization courses in NBC warfare, while scientist conducted courses at brigade level. Moreover, a series of studies were undertaken to provide for both active and passive defence against nuclear attack for army combat formations.

As regards equipment, the Indian Ministry of Defence has obviously allocated high priority to the indigenous production of NBC gear.

This has also involved the participation of the private sector for the manufacture of both NBC suits and respirators. In addition, the Indian army has retained its old Second World War respirators - these are old, but would still offer significant protection. India would not find it particularly difficult to produce enough NBC personal gear - respirators and NBC suits - for its armed forces in a relatively short period of time - though this equipment might be placed in storage. Mention should also be made of the fact that a new decontamination vehicle has entered production.

While it is abundantly clear that NBC warfare has been accorded a much higher priority in the Indian army, it remains unclear as to the exact status of NBC preparedness and training in the Indian army. Attempts to contact senior military officers on this subject proved unsuccessful, though some retired officers offered some vague information that leads to the conclusion that some training is in progress.

It has become clear that India's Army Training Command has conducted detailed studies into NBC warfare. Indeed, given India's perception of its nuclear threat, it is not surprising that the Indian army schools of instruction and combat include NBC scenarios. Moreover, the publisher of the prestigious Indian Defence Review stated that the forces earmarked for use against Pakistan are well equipped to deal with NBC warfare.

It would be natural for India's Strike Corps to be the first to be fully equipped and prepared for NBC warfare and there are some indications of this beginning to occur. It is highly probable that at least one Corps is fully prepared - trained and equipped for NBC warfare. The other formations would probably receive personal NBC gear - but will be allocated a lower priority for receiving decontamination and monitoring equipment. It should be pointed out that the RAPIDS require virtually no modifications for deployment in an NBC environment.

It can probably be assumed that the state of NBC warfare in Pakistan is in a similar state to that of India, except that Pakistan's industry is not yet capable of meeting all NBC needs and that the country lacks the massive R & D infrastructure of India. Indian sources assume that Pakistan has a nucleus of NBC trained personnel - with Chinese NBC gear.

One thing is clear, however, both countries have now made NBC warfare something of a priority and are making efforts - covertly - to train and equip themselves. Nonetheless, there may be a large gap between what the military wants and reality.

While there is some reference to NBC warfare and the necessity to fight under such conditions in both armies, there have never been any major NBC exercises conducted by either side. It is therefore not inconceivable that the principal focus of NBC training and equipment programs in both countries is more geared towards meeting an emergency that might arise after one side uses such weapons. This would involve stockpiling equipment and drafting rapid training instructions - aimed at rapidly familiarizing troops who have to enter an NBC contaminated area. It does not seem that either country intends to develop a tactical nuclear warfare doctrine.

One of the reasons for the lack of NBC exercises could be the extremely severe environmental conditions prevailing on the South Asian battlefield. These conditions range from the intense cold of the Siachen glacier to the blistering heat of the Thar desert. Under normal peacetime conditions these climates pose great difficulties for human endurance, if the troops were clad in full NBC gear and armoured vehicles 'buttoned-up', there would be more casualties from heat-stroke than from exposure.

This brings us to the other issue that needs to be considered - where on the South Asian battlefield could tactical nuclear weapons possibly be used ? The answer to this question will determine whether or not there is any battlefield use for nuclear weapons.

7

Modernising the Indian Air Force and Air Power Projection

MODERNISING THE INDIAN AIR FORCE

The induction of the first fourth-generation aircraft, the Su-30 MKI began in 1997 and the IAF is expected to build-up to full strength of 230 by 2014. It is understood that another 42 have been ordered taking the total fleet strength to 272 aircraft. There is a proposal from Russia to eventually upgrade the IAF Su-30 MKI fleet to fifth generation standards.

In the meantime, the MiG-23 fleet has already been phased out and the MiG-21 fleet with its different variants would be extinct in another five to seven years at best. The fleet of Jaguars, MiG-27, MiG-29 and even the Mirage-2000 all with upgrades, would last for another 10 to 15 years; but being of third generation vintage, would not really be able to project frontline capability. The strength of the combat fleet currently is reported to be down to 34 squadrons as against the authorised 39.5 and by 2015, is expected to reduce further to possibly well under 30 seriously eroding combat capability of the IAF. This situation will be incongruous for an emerging regional power and catastrophic in two-front war scenario.

The emerging geopolitical and security scenario requires our nation to possess comprehensive military capability, characterised by flexibility and speed of response, the mobility and transportability of all forms of national power, long-reach, precision targeting, minimum collateral damage and reduced visibility. Aerospace power fits the bill perfectly. The 21st century belongs to aerospace power and given the Indian situation, concerns and aspirations, the need for a strong and comprehensive aerospace capability is inescapable

Backed by a resurgent economy, two decades into the post-cold war era, India is beginning to emerge as a regional power and given competent political and bureaucratic management, has the attributes to rise to the status of a super power.

The growing status of the nation is accompanied by enhanced responsibilities wherein India may be called upon to intervene decisively in the region militarily to safeguard national interests that transcend our geographical boundaries and extend from the Persian Gulf to the Strait of Malacca. As a regional power, the nation may be called upon to respond to calamities, man-made or natural, to humanitarian crisis, to restore order or to ensure peace and stability.

While economic strength is the main pillar of national power, the military capability of a nation must be enhanced in tandem to secure its economic status and provide the environment for further growth. This philosophy was echoed by Air Chief Marshal F H Major, the then Chief of Air Staff, Indian Air Force (IAF) on the occasion of its platinum jubilee celebrations in October 2007 when he said "The emerging geopolitical and security scenario requires our nation to possess comprehensive military capability, characterised by flexibility and speed of response, the mobility and transportability of all forms of national power,

long reach, precision targeting, minimum collateral damage and reduced visibility. Aerospace power fits the bill perfectly. The 21st century belongs to aerospace power and given the Indian situation, concerns and aspirations, the need for a strong and comprehensive aerospace capability is inescapable".

Stated in simple terms, the nation's aerospace power must possess the capability to project power effectively in the region for which it must have combat aircraft with adequate reach, lethal firepower through modern stand-off / precision guided munitions and stealth characteristics. It must have strategic airlift aircraft with the capability to move large forces by air over long distances, tactical transport aircraft to operate over shorter distances and a fleet of helicopters to provide mobility and firepower in the tactical battle area. Two things follow from this, one being that the nation must possess multi-layered air defence system to protect its offensive operations capability and secondly that development of aerospace power must not only cater to perceived threats but more importantly, must be capability-based to respond to a wide variety of threats, existing or unforeseen.

NEW 'SPECIAL MISSION' AIRCRAFT FOR THE INDIAN AIR FORCE

In recent years the Indian Air force (IAF) as part of its 'transformation' has been progressively augmenting its fleet of special mission aircraft beyond the usual fighter and transport squadrons. After having brought in refuellers and airborne early warning aircraft, the IAF is now quite keen to augment its electronic warfare (EW) capabilities with more specialised aircraft in such roles. In late April last year, the Defence Acquisition Council put its stamp of approval on the IAF's proposal to procure nine 'special mission' aircraft for 1100 crore rupees or more. The status of the request for proposal (RFP) that the IAF was supposed to issue subsequently is unclear. But it is still worthwhile to look at this program more closely.

The IAF's RFI for the nine aircraft issued way back in 2012 specifies that two of the nine aircraft should be certified to perform the signals intelligence (SIGINT) role, given that the mission package for SIGINT commonly requires permanent modifications to the airframe. The remaining seven aircraft according to the RFI are to be configured by the prime contractor for the multi-mission role, 'supporting aerial survey, target towing, communications jamming (COMJAM) and flaring'. The RFI further specified that these missions i.e. for the seven COMJAM aircraft will be flown in addition to their original passenger and cargo roles.

Now what the IAF is essentially looking for has emerged as a classic combination over the last two decades. The special mission aircraft sought by the IAF are essentially militarized business jets that give a very good mix of deployability and endurance. The RFI issued last year spells this out by explicitly wanting 'aircraft powered by twin turbofan engines with low noise and vibration levels, with hot-and-high capability in all roles, certified for deployments at air bases up to 3,300 meters (10,000 ft.) above mean sea level.' The certification according to the RFI must be done by the airframe supplier. Reportedly the IAF may be looking for a biz jet platform with a cruise speed of Mach 0.75-0.80 and a minimum range capability of 4500 kms.

While all nine are to be based on a single platform the requirement for only two of them to be specialized for SIGINT probably follows from the fact that the IAF already operates two Learjet 29A and three Gulfstream III SRA platforms in that role for the Aviation Research Centre (ARC). The seven COMJAM units will therefore be filling the shoes of the IAF's retired Canberras and Avros.

The RFI however does suggest that the IAF wants the best that is out there when it says that '[sigint] system must be a futuristic, state-of-the-art system using cutting edge technologies, algorithms and software.' Furthermore the IAF wants that the set up should be up to the task of 'rapid system acquisitions and data processing with a high degree of automation', besides being 'capable of transmitting data to the ground through data links'. Interestingly the IAF also seems to be looking to move to systems that merge cyber and EW techniques. According to the RFI apart from the usual profiles, 'electronic countermeasure (ECM) systems on board the COMJAM specialized units need to be able to deceive adversaries by introducing false information into the enemy's communications' network and degrading enemy communications'. This kind of capability is akin to what the United States is looking for in its next generation jammer (NGJ) initiative wherein mutating algorithms are sought to be 'fired' through the aperture of enemy radar antennae to take over as 'system administrator' or at least 'infect' the enemy's network. Of course technologies of this kind are being developed by the US under the aegis of a program known as Senior Suter.

On the other hand the IAF wants the electronic support measures (ESM) used by the SIGINT aircraft to have the ability 'to intercept, identify, fingerprint and locate the source of electromagnetic emissions from radars, ECMs, Identification Friend or Foe/Successor interrogators (1030 mhz), transponders (1090 mhz), Tactical air navigation/Distance Measuring Equipment interrogators signals (1025-1150 mhz) and communication signals.' Making these acquisitions a full blown intelligence surveillance reconnaissance (ISR) buy is the fact that seven of the aircraft for their 'aerial survey' role will have to be outfitted with 'microprocessor-based high-performance aerial survey camera systems with camera magazines, gyro-stabilized mounts, cockpit displays and automatic GPS-controlled photo flight systems. '

For COMJAM missions the IAF requires that the aircraft have enough space to accommodate up to five operator workstations and other related equipment with the overall ability to carry up to 10 passengers.

This requirement to carry up to 10 passengers represents an enlargement of mission requirements compared to what was laid out in a previous RFP issued in 2009 for this same procurement category which had seen Embraer and Israel Aerospace Industries (IAI) shortlisted with both vendors offering ELTA's EL/I-3001 Airborne Integrated Signal Intelligence System (AISIS) mission system. That time over the Ministry of Defence (MoD) cancelled the RFP since vendors escalated prices based on an apparent lack of clarity in India's offset policy at the time.

This time over both Embraer and IAI are likely to bid again offering ELTA's AISIS which clearly has found favour with the IAF once before. In the words of its manufacturer 'AISIS is an aircraft mounted suite designed to perform long-range, high-endurance missions thus providing tactical and strategic intelligence. The system comprises ELINT (Electronic Intelligence) and COMINT (Communications Intelligence) sensors to search, intercept, measure, locate, analyze, classify and monitor communication and radar transmissions. The Electronic Order of Battle (OEB) picture generated by the

EL/I-3001 suite is transmitted in real-time to ground stations for its exploitation via secure line-of-sight data-links, satellite communications and/or HF/VHF/UHF radio sets.' Elta also claims that the system is 'optimized' to effectively deal with low probability of intercept transmission sources and is of course in use with the Israeli defence forces.

Now the last time over Embraer offered a derivative of the EMB-145 with the pull of commonality of platform between these proposed special mission aircraft and the DRDO developed AEW&C currently in the process of being inducted by the IAF. On the other hand IAI had chipped in with the Gulfstream G200 which it manufactures under license in Israel. This time over IAI may offer the new super mid-size it is building- the Gulfstream G280. Indeed G280 based EW platforms are being touted by IAI as an affordable way forward in procuring special mission aicraft.

Affordability will certainly be a key factor in determining success in this tender, given that it has already been shot down by the MoD once before on those grounds. More than the mission systems the basic cost of the airframe and integration both of which are to be done by the airframe provider are likely to carry the day. Thus vendors who have cobbled up such offerings before with decent maintenance support will have a good chance at winning this tender. Of course, given the requirement for a larger aircraft as compared to the previous tender and current prices it remains to be seen how much more than the ball park 1100 crores would the Indian government be willing to expend on this proposal. Naturally something like a Gulfstream G550 based offering is ruled out because that would inflate costs rather considerably. On the other hand G280 sized jets are likely to be in the sweet spot for this tender. Apart from Embraer and IAI, Saab too is likely to bid again even though it was not down-selected the last time over.

From the US, offerings are likely to be made by Hawker Beechcraft in partnership with Raytheon, L-3 communications, Lockheed Martin or Boeing who will provide the mission package. Hawker Beechcraft's Hawker 800 after all already serves in a similar role with the South Koreans with eight specially-equipped aircraft delivered back in 2000. Of course the mission systems providers could also team up with other super mid-size manufacturers such as Bombardier or Cessna. L-3 communications Mission Integration Division (MID) in Greenville, Texas has racked up successes in the special mission space in recent times by integrating ISR capabilities on to business aircraft and is executing a contract for the Saudis along with Hawker Beechcraft at the moment besides on going work with the US Air force on 'Project Liberty'. Incidentally ARC's first SIGINT platform, a Boeing 707 SIGINT, was originally modified for the role by then-US contractor E-Systems which has since then been subsumed by Raytheon. But participation from US manufacturers, one suspects, may also depend on how much the Indians are willing to pay in the final analysis. For India, familiarity with a manufacturer and technology sharing are likely to be very important considerations for this tender. In that sense Embraer and IAI are probably ahead. In any case successfully completing this tender within a decent timeframe will certainly go a long way in dealing with the constant needling that India's neighbours are resorting to on both fronts.

COMBAT FLEET OF THE IAF

The IAF went through a partial upgrade of its combat fleet between the period 1979 to 1989 when its fleet of *Gnats, Hunters* and *Maruts*were approaching the end of their Total Technical Life and were due to be phased out leaving only the *MiG-21* as the mainstay. In this period, the combat capability of the IAF was upgraded through the induction of the British *Jaguar*, Russian *MiG-23, MiG-27, MiG-29* and the French *Mirage-2000.*

The *C-130J* has the capability to undertake deployment of Special Forces in all-weather conditions by day or night even in complete darkness. It is capable of receiving fuel in flight at low level and apart from special operations, can be employed for airborne assault, air transported operations

The induction of the first fourth-generation aircraft, the *Su-30 MKI* began in 1997 and the IAF is expected to build-up to full strength of 230 by 2014. It is understood that another 42 have been ordered taking the total fleet strength to 272 aircraft. It is also understood that there is a proposal from Russia to eventually upgrade the IAF *Su-30 MKI* fleet to fifth generation standards. In the meantime, the *MiG-23* fleet has already been phased out and the *MiG-21* fleet with its different variants would be extinct in another five to seven years at best. The fleet of*Jaguars, MiG-27, MiG-29* and even the *Mirage-2000* all with upgrades, would last for another 10 to 15 years; but being of third generation vintage, would not really be able to project frontline capability. The strength of the combat fleet currently is reported to be down to 34 squadrons as against the authorised 39.5 and by 2015, is expected to reduce further to possibly well under 30 seriously eroding combat capability of the IAF. This situation will be incongruous for an emerging regional power and catastrophic in two-front war scenario.

There is therefore an imperative need for total revamp of the fleet with fourth and fifth generation aircraft beginning not later than 2015 and to build-up to the sanctioned level of 42 squadrons by 2022.

As there was considerable uncertainty at the turn of the century with regard to the operationalisation of the indigenous Light Combat Aircraft, *Tejas,* over a decade ago, the IAF had projected a requirement of six squadrons of fighter aircraft to replace part of the *MiG-21*fleet being phased out.

It has been five years since the tender was issued by the Ministry of Defence and nine months since selection of the French *Rafale* was made public, contract with Dassault is yet to be signed.

If all goes well, the contract may be concluded sometime in 2013 at the earliest and delivery will commence four years later. Thereafter it may take a decade for the *Rafale* fleet to reach full strength and operational status. All this presuming that there are no fresh impediments.

In the meantime, Hindustan Aeronautics Limited (HAL) has entered into a contract with Russian companies Rosoboron export and Sukhoi to develop the Fifth Generation Fighter Aircraft (FGFA), a stealth fighter in the class of the American *F-22 Raptor*. A derivative of the Russian *PAK FA* whose single-seat prototype *T-50* is already undergoing flight tests, the FGFA will be a twin-seat version customised to conform to the new doctrine of the IAF. To be produced in India by HAL, the initial order by the IAF will be for 214 aircraft (roughly ten squadrons) at a cost of US$ 100 million per aircraft and the total outlay of US$ 25 billion apart from development cost. Series production of the FGFA is scheduled to commence in 2019. The IAF can hope to have the complete initial order delivered and squadrons fully operational by 2029 at the earliest.

IAF MODERNISATION: AN OVERVIEW

In the words of the Air Chief Marshal Norman Browne, Chief of the Air Staff (CAS) of the IAF, the "IAF is witnessing an unprecedented phase of modernisation and capability enhancement [which can be] witnessed across the capability spectrum ..." The most vital capability enhancement is perhaps the IAF's modernisation of its fighter fleet, which has caused some concern in recent years due to the shrinking number of combat squadrons. According to the Parliamentary Standing Committee on Defence (15th Lok Sabha), the present number of combat squadron has dwindled to 34 against the sanction strength of 42. Moreover, the number is likely to reduce further to 31 during the 12th Plan (2012-2017). To arrest the declining trend, the IAF has made a two-prong approach: upgrading existing fighters (MiG-29, Jaguar and Mirage 2000) while inducting new ones. The aim of the IAF is to increase its combat squadron strength to 40-42 by the end of 14th Plan (2022-27) and eventually to 45 squadrons by the 15th Plan (2027-2032).

Upgrades

The contract for upgrading MiG-29s was signed in 2008 with RAC MIG of Russia at a cost of US $964 million. This program is to be completed by

2014. The first three upgraded MiG-29s (known as MiG-29UPG) were handed over to India by the Russian company in December 2012. Three more fighters are to be upgraded in Russia and the remaining 63-odd planes are to be upgraded in India with support from the Russian partner. The service life of the upgraded aircraft has been extended to 40 years. Among other features the upgraded MiG include Phazatron Zhuk-M radar, beyond-visual-range combat ability and the mid-air refuelling.

The contract for modernising Jaguars to DARIN-III Standard was signed with India's state-owned Hindustan Aeronautics Ltd (HAL) in 2009 at the cost of Rs 31.1 billion. The work is scheduled for completion by 2017. The first upgraded Jaguar was successfully flight tested by the HAL on November 28, 2012. Among other features the upgraded aircraft incorporates new state-of-the-art avionics architecture including Mission Computer (MC), Engine and Flight Instrument System (EFIS), and autopilot. The retrofitted Jaguar will "result in a major operational improvement with regard to all weather air to ground, air to sea and air to air capabilities through incorporation of multi mode radar", says R. K. Tyagi, Chairman, HAL. In July 2011, the MoD signed a $2.4 billion contract with French companies Thales, and Dassault Aviation and HAL for upgrades to the IAF's Mirage-2000 fleet procured in eighties. As per the contract, out of 50-odd fighters, two will be upgraded in France, two at HAL with French support, and the rest by the HAL. The entire process is expected to be completed by 2021. The improvements include new avionics, radars, mission computers, glass cockpits, helmet-mounted displays, electronic warfare suites, weapon delivery and precision-targeting systems, which will bring the fleet to Mirage 2000-5 standards and extend the service life by 20 years. A separate contract valued €959 million has also been signed with MBDA to provide 450 MICA missiles to arm the upgraded fighters.

Fighter

The IAF is all set to induct in its fleet over 400 new fighters that include three new types of combat planes - Light Combat Aircraft (LCA), French Rafale and Fifth Generation Fighter Aircraft (FGFA) – and an additional 42 SU-30MKIs. The additional SU-30 MKI is part of the $4.5 billion defence deal signed between India and Russia during President Putin's December 2012 visit to New Delhi. The newly contracted SU-30 MKI will be license produced by the HAL, taking Indian aerospace company's total order of the fighter to 222, and the total cost of procurement of 272 Su-30MKIs to $12 billion.

Beginning with inductions of new type of fighters, the IAF has already placed orders for 40 LCAs (20 each in Initial Operational Clearance (IOC) and Final Operational (FOC) standards) of MK-I version with GE404 engine. These planes are planned for induction in the 12th Plan (2012-2017). There is also a further plan to induct more LCAs of MK-II version with superior GE F414 engines, 99 units of which have been contracted for $800 million. All together, as many as six LCA squadrons (108 fighters) are to be inducted by the end of the 13th Plan (2017-2022). The much touted approximately $20 billion medium multi role combat aircraft (MMRCA) deal, in which French Rafale emerged as the winner, looks set for contract finalisation in early part of the next financial year (2013-14). As per the plan, the first Rafale squadron comprising of 18 aircrafts will be inducted in 3-4 years after contract signing. The rest 108 aircraft, which will be manufactured by the HAL under the transfer of technology agreement with France, are to be inducted in the following seven years.

The induction of LCA and MMRCA is soon going to be over-shadowed by what is poised as India's biggest ever defence programme to acquire 200-250 Fifth Generation Fighter Aircrafts (FGFA) – though in a recent interview the Air Chief has however indicated a lower figure of 144 fighters. Consequent to 2007 inter-governmental agreement between India and Russia for joint development of FGFA, both the sides signed a Preliminary Design contract in 2010 at the cost of $295 million to be shared equally. Drawning upon the basic structural and systems design of the Russian PAF-FA, the FGFA for the IAF is now visualised as a single seat fighter with advanced features such as stealth, super-cruise, and ultra-manoeuvrability. HAL, the Indian joint partner in the developmental efforts of the FGFA, has committed $6 billion dollars for the initial developmental efforts. Total programme cost on the Indian side including for the induction is estimated to be $30 billion. The IAF is hopeful of inducting the aircraft from 2020 onwards.

TRANSPORT AIRCRAFT

Like the fighter fleet, the transport fleet of the IAF is on a major course transformation, by way of upgrades and replacement of existing fleet, and induction of new planes. Beginning in this regard was made in 2007 when India and Russia signed another intergovernmental agreement for joint development and production of 15-29 ton class Multi-role Transport Aircraft (MTA). Post the 2007 agreement, both the sides have formed a joint venture in India as an equal partnership. Of the total projected requirement of 205 MTAs, the IAF's share is 45 (100 for Russia and the rest 60 for exports).

The big boost for IAF's transport fleet however came in January 2008 when India signed the Letter of Offer and Acceptance (LOA) with the US government for procurement of six C-130J-30 Super Hercules at the cost of $962.5 million. Intended for use by the Indian Special Forces, the aircraft were all delivered by 2010-11 - ahead of the schedule. Happy with the performance of the new aircraft and the delivery schedule, the IAF is planning to induct six more C-130Js in the near future. Lockheed Martin's success in bagging the first major IAF order was then replicated by the Boeing when Indian signed another LOA in June 2011 for procurement of 10 C-17 Globemaster III heavy lift aircraft at the cost of $4.116 billion. The delivery of the aircraft is scheduled for completion between June 2013 and June 2015. Like in the case of C-130J, IAF also plans to increase its C-17 fleet by 10 more of such planes.

The IAF's AN-32 fleet inducted between 1984 and 1991 is presently going through a major modernisation under a $400 million contract signed with Ukraine in 2009. Of the total 105 AN-32s, 40 are being upgraded in Ukraine and rest will be done India. The upgrades, which will increase the service life by 15 years to upto 40 years, also include noise suspension, collision avoidance and ground proximity warning systems, and satellite navigation - among others.

In a major boost to the Indian private sector, the Defence Acquisition Council (DAC) – the highest decision making body in the MoD – in a July 2012 meeting gave its nod to the IAF's Rs. 119 billion proposal to procure 56 aircraft (of 6-8 tonne class) as replacement of HAL-built Hawker Siddeley 748M Avro aircraft. The decision was then followed by issuance of RFP in November 2012 to five global manufactures - Russian Ilyushin, Ukrainian Antonov, European EADS, Italian Alenia Aeronautica and Swedish SAAB. As per the RFP terms, the aircraft are to be procured through the 'Buy and Make' route of the MoD's Defence Procurement Procedure- 2011, with the condition that the foreign vendor will select a private Indian company for manufacturing 40 aircraft in India (initial 16 aircrafts to be procured off-the-shelf). The deliveries of aircraft would commence within 24 months from the date of signing the contract and would be completed over a period of eight years. The RFP also stipulates that of the 40 aircraft to be manufacture in India, 16 must have 30 per cent indigenous content which would increase to 60 per cent for the rest 24 aircrafts.

Trainer

The IAF's basic flying training (or Stage-I training) got a shot in arm when the government after some delay and controversy finally signed a contract on May 24, 2012 with Swiss company Pilatus Aircraft Ltd for supply of 75 PC-7 Mk-II turbo prop basic trainer aircrafts (BTA). As per the contract, valued Rs 29 billion, all the aircraft are scheduled for delivery between February 2013 and August 2015. The Pilatus contract may further be swelled with the MoD reportedly 'rejecting' on cost ground the state-owned aerospace major HAL's proposal to supply 106 trainers from 2016 onwards. If the Swiss company succeeds in fishing in HAL's misery, it may end up meeting IAF's entire BTA fleet. Presently the IAF does not have a BTA since the entire fleet of HPT-32 (114 aircraft) was grounded after a fatal accident in July 2009.

Apart from the BTA, IAF has also set its eye on modernising its fleet of Intermediate jet Trainers (IJT) – for stage-II training - as its current fleet of 81 IJT Kirans inducted in seventies is on the verge of retirement. Although HAL has an order to produce 85 IJTs (including 12 Limited Series Production), the project is running behind the schedule. As against planned delivery from June 2012 onwards, the HAL is still struggling with the flight testing. This has not only displeased the IAF but could lead to procurement from the foreign sources given the criticality of training and the obsolescence of Kirans.

Unlike the basic and intermediate trainers, the IAF is however comfortable with its advanced jet trainers. So far IAF has contracted 106 AJT Hawks (as against the requirement of same number) from UK through two separate agreements signed in 2004 and 2010.

Force Multiplier

Among other major aerial platforms, the IAF has inducted or in the process of inducting aerial refuelling and airborne surveillance aircraft, in a move to enhance its force multiplier capability. The IAF, which is looking at midair refuelling a mandatory capability in its all on-going and future aerial platform purchases, is hoping that it is second time luck in concluding the $1.0 billion tender for 6 mid-air refuellers, to add to the six IL 78 procured in early 2000s. Pending the government announcement, Airbus has already issued a statement (on January 7th), stating that it has been 'selected' as the 'preferred bidder to supply its A330 MRTT Multi Role Tanker Transport to the Indian Air Force (IAF)." Airbus's win, which comes against Russian IL 78, also means Moscow's third straight defeat in India's competitive bidding process. Earlier, Russia lost to the US for two IAF tenders for attack and heavy lift helicopters.

India has a total requirement of at least 20 AWACS (airborne warning and control system), and AEW&C (airborne early warning and control) aircraft to maintain border and coastline surveillance. So far, the IAF has already inducted three IL-76-based Phalcon AWACS with two more under the pipeline. The first three AWACS, the contract of which was singed in March 2004 under a tripartite $1.1 billion deal among India, Israel and Russia, were the delivered in 2009 and 2010 and 2011, respectively. As a follow-on order to the 2004, agreement, the MoD has in December 2012 given its nod to procure two more AWACS, thus eventually increasing the total AWACS fleet to five. The imported

AWACS fleet is soon going to be joined by three indigenous AEW&C systems based on the Brazilian Embraer platform. The first Embaraer aircraft fitted with the DRDO-developed AEW&C reached India in September 2012 for further testing before its induction in IAF.

Miscellaneous

Apart from the major platforms, the IAF modernization also includes induction of other systems, including simulators, air defence system and precision-guided weapons. Presently out of 46 simulators, 30 are operational, with others in the process of being replaced. Regarding radars, the IAF apart from the induction and imminent induction of AWACS and indigenous AW&CS, is in process of fielding a host of radars including Medium Powered Radars (MPR), Low Level Transportable Radars (LLTR), Low Light Weight Radars (LLWR), and Aerostat Systems. To give a further push to the Air Defence sector, a range of missile systems comprising of short range surface to air missile (SAM), medium range SAM and long range SAM are being introduced.

AIR DOMINANCE AND FORCE PROJECTION

Indian subcontinent witnessed exponential increase in acquisition and/ or development of conventional aeroplanes as early as 1950s. Immediately after independence in 1947, both India and Pakistan started acquiring aeroplanes from the western nations viz, France, UK and USA. China too was busy acquiring vintage, but still airworthy variants of MiG family from the erstwhile USSR.

India took a giant leap in the sphere of producing indigenous fighter when the first home production, the HF-24 flew on 24th June, 1961. HF-24 was a twin engine, swept wing design fighter with power controls, which could fly at speeds in excess of 900 kmph, inspite of being relatively under powered keeping in view its overall weight. Notwithstanding numerous shortcomings/limitations, HF-24 raised quite a few eyebrows in the developed and militarily advanced nations viz USA and USSR. These nations considered entry of a third world nation in the exclusive domain of production of state of art fighter aeroplane as threat to their continued primacy, not only in the sphere of military aviation but also in the economic arena. Sale of military hardware has been and continues to remain the most prominent money chirner for advanced nations viz USA, Russia, France and UK etc after the end of second world war.

By any standards, it was a crowning achievement of scientists and technicians of a fledgling nation within 14 years of getting independence. India was well on its way to become a formidable Air Power in South Asia.

Three successive wars in 62, 65 and 71 changed the scenario of indigenous development of aeroplanes. Military and Political leadership led by less than informed bureaucrats decided for acquisition from foreign vendors. On the face of it, such option might not appear to be a wrong option because we needed military hardware, aeroplanes included, in large numbers almost immediately. Home production was in no position to meet the demands. But what is incomprehensible is the fact that we deliberately opted to slow down and finally stop indigenous development, which is what we did by consigning HF-24 to museums in late seventies/early eighties.

HF-24 PROGRAMME closure would perhaps rank as the worst ever collectivedecision taken by Military (IAF in particular), Bureaucratic and Political leadership against the national interests and Security. Without doubt foreign vendors must have popped the champagne to celebrate their unbridled primacy in the field of aeroplane manufacturing. Had we continued development of further variants, we would indeed have become an Aerospace power in the 80s itself.

Perhaps our decision to discontinue the HF-24 programme was also influenced by an equally myopic decision by UK in opting to discontinue the TSR-2 development programme around the same time.Mr Duncan Sandys, a British Member of Parliament, was instrumental in discontinuance of TSR-2 development programme. The learned but ill-informed MP argued that due to advent of HEAT SEEKING Air-to-Air Missiles, the days of manned fighters were over. Rest is history.

An objective analysis would indicate that weare truly not an Aerospace Power. We have, as yet, not become a substantive Aerospace Power primarily because of two reasons. Firstly the lopsided and flawed Defence Procurement Policy and secondly, near total absence of any worthwhile R&D during the period 1960 till 1980s. Merely establishing defence laboratories and ordnance factories was not enough. Had we continued with the HF -24 programme and taken it to higher levels, we might have had indigenous force multipliers, fighter aeroplanes, heavy lift helicopters and transport, radars, SAMs etc of proven operational capability matching in performance with the best systems available.

A nation does not become Aerospace Power on borrowed(read imported) hardware. Nation's Defence Establishment over the years comprising of RakshaMantris, DefenceSecrataries and Service Chiefs have not exerted themselves as they should have over the years. Euphoria of 1971 victory and almost self defeating decision by the then Prime Minister Smt Indira Gandhi to keep Defence portfolio with herself led to the "defence minister as PM" becoming inaccessible to the executives of the defence establishment. Everything related to defence affairs slowed down. Her autocratic style of functioning made the matters even worse. Service Chiefs could hardly find the ears of the RakshaMantri, the PM.

Ordnance Factories, most of these, have merely attained the status of money guzzlers with hardly anything to show for such massive infra-structure and investment in place. Ordnance Factory Board, the controlling apex organization has been worthless and has done immense dis-service to the nation. Most of these factories deserve to be shut down and an entirely new techno-management organization should be structured.

Defence Research Development Organisation (DRDO) is yet another bureaucratic behemoth with nothing spectacular to its credit. All projects, without exception, have never met pre decided time lines. Even the quality of finished product continues to be questionable.

Indeed there has been a silver lining in an otherwise bleak military hardware development programme. The Surface to Surface Missile programme under civilian control led by our erstwhile President Dr APJ Abdul Kalam has become a world class SSM programme. We have already perfected technology to mass produce SSMs of 5,000km range. However we still have to pefect cryogenic engine technology.

Satellite fabrication technology has also achieved many landmarks. Our scientists have manufactured sensors installed on satellites for multi-dimensional use from weather monitoring, education, TV transmission, agricultural information etc. At the same time few of these could even monitor ballistic missile launch etc. It might appear to be irony of sorts; the SSM and Satellite development programmes have been totally civilian with hardly any military control. Indian military leadership, past and present, may like to ponder over this.

Our capability to produce force multipliers viz AEW/AWACS, Mid Air Refuellers, ECM Systems, Reliable Cryogenic Engines, SAMs etc remains woefully inadequate. What is worse is that it is not likely to be any better in foreseeable future.

Before entering into the domain of what constitutes an Aerospace Power, the difference between Air Power and Aerospace Power must be understood. Except in case of the erstwhile super powers, USA and USSR, almost all other nations have acquired air power components based on regional threat. Conventional Air Power comprises of three elementsviz the Strike Element (fighter aeroplanes, Attack Helicopters etc), the Logistic Element (Transport aeroplanes, Helicopters etc) and Ground Based elements, viz Radars etc. A fourth element has been added in recent years in the form of Force Multipliers viz Mid Air Refuellers, AEW/AWACS, RPVs, Drones, SSMs etc. Relatively more expensive component of Air Power, the Strike Element has little or no use for the nation during peace time. Indeed it remains as the most effective deterrent as a FORCE IN BEING that must remain operational so that if the need arises it can be brought to bear upon the adversary almost instantaneously. Logistic Element of Air Power is the most important component during peace time. Aid to civil power becomes a major commitment during peace time and in times of natural calamity, civil disturbance etc.

Strike element of Indian Air Power has been used only twice during peace time. Once during the Nagaland crisis led by Phizo, when Mysteres were used for straffing the Naga rebels hideouts. Second occasion was during Goa operations, when Canberras were used for bombing.

Aerospace Power on the other hand has numerous other functions to support national requirements related directly to economic development and is constituted keeping in view the Global scenario. Other than support to Military, Aerospace Power contributes to following areas, which cannot be taken care of by conventional air power:-

- Telecommunication
- Academics
- Tele-medicine
- Cartography
- Weather Monitoring
- Monitoring Bio-diversity
- Soil Conservation
- Forestry Management
- Land Cover for Wild Life Sanctuaries
- Agricultural Produce Estimates
- Flood Inundation Mapping

Thus Air Power is actually a constituent of Aerospace Power. Global militarization on a very large scale, induction of sophisticated weapons has led to an uneasy state of peace. The situation is almost akin to the cold war period when the two super powers could not risk to escalate tensions and wage a nuclear war. Consequences of such miscalculation were bound to be disastrous for the entire world. "Mutually assured Destruction", a term coined during the height of cold war is applicable in modern times more than ever before. Crippling damage can result even with conventional weapons.

Rapidly changing global world order, which has moved from conflict between nations to conflict based onideology and religion coupled withmisplaced/irrational beliefs of few nations about their right to interfere in governance in the contiguous region. For instance birth of ISIS, Russia's unilateral action in Ukraine and China's continued attempt at throwing the gauntlet in South China Sea emerging as one of the foremost maritime challenge after second world war. It is in this context that it becomes imperative that India move towards becoming a substantive Aerospace Power. But for that to translate into action, Indian leadership, both political and military, must adopt a doctrinal approach.

Hence in order to maintain primacy in the comity of nations in the international arena, nations have taken a conscious decision to become aerospace power rather than remain content from being a formidable Air Power. Primary constituents/capability of an aerospace power could be broadly termed as:-

- Proven Launch Vehicle/s.
- Outstanding expertise in Satellite Fabrication.
- Development of Electro-optical Sensors.
- Sustainable and Consistent rate of Satellite Production.
- Development of Reusable Launch Vehicles.
- Miniature Warheads: Conventional and Nuclear.
- Advanced Metallurgy.
- Ground Infra-structure viz monitoring/tracking stations etc.
- Advanced Ground Testing Facilities.
- Launch Pads.
- Suitable Parking Slot/s for Geo-stationary Satellites.
- Operationally Deployed BMEWS/BMD Systems.
- Anti-satellite(ASAT) Weapons.

At this stage it would be pertinent to clarify that possession of launch vehicles, indigenous or imported and warheads alone does not qualify a nation from becoming an Aerospace Power. Indeed launch vehicle and warheads are two of the prime constituents of an Aerospace Power, but merely their presence not supported by capabilities listed above, does not make them an Aerospace power. Pakistan and North Korea would then be termed as an Aerospace Power. Ballistic missile threat has become the most feared situation in the event of hostilities. Thus alongwith development of strike capability by using ballistic missiles, nations have embarked on systems that would protect against a ballistic missile threat. Hence nations have concentrated on developing Ballistic Missile Early Warning Systems(BMEWS) and a protective shield, the Ballistic Missile Defence Systems(BMDS). Efficacy of each of these will now be highlighted.

Famous US project/system codenamed STAR WARS was developed during the height of cold war. Operational capability/effectiveness of this system can be at best a matter of conjecture even as on date. Proposed European Ballistic Missile Shield to protect against Ballistic Missile attacks is the latest system under development at cost of billions of dollars. BMEWS and BMDS, irrespective of their origin, have never been tested under operational(warlike) conditions, hence the degree of reliability claimed by systems manufacturers cannot be trusted.

What should ring alarm bells amongst the protagonists of BMEW/BMD is a recent update by Pentagon, wherein operational efficacy of THAAD, Aegis and Patriot Systems has been questioned.All tests involving destruction of an incoming ballistic missile threat by all nations have been conducted in highly controlled environment, in which vital parameters of the 'enemy' ballistic missile were already knownviz launch window, likely trajectory etc, which will not be the case in an actual war scenario. Interceptor was ready for engagement. To elaborate further without going into technological details a ballistic missile threat can be neutralized only and only if the exact launch window, trajectory and probable target is known. In case of actual war scenario, the launch window will never be known. Suffice to say thatneither the existing BMEW/BMD systems nor the systems likely to be developed in foreseeable future, could be termed as fool proof that would provide assured protection against an incoming ballistic missile. Lessons learnt from anti-aircraft missiles (air to air and SAMs)kill capabilitywould suffice to prove the likely effectiveness of the BMDsystem/s for a successful intercept of an incoming ballistic missile with extremely small radar signature. Guaranteed protection is a far cry. ICBMs deployed all over the world carry multiple warheads alongwith dummies that behave in exactly the same manner as a live warhead. There is no technology available to differentiate between the two. Further it is extremely difficult, if not impossible,to guarantee intercept during the ballistic phase, when radar signatures are feeble. A ballistic missile has most prominent heat signature during launch phase but the window of intercept during this phase is extremely narrow. Even if it was to be assumed that the missile shield will provide 100% guarantee of successful intercept, the fact remains that warhead will explode and cause radio activity to spread not necessarily over the intended target. Exo-atmospheric interception would remain a better option as compared with endo-atmospheric intercept either during launch or re-entry phase.

Utopian thoughts such as making the world free of nuclear weapons will remain a distant dream. Nuclear tipped missiles will continue to remain on top of the list of most devastating weapon systems against which there is/will be no assured protection. Launch vehicle capability will decide the distance to which the warhead could be hurled.

Possibility of an armed conflict between nations is slowly but surely receding. Unfortunately, however, there is no cause for mankind to rejoice because a far more dangerous and unpredictable power in form of radicals has emerged/is emerging all over the world. These groups have no international boundaries as exists between nations. Alignment of such extremist groups with rogue nations can translate into violence of gigantic proportions. If such extremist elements/organisationscould get hold of a nuclear tipped ballistic missile system and/or sufficient quantities of fissile material from rogue nations having launch platforms and warheads, threat of nuclear tipped missile launch cannot be ruled out. No military strategist can even hazard a guess/predict the intended time/target for such cases. An organization like ISIS, which burns and beheads human beings with impunity can, rather will resort to such actions without doubt.

In the prevailing geo-political scenario, India as an Aerospace Power should not only develop the above stated capabilities but also may have to re-examine the"NO FIRST USE" policy with respect to use of nuclear weapons against a rogue nation/group. A rogue nation and/or group must be conveyed that should our national interests be threatened, we will not hesitate in carrying out a pre-emptive nuclear strike. Such resolve/policy would be a far better deterrent and protect our national interests rather than a ballistic missile shield. The age old principle of "Threat in being" neutralized by "Forces in being" is not applicable in the case of rogue nations/groups.

Our stated policy of non-alignment has kept us out of any military alliance viz NATO, Warsaw Pact etc. However in reality we have had to concede ground to nations from which we import military hardware.In order to remain trulynon-aligned, a nation must be nearly self sufficient with respect to security issues.

Unfortunately our myopic leadership and flawed acquisition/indigenous manufacturing policies over the years have made Indian Military entirely dependent on imported hardware. Nearly 80% of our military hardware is of Russian origin.

Even the ammunition/missiles/bombs/PGMs etc are imported. In the recent years our shift to other nations viz France, Israel and USA has not been taken very kindly by the Russians. We continue to occupy the top position as the largest exporter of military hardware.

In strictest sense our non-aligned status remains on paper. The truth and harsh fact is that for our security needs we are and will continue to remain dependent on nations from which military hardware is importedviz Russia, USA, France, Israel etc. Selling of arms is the top money earner for any nation. Our position as arms exporter is perhaps at the bottom of the list, primarily because our inefficient and poorly managed defence industry. Fortunately our diplomacy has been able to sustain our military posturing in the region.We, however, continue to remain at the "mercy" of military hardware exporting nations because of long term dependence on the exporting nation. Inspite of being an export oriented Air Power, a recent study published placesIAF seventh amongst top ten Air Powers in the world.

Creating, maintaining, sustaining and finally deploying the military assets define the national power. Overall power of a nation can be subdivided/ classified as under:-

- Military Power
- Economic Power
- Soft Power

Achieving top military/economic power status by India, even in Asia would be a difficult, if not impossible. However current economic growth and future projections as per IMF, our economy might double by 2020. To sustain unbridled national growth in all spheres, we must be 'militarily' strong. That can be achieved if we focus on attaining a top SOFT POWER status, which is possible.

It would neither be prudent nor technologically possible to bridge the yawning technological and manufacturing capability gap in the field of shipping, aeroplanes, weapons etc. The only option we have is to expand in the field of our strength, which are satellite manufacturing and launch vehicle design and production.

We can safely move into the top echelons of Aerospace Powers by manufacturing and demonstrating that not only can we fabricate satellites embedded with suitable sensors for national applications but also have thesatellite neutralization/destruction capability. Wasting time, effort and money in indigenous manufacture/imports to acquire BMEW/BMD systems will be counter productive.

The world today has become increasingly dependent on transponders embedded in satellites. Destroying few important functional satellites can virtually 'blind' the nation to which those satellites belonged. Deployed satellites are in different parking slots allotted to each nation in case of Geo-stationary satellites. Others are in Geo-synchronous orbit around the earth and many more in Molniya orbit. Thus orbit parameters of most of the satellites in orbit are known to everyone.

We must adopt a fundamentally different approach in acquiring Aerospace Power status. In that we must firstly aim to achieve fabrication of satellites embedded with sensors required towards national development thus becoming a prominent SOFT POWER. Currently transponders numbering around 200 are installed in various satellites of Indian origin.

We need to increase this number to around 500 by 2020. Secondly, in order to maintain a viable, effective and strong deterrent we should focus on satellite destruction capability of our adversaries, if and when the need arises. We can accomplish this within ourexisting technological capability envelope. Nations are developing missiles to destroy satellites. Few nations have attempted it but success rate is unlikely to be high and/or guaranteed.

Position of all satellites in their respective orbits is known. As a concept, if a nation desires to destroy the satellite of her adversary, placing an explosive laden satellite in close proximity of intended target satellite and exploding it would cripple the target satellite.

Geo-stationary and Geo-synchronous satellites could be engaged with relative ease as compared to satellites in Molniya orbit. Engaging a satellite in Molniya orbit at/or near the perigee might be relatively more difficult than engaging it at the Apogee, when target satellite would be at the slowest speed in its orbit.

Satellite destruction capability would have an adverse fall out as well. It will give rise to uncontrollable space debris, which would remain in orbit for years. Anti-satellite weapon development, viable economically and technically, therefore, is a distinct possibility and should be explored.

Anti missile weapon system will require extensive and highly advanced tracking infra-structure spread all over the world. Still guarantee for successful intercept cannot be assumed because each strike missile will have a different trajectory. Even if a small portion of the missile trajectory falls in no radar coverage area, chances of intercept would virtually be Zero. However in case of anti satellite system no such dilemma exists because satellite orbits are known since these are pre-designated.

Most nations, India included, which are involved in development of BMEW/BMD systems are actually influenced by US infatuation with ballistic missile defence shield and incurring huge amounts in procuring a non-functional and unreliable system. In order to influence other nations US strategists have successfully embarked on linking Nuclear Deterrence and Ballistic Missile Shield and have succeeded.

An objective analysis would reveal that development programme of Ballistic Missile Defence Systems was in fact a planned "Economic Weapon" against the erstwhile USSR to bleed it economically. Indeed the US succeeded in its plan beyond its wildest imagination.

Each nation, individually as well as in a group, is spending (read wasting) huge amounts of money in developing a system that is bound to under perform under operational conditions. In a make believe world of ballistic missile defence systems, new technologies and systems are being sold to less than informed nations. All known/proclaimed ballistic missile defence systems are highly localized and their effectiveness against supersonic missiles with extremely small radar cross section is highly questionable notwithstanding various test results under controlled conditions.

A key component of Aerospace Power is development of Drone technology, both for surveillance and attack purposes. Our progress in this field has been tardy. Extensive and deliberate effort in R&D to develop high quality/capability drones must become one of our top priorities.

Budgetary support for R&D merits a total overhaul in our thinking so far. DRDO is assumed to be the sole proprietor of R&D. In order to retain our top class engineers from IITs, we must offer them better R&D facilities than USA to reduce/prevent the brain drain. At least 1% of the GDP must be allocated for R&D in diverse fields. R&D has been our weakest link in overall national development.While our software engineers rule the world but we have virtually nothing to show in the hardware domain. We cannot, should not and must not subjugate ourselves voluntarily to wear a tag of a "Data-entry" nation. Unless we change our outlook towards investment in R&D, we as a nation would never become the global power that we can become.

For all or some of the above suggestions to fructify, we have to alter our thinking radically. Aerospace Power is not to be assumed as an extension of Air Power. In fact Air Power is one of the many constituents of Aerospace Power.

In short term Strike element of Air Power will continue to remain a formidable and most preferred option in the event almost instantaneous pre-emptive/retaliatory strike is required against an adversary. In long term Aerospace Power can be used to strike telling blow by destroying satellites belonging to adversary. During peace time Aerospace Power would contribute significantly to overall growth of the nation. Every component of Aerospace Power listed above has a definite function towards making us a potent Soft Power.

INDIAN AIR FORCE UPGRADES IN THE NEXT DECADE

THE threat scenario is periodically reviewed by the Indian Air Force and steps taken to meet any eventuality. This includes induction of new aircraft and air defence assets as well as upgrade of the operational capability of existing assets.

The IAF has prepared a comprehensive Long Term Perspective Pan (LTPP) till the year 2027 for modernization of its fleet to meet the security challenges. The IAF is in the process of inducting various types of fighter aircraft like Medium, Multi Role Combat Aircraft (MMRCA), Light Combat Aircraft (LCA), SU-30 MK1 and Fifth Generation Fighter Aircraft (FGFA). The Government has allocated adequate funds for the purpose.

The Indian Air Force (IAF) has ambitious plans to transform itself into one of the most modern air forces in the world by acquiring capabilities across the entire spectrum of war fighting over the next decade. Indian Air force will be spending US$70 billion on procurement and upgrades in the next decade.

The IAF envisages transforming itself into a potent and networked aerospace power through three aspects. For decades the IAF had largely been tethered to one non-western source. Much of the inventory acquired through this route has now been overtaken by obsolescence. As a result, in recent years, there has been an alarming erosion in combat power and other capabilities. Even after prolonged and reportedly vigorous effort, the indigenous Research & Development Organisations and the Aerospace Industry have not been able to provide a respectable degree of self reliance to the IAF. The near total dependence on foreign sources for cutting edge technology and frontline equipment is potentially perhaps the most debilitating factor that often threatens to seriously undermine the capability of the IAF.

First and foremost priority for IAF has been to induct and integrate new technology weapon platforms and upgrade the existing inventory. IAF has a long list of acquisitions which includes 126 MMRCA; 214 fifth generation fighter aircraft which will be coming around 2017; additional 42 SU30's for which IAF has already issued RFP to HAL; 75 trainers for which process is well on its way; two more AWACS of IL-76 base; ten C-17s; 80 + 59 medium-lift helicopters; 22 attack helicopters; 12 VVIP helicopters.

There are upgrades also going on for weapon systems: 63 MiG-29's, that upgrade is well on its way in Russia. Mirage 2000 upgrade has gone to the CCS and Jaguar re-engineering, that is another major project for which a new RFP has been issued already.

In the Missiles segment, IAF has 18 firing units of MRSAM (Medium Range Surface to Air Missiles), four Spyders, 49 SR-SAM that is short range, 8 Aakash missiles. There are different stages of missiles coming — a multi-layered defence which is what is desirable in air defence. Plus it has the AWACS and from the AWACS to the IACCS.

In radars, IAF has got Rohinis, aerostats, medium-power radars, low-level tactical radars, low-level light weight radars, AFNET which is already active, besides the MAFI (Modernisation of Airport Infrastructure) which is going on. The first airfield to convert on to MAFI would be Bhatinda. IAF has the IACCS which is active, so all-round development of the Indian Air Force is in the offing.

IAF radars have complete coverage at medium and high levels. It has some gap at the low levels because the capability of ground base radars is limited because of the earth's curvature. To fill these gaps, IAF has many other schemes in place. Firstly low-level radars, the medium-power radars, the LLTRS, the LLWRs, they fill in the low-level gap.

It has got the AWACS and the aerostats which actually raises the platform of the radar so it increases the range of the radar. Most of them are on track and 2012 onward, they will start ramping up. The first medium-powered radar at Naliya - was inaugurated earlier this year. The second important aspect is the induction and training of manpower to handle the new inventory. Though the manpower intake has improved a little bit, but it is still not up to the desired standards.

IAF is taking various measures such as inducting candidates before their 12th standard and degree and giving them a degree in the Air Force. IAF is approaching various regions to find new talent. Also, the emphasis is been made to retain them. It is improving the training patterns. Not surprisingly, in the last three financial years the IAF has been allocated more money for capital acquisition than the other two services and is likely to get more funds than the Army and the Navy in the next few years.

Despite the limitations, the IAF has managed to attain and project an image of a potent force capable to preserving the sovereignty of the Indian skies and in more recent times, to project power albeit limited in quantum and reach. And even in the future there appears to be no option but to procure advanced technology and hardware from abroad. There is however an attempt to indigenize products through co-development, co-production and the difficult, but innovative, concept of "Offsets". This route is the most expedient under the circumstances to accord military hardware a semblance of Indian character.

Life of a modern weapon system is in the region of thirty years which is normally extendable by another 10 to 15 years after a mid-life upgrade. New equipment procured for the IAF over the next decade will remain operational up to 2050 at the very least, possibly up to 2060. As the nature of warfare itself is undergoing transformation, it is necessary to make a comprehensive reassessment of the contours of the operational scenario that the IAF will have to contend with and reconfigure its inventory accordingly. To do this at this point in time, the IAF needs to take note of India's regional power status in the emerging world order and assess its possible role and responsibility in the new geopolitical and geostrategic environment.

Tejas—India's Big Defence Leap

The Indian Defence industry has posted a significant milestone on January 10, when the Indian Air Force formally granted initial operational clearance to the country's first indigenously manufactured light combat aircraft, marking the culmination of nearly two decades of work by Indian defence scientists and technicians. Named the Tejas, the aircraft will initially form one squadron (20 aircraft) in the IAF.

The Tejas was designed by the Aeronautical Development Agency (ADA) under the Defence Ministry-controlled Defence Research and Development Organisation. The project was conceived and launched in 1983, with an expected budget of Rs560 crore (about $5.6 billion), but test flights weren't launched until 2001.

The project, which has its fair share of critics in India—and even within the Indian Air Force—has seen numerous ups and downs during the course of its long journey to service. But 10 years after the initial test flights, the fourth-generation plus aircraft has finally arrived. Admittedly, there are still some doubts over the fact that the LCA's engine, radar, some navigation technologies and some of its displays are imported. But officials at the ADA asserted ahead of the launch that the design, development, testing, certification and mastery of the system engineering are completely Indian.

There are just six to eight countries in the world that can design, develop, test and certify a fighter aircraft—India is now one among them. ADA already has a road map in place for future development of the Tejas. Over the next five years, the Tejas will be completely indigenous and the higher variant will be ready by 2014. Even without any further refinement, the current batch of Tejas aircraft is comparable with Sweden's Gripen, the Chinese-Pakistan J-17 Thunder and the South Korean T-50 jets. If all goes well, over the next decade, both the manufacturers and the Indian Air Force are planning to increase that number to 200 aircraft, if not more. But even without these kinds of numbers, India's Defence Ministry will be celebrating the induction of the LCA Tejas as a major turning point in its effort to indigenise the country's defence production sector.

Procurement of Combat Aircraft

Su-30 MKI aircraft and Tejas Light Combat Aircraft are the major modern combat aircraft that have been contracted for induction into the Indian Air

Force (IAF). The total cost of procurement of the Su-30 MKI is over Rs55,717 crore while the cost of procurement of the Teja Light Combat Aircraft is about Rs8691 crore. Capacity for design and manufacture of modern combat aircraft involves development of very high and sophisticated technology skills which is a gradual process.

Technology denial regimes have thwarted this effort in the past. The Defence Procurement Procedure provides for procurement of aircraft and their subsequent manufacture in India. Hence, major aircraft procurement programme entail a mix of outright purchase from abroad and subsequent manufacture in India with increasing levels of indigenization. Hindustan Aeronautics Limited (HAL) is already manufacturing the Su-30 MKI aircraft as well as the Tejas Light Combat Aircraft for the IAF. Further, HAL would also eventually be manufacturing the Medium Multi-Role Combat Aircraft (MMRCA) and Fifth Generation Fighter Aircraft (FGFA) planned for induction into the IAF.

AIR FORCE MODERNIZATION: AIR DOMINANCE AND FORCE PROJECTION

Until recently, India's traditional strategic sphere lay between the Gulf of Aden and the Strait of Malacca; but with India's global footprint expanding, the Indian Air Force should be ready to serve wherever the country's future strategic interests lie. The air force is gearing up to provide the strategic outreach that India needs as a growing regional power and to project power where necessary in order to defend vital national interests. According to Kapil Kak, a retired air vice marshal and senior defense analyst, although there is a gap between vision and capability with regard to shaping India's strategic neighborhood, forward movement is now visible. In his view, the modernization plans of the air force are aimed at achieving the following objectives:

- Air dominance and control of the air
- Deterrence, by both denial and punishment
- Long-range offensive reach—penetration, precision, persistence, and parallelity—in simultaneous operations at the tactical, operational, and strategic levels
- Strategic air-lift capability for power projection through both hard and soft power, such as humanitarian assistance and disaster relief operations and diaspora evacuation
- Build-up of capability for coercion
- Acquisition of force enablers and multipliers and related combat-support systems, including networking for tri-service command and control

- Capability of conducting cyberspace and information operations
- Indigenization of future capabilities for design and development

From a sanctioned strength of 39 squadrons, the Indian Air Force is down to 34 squadrons at present, due to decades of neglect, but hopes to enhance its strength to 42 squadrons by 2022. Yet plans to acquire 126 multi-mission, medium-range combat aircraft—in order to maintain an edge over the regional air forces—are stuck in the procurement quagmire. Tejas, the indigenously designed light combat aircraft, which is expected to replace the obsolescent Mig-21, is still a few years away from becoming fully operational. India is also developing a fifth-generation fighter jointly with Russia and aims to fly it in 2015. New fighter bombers include a fleet of 272 Sukhoi-30 MKIs, half of which have already been built. AEW aircraft are being acquired from Israel as well as being developed indigenously. India has also acquired 6 C-130J Super Hercules aircraft for its special forces and will likely order 6 more from the United States. C-17 Globemaster heavy-lift aircraft are also likely to be acquired shortly, which will take India's defense cooperation with the United States to a new level. Although a contract has been signed with a Swiss firm for 75 Pilatus PC-7 basic trainer aircraft, India's fleet of jet trainers continues to be deficient. In the rotary-wing category, the indigenously manufactured Dhruv utility helicopter has entered service. The air force is also in the process of acquiring medium-lift transport helicopters and attack helicopters.

In keeping with developments in the region, India's strategic forces are also modernizing at a steady pace. The Agni-I and Agni-II missiles are now fully operational. Immediate requirements include the Agni-V intermediate-range ballistic missile, which has a 5,000-km range, and nuclear-powered submarines with suitable ballistic missiles to provide genuine second-strike capability. As noted above, the INS *Arihant,* India's first indigenously built nuclear submarine, will likely become fully operational by late 2014. While India's emphasis is on mobile missile launchers, a small number of hardened silos are also being constructed.

The armed forces do not currently have a truly integrated tri-service C4I2SR system suitable for network-centric warfare, which would allow them to optimize their individual capabilities; however, plans have been made to develop such a system in the next five to ten years. In fact, all new weapons and equipment acquisitions are now being planned on a tri-service basis to ensure interoperability.

INDIA: AIRPORT PROJECTS IN INDIA: THE PRIVATISATION PROCESS

India is at the threshold of emerging as an economic power. However, it is recognised that infrastructure holds the key to this transformation. The infrastructure gap in India is obvious to all. Of late the Government has dedicated itself to address this on a war footing. The task is huge. It involves not only harnessing financial resources but also technology and know-how. Around the world more and more airports are moving towards privatization. This is the trend in Asia, Europe and Latin America. In India too private participation is felt necessary and therefore the Government has opened up this sector to the Public Private Participation (PPP) route.

At first blush, it may seem that Government's efforts are too little too late but it may be worthwhile to bear in mind that air traffic in India has witnessed a 35 percent average growth, year upon year, for the past about 6 years, as against the global growth of only 9 percent per annum. In this chapter we explore the path adopted by the Government so far in airport privatisation. Essentially we look at three segments:

First, we examine the basic approach in the Concession Agreements (Agreements), comparing both the Greenfield and Brownfield sectors.

Second, we draw attention to the need to have an independent Regulator in place and

Third, we examine the dispute resolution mechanism put in place in the Agreements.

Basic approach in the Concession Agreements:

So far the Government has signed off four Concession Agreements - two in the Greenfield sector (Bangalore and Hyderabad) and two in the Brownfield sector (Delhi and Mumbai).

For the purposes of this chapter we take up the Agreements for Bangalore and New Delhi as our model (i.e. one in the Greenfield and the other in the Brownfield sector).

Notwithstanding the privatization route, the Government has retained in these airports 26 percent shareholding (either through the Airport Authority of India or through the State Government).

This crucial 26 percent shareholding ensures that the Government is able to veto certain "fundamental resolutions", which as per the Companies Act requires a minimum of 75 percent shareholders vote (for instance, issuance of new shares; change of directors; change of auditors etc).

Hence the Government does continue to retain some level of control over the private entity.

The commercial backbone of the project is the large chunk of land the private entity is "gifted" i.e. allowed to develop along with the airport for any commercial purpose it may please (subject to local laws). Here it may set up not only hotels or malls - it can even go for Special Economic Zones, manufacturing factories, country clubs, golf courses, power plant etc. At Bangalore the concessionaire got about 300 acres of land and at New Delhi 250 acres for free commercial development.

Nature of the concession

Basically the concession is for construction, development, operation and maintenance of the airport over a period of 30 years (concession period) extendable at the sole option of the concessionaire by another 30 years - (i.e. total 60 years). The land is leased out to the concessionaire by the State Government at a nominal rent.

The Government has extended its full commitment and support for the project; for instance, the Bangalore concession Agreement states, "GOI acknowledges and supports the implementation of project". It further states that the Government of India will not take any steps or action in contradiction with the concession Agreement which results in or would result in its shareholders or the lenders being deprived or substantially deprived of their investment or economic interest in the project. Further all statutory and non-statutory bodies under the control of the central Government will act in compliance with the concession agreement as if they are a party thereto and the Government of India shall ensure that all statutory compliances as may be required are granted promptly. The State Governments have similarly entered into State Support Agreements. This is a unique feature in airport privatization Agreements. The Port sector or Road sector do not have similar obligations on the Government.

Types of construction

Here we find a departure between the approach taken in the Greenfield sector and the Brownfield sector While the Greenfield projects, pretty much leave it to the concessionaire to plan the construction, as per the approved Master Plan, the Brownfield agreements are far more specific. The agreement for New Delhi for instance stipulates development of a Master Plan within six months of the agreement.

This is to be updated and reviewed every 10 years. Any delay in submission of the Master-Plan would entail liquidated damages at the rate of US$ 65000 per day. The concession Agreement sets out certain type of works called the "Mandatory Capital Projects" (which are set forth in a Schedule). For instance, for New Delhi airport, a parallel runway is listed as one such work, which is required to be completed within 24 months of the signing of the agreement and if it is not, liquidated damages would follow. Then, there is a category of works which fall under the heading of "Major Development Plan". These comprise of projects expected to have a capital cost in excess of US $ 25 million.

All the above are subject to review and approval by the Government. While strict time lines are stipulated for submissions of the Plans for approval, the AAI or the Government concerned is not obliged to revert with their approval/ suggestions within any time stipulation. This can lead to a situation where work is commenced (as it has to in order to meet the time deadline) and belatedly the same is not approved, or some modification is required by the Government.

Adherence to standards

Here again we find that the approach of the Government in the Greenfield versus Brownfield sector is not consistent. In the Brownfield sector (Delhi and Mumbai) the concessionaire is required to:

i. adhere to Good Industry Practices;

ii. adhere to Development Standards and Requirements - these are specified in a Schedule. For instance, it is stated that the airport must conform to the ICAO Aerodrome Design Manual (DOC 9157); the Airport Services Manual (DOC 9137); the National Building Code of India etc;

iii. adhere to Operations and Maintenance Standards and Requirements. These again are set forth in a Schedule. For instance, it is stated that the relevant standards prescribed by the ICAO (Chicago Convention) are to be followed.

However in the Greenfield sector the approach is far more hands off. The specifications are very broad and vague.

Monitoring of the project

The inconsistent approach of the Government between the Greenfield and Brownfield sector comes out most dramatically when it comes to monitoring of the project and imposition of damages for default. In the Brownfield sector the agreement has in place an aggressive manifold monitoring mechanism. To begin with "objective" and "subjective" service quality requirements are set forth in separate Schedules. To illustrate one "objective" service requirement states that the maximum queue - in time for check in should be 5 minutes for business class and 20 minutes for economy passengers. The waiting time for security checking should be less than 10 minutes for 95% of the passengers. "Subjective" requirement are based on passenger feedback survey as per IATA SCIA / AETRA guidelines. If a certain specific rating is not achieved within a stipulated period then liquidated damages follow.

Further the concessionaire is required to achieve ISO 9001-2000 Certification. This is to be done within 2 years of the Agreement coming into force and if the same is not achieved, liquidated damages are to follow.

In contrast, in the Greenfield sector (Bangalore and Hyderabad) monitoring is only through passenger survey. Further (unlike the Brownfield sector), liquidated damages do not necessarily follow but if the rating through passenger surveys is consistently below the stipulated norms (over a period of years) and if the targets for rectification are not met, it may become an "event of default" leading to termination.

While examining the inconsistent approach between Greenfield and Brownfield sectors we may lastly take a look at the liquidated damages provision. In the Greenfield sector, even where there is delay in opening of the airport (something which ought to be a matter of serious concern), the concessionaire is allowed 6 months extension of time if it can show that the delay was allegedly on account of failure by the Government in the performance of its obligations (a provision which is easily capable of abuse and likely to lead to disputes).

After this, liquidated damages follow at the rate of only US$ 2500 per day upto the next six months of delay - surely a very nominal amount considering the consequences of delay (even one aeroplane hovering for landing permission can incur costs of more than the LD stipulated). In contrast, in the Brownfield sector, the concessionaire faces a prospect of liquidated damages of about US$ 65000 per day merely on account of delay in submission of the Master Plan beyond the stipulated period of 6 months even though prior to the agreement it had already submitted an Initial Master Plan (on the basis of which its bid was selected).

In fact Brownfield operators run the risk of paying liquidated damages (ultimately leading to termination of the contract) on at least 20 different counts - many of which are beyond their control e.g. security delay, check-in-delay etc., which can all result in liquidated damages and finally cancellation of the contract, (even though these are matters arguably beyond the control of the concessionaire). Airport security is a matter within the control of the Government and check-in formalities and efficiency is within the domain of the airline concerned. It seems unreasonable to penalize the concessionaire for shortfalls in targets here.

A Greenfield operator pays liquidated damages on only one count i.e. delay in opening of the airport. Here delay for six months mount up to less than half a million US$. Contrast this with the 10 million US$ a Brownfield operator may have to end up paying for a delay of 6 months for mere delay on account of submission of the Master Plan.

Absence of Regulator

In infrastructure projects concerning the public, an independent regulatory authority has become necessary. Accordingly the Agreements stipulate that an Independent Regulatory Authority would be set up to regulate all aspects of the airport. Vast powers are envisaged to be cast upon the Regulator. The Regulator would lay down and regulate standards, approve charges, impose penalties etc. Further the Regulator would be empowered not only to settle disputes between the public and the Government but also contractual disputes between the Government and the Concessionaire, as it is stipulated that once the Regulator is in place, the arbitration agreement as per the Agreements shall stand overridden. Firstly, the Regulator is not yet in place and considering that the Bangalore airport agreement was signed as far back as July 2004 the delay is unexplainable. Further the Regulator would work only if there is a mechanism to ensure that people of highest caliber, independent of Government control occupy the position. Once the Regulator is appointed the Regulatory philosophy has to evolve and there has to be transparency. All this will take time. We are years away from any of this as the Government is still discussing and deliberating preliminary issues. Even a Bill has not yet been placed before Parliament.

Secondly pure contractual disputes between the Government and the Concessionaire need not be referred to the Regulator. These, (in the event of dispute) need to go to the arbitrator. To override the arbitration agreement is bound to discourage foreign players. Resolution of disputes through the Regulator would cause serious problems of lack of confidence (amongst foreign parties) and also result in delay. The Regulator would naturally be subject to the hierarchy of the Indian legal system. Any decision of the Regulator would be appealable to the appellate authority. One is actually looking at three or four stages in dispute resolution - first, a decision by the Regulator followed by that of the appellate authority, followed by a Writ to the High Court, followed by an appeal to the Supreme Court. Given the delays under the Indian legal system, dispute resolution would become inefficient and expensive. Perhaps the Government should have segregated pure contractual disputes between the concessionaire and the Government and reserved these for international arbitration (which would have been as per the expectations of the international investing community also). The Regulator should step in only where public interest is involved.

Dispute Resolution

Planners (and contract writers) apparently tire out by the time they reach the dispute resolution clause (tucked away at the end of the Contract). Most dispute resolution provisions do not get the attention they deserve. Here too, we find the Agreements very unimaginative in their approach. Briefly, the concession Agreements stipulate that dispute resolution shall be through adhoc arbitration through a panel of 3 arbitrators, with the venue of arbitration as India. To understand what is wrong with this clause we need to step back and see the nature of the project. These are no ordinary construction or management contracts.

These are mammoth and diverse projects involving public interest as well. What is most significant is that we are looking at a project which is to have a longevity of 60 years. Considering that the history of independent India is just about 60 years it can well be imagined what a long period of time 60 years can be in the history of a nation! The technological, political and social changes which may happen in the contractual period of 60 years cannot be visualized and therefore captured within the four corners of any contract (no matter how thoughtfully written). Therefore the dispute resolution clause must be flexible and geared to handle contingencies which may arise in the working of the contract. One possibility is that in matters of this type the arbitrators must be empowered to even modify or alter the contract if subsequent developments so warrant. This is no doubt a revolutionary concept but one which may well meet the demands of a situation where parties enter into such long term commitments and then events overtake them. The dispute resolution mechanism must not be found to be wanting in such situation. Indeed there is no mechanism for mediation or conciliation or Dispute Review Boards in the Agreements, all of which could have worked towards a just, fair and expeditious resolution to disputes.

8

Developing the Air Defence System

AIR DEFENCE

Air defence was the primary function of the IAF until offensive air operations were also accorded the same priority. It remains an important component of the air power doctrine and the IAF has invested heavily in upgrading it. The air defence set up has three components – namely-armed interceptors, surface to air missiles and an extensive sensor network.

The backbone of the IAF's air defence fleet comprises of MiG-21s. Almost 16 operational squadrons fly in the air defence role. The oldest MiG-21 sub-types are being progressively retired, but both the MiG-21M and MiG-21bis continue to carry the IAF's primary air defence mantle. They continue to pull all the routine alerts along the border and form an important component of the air force's tactical reconnaissance force. The Gulf War and conflicts since have highlighted the need for aircraft with sensors that are more advanced and the ability to engage targets at increasing ranges. The baseline MiG-21M and MiG-21bis, given the vintage of their designs, are sorely lacking in these capabilities. However, the sheer size of the IAF's MiG-21 fleet has meant that any modernization plans would have to include these aircraft. While the MiG-21FL/Ms are now over 25 years old, the oldest MiG-21bis airframe is only 18 years old and the latter type is eminently upgradable. In the 1980s, the IAF did carry out a limited upgrade to configure the MiG-21Ms and MiG-21bis to carry the Matra Magic II air-air missile (AAM), and later for the R-60 AAM. A number of MiG-21bis were also fitted with head-up displays (HUD), but the aircraft remained sorely lacking in sensor ability.

Until the mid-1990s, a comprehensive upgrade of the MiG-21 had to be repeatedly postponed for either a lack of funds, or a dearth of suitable upgrade packages. However, a comprehensive upgrade of 125 "new" MiG-21bis is now underway. The program is almost two years behind schedule. The delay has been caused primarily due to re-design problems. The replacement of the MiG-21's original avionics by newer generation lightweight systems had altered the aircraft's center-of-gravity. These have now been overcome and the first 36 upgrade kits arrived in India during the last quarter of 1999. Under this program, the MiG-21 will be fitted with new avionics, the lightweight Super Kopyo multi-mode radar, IRST, and a comprehensive self-defence suite. While endurance and payload restrictions will remain, the MiG-21s will now be able to deploy almost as wide a range of air-air and air-surface ordnance as the most modern aircraft – including the R-77 AAM (AA-12 "Amraamski") and the Kh-31 ASM. One can expect to see this potent point defence fighter remain in service well into the second decade of the 21st century. Indeed the MiG-21s proposed replacement – the LCA – is not expected to begin entering service until 2010.

The move to make the MiG-21 fleet BVR capable, underscores the importance that the IAF accords staying on the cutting edge. The benefits of a BVR capable air defence force was much appreciated during operations over Kargil, where offensive air operations went unchallenged by the Pakistan Air Force. By all accounts, R-77 and R-27 armed MiG-29s on escort duty and CAP, ensured that PAF fighters stayed well over 40 km away from the border.

Even more modern types are undergoing comprehensive upgrades as well. The MiG-23MF, however, is an exception, with the sole remaining unit, filling an important role as a BVR training unit. Both the IAF's second-generation BVR types – the MiG-29 and Mirage 2000 – are also being upgraded with sensors that are more modern. In case of the former, it is expected that all aircraft will have their N-109 radar replaced by an electronically scanned Phazatron system. The older "A" versions are also being upgraded to fire the R-77s, like the newer "SE" variant. While the latter has more capable radar (NO-19M), it too will be the subject of an avionics upgrade.

The MiG-29 is also being equipped for air-air refueling to increase endurance. A major component of upgrade programs for air-superiority fighters across the board will eventually see them equipped with the HMS/R-73 combination. Both squadrons of Mirage 2000s will undergo an avionics upgrade, although the exact nature of the upgrades remains unclear.

The Mirage 2000 was India's first second-generation BVR capable aircraft and its multi-role capabilities came in very handy during PGM strikes over

Kargil in 1999. The aircraft has consistently maintained the highest serviceability of any type in IAF service (>90%) and has a superb safety record. The flexibility offered by the type has led the IAF to consider "topping up" existing units with a purchase of ten additional Mirage 2000Hs. Also under consideration is the purchase of the up to two squadrons of Mirage 2000Ds. Whether the latter deal comes through will depend as much on finances as on a successful completion of the Su-30MKI development program. Russia is currently filling an order for 50 Su-30MKIs. Eighteen Su-30MKs are already in service with No.24 squadron and a second squadron (No.20) has been earmarked for conversion.

In an effort to simplify logistics, the IAF has successfully integrated western missiles with its Soviet designed aircraft and vice versa. Under the first such program, MiG-21s were retrofitted with a capability to launch the Magic II AAM. More recently, MiG-29s have been adapted to carry the Super-530D. Integrating Soviet missiles with the Mirage 2000s proved more of a challenge, but was overcome by the mid-1990s. Indeed Mirage 2000s on missions over Kargil in the summer of 1999 were carrying R-73 AAM. The Mirage 2000 is also capable of deploying the R-27 AAM. It is more than likely that once the R-77 enters service in quantity, it will be integrated with the Mirage 2000.

The IAF's APD now puts offensive air operations on par with air defence. Allied air campaigns since the Gulf War have been very closely studied by the Indian Air Force. A series of studies from the College of Air Warfare (CAW) have acknowledged that the quickest way to bring a military campaign to a successful conclusion is to destroy the enemy's war making potential. Not surprisingly, the IAF's attack fleet is increasingly being equipped with enhanced standoff attack capabilities. Since the early 1990s, the IAF has made a determined effort to build up stocks of PGMs.

There has been an increase in the number of armed helicopters within both the IAF and the Army Aviation Corps (AAC). This has allowed the IAF to reorient its attack away from the role of "flying artillery" that has been demanded of it in the past.

Indeed as the air campaign over Kargil demonstrated, the IAF achieved the best results only when it was able to persuade the Indian Army that it's fighters were better utilized in closing enemy supply lines and taking out C3I nodes, rather than providing support to company and battalion sized operations. It should be recognized that the situation in Kargil was unique, and that close air support still has some applicability in the plains. Joint exercises since Kargil have convincingly demonstrated the merits of the IAF's re-orientation of its air support doctrine.

Kargil provided the air force with unique environment to hone its attack skills. The IAF launched PGMs in anger for the first time. Mirage 2000s, MiG-27s, and MiG-23BNs carried out devastating attacks against enemy command nodes and logistics in the area. In what became a much-celebrated event, Litening equipped Mirage 2000s took out the Pakistani battalion HQ atop Tiger Hill with pinpoint accuracy. 1000 lb. bombs fitted with IR seekers were used extensively against vital C3I facilities. The Mirages tracked ground targets from 15 km out and then released their weapons at about 6km and holding the lasers onto target at the closest of about 3-4 km. This allowed them to remain well outside the envelope of enemy air defences. As mentioned earlier, the conflict also exposed some of the limitations of the attack fleet and tactics. In particular, battlefield interdiction was found to be of greater utility than close air support in the mountains.

It also alerted the air force to the ever present dangers of operating in a MANPADS (and indeed SAM) rich environment. The IAF lost two fighters, one MiG-27 and one MiG-21M, and an attack helicopter over Kargil.

While the MiG-27 was lost because of an engine flameout due to ingestion of smoke and debris, the MiG-21 was lost to a SAM while searching for the downed MiG-27. It is now appreciated that a lack comprehensive of countermeasures (chaff/flare dispensers) across the MiG-21 fleet contributed significantly to the tragedy. Until Kargil, only the MiG-23BN, few Jaguars, and a handful of MiG-27s were fitted with automated countermeasures (in addition to the air defence types). Upgrading the self-defence and jamming capabilities of the rest of the attack fleet has now assumed a sense of urgency and base repair depots have taken on the task of upgrading chaff/flare dispensers.

The bulk of the IAF's attack fleet is relatively young, most of the aircraft having been procured since the 1980s. The MiG-27 forms the backbone of the IAF's tactical strike aircraft, equipping some eight squadrons and one training establishment. Three squadrons of MiG-23BNs support these. Their sophisticated electronic warfare capability has caused them to be called "most modern" of IAF strike aircraft.

Five squadrons of Jaguars form the IAF's deep penetration strike fleet. The IAF expects all of these types to remain viable for the near future. Both the MiG-27 and Jaguar are expected to remain in service until 2020. To this end, a comprehensive sensor and electronic warfare upgrade program has been initiated. The IAF's commitment to keeping the Jaguar in service for many years to come has been re-affirmed by its decision to order two more batches of the type. A 1999 order for 17 two-seaters is currently under production. An additional 20 single-seaters have been ordered this year.

Extremely versatile Mirage 2000s and Su-30s complement the dedicated strike fleet.

In addition to fulfilling overland strike duties, the IAF is tasked with the providing tactical air support to the navy. One Jaguar squadron has been specifically earmarked for this role on the western coast and is equipped with a mix of Sea Eagle armed Jaguar IS and IMs. Additionally, the IAF is in the process converting a MiG-27 squadron to cover the eastern coast. These aircraft operate in conjunction with the Navy's own air assets – including Sea Harriers and Tu-142s.

The 1990s have seen the IAF's strike fleet take on the additional task of delivering nuclear weapons. The Jaguar was the first aircraft evaluated for the role and was found too sluggish with the first generation gravity bombs. Consequently, Antilope equipped Mirage 2000s have taken on the task of providing India with a viable nuclear deterrent. It is now believed that the compactness of the second generation of nuclear warhead has allowed the nuclear delivery role to be taken on a by a larger number of aircraft – namely MiG-27s and Jaguars. It can reasonably be expected that in the future the Su-30 is likely to provide the backbone of India's manned deterrent force. It is also believed that the IAF is entrusted with the operation of India's emerging nuclear missile force.

Unspecified numbers of Prithvi SRBMs and Agni IRBMs form the basis of this force. It should be noted that as the size and sophistication of the missile arsenal grows manned delivery platforms will loose a great deal of their importance. As things stand today, the IAF offers adequate deterrence vis-à-vis Pakistan, however the situation vis-à-vis China is less clear. Unfortunately, until the Indian missile arsenal reaches maturity, India's ability to inflict unacceptable damage on China remain restricted. While the IAF is likely to remain the sole strategic service for some time, it is likely to be joined by the navy when the latter deploys cruise missiles and if its lease/purchase of Tu-22Ms materializes.

AIR DEFENCE SYSTEMS IN OTHER NATIONS

Pakistan

Pakistan is one of the vulnerable nations to air threats. As is commonly known the country had fought three wars with India. Hence, they have given more priority to the AD syatem. In their system any air craft intruding in to their territory can be easily identified. The recent act of firing at flying objects near angoor adda in south Waziristan, while attempting to cross the border, under the cover of darkness is proof of the level of AD in Pakistan. It was also reported that the flying objects upon being fired turned back and proceeded towards Afghanistan.

The Pakistan military has always purchased its AD hardware to bear, in any offer to deter such invasion especially from India. Given the terrain, Pakistan AD assets would also be hard to bring to tolerate very isolated point defence roles and given their short supply, The Pakistan military would likely be uncertain to put these AD hardware at undo risk of being destroyed.

Also, more dispersed efforts using gun fire and MANPADS would be challenging as well. Using this sort of defence effectively would be required a widespread deployment long the border. Pakistan forces probably would not have bandwidth for its at this time. Even if did it this would be very limited in capability given the limitations of both older MANPADS, anti air craft artillery and crude sensors in rough terrain.

In fact Pakistan had used American technology for their surveillance activities. But with the attack of 9/11 and the nuclear pact between America and India, Pakistan has now moved towards china for its requirements. The size of Pakistan is 5 times smaller when compared to India against whom it has fought three wars. In their strategy to counter the threat of Indian air power, Pakistan will not go the route of acquiring more expensive air craft as they have other options such as more shoulder fired missile systems, self propelled SAMs and guns along with greater mechanization of the ground forces, which gives much greater security from air threats and also allows ground forces to build enough thrust to smash through enemy defences, such that opponents air capability is provide ineffectively. At present Pakistan uses very high sensitive RADRAs such as AN/TPS-77, YLC-6 2D and YLC-6 3D.

The destruction capability of m1 Pakistan is consisted of large amount of ADA ranging from 14.5mm to ZPU 57mm calibre radar controlled guns such as the 35mm oerlikon RADAR controlled guns, 37mm manually operated guns and interceptor such as F-16.

India

In respect of now the AD of India, the Indians have a much bigger AD system than many of the other countries. As the regional leader India processes a strong AD system especially in fear of their neighbour Pakistan and their arch rival in the region China. India has already fought 5 wars with these two neighbours. Since recent times India has involved it self with the USA concerning matters of AD. Thus with the advance technology that they have acquired from the USA with regards to AD including AD interceptors and RADARs, they are now considered as the nation which has the strongest AD system in the region. Apart from such important acts India has commenced to train soldiers to be capable spot and identified enemy air craft with their naked eyes. This discourages the enemy from undertaking any sort of adventure in the Indian skies. Such is the fly catcher precision of these men from the AD arty, that they could distinguish the air craft as hostile or friendly within a split of a second. If the air craft turns out to be hostile, it is welcomed with a barrage from the anti air craft turns, mainly the L/70s. The solid backup provided by the regiment to the Indian air force, was well recognize in the Goa liberation operation-Indo –Pak wars in 1965 and 1971 and operation Rakshak I and 11 in Punjab.

The eagle eyed regiment put down 13 Pakistani air craft, including the saber B-57, bombers during "operation riddle" in 1965. The regiment, which has many success to its credit, was awarded with the battle honour 'Basanthar River' after the 1971 Indo –Pak war for its contribution with providing AD. During the war, the regiment put down several F 16 sabre air crafts and Mig -19 fighters by deploying the L -70 guns. Also during the 1961 Goa liberation operation, the regiment was involved in capturing 13 officers 21 men of the Portuguese artillery battery.

The regiment has a separate air craft identification centre, where the men are trained to identify over 70 air crafts with their naked eyes, even when an air craft is miles away. In this training, centre takes helps over 12,000 slides, several models and the latest jane's air craft recognition guide, which has the details of over 500 passenger, transport and fighter air craft that are used all over the world.

Through the regiment uses sophisticated radars the approaching air craft if flies at a low level may escape the vision of radars but it does not escape the eyes of these men. As soon as a hostile air craft is spotted, the massage is sent and within seconds it is gunned down. There is a capability required for the defence of vital point and area targets, against stealth, supersonic and subsonic air attack weapons, ranging from tactical air craft, attack helicopters and remotely piloted vehicles to precision –guided munitions.

Apart from the above the USA has developed the low level AD system in to a medium level AD system. The common example is the medium extended air defence system. This is a highly mobile, low to medium AD system was designed to replace the HAWK and PATRIOT PAC -3 AD system. That will be a key element of theatre missile defence in the army, Air and missile defence planning.

The MEADS weapon system are needed to provide protection to maneuver forces. The system will provide area and point defence capabilities against each tactical missiles, which includes tactical ballistics, air to surface, and anti radiation missiles and air breathing threats which consisting of fixed and rotary wing air craft, cruise missiles and unmanned areal vehicles. The system will be consisting a sensor, launcher, missile, and tactical operations centre and will be capable of independent operations. As part of the army air and missile defence architecture, the system will be well-matched and interoperable with the other army AD systems and will interface with joint and allied sensors and battle management command, control, communication, computer and intelligence network.

The MEADS systems are responses to ensure protection of maneuvering of forces. The system will provide area and point defence capabilities against tactical missiles and air breathing threats. MEADS integrate state of the art technologies in its sensor, weapon, and BM/C41 systems. Information superiority will enable MEADS to be fully capable of operating separately or in a network, receiving and exchanging data with other theatre air and missile defence systems and external sensors. The MEADS will also help joint forces with the theatre by contributing to full dimensional protection for the dominant manoueuvre forces through accurate engagement of threat tactical missiles and air breathing threats.

When comparing with the AD system of India, Pakistan, and the USA with that of Sri Lanka's AD it is observed that a few advance steps have to be taken immediately to counter the existing LTTE threats. The example that could be highlighted here is the monitoring of a spy air craft by the Pakistani military. Now the question arises as to why Sri Lanka AD AD system could not destroy the LTTE light air craft which was intruded more than eight times since those air crafts were put down by the AD system. It can highlighted that the LTTE air craft has intruded only at nights and due to non availability of night capability in most of the air crafts and the weapon system of our land based air defence system.

In case of India, the country processes abundant man power. Indian AD authorities have decided to utilize the abundant human resources in to maximum use. The Indian believe that the human eye is the most accurate when it comes to detecting any incoming hostile air crafts in respect of AD. Hence, they have specialized training programs carried out on this human aspect apart from the availability of highly integrated electronic devices. However in Sri Lanka we do not use manpower as much as what India do.

As we know that USA is second to non in respect of air defence. They have spent more on highly sophisticated low and medium level AD systems. They have stealth technology, sensors, and integrated AD systems automatic AD guns. However Sri lankan government can not spent such amount of money to purchase such advance Air defence systems. It is pertinent to mentioned that after the 9/11 attack in USA by Al qaeda, more concentration was given to unconventional terrorists groups such as LTTE. The USA banned many terrorists organizations and provided support the countries mostly affected by such terrorists organizations. Although the Sri Lankan government had opportunities to get some kind of assistance from the USA, it can not do so due to political barriers within the region.

CHINA'S AIR DEFENCE ZONE IN SOUTHEAST ASIA

Beijing's recent announcement of an East China Sea Air Defence Identification Zone(ADIZ) has the region wondering whether similar zones will follow, especially in the highly disputed South China Sea. China's ambassador to Manila has said that Beijing reserves the right to set up an ADIZ over the South China Sea, a statement that sent chills through the region. But the real question is not whether China will assert more ADIZs in disputed waters, but what its new zone says about Beijing's evolving strategy in Asia and how the United States and its regional partners should respond to future developments.

Beijing is unlikely to announce an ADIZ in the South China Sea in the immediate future, and its newly announced good neighbour policy offers U.S. policymakers a window to begin thinking about contingency plans for a future, more aggressive Chinese course of action.

Southeast Asian countries are puzzled by the ADIZ and China's other mixed signals. A little more than a month ago, President Xi Jinping and Premier Li Keqiang went on a diplomatic blitz to five ASEAN countries. Xi then told a closed-door meeting of high-level party leaders that the country was launching a new policy whose guiding principle would be to treat neighbouring countries as friends and partners. The new neighbourhood policy calls for the "best use of strategic opportunities" and the "creation of a close network of common interests," emphasizing above all that national rejuvenation would be the goal of China's regional diplomacy.

In this context, China has been investing in strategic bilateral ties with select ASEAN members. Trade and infrastructure are expected to be the two main drivers of future China-ASEAN ties. Xi and Li seem to understand the need to soften the hostility and heavy-handedness that characterized Beijing's regional diplomacy during the latter years of the Hu Jintao-Wen Jiabao government. That heavy-handedness was exemplified by the pressure China placed on Cambodia to wreck consensus on the South China Sea at the ASEAN Ministerial Meeting in 2011.

China's relationships with Malaysia and Vietnam, both claimants in the South China Sea, offer a valuable glimpse into its more nuanced engagement with Southeast Asia.

Malaysia is a significant trading partner for China and an important piece in its new regional strategy. For China, getting its relationship with Malaysia right has two goals. First, it could set an important precedent for how Beijing handles foreign policy with neighbours with whom it has outstanding conflicts. Second, it could serve as a showcase of the new policy toward its neighbours and a reminder to other countries that they have much to gain from cooperating with China.

Malaysia has often looked to China as the engine of regional growth and has supported a greater role for Beijing in regional institutions. Weeks after President Xi's trip, Malaysian defence minister Hishammuddin Hussein met with his Chinese counterpart, General Chang Wanqan, in Beijing, where both agreed to hold their first joint military exercises next year. Malaysia does not take for granted its claims in the South China Sea—the government decided in mid-October to build a new naval base along the disputed waters off the coast of Borneo—but plans are reportedly in the making to launch direct contact between Malaysia's Naval Sea Region 2 and China's South Sea Fleet.

Chinese leaders have also invested in revamping their oftentimes fraught relationship with Vietnam. Chinese policymakers recognize a shared heritage and ideological affinity between the two countries and their ruling Communist parties. While bilateral economic ties have forged ahead, Hanoi is anxious about its large trade deficit with China and overdependence on Chinese imports to fuel its manufacturing sector. Beijing hopes to assuage that concern with new infrastructure initiatives and border area policy.

During the past year, China and Vietnam have both refrained from heated rhetoric. Beijing even played up the significance of a recent joint agreement between the two governments on the delimitation of the Tonkin Gulf and fishery cooperation in the South China Sea. Like with Malaysia, China is counting on the established government-to-government consultation mechanisms, and strong party-to-party ties, with Vietnam to pay off in the long run.

But China is unlikely to permanently forego aggressive actions for the sake of good bilateral relations. This is one lesson of the new ADIZ, which has provoked both Japan and South Korea, and of China's ongoing efforts to isolate the Philippines and pressure it to drop its UN arbitration case against Beijing's South China Sea claims. Days after Beijing announced the East China Sea ADIZ, it deployed an aircraft carrier, the *Liaoning,* and four escorting warships to the South China Sea for the first time on what the government described as a routine training mission. Against this backdrop, the United States has in place frameworks, especially with Vietnam and the Philippines, that it can use to begin strategic planning for future scenarios in the South China Sea.

The U.S.-Vietnam comprehensive partnership launched in July opened up new avenues for training and cooperation on maritime security and domain awareness. Both the United States and Vietnam should move beyond diplomatic language in their annual Defence Policy Dialogue, which is currently convened at the vice ministerial level, and utilize it as a serious platform to discuss ways in which the two militaries could better coordinate on regional maritime security. The recent agreement signed between the two countries' coast guards at this year's defence dialogue is a welcome first step. In addition, Hanoi should rethink its lukewarm approach in recent years toward enhanced military cooperation with Washington in light of Beijing's long-term game in the East and South China Seas.

It is imperative for the United States to conclude negotiations with the Philippines on an enhanced U.S. troop rotational presence. Bilateral talks stalled just before Typhoon Haiyan hit the central Philippines, due to what Manila said were disagreements over access for Philippine forces to U.S. facilities. Reaching a mutually agreed-upon framework will not only allow the United States to strengthen its force posture in the Western Pacific, but also pave the way for U.S. and Japanese military personnel to provide better training to their Philippine counterparts. In the meantime, the United States should show continuous support for the Philippines' arbitration case against China and for resolving conflicts in accordance with international law. Secretary of State John Kerry has a timely window of opportunity when he visits both Vietnam and the Philippines next week. In Vietnam, Kerry should stress the strategic importance Washington places on its economic and military cooperation with Hanoi, and call on Vietnam to play a greater role in regional security within ASEAN.

In the Philippines, Kerry should try to reinvigorate the negotiations on U.S. troop rotations, and indicate steadfast support for Manila's efforts to peacefully handle the South China Sea conflicts. U.S. policymakers need to begin planning for ways to best coordinate with, and among, partners in Southeast Asia in order to avoid a discordant response as that seen between Japan and South Korea to China's ADIZ.

Neither the United States nor ASEAN should assume they know what China's next move in Asian waters will be. They certainly did not expect the recent ADIZ announcement. It is therefore important for the Obama administration to start working with friends and allies to be better prepared for coordinated responses to unexpected developments.

CHINA AIR DEFENCE ZONE A THREAT TO REGION

The Philippines expressed concern Thursday that China may seek control of air space over contested areas of the South China Sea, after Beijing declared an air defence zone above other disputed waters. Foreign Secretary Albert del Rosario said China's announcement of an Air Defence Identification Zone (ADIZ) in the East China Sea on the weekend raised the prospect of it doing the same for the South China Sea.

"There's this threat that China will control the air space [in the South China Sea]," del Rosario said in an interview on ABS-CBN television. The Philippines, China, Vietnam, Malaysia, Brunei and Taiwan have overlapping claims to parts of the strategically vital and potentially resource-rich South China Sea. China insists it has sovereign rights to most of the sea, even waters and islands close to its neighbours. China has been steadily increasing its military and coast guard presence in the sea in recent years to assert its claim, causing diplomatic tensions to rise and stoking concerns in the Philippines about perceived Chinese bullying.

Del Rosario also voiced concern over China's declaration of the air defence zone in the East China Sea, where it is embroiled in a territorial dispute with Japan. "It transforms an entire air zone into China's domestic air space. And that is an infringement, and compromises the safety of civil aviation," del Rosario said.

"It also compromises the national security of affected states." The air defence zone requires aircraft to provide their flight plan, declare their nationality and maintain two-way radio communication, or face "emergency defensive measures."

The zone covers Tokyo-controlled islands—known as Senkaku in Japan and Diaoyu in China—where ships and aircraft from the two countries already shadow each other. In a statement issued Thursday, the Japanese Foreign Ministry said the setting up of the ADIZ could cause "unintended consequences" in the region.

The ministry said it is consulting with the United States, which has military bases in Tokyo, and coordinating with other "relevant countries and partners" that have common interests in ensuring the stability and the safety of the region. "Japan will, in partnership with the international community, strongly urge China to exercise self-restraint," it said.

The ministry said China's establishment of the zone, which overlaps with Tokyo's own air defence zone, is a "profoundly dangerous [act] that unilaterally change the status quo in the East China Sea, escalating the situation, and that may cause unintended consequences in the [region]." The United States defied Beijing's air defence zone on Wednesday by flying two B-52 bombers through the area.

The exercise was described as a training mission, although analysts said US was clear in its message that it will not recognize the new territorial claims Beijing imposed over the weekend. China did not respond to what Chinese netizens referred to as provocation and defiance from Washington. The Japanese ministry insisted it will not recognize China's air defence zone, and that such measures "have no validity whatsoever in Japan." "Japan demands China to revoke any measures that could infringe upon the freedom of flight in international airspace," the statement said.

Japan has already protested China's actions and expressed its concerns to Beijing. It also demanded China to revoke such measures. "Japan will continue to respond firmly but in a calm manner against China's attempt to unilaterally alter the status quo by coercive measures with determination to defend resolutely its territorial land, sea and airspace," the ministry said.

Beijing was incensed by Tokyo's move to nationalize the chain of islands in the East China Sea in September 2012. The islands are called Senkaku by the Japanese and Diaoyu by the Chinese. Chinese and Japanese coast guards have regularly confronted each other in the surrounding waters, with China being angered by Japan's threat to shoot down Chinese surveillance vessels in the disputed waters.

The Senkaku Islands stretch out to a total of seven square kilometers, and is located northeast of Taiwan, east of mainland China and southwest of Okinawa. The uninhabited chain of islands is close to major shipping lanes, offers rich fishing grounds and believed to contain oil deposits. China's claim is founded on ancient times while Japan incorporated the islands into its Nansei and Shoto islands back in 1985.

CHINA'S MILITARY MODERNIZATION

China has been steadily building up its strategic and conventional capabilities since the 1990s. Eighteen years ago, experts say, China had a "bare-bones" military: basic capabilities, but nothing sophisticated or top-of-the-line.

But two decades of double-digit spending increases have changed that picture. China says its 2008 defence budget is $61 billion, though the Pentagon has historically challenged Beijing's reported figures.

In its annual report to Congress, the U.S. Defence Department estimated China's total military-related spending for 2007 to be between $97 billion and $139 billion, as compared to $52 billion reported by China. All that spending has gone to building a sophisticated, modern military: a large, increasingly capable submarine fleet, an air force stocked with Russian warplanes, and technical strides which have improved China's ballistic missile arsenal, as well as satellite surveillance, radar, and interception capabilities.

China continues to stress that its military modernization is in line with its peaceful rise in the world. Its latest White Paper on national defence emphasizes it will never seek hegemony or engage in military expansionism.

However, this has not alleviated concerns among its neighbours and regional rivals, say experts. A CFR Independent Task Force report (PDF) in 2007 on U.S.-China relations noted that many of China's neighbours and potential adversaries were making adjustments to their own defence plans and expenditures to balance China's growing military capabilities.

Japan: Japan and China compete over a host of issues, from regional security to international trade to access to energy. The two countries have a centuries-old history of conflict, including two Sino-Japanese wars that began in 1894 and 1931, and a bloody Japanese occupation of China during World War II. As this Backgrounder points out these animosities surface in recurring cycles, often involving Chinese anger over Japan's perceived lack of contrition for wartime crimes.

But concrete territorial and economic issues also aggravate the relationship, including Japan's close alliance with the United States, trade frictions, and ongoing disputes over ownership of various islands in the East China Sea. In 2007, China and Japan ranked third and fifth respectively in national defence expenditures (PBS), both spending only a small fraction of the U.S. budget even after adjusting for gross underreporting by Beijing.

China's military modernization fuels Japanese fears that China will use its growing economic leverage and military prowess to throw its weight around and dominate the region. Tanaka Akihiko of the University of Tokyo, speaking at a December 2008 CFR symposium on U.S.-Japan relations said China's growing military forces might change the balance of power in East Asia, which "would necessitate for Japan and the United States to readjust its force structure and other military management."

Japan has significantly upgraded capabilities over the past 15 years, deploying the Aegis radar and accompanying missile systems for its navy and warplanes armed with advanced air-to-air missiles for its air force. Since 1998, when a North Korean missile test violated Japanese airspace, Toyko has been working in partnership with the United States to develop theatre missile defences which have obvious application in the event of any conflict with China.

Over the past decade the U.S.-Japanese security alliance has been strengthened through revised defence guidelines, which expand Japan's noncombatant role in a regional contingency, allows for the deployment of an X-Band radar system in Japan as part of a missile defence system, expands bilateral cooperation in training and intelligence sharing, and allows a nuclear-powered U.S. aircraft carrier in the Yokosuka Naval Base. In September 2007 Japan joined a multinational naval exercise with the United States, Australia, Singapore, and India in the area west of the Malacca Straits.

The exercise reinforced the U.S.-led campaign of strengthening security ties among its democratic allies and "the strategic countering (PDF) of Chinese military power," argues a December 2008 U.S. Congressional Research Service report.

In 2005, a joint statement by U.S.-Japan Security Consultative Committee 2005 for the first time included Taiwan as a common strategic objective where the parties would "encourage the peaceful resolution of issues" through dialogue. Though Japan's foreign affairs ministry said this did not change the country's position on Taiwan, many experts believe the shift indicates that Japan is increasingly concerned with China's growing military capabilities.

Taiwan: It is the main driver for China's militarization drive and biggest concern for the United States as this Backgrounder points out. Taiwan is also pursuing modernization goals which include procurement of army attack helicopters, army utility helicopters, PAC-3 missile defence systems, fighter jets, and diesel-electric submarines, as well as transformation of the military.

Relations between China and Taiwan have improved dramatically under the administration of President Ma Ying-jeou, although U.S. arms sales to Taiwan remains contentious. In its white paper on national defence, China says the United States continues to sell arms to Taiwan "causing serious harm to Sino-US relations as well as peace and stability across the Taiwan Strait." In October 2008, Beijing suspended military contacts with the United States in protest of the U.S. decision to sell $6.4 billion in defence equipment and services to Taiwan.

South Korea: It has undertaken a major modernization drive, replacing antiquated fighter aircraft, frigates, tanks, and artillery pieces with advanced systems, many of them purchased from the United States or developed in partnership with U.S. defence industries, notes the 2007 CFR report (PDF). However, most experts say South Korea's military initiatives are more in response to a possible conflict with a nuclear North Korea.A thorough look at the status of South Korea's military is contained in CFR's Crisis Guide: The Korean Peninsula.

Russia: The country is China's largest supplier of advanced military hardware as well as a potential great power rival. Moscow experienced a significant decline in its overall military capabilities during the 1990s, but buoyed by strong oil revenues in the past decade, it has been increasing its defence expenditure, in what most experts see as a sign to counter U.S. influence in the region.

The 2009 defence budget is expected to be $50 billion, a 25.7 percent increase from previous year. Fedor Lukyanov, chief editor of *Russia in Global Affairs,* told a January 2009 CFR meeting that there are limits to Russian military cooperation and arms sales to China. "We sold everything we could without making damage to Russian security," he said. CFR's Senior Fellow on Russian and Eurasian Studies, Stephen Sestanovich says Russia's relationship with China is based on the interests of some elites—those in the energy sector, the nuclear power sector, and the arms exports, that see China as an important market.

China and Russia also formed a security alliance to solve border disputes, which has grown into an important regional organization, the Shanghai Cooperation Organization (SCO), and includes Central Asian countries Kazakhstan, Kyrgyzstan, Tajikistan, and Uzbekistan. China and Russia have held a number of joint military exercises under the SCO. In October 2007, the SCO also signed a memorandum of understanding with the Collective Security Treaty Organization, a military alliance of several former Soviet states. Some analysts see the SCO as a vehicle for Russia and China to curb U.S. access to the region's vast energy supplies. But others say Russia and China have very different objectives in Central Asia. Russia wants to reassert its regional leadership there, while China seeks energy ties, note some analysts. In 2008, China and Russia resolved (BBC) their last remaining border dispute involving islands in the eastern part of the border which had seen armed clashes between the two sides during the Cold War.

Southeast Asia: Experts say Southeast Asian countries, including Indonesia, the Philippines, and Thailand, are currently calculating whether the political and economic benefits of closer ties with a strong China outweigh the military risks. Bilateral trade between China and all ten countries within the Association of Southeast Asian Nations (ASEAN) is expected to exceed $200 billion in 2008 up from $ 190 billion in 2007.

The region is now China's fourth-largest trading partner. Despite the economic windfall, ASEAN countries want the United States to pay more attention to the new security trends in the region, experts say. While these countries are not very vocal about their fears, experts say they are nervously looking over their shoulders at China's military buildup and wondering where it's headed.

Border disputes with some countries also complicate China's relations with its Southeast Asian neighbours. Vietnam and China each assert claims to the Spratly and Paracel Islands, archipelagos in a potentially oil-rich area of the South China Sea. Malaysia, the Philippines, and Taiwan also claim all or part of the South China Sea.

China's assertion of "indisputable sovereignty" over the Spratly Islands and the entire South China Sea has elicited concern from Vietnam and its Southeast Asia neighbours, according to the U.S. State Department. Vietnam has been pursuing closer military relations with the United States through joint military exercises, and sharing intelligence on terrorism, drugs, and other transnational threats. Vietnam has also hosted U.S. warships at its ports.

India: It has long-time rivalry with China over disputed borders and these two Asian giants also fought a war in 1962. New Delhi watches Beijing's military buildup closely and has undertaken military reforms of its own. It is currently building a nuclear submarine and is trying to acquire two more aircraft carriers in addition to the one it possesses.

It also launched its first unmanned moon mission in October 2008, another step in what many analysts see as a race with China in space. It has also been expanding its military cooperation with the United States. In June 2005, New Delhi and Washington agreed on a new framework for their defence relationship, including increases in defence trade, technology transfers, and joint exercises for the next ten years.

China's close military cooperation with Pakistan also concerns New Delhi. Each country helps the other to check India's power, say experts. China remains a key supplier of arms to Pakistan and in 2008, agreed to help Pakistan build two nuclear power plants. China also supplies Pakistan with nuclear technology and assistance, including what many experts suspect was the blueprint for Pakistan's nuclear bomb.

Pakistan's army has both short- and medium-range ballistic missiles that experts say came from China. According to Thomas C. Reed, a former U.S. Air Force secretary, China probably helped Pakistan test a nuclear weapon inside China in 1990. Reed adds that this weapon was most likely based on a Chinese design.

Central Asia: Several Central Asian countries— Kazakhstan, Kyrgyzstan, Tajikistan, and Uzbekistan —have forged closer relations with China as part of the Shanghai Cooperation Organization. Experts say tensions in China's western province of Xinjiang is one of the major reasons behind Beijing's eagerness to improve relations with the Central Asian states.

Xinjiang is largely made up of Uighurs, predominantly a Muslim community with ties to Central Asia, and China has been concerned that Central Asian states may back a separatist movement in Xinjiang. Beijing also seeks energy ties in the region. Under the SCO, the countries conduct joint military exercises. Problems with their own Muslim fundamentalist groups have led these countries to assist China in its struggle against separatists from Xinjiang, say experts. However, some experts say the Central Asian states still view China and Russia as possible hegemonic powers.

IMPLICATIONS FOR THE UNITED STATES

China clearly complicates U.S. defence planning in Asia, says CFR's Senior Fellow for China Studies, Adam Segal. The Pentagon's 2008 report to Congress states: "Current trends in China's military capabilities are a major factor in changing East Asian military balances, and could provide China with a force capable of prosecuting a range of military operations in Asia-well beyond Taiwan." Most countries in the region have some degree of caution in their relationship with China, says James Mulvenon, director of Washington-based Centre for Intelligence Research and Analysis. However, none of them, he adds, want to engage in any form of containment policy with the United States. Meanwhile, though China is wary of U.S. military presence close to its border, its troubles with Uighurs has led it to support U.S. military actions inside Afghanistan, say experts.

The best way for the United States to ensure that its security interests in the region are not compromised by China's growing military capabilities is to strengthen security alliances with China's neighbours, notes the 2007 Council Task Force report. The report says the United States should better coordinate U.S.-South Korea-Japan security planning, give greater attention to ASEAN, work with ASEAN members to help draw China into constructive security relationships, and pursue a deeper military relationship with India.

AIR DEFENCE IDENTIFICATION ZONE (EAST CHINA SEA)

The East China Sea Air Defence Identification Zone is an Air Defence Identification Zone covering most of the East China Sea where the People's Republic of China announced that it was introducing new air traffic restrictions in November 2013. The area consists of the airspace from about, and including, the Japanese controlled Senkaku Islands (which are known as the Diaoyu Islands inmainland China and are claimed by mainland China as well as

Taiwan) north to South Korean-claimed Socotra Rock (known as Suyan Jiao in China).

About half of the area overlaps with a Japanese ADIZ, while also overlapping to a small extent with the South Korean and Taiwanese ADIZ. When introduced the Chinese initiative was controversial as requirements were imposed that other countries with air defence identification zones do not impose and it included contested maritime areas. Critics said the move escalated the Senkaku Islands territorial dispute between China and Japan.

History

The first ADIZ was established by the United States in 1950 when it created a joint North American ADIZ with Canada, citing the legal right of a nation to establish reasonable conditions of entry into its territory. The U.S. does not apply its ADIZ procedures to foreign aircraft not intending to enter U.S. airspace and does not recognize the right of a coastal nation to apply its ADIZ procedures to foreign aircraft not intending to enter their national airspace.

South Korea's ADIZ was established in 1951 during the Korean War, also by the United States. It currently does not cover Socotra Rock, known to Koreans as Ieodo. Korean Defence Minister Kim Kwan-jin said that Korea would consider extending its ADIZ in light of the extent of the Chinese ADIZ but an announcement of a change was postponed after a meeting with the United States ambassador.

Japan's ADIZ was created by the U.S. during its post-World War II occupation of Japan. Management of the ADIZ was transferred in Japan in 1969. The Japanese ADIZ is not recognized by China or Russia. Japan unilaterally expanded its ADIZ twice after the US transfer, once in 1972 and once in 2010. On 25 June 2010, Japan extended its ADIZ 26 km west to cover the whole Yonaguni Island, which was previously intersected by the original Taiwan/Japan ADIZ lines drawn by the U.S. The government of the Taiwan expressed its "extreme regret" over Japan's handling of the move.

The People's Republic of China announced the establishment of what it called its East China Sea Air Defence Identification Zone on 23 November 2013 defining an ADIZ as a zone that allowed a coastal state to "identify, monitor, control and react to aircraft entering this zone with potential air threats." Despite several international protests, China's move received broad domestic support.

According to a 2011 study of the justifications for establishing an ADIZ, at that time there had not yet been a "recorded instance of protest" against the initial establishment of an ADIZ.

The Chinese Air Force Command Academy began planning for an ADIZ after the Hainan Island incident and in May 2013 had suggested an ADIZ that covered China's exclusive economic zone, but this was expanded during review by the PLA to the current area.

EVALUATION OF PAST AND FUTURE AREAL THREATS

As per the past LTTE air threat experiences, LTTE air wing had carried out several areal attacks on some vital points in the country. In each time of attacks other than the last our AD system could not put them down or disrupt them when entering in to our vital areas. Though the effects of the attacks were minimal they entered in to the areas like BIA, Kolonnawa, Harbour some of the economical valued places with their so called air craft Zlin 143 light air craft and released bombs or payloads. All the times they used to fly at nights without lights as it cannot be seen.

More over, the LTTE is in the position that use of air craft in attacks against government forces boosts up the morale of their carders. In addition the LTTE also wished to prove to the Tamil community that its strength had not waned due to reverses in the east.

It wanted to demonstrate that it was equally capable of countering the Sri Lanka government forces on land, sea or air. At the same time, by attacking only the air base and not adjacent civil air ports, the tiger wanted to signal to the international community that they were not a terrorist organization, but well organized freedom fighters.

The recent past raids have been exposed limitations of security of the vital places from stealth raids. Air space can not be sealed completely, particularly from light air crafts with its less radar signature and such air craft flying low at tree top level bellow the AD radars horizon can manage to enter the air space. Some years back, light air craft managed to fly over the white house despite its strong AD system.

Hence conventional measures would not be adequate to defend military and vital installations against the air threat by terrorists. An integrated plan involving counter intelligence measures to eliminate moles, Intelligence acquirement efforts directed to gain early warning on coming operations, a modern AD systems and physical security measure with well prepared operational readiness drill will have to be work out.

As per the present situation, after ending humanitarian war so many repercussions are been arisen from the world community. It seems that still the LTTE Diaspora is functioning and pro LTTE sympathizers are trying re organize within and out of the country. The AD system of the country has to be 100% vigilant to detect any situation like suicide areal attack using high jacked commercial air line and spying using UAV's having capability climb and fly with more capabilities.

PROCUREMENT AND SYSTEM DEVELOPMENT

Everyone rails at the procurement system as the source of all unjustified expense and interminable delays. We will not repeat the well known arguments. We will only suggest that completion dates have the same status as other specifications of a system. Many of the systems suggested by *New World Vistas* can be built a piece at a time, and funding reductions should be reflected in the extent of the system rather than by extending the procurement time. The systems need to mesh with one another, and, therefore the relative phasing of procurements is important. These considerations suggest that systems be procured in blocks which continuously replace older blocks and continuously insert new technology in later blocks. One can argue that this has been the philosophy of many procurements, and we have chosen the nomenclature to suggest this argument. While this is true to some extent, the procurement cycle time for many of the concepts in New World Vistas should be no more than two years, and replacement time for information systems should be no more than 5 years. The system should be redesigned to accommodate these times. It is known in the commercial world that extended development periods lead to excessive costs. The Defence procurement system stretches programs in time so that many programs can be pursued in parallel. Both Government and Contractor have become too comfortable with this situation. We should consider the possibility that programs in series with rapid completion may be more economical.

The existing organization is optimized for the development and procurement of independent systems. It was emphasized many times that the effectiveness and affordability of capabilities depends on their close integration. The ideal situation would be one in which all participants in all procurement and development projects interacted at all times to produce systems which naturally worked together in the most efficient way. The ideal situation is impossible. Even if people could be convinced to behave in the proper way, they would spend so much time cooperating that they could get no work done. While we must instill the importance of the concepts of integration and cooperation of systems in all Air Force people, government and contractor, we must realize that focus on an individual product is the natural tendency of techno-humans.

Therefore, integration and interoperability must be assured at a higher level than that of individual system development and procurement. We recommend that an Integration Authority be established to guarantee integration and interoperability. We use the terms assured and guaranteed rather than dictate to indicate that the function of the Integration Authority is not to hand down specifications. That has been tried before, and it tends to stifle innovation and to stagnate technology. The specification of Ada is an example. Rather, we envision an Integration Integrated Product Team (IIPT) approach under the command of the Integration Authority. The IIPT would be composed of knowledgeable members of all interacting development projects. They would be responsible for proposing program and system modifications to facilitate integration and interoperability. The teams could also specify common components which could be separated from several projects into a common procurement to reduce cost. The purpose of the IIPT's would be to produce global optimization of systems rather than the sum of local optimizations that we have today.

We believe that the Integration Authority and IIPT approach could produce significant economies even in the short term. Avionics modernization of existing aircraft, and GPS installation in those aircraft are areas where enforced commonality could result in substantial savings Air Force wide.

9

Development of the Aviation and Aerospace Power

RATIONALE

The development of the aviation and aerospace industries has been one of the most exciting and challenging adventures in human history. In a single lifetime the technology of powered flight has progressed from a faltering hop of a few metres to giant machines efficiently carrying hundreds of passengers and cargo, non-stop half way around the planet.

Today, military aircraft routinely conduct missions with pinpoint accuracy, often at supersonic speeds. Satellite technology facilitates instant global communication, and the Earth and the rest of the universe are being surveyed in ever-increasing detail. Men have visited the Moon and a permanently inhabited space station is now a reality.

Aviation is an extremely important industry in Australia, due to the large distances and sometimes challenging terrain that separate population centres. In areas such as northern Queensland, for example, many remote settlements are inaccessible by road for much of the year, and the only way in or out is by air. In addition, rapid economic growth in many countries in the Asia-Pacific region has been mirrored by the proliferation of air travel and transport. Major aircraft manufacturers forecast massively increased demand for air travel in the region in the years to 2025.

Government has identified aviation as a priority industry, and Queensland's aerospace industry is consequently experiencing rapid and significant growth. Aircraft manufacturers, aerospace companies and airlines have aircraft construction, maintenance, operations and training centres in

Queensland established to meet the projected increased demand for aviation and aerospace services. Meanwhile, projects at Australian universities and research centres represent the cutting edge of aerospace technology. These activities demand well-trained, technologically literate personnel. People planning careers in aviation and aerospace should anticipate the need to be flexible, adaptable, creative and innovative in a fast-moving, highly competitive environment. The Queensland Studies Authority recognises the importance of aviation and aerospace in the future growth and development of Queensland industry. The senior syllabus in Aerospace Studies provides students with an opportunity to gain an understanding of the underlying concepts and principles of aviation and aerospace. It is concerned with concepts related to the design, construction, operation and maintenance of aircraft and spacecraft; the safety management systems that have been developed to ensure the safe operation of the aviation and aerospace industries; the structures and management of aviation and aerospace businesses; and various factors that affect day-to-day aviation operations. A course developed from this syllabus will combine elements of many disciplines, including mathematics, physics, English, information and communications technologies, business, engineering, history and law, and encourage a positive interest in the aviation/aerospace industry as a whole.

All seven key competencies are relevant to Aerospace Studies:

KC 1: collecting, analysing and organising information

KC 2: communicating ideas and information

KC 3: planning and organising activities

KC 4: working with others and in teams

KC 5: using mathematical ideas and techniques

KC 6: solving problems

KC 7: using technology.

In Aerospace Studies, students will collect, analyse and organise information and data pertaining to aviation and aerospace from a variety of sources and communicate ideas and information using a range of media. Individually and in teams, students will research, plan and organise diverse activities, including conducting experiments, modelling structures, and analysing business and operational systems. Students will use mathematical concepts and techniques in preparing and interpreting data, and develop skills of critical thinking, problem solving and decision making in the context of theoretical and practical situations, case studies, scenarios or projects relating to aviation and aerospace. They may also use and apply a range of information and communication technologies, and software packages. Opportunities may exist for interaction with industry including excursions and field research. Aerospace Studies is designed to facilitate the entry of students into the aviation and aerospace industries upon completion of Year 12 by providing a firm foundation of knowledge relevant to an array of career pathways and further education and training.

Progression is possible in careers as diverse as aerospace and aircraft engineering, aviation business management, human resource management, customer services, aircraft pilot, and air traffic control, both within Australia and overseas. The syllabus also supports the existing tertiary offerings related to aviation and aerospace in universities throughout Australia.

The breadth of learning in Aerospace Studies provides scope for students who may choose to follow career paths in other industries or professions. The knowledge and understanding gained from the range of disciplines involved, as well as the required critical thinking and communication skills, could be applicable to a diversity of employment, further education and life-long learning opportunities.

Global Aims

Aerospace Studies aims to:

- raise students' awareness of the aviation and aerospace industries
- encourage students' future participation in the aerospace industry
- increase the skills and knowledge that would enhance students' future employment prospects
- foster and develop inquiring minds and intellectual skills that will help students think critically and purposefully about the aviation and aerospace environments
- promote students' appreciation of the need to become lifelong learners in the aerospace industry
- develop in students an appreciation of the need, and willingness to operate within a highly regulated environment, while adapting to rapid technological change
- assist students to recognise the need for, and develop, effective communication skills in an aerospace context
- promote both individual and team work
- promote students' appreciation of the overarching safety culture within the aviation and aerospace industries.

RESEARCH AND DEVELOPMENT OF ARMOR

The manufacture of tanks and armoured vehicles, which started from zero in China, initially began with imitations but now has been replaced with our own designs and manufacturing. As early as the end of 1945, the PLA set up its first tank corps using tanks captured from its enemies during battles. By 1949, when the People's Republic of China was founded, the PLA already had two armoured divisions and two armoured regiments, and equipped these corps with 410 American or Japanese tanks and 367 armoured vehicles, all captured equipment. On the basis of this we started constructing and developing our own armoured weaponry.

On September 1, 1950, our Armoured Corps was officially established. To meet the needs of the tanks corps we bought over 400 tanks and mobile guns from the Soviet Union. Immediately after that, the tank corps made use of the equipment during the war to Resist U.S. Aggression and Aid Korea, and forcefully backed the infantry's operations. In 1956, we began to set up the tank industry. Until 1959, we copied designs to make medium-sized tanks (model 59) for our troops. Then, starting from the latter half of 1958, a magnificent stage in the history of the developing of our tanks began, a time when we designed and made our own tanks. After a hard struggle of 4 to 5 years, as we manufactured model 62 light tanks, we finalized the designs of model 63 amphibious tanks and model 63 armoured vehicles. Then four major series were gradually formed according to the requirements of our operations and capacities that would adjust to specific terrains and climates. They were medium-size, light, amphibious, and armoured carrier tanks. Step by step, they became the mainstay of our armoured weaponry.

During the Cultural Revolution, the research and production of tanks were seriously damaged. Though the scientists, technicians, officers and men in our defence industry worked hard to achieve some progress, and the design of the medium-sized model 69 tank was finalized along with a number of accessory automobiles during this time, on the whole, the level of technology and the quality of the equipment was not much improved, and the distance between the most advanced technology and ours grew.

Since the Third Plenary Session of the 11th Party Committee, the policy of reform and opening to the outside world has brought opportunities for the rapid development of science and technology in our national defence. In the wake of a strategic transformation in the guiding concept on the construction of our army, we have strengthened the strategic research about how to develop weapons and developed an overall plan of development. The plan and the policies we put into practice in developing weapons were constructive and reliable, so the research and development of tanks and armoured vehicles embarked on a steady and healthy road and achieved much progress. During this period, we did much research and finally manufactured over 10 new types of weapons, including the main battle tanks, caterpillar infantry battle vehicles, armoured carriers, mobile antiaircraft guns, antitank missile launchers, armoured command vehicles, tank bridge-making vehicles, tank rescue haulers, and tank transporters. Using advanced foreign technology, we actively improved our existing weapons, improving fighting capability and increasing the amount of equipment and weapons in every unit of the armed forces. Our armoured weaponry has played an important role in training and preparing to prevent war, as well as in self defence.

We have achieved great progress in the development of armoured weaponry after a tortuous experience. The many successes and failures have made us understand better the characteristics and rules of development:

- Strengthen research on developing weapons, and base macro decisionmaking on science. In the past, weapons development was much affected by political movements, the organizational system, and factors like personnel changes. We did not work according to scientific rules. In recent years we have, through wide discussion, decided upon an active and cautious policy for weapons development. We have formulated development principles with Chinese characteristics for the tanks and armoured vehicles and made long-and medium-term development strategy and plans. Therefore our weapons construction is done through long-term planning, good coordination, and priority development. The democratic and scientific method we adopt in our models and decisionmaking process is the important foundation for the constant and steady development of our weaponry.
- In weapons development, we should consult with the department that uses them. The armed forces are the direct users of weapons. In the making of set models, they should pay attention to the testing of these models. In recent years, we have verified our weapons models in actual battle and paid attention to the integration of tactics and technology as well. We have strictly carried out model testing according to testing standards, regional adaptation testing, and special testing under nuclear and chemical conditions. We have asked representatives from the armed forces to take part in the management of scientific research. This is of extreme importance for meeting the battle requirements of the armed forces and ensuring weapons quality. As reform of defence science and technology progresses, we should actively carry out contract systems under the guidance of the defence industry, respecting the decision of the chief engineer in matters of technology, and encouraging the initiative and creativity of the broad mass of scientists and technicians.

- We must uphold the policy of taking the initiative and actively importing technology, which is a shortcut for the development of weapons. Independence and self reliance comprise our basic national policy; this is also the policy we must follow in weapons development. But in the development of technology, we should try to create anew and be good at learning and inheriting these two are complementary. In the early days of our new Republic, we learned from the advanced experience and technology of the Soviet Union, jumping over the traditional technical development stage. This way the research and manufacturing of tanks were quickly on the track, and we were able to shift from copying to designing and manufacturing our own tanks. At the end of the 1970s, through importing advanced technology, we were able to facilitate the quick development of our tanks and armoured vehicles and shorten the distance between the advanced-level and our own. Today we take the initiative with imported technology, stressing utilization and development and gradually form weapons systems that have our own characteristics.
- We need to step up innovation and expand the accumulation of technology, key factors in weapons development progress. The research of weaponry in the past followed the traditional way, that is, a model led the research work or even the production of accessories. This resulted in a lack of accumulation of technology, passive and insufficient research on models, a long research period, and many unnecessary repetitions. It should be a profound lesson for us. In recent years, we supported and directed innovation that correlates to the background of the models. We adhere to a principle that the component parts take priority over sets of equipment. In addition, we imitated the good points of advanced scientific and technological results from abroad and make use of them in some projects. We broke through the line of demarcation between the departments and the industries and encouraged competition. All the efforts produced a remarkable effect.
- The development of tanks and armoured vehicles must follow a process in which the vehicles are classified and grouped and put in a standardized series. If the army wants to enhance the overall operation capability of the armoured corps, there will be a variety of requirements for weaponry. Since the 1960s we have believed that all kinds of accessory vehicles should be derived from a basic model design that can be flexibly changed. In weapons research and manufacture, besides carrying out the principle of standardization from beginning to end, we tried every possible means to enhance the universality of the

component parts. This universal concept is useful not only to help crate standardized products but also to lower the costs of contract work, simplify the training of our army, and ensure logistics supplies.

- The development of weaponry needs a stable troop of scientists and technicians. In the early 1960s, along with the modernization construction of the armoured corps, we founded the Scientific and Technical Research Institute of the Armoured Corps and the Institute of Engineers for the Armoured Corps. We gradually had a team of scientists and technicians that combined theory with practice. They worked together with the national defence industry department and made contributions to our first generation of tanks. Because of the advent of the cultural revolution, the teaching system and research institute of the armoured corps suffered great damage and much talent was lost. Both the positive and negative experiences have made us realize that in order to develop weapons it is important to have a team of scientists and technicians rich in practical experience and full of creativity. Under the current new situation, we should take strong measures to ensure the stability of the team, and create favorable conditions for the upgrading of knowledge and the growth of talents.
- The organization that uses weapons should create a favorable technical system and environment for the development of new weapons. "Without technology there would be no armoured corps," these were the famous words that former Commander of the Armoured Corps General Xu Guangda used to say about the construction of the armoured corps. At the founding of our armoured corps, we established the department of technology and laid the organizational foundation for weapons development. When the first generation of new weapons was decided upon, documents for the use, repair, testing, and technology were edited, weapons were tested and their fighting capability, ease of use, and reliabilty were constantly improved. We created favorable conditions for the development of new types of weapons. Tradition and experience in this area should be upheld and carried forward.

We are facing new opportunities and challenges at a time when modernization is our central task and there is a new technological revolution going on. We should grasp the opportunity and gradually establish a weapons system that has Chinese characteristics and that meets the requirements of future anti-aggression war.

The development of armoured weaponry should proceed from reality and in accordance with the actual conditions of our country and our army. We should go our own way and not follow the footsteps of the others. The future development of tanks and armoured vehicles should follow these principles:

- Pay attention to fire power, improve overall quality, and increase survival capability.
- Reform current weaponry in a planned way and strengthen combat capability.
- Take into account terrain and weather conditions and improve adaptability.
- Form modular sets with fewer basic models but higher standardization.
- Strive for advanced, reliable, economical, and easier-to-operate weapons.

These principles were established after summing up the experiences of developing armoured weaponry.

In our future development work, we should put them into practice, strengthen test methods to ensure a weapon's long life, gradually certify, research, manufacture and equip for a complete set and arrange for advanced research, manufacture, production and improvement. At the same time, we should speed up the training of personnel and technical research so as to maintain good development momentum.

Motorization and armoring our troops are the developing trends for the modernization of our army. Fast-reaction and quick-strike capabilities will be important factors for our armoured corps in winning future anti-aggression wars.

Weapons for our armoured corps in the year 2000 must meet the requirements of future warfare. Our armoured corps should improve the ability to strike deep, react fast, and coordinate well with the air force. The overall efficiency and adaptability should be improved, and weapons systems with appropriate combinations of different levels of quality should be formed. At present, we should give priority to the development of new types of main battle tanks, infantry fighting vehicles, automatic battle command complexes, and anti-aircraft vehicles. At the same time, we should selectively improve our current weapons and improve their reliability and fighting capability.

We are confident that under the correct leadership of the Central Committee of our Party and the Central Military Committee, and with the great efforts of all people in the defence industry and armoured corps, the working capacity of our armoured weaponry will be greatly improved, and the capacity of combined-operations will reach a new level. It is a difficult and heavy task, however, as long as we persist in our efforts, we will definitely achieve our aim.

REFORMING DEFENCE SCIENCE, TECHNOLOGY, AND INDUSTRY

The development and reform of defence science, technology, and industry are now in a key stage. A new situation and some arduous tasks lie ahead of us. This is mainly reflected in the following:

- Owing to the needs of modern technology, especially in a high-tech regional war, we have to speed up research and development of new weapons and develop our national defence science and technology in order to reach the advanced world level.
- The second strategic goal of socialist modernization is for us to continue to carry out a policy of linking the army and civilians and to accelerate this step of strategic transition so as to release more power into the main battle field of national economic construction.
- The basic object and whole plan of national economic system reform call for further liberating and developing military productive forces to form a new system suited for socialist market economy that would combine with the practices and special features of the national defence industry. The necessary prerequisites to complete these tasks are to uphold a practical and realistic style of work, emancipate the mind, and under the guidance of Deng Xiaoping's thoughts on building a socialist society with Chinese characteristics, to research and approach the major problems, to enhance our sense of principle, orderliness, predictiveness and creativity.

Position and Effect in National Strategy

Faced with new conditions and wanting to speed up the reform and development of defence science and technology, we must first of all fully understand its vital importance. President Jiang Zemin pays great attention to this. He asserts that the key to developing defence science and technology is to heighten its level. This is not only the requirement of the new military strategy but also that of the whole modernization drive. We can deepen our understanding of these points from the following three aspects:

- Defence science, technology, and industry are the major material bases on which we can realize our army modernization. The use of modern weapons is a sign of a modernized army, and is also one of the factors for improving the combat effectiveness of an army. The biggest problem we have in the construction of a modern army is the lack of up-to-date weapons. With the deployment of high technology in the military domain, the precision of weaponry has improved, the intensity of the battle has greatly increased, and other characteristics of war like swiftness, abruptness, three dimensions, mobility etc. have become more conspicuous. As the Gulf War clearly showed, the one who possesses high-tech superiority will have the upper hand on the battlefield. To fundamentally change the backwardness of our army's weapons, and strengthen the material base we count on to deal with local wars of modern technology, especially those under high-tech conditions, we must speed up the research of new and high-tech weapons, and raise the level of modernization of our weaponry. Weapons modernization is, in the final analysis, determined by the modernization of our defence science, technology, and industry. Therefore, we must seize the opportunity and speed up the development of our defence science, technology and industry, to ensure the realization of the modernization of defence.

- Defence science, technology, and industry are important symbols of our comprehensive national power. At a time of peace and development, world competition is essentially about comprehensive national power, and the key is the competition in science and technology. National defence science, technology, and industry represent a nation's economic and technological power and are important pillars of the comprehensive national power. They are also essential for the raising of the nation's status. China is a developing country with a low per capita income. One of the reasons that we are not looked down upon in the world is that we have built a relatively complete defence industry, and we have been able to research and manufacture various types of conventional and strategic nuclear weapons independently. Deng Xiaoping said, "If China did not have atom bombs and hydrogen bombs, and had not launched satellites since the '60s, China would not be called an important, influential country and would not enjoy the international status that it does today." Such things reflect the ability of a nation, and also symbolize the prosperity and development of a nation. In the last few years, we have achieved a series of breakthroughs in defence science, technology and industry. Both the new developments in the research of weaponry and the successful launching of satellites for foreign countries further promote the strengthening of comprehensive national power and raise our international status.
- Defence science and technology are the leading forces for the development of our national high-tech industries. Nowadays, more and more countries attach great importance to science and technology and are developing their high-tech industries as if they were in a race. It has become a strategic focal point and a common practice. Deng

Xiaoping once said, "Whether it was in the past, at present, or in the future, China is determined to develop its own high technology and to occupy a position in the domain of high technology in the world." On the whole, defence science, technology, and industry belong to high-tech industry, and they can stimulate high-tech industry and cause great advances in it, especially in three aspects:

- To go through the processes of research, experimentation, and production in the defence industry, we need a lot of new materials, new technologies, experiments with new methods, and efficient facilities for production. This is bound to make strict demands on basic industry and result in a series of industrial breakthroughs and improvements.
- Then, some new high technologies, such as nuclear technology, telemetry and remote sensing technology, automatic control, electronics and computer science, precision machinery, meticulous chemical, etc. were originally and successfully used in the defence industry and have gradually formed some new competitive industries through their application in the civilian sector.-Finally, the military departments and enterprises make full use of their superiority in equipment, technology, and talented personnel directly to develop new high technology products, which, to a certain degree, have filled in the gaps in the fields of science and technology and raised the overall level of the national economy.

Contradictions in the Development of Defence Science and Technology

With changes in international affairs and hot competition in the high-tech world, all countries are readjusting their national strategy and defence strategy and pursuing the development of modern technology, especially high technology, as the key measures to strengthen comprehensive national power and defence strength, and thus gain the strategic initiative. Historical experience has proven that all starting points and guiding ideology in our work should alter with changing situations. Analyzing the distinguishing features of modern technology, especially high technology, and taking into consideration our national and military conditions, we need to seize the opportunity to speed up the development of defence science and technology. We also need to correctly understand and handle some important relationships:

- The relationship between the part and the whole. Defence science and technology are parts of a complicated system involving a wide range of areas. Some of them are urgent in the short view but not so from the longer view. Therefore, we must pay special attention to the overall balance, clearly defining our priorities and tilting toward the major projects. When we form development strategy or policy on technology, we should start from the overall development of defence science and weapons research and manufacturing. We should focus on raising overall efficiency and properly handling the relationship between the part and the whole. The relationship between requirements and possibility. For a considerably long time, the gap between available funds and the large investment needed for developing high-tech weapons will be a restriction on development. For this reason we must make great efforts to balance production with rational disposition of funds in all projects. Additionally, we should get rid of and guard against extravagance for instant benefit, repeatedly spending money for quick results followed by a quick reversal, and so on.

- The relationship between making the focal points stand out and coordinating the different branches of development. It would be best if we choose projects that will play both an important role in strengthening the fighting capacity and the deterrent power of our armed forces, and a vanguard role in raising the level of defence science or the level of the whole nation's science and technology. For the major projects, we should concentrate manpower, material resources, and financial resources to ensure their implementation. Meanwhile, we need to coordinate the overall development of all weapons with science and technology.
- The relationship between the requirements of demand and the push of technology. To program weapons development we have to adhere to the principle of linking demand requirements with the push of technology. On the one hand we should make thorough studies of the requirements of local war under the circumstances of modern technology, especially high-technology. On the other hand, we should lay stress on discoveries in the development of new and high technology, which will raise the effectiveness of weaponry. A new concept and a new system of weaponry should be formed and the structure of weaponry renewed and optimized constantly.
- The relationship between long-term and short-term interests. Proceeding from the requirements of high-tech war, we ought to manage to do research on some weapons with a higher starting point in accord with the plan and the focal point, and utilize results in scientific research to improve existing weaponry and military equipment. To obtain staying power, we should also do research in advance, reserve more technical

capacities and keep up with the advanced world technology, so as to raise the overall level of defence science and technology.

- The relationship between the efficiency of the whole and the efficiency of a single unit. A local war under the circumstances of modern high technology is a confrontation between two systems within a given battleground. We need to study both operational policy and weapons development from the standpoint of systematic operations to raise the efficiency of the whole and hence the quality of our weapons system. If we do not examine the quality of our weapons system as a whole, even if we have numerical superiority or an advanced single weapon, we can not make the most of these weapons as a whole.
- The relationship between the offensive and defensive. In a future anti-aggression war, our country will uphold the concept of active defence. It means that active defence is not just defensive, it is offensive as well. Our air-defence weapons system and even the whole weapons system should have two capabilities. It could greatly help overall quality and effectiveness if we possess one or two effective weapons that can assume the offensive.
- The relationship between defence and commercial use. With the development of modern science and technology, defence and commercial products become more and more compatible. While we emphasize the conversion of defence technology into commercial use, we must study defence-commercial dual purpose technology and possible transfers from commercial technology to defence use. Development of defence products should actively use commercial technology, so that it will have a solid foundation for development.

Optimum Disposition and Proper Use of Resources

A problem that restricts or affects the development of the defence industry is the improper defence industrial structure. For this reason, our fundamental goal for modernizing the structure is the optimum disposition and full liberation of the military productive force. As the international situation changes and new technology steadily develops, many developed and developing countries find a flexible military industrial structure to be an important strategic measure in restructuring their national defence industry. Currently, we have made good progress in defence industry adaptation, but the situation is still short of what is expected for example, problems such as activities too large in scale, overextended battle lines, low-level production, inefficiency and so on still exist. In the future, any defence industry should follow and serve the needs of the military strategy in the new era and be suited to the building of the country's socialist market economy system. Additionally, we should pay attention to the following points in our guiding ideology:

- Speed up modernization by relying on progress in science and technology. Science and technology are the number one factors in the productive force. With the rapid development in science and technology, economic competition in the world has more and more become the competition of a product's level of technology. Modern warfare is also, to a degree, the competition of high technologies. Adjustment in the structure of the defence industry and improvements in its of research and manufacturing capabilities should be conducive not only to the rapid development of national defence science and technology but also to research and manufacturing of high-tech weapons, and to the integration of research and production. We should pay attention to the development of mature technological products and useful foreign products to improve our existing equipment, and to raise its technological level. We should also be aware of the requirements of a high-tech local war and focus on the research and manufacturing of high-tech weaponry. To raise the level of technology, and to have rapid development, we should put advanced research in a strategic position and concentrate our resources on breakthroughs in key technologies. At the same time, we should pay close attention to the improvement and renewal of technology and the coordinated development of technology, equipment, and materials. Additionally, we should conduct our research and production of military supplies by relying on science and technology and by improving the quality of our workers.
- Adhere to the principle of contracting the front and stressing the main point. At the present time, the units that are responsible for research and manufacturing of military products do not have that many projects or funds. In addition, some shortcomings like scattered resources and repeated projects still exist, causing a longer period of research or manufacturing and a lower productive level. In future modernization, we should cut down those projects that are outdated and make allowances for those that are really advanced. We will mainly derive our plan from the tasks, and take the investment as the foundation, concentrating the research and production in some major enterprises and academies or scientific institutes. Moreover, we should concentrate them in a number of workshops or laboratories within an enterprise or an institute. As a number of scientific bases and major production bases are formed, we will concentrate resources and try to fulfil the

task of manufacturing military products on time, guaranteeing quality and quantity.

- Apply economic methods to promote modernization. In the past, we adjusted the defence industry structure depending on the plan and administrative method. Under the overall situation of building a market economy system, we should apply more economic methods, particularly insisting upon the role of the market and giving full play to the function of our market system. For instance, the start or the abandonment of our scientific projects, or the increase or decrease of production power, should be decided according to the requirements of the domestic and international markets. The market will play a fundamental role under the macro adjustments and be controlled by the state.

The Transition from Military Industry to Market Economy System

The Fourteenth Party Congress made it clear that the goal of our economic system reforms is to build up and improve the socialist market economy system. The third plenary session of the Fourteenth Party Congress further confirmed the framework of our socialist market economy system and put forward requirements for the initial buildup of the socialist market economy system at the end of this century. How to speed up the reform of the military industry, and build a new system that meets the requirements of the market economy are important issues to study and answer.

The military industry is an component part of the whole economic system of the country. Its production, circulation, distribution, and exchange activities cannot be separated from the national economy. Therefore, it must be subordinated to the need to set up a new economic system in the country, and speed up the transition to the socialist market economy. The transition from a highly centralized, command and planned economic system to a market economic system is a great change of strategic significance for the military industry. The key to what is actually a profound revolution is the proper handling of the relationship between the plan and the market. Deng Xiaoping has emphasized on many occasions that both the plan and the market are tools of economics. President Jiang Zemin pointed out, "The scope, degree, and forms of integration of the planned and market economic scan be different at different times, in different areas and regions." According to the realities and characteristics of the military industry, we should pay attention to the following three points for the present time:

- National security is the foremost reason for the research and production of military products. Its funding mainly relies on investment by the state, and the state is the monopoly buyer of the products. There should be strict planning and management of the research and production of military products by the state. The state should purchase these products, and production should not be regulated by the market. Concerning the allocation of resources, the state plan should still play the leading role and be the main control point.

- Reform of the research and production of military products should be directed toward designing a contract system. Through economic contracts, there should be clear relations of interests between the supply and the demand sides, and there should be unity of responsibility, rights, and interests. The essence of a purchaser/contract system is to shift to the market economy, changing administrative management to management by economic means.
- As an economic activity, the research and production of military products should follow the law of value, and adapt to the changes in supply and demand, making full use of the role of the market. At the same time, control by the state should not be weakened or negated. During a shortage of resources, or an imperfect market, the strengthening of state control would be conducive to giving full play to the advantage of socialism in concentrating resources on big projects, and achieving better results and efficiency from limited resources.

The resolution of the third plenary session of the Fourteenth Central Committee of our Party pointed out that the building of the socialist market economic system is to use the market system as the principle means to allocate resources under the authority of the state. Through several years of experiment and practice we have found that in order to have the market play a role in the defence industry, we need to recognize the importance of using price as a lever and introducing competition to gain efficiency in the allocation of resources, to motivate enterprises. Currently, there is a strong desire to reform the pricing of defence products. But the budget for the armed forces is very tight, and because there have been big increases in the prices of raw materials, it would be very difficult to carry out such reform.

Further, a reform would involve big adjustment of interests in supply and demand, and is closely related to financial and monetary system reform, as well as enterprise reform. Therefore, to have military products appropriately priced, and to have a new pricing system, we need to ask the government to have an overall plan to solve the problem. To conduct the reform in the pricing of defence products, with a smooth transition, we should price military products on the basis of actual value and not the market-bearing price, as with civilian products. In principle, we should use both adjustment and the role of the market, with emphasis on adjustment. The government may apply the laws of value and supply and demand, taking into consideration the ability of different sides to cope with the reform and adjusting unreasonable pricing of major military products at an appropriate time. With regard to generally low-priced military products and their accessories, apply a price based on supply and demand, and gradually adjust prices to reflect the market price.

Another outstanding problem is the introduction of competition into defence industry reform. Competition is necessary to encourage creativity and to raise efficiency. In the early 1980s Deng Xiaoping said that there can be competition in weapons production. Some weapons can be produced by more than one department, and the army can choose to buy the better products. But in recent years, because of the unsmooth structure, the unclear division of government and enterprise, interference by the administration, and the weak concept of market, the competition mechanism has not been given full play in the research and production of military products. According to the experiences of the developed countries, and in light of the actual conditions in our country, we should actively introduce competition in the research and production of military products. But the scope, items, and forms of competition should be chosen according to actual situations. For example, in terms of scope, competition can be carried out in the same trade, in the defence industry system or in the whole country in certain cases. In terms of weapons systems, there can be competition in subsystem or in single unit equipment. In terms of items, we can start out in small and medium projects, and when we have more experience, we can then gradually press forward. In terms of forms, we can have competition among units and even within the same unit.

Opening to the World

The current world is an open world. We must notice that the general trend of development in the world economy and in science and technology is increased mutual infiltration, interdependence, and integration. Any country that wants to speed up development has to carry out an open policy. Deng Xiaoping said, "Opening to the outside world is of great significance. It is impossible for any country to have development in isolation and with its door closed, neither would it be possible without the strengthening of international exchanges, and importation of advanced experiences, science and technology, and funds from the developed countries." In fact, even in the confidential and sensitive military sphere, the countries of the world are not closed to each other. Many countries not only import advanced technology and equipment from abroad, but also carry out broad cooperation in the area of military high technology, and have joint research and production of new types of weapons.

There is still a gap between the level of our national defence science, technology, and weaponry and that of developed countries. To make quick advances, we need to be self-reliant, but at the same time we should open wider to the outside world. There are two key points in the opening of national defence science, technology and industry:

- Increase exports. To satisfy domestic needs, the defence industry should try to develop products for export and expand exports. This will then open a source of income and accumulate funds to be used for imports. It will facilitate links with the international market, and through competing in the international market, the quality and character of our products will improve. Domestic and international needs can be considered as a whole, and scientific research and production will increase. It will also help to break the international monopoly and raise our international status. We must be aware that our products for export are not very competitive or cost effective. To achieve some breakthroughs in the international market, we need to dare to compete and carefully plan for long-term benefits. We should formulate a correct export strategy and adopt effective measures. For instance, we should try to open new markets, and concentrate on large and new projects. In response to market needs, we should promote the research and development of new types of products for export, raising the technological level of our export products so as to increase our competitiveness. Management of enterprises engaging in foreign trade should be further changed. We should increase the motivation for developing new products, improving quality, lowering cost, and increasing foreign exchange. We should constantly strengthen our competitiveness in the international market and open new venues for our foreign trade.
- Import technology. Deng Xiaoping pays special attention to the importation of technology. He has clearly pointed out, "Science and technology are the common treasures of mankind. Every nation, every country should learn from the strong points of other nations and countries, and learn from the advanced science and technology of others." In the process of our opening to the world, we should seize every favorable opportunity to import advanced technology from abroad, especially new and high technology. We should expand our technology cooperation and exchange with foreign countries. We should be good at linking imports with our own creations. Imported technology should be well digested and widely applied and used. The starting point of our research should be raised, and our ability to be self-reliant

should be strengthened. While doing a good job in importing technology, we should create favorable conditions and adopt flexible measures to attract talented people from abroad. This will be beneficial to the acceleration of the development of national defence science and technology, as well as the training of talented people for national science and technology.

Training Defence Scientists and Technological Experts

Scientists and technology experts are the creators of science and technology. Science and technology experts in the defence industry play a special role in the development of national defence science and technology and weaponry, and to a large degree determine the development progress of new high-technology weapons, and even the successful realization of the goals of modernization for national defence and army building.

Under the overall situation of reform and opening up, and the development of a market economy, the conditions for the existence and development of national defence science and technology personnel have undergone great changes.

We need to use new thinking to select and train talent. Deng Xiaoping once said, "We need to open up a way, so that talented people will grow to maturity quickly. We should not block talent. The constant emergence of talents means the success of our cause." Under the new situation, the building of the national defence corps of science and technology experts should pay special attention to the following three points:

- Liberate our minds and change our way of thinking. We should not simply rely on the state to supply us with experts. A new way is to attract and train science and technology experts through competition and promotion. The building of a high-level national defence corps of science and technology experts would not be possible without the support of the state and the improvement of the overall situation. But the national defence departments and units of science and technology should realize that reform and opening up have provided opportunities for them to attract more talent. They should focus on strengthening vitality and competitiveness and creating fine conditions to attract talent. They should be good at discovering, uniting, and making use of talent and maintaining a degree of superiority in the competition for talent.
- Change the environment for talent. What Deng Xiaoping once said is significant and worth pondering: The most important point, which I am most concerned with in the reform of the economic system is talent.

In the reform of the scientific and technological system, what I am most concerned with is also talent.... We should create an environment, in which talents showing themselves could appear. The reforms should create such an environment. Under the traditional planned economy system and personnel system, national defence science and technology experts were normally assigned through state planning and administrative means. As the development of the market economy and the reform of personnel system moves forward, we should, under the guidance of the state, pay attention to exploring the opportunities for recruiting and selection through labour markets and facilitate the appropriate promotion of talent, to create a balance of supply and demand. We should also gradually set up a system of training, evaluation, examination, recruiting, promotion, and awards for talented people.

- Take a long-term point of view and train talent for the next century. In the competition for talent in the world today, competition for young and middle-aged talent is very intense. Many developed countries believe that the greatest challenge facing national defence science and technology is attracting and retaining needed talent, especially for key technologies. To strengthen the building of our national defence corps of science and technology, we should face up to modernization, the world, and the future, and focus on selecting and training a group of young and middle-aged leaders in science and technology who will advance to the forefront of global science and technology in the next century. Senior scientists and technological experts should make the historical responsibility of training young people their first priority. At the same time, concerned departments and units should not stick to a certain pattern but select talent, especially young talent, and boldly make use of them, letting them shoulder heavy responsibility in making technological breakthroughs, accumulate experience, and grow to maturity quickly.

A Scientific, Authoritative and Effective Overall System

National defence science, technology, and industry are very important strategically and have a unique pattern of development. Only by strengthening overall control can we take into consideration national and military strategic requirements and make timely decisions and arrangements in light of national economic, scientific, and technological realities based on collective wisdom and scientific proof. According to historical experiences and future trends of development, we should pay attention to the following if we want to raise the authoritativeness and effectiveness of the overall control system:

- Strengthen the centralized and unified leadership of the Party and the state. During the 1950s and 1960s, we lacked economic power and qualified technical personnel, and we faced a very serious international situation. We made atom bombs, hydrogen bombs, and satellites, and we made major breakthroughs in other fields of high technology. The most important reasons for these successes were the wise decisions of Chairman Mao and the Party Central Committee, and the high prestige enjoyed by the central government headed by Premier Zhou Enlai. Judging from the experiences of foreign countries, the development of high technology, especially military high technology, is strictly regulated and controlled by the state. Under our current system, the strengthening of centralized and unified leadership is mainly the strengthening of decisionmaking, at high levels on the development of the defence industry, major projects, and important issues like the integration of defence and commercial industries. Under centralized and unified leadership, the different levels of administration should be responsible for their own management work.
- Decisionmaking on the major issues should be scientific and democratic. One important lesson we learned from both positive and negative experiences in the past is to ensure correctness in decisionmaking and efficiency and effectiveness in execution. The key to both of these is that decisionmaking should be scientific and democratic. Along with the steady development of new-tech revolution, modern weaponry is increasingly associated with high technology, and its cost has more than doubled. In addition to the changeable and unstable international situation, various intricate problems place higher demands on decisionmaking. Those important decisions related to development strategy, planning, goals, and focal points of the defence industry and weapons development are related to complicated systems engineering, and they should be suited to the changes in the international situation and rely on possible national power. The modernization of our army places demands on national defence research and production and science and technology; it is especially high technology that provides a great push in the development of weapons and equipment. These two points should be emphasized. Only through an all-around assessment and a comprehensive balance of strategy, tactics, economics, and technologies can we ensure that any decisionmaking is correct and its execution effective. To make fewer false starts and avoid mistakes, we should adhere to a strict decisionmaking process while making decisions. The decisionmaking system should be improved, and we

should give full play to the consulting departments' role in the making of decisions, especially paying attention to the advice by experts. We should also pool the wisdom of the masses, and the basis for the decisionmaking should be scientific and democratic.

- State planning should be based on scientific methods and earnestly carried out. The state command plan for the research and production of military products has the effect of law and should not be changed by any one or any unit without authorization. Of course, under the overall situation of a market economy, the command plan should also strictly follow the law of value, reflect the changes in supply and demand and give play to the economic lever. On the premise that energy supply, main materials supply, and transportation are provided by the state, all departments and enterprises should give priority to fulfilling the research and production tasks for military products, and strictly carry out contracts according to the law. Those who have violated the state plan or can not fulfil the plan, should be seriously dealt with. Set up a fairly complete law system. We could say that a market economy is a legal economy. In order to carry on the research and the production of military products in a systematic fashion and achieve standardization, regularization, and legalization, we should continue improving the existing laws and regulations, emphasizing development of the basic law of research and production in the defence industry. Moreover, we need to make and issue new administrative decrees in accordance with the new problems or new situations we might be facing in research and production. We should have strict management procedures, work according to objective laws, and ensure the sustained, rapid, and healthy development of the national defence industry.

10

Air Force Planning

The Air Force could cut beyond the thousands of airmen and hundreds of aircraft the service plans to draw down if sequestration returns in fiscal year 2016, according to a budget document.

Although the Air Force and the Defense Department received some spending relief from the scale of the cuts originally expected in fiscal year 2014, and hopes for the same with the proposed budget in 2015, "a lot of uncertainty remains" in 2016 and beyond, said Kathy L. Watern, Air Force deputy assistant secretary for cost and economics.

Watern, who spent two decades of her civilian career at Wright-Patterson, spoke to dozens of members of the Dayton Area Defense Contractors Association on Monday at the Hope Hotel and Conference Center.

Under the full impact of sequestration, the Air Force could withdraw the entire KC-10 Extender refueling tanker fleet of 59 jumbo jets. It also might reduce the number of RQ-4 Global Hawk Block 40 spy drones, buy fewer fifth-generation F-35A Joint Strike Fighters, bypass modification of fourth-generation fighter jets, such as the F-16, and spend no money on a next-generation jet engine, according to the Air Force.

Watern said the service branch anticipated solidifying what might happen in 2016 in the weeks ahead. A baseline $109.3 billion proposed budget in 2015, compared with an enacted baseline budget of $108.8 billion this year, would cut the number of airmen by 20,400 and civilian jobs by 2,700.

By 2019, the Air Force could retire 500 aircraft among the three components of active-duty, Air Force Reserve and Air National Guard. The Air Force has put a priority on new aircraft and restoring readiness it says was affected by sequestration.

The military wants to retire the U-2 spy plane and withdraw the A-10 Thunderbolt II ground attack jet, better known as the Warthog, which gained fame in the Persian Gulf War and has ardent backers in Congress and among ground troop advocates. The Global Hawk would replace the U-2.

The F-35, KC-46 Pegasus, and a long-range strike bomber have top billing. Additional priorities would replace the aging T-38 Talon jet trainer aircraft, pursue a next-generation E-8 Joint STARS aircraft, buy more sensors and munitions, and schedule more training exercises and invest in space-based systems. The Air Force operations and maintenance budget would decline to $44.3 billion from $45 billion this year. In two major areas affecting Wright-Patterson, the Air Force-wide acquisition budget could rise to $18.5 billion next year compared to $16.8 billion today, and spending on research, development, test and evaluation would remain flat at $16 billion. The base is headquarters for the Air Force Materiel Command and the Air Force Research Laboratory. Watern said much of the increase in the acquisition budget is for new aircraft, including 26 F-35s at a cost of $4.2 billion, and seven KC-46 tankers for $1.5 billion.

The budget is part of a proposed $495.6 billion Pentagon spending plan proposed by President Barack Obama. Obama has asked Congress to approve a $26 billion "Opportunity, Growth and Security Initiative" to recover from sequestration cuts. The Air Force share would amount to $7 billion spent to restore readiness, buy two more F-35As, and modify aircraft, among other priorities. The Air Force has initiated early retirement incentives and other force reduction measures prior to involuntarily eliminating positions, Watern said. In a move to reign in compensation costs, the Pentagon has proposed a 1 percent pay raise for service members and a pay freeze for generals and admirals. Following a Pentagon directive, the Air Force will cut headquarters staff by 20 percent.

THE AIR FORCE

The Air Force is a strategic service of the PLA, and the main force for carrying out air operations. It is responsible for such tasks as safeguarding the country's territorial air space and territorial sovereignty, and maintaining a stable air defence posture nationwide. It is mainly composed of aviation, ground air defence, airborne, signal, radar, ECM, technical reconnaissance and chemical defence sections.

History of Development

The Air Force was founded on November 11, 1949. The years from 1949 to 1953 witnessed the establishment of an Air Force leading organs in the CMC and in each of the military area commands; the creation of the fighter, bomber, attacker, reconnaissance and transport, airborne forces and a number of educational institutions; and the organization of the Air Force of the Chinese People's Volunteers to take part in the War to Resist U.S. Aggression and Aid Korea (1950-1953). The Air Force was merged with the Air Defence Force in 1957, by adopting a system combining air operations with air defence. In the 1960s and 1970s the Air Force formed the guiding principle of giving priority to the development of air defence forces, and gradually grew into an air force for territorial air defence.

Since the 1990s the Air Force has been in a phase of rapid development. It has deployed third-generation combat aircraft, third-generation ground-to-air missiles, and a series of relatively advanced and computerized weapons and equipment. It has stepped up the development of military theories with strategic theories at the core, and introduced a strategic concept that the Air Force should be capable of both offensive and defensive operations. As a result, the Air Force has begun its transition from territorial air defence to both offensive and defensive operations. After nearly six decades of development, the Air Force has initially developed into a strategic service comprising more than one wings. It now has relatively strong capabilities to conduct air defensive and offensive operations, and certain capabilities to execute long-range precision strikes and strategic projection operations.

Structure and Organization

In peacetime, the Air Force practices a leadership system which combines operational command with building and administration, and which consists of the Air Force Headquarters, air commands under military area commands, corps-level (division-level) command posts, divisions (brigades) and regiments. The Air Force has under it an air command in each of the seven military area commands of Shenyang, Beijing, Lanzhou, Jinan, Nanjing, Guangzhou and Chengdu. It has also under it an airborne corps as well as various institutions of education, research and experimentation. Under each air command at the military area command level are aviation divisions, ground-to-air missile divisions (brigades and regiments), antiaircraft artillery brigades (regiments), radar brigades (regiments), ECM brigades (regiments and battalions), and other specialized service units. In key areas there are also corps-or division-level command posts. The Air Force has also a number of educational and training institutions, including the Air Force Command College, Air Force Engineering University, Air Force Aviation University, Air Force Radar College, Air Force College at Guilin, Air Force College at Xuzhou, Air Force School for Noncommissioned Officers at Dalian and seven flying colleges.

An aviation division usually consists of regiments, groups and squadrons, and has such types of aircraft as fighters, attackers, fighter-bombers, bombers, transports and combat support aircraft. It has under it aviation regiments and related stations. The aviation regiment is the basic tactical unit. With battalions as the basic fighting units, the ground-to-air missile force is usually organized into divisions, regiments and battalions or into brigades (regiments) and battalions. With batteries as basic fighting units, the antiaircraft artillery force is usually organized into brigades (regiments), battalions and companies. The airborne forces are organized into corps, divisions, regiments, battalions and companies.

Force Building

To meet the requirements of informationized warfare, the Air Force is working to accelerate its transition from territorial air defence to both offensive and defensive operations, and increase its capabilities for carrying out reconnaissance and early warning, air strikes, air and missile defence, and strategic projection, in an effort to build itself into a modernized strategic air force.

Taking into full account preparations for combat and its own transformation and development, the Air Force is exploring training systems and methods tailored to the development of the latest generation of weaponry and equipment.

It stresses technical and tactical training in complex environments, combined training of different arms and aircraft types, and joint training; conducts mission-oriented and confrontational training; and is increasing on-base, simulated and web-based training. It is working to optimize the tripartite pilot training system composed of flying colleges, training bases and combat units, and intensifying the training of aviation units in counter-air operations, air-to-ground attacks and joint operations.

It is deepening reforms and innovations in institutional education by improving the system of discipline, and making innovations in teaching programs, means and methods. It is strengthening on-the-job training, and exploring a new model of personnel development, namely the triad of institutional education, training in units and professional military education. For this purpose, the Air Force Military Professional University was established in July 2008.

To satisfy the strategic requirements of conducting both offensive and defensive operations, the Air Force attaches importance to developing new types of fighters, air and anti-missile defence weapons, and command automation systems. It has deployed some relatively advanced computerized equipment, and air-to-air and air-to-ground precision-guided munitions, upgraded the electronic information systems of the equipment on active service, and improved the basic networks for intelligence and early warning, command and control, and communications. It has in the main established a major battle weaponry and equipment system with third-generation aircraft and ground-to-air missiles as the mainstay, and modified second-generation aircraft and ground-to-air missiles as the supplement.

Centring on the improvement of the capabilities and quality of its personnel, the Air Force pursues a road of personnel development which takes new-and high-tech talents as the driving force, makes breakthroughs in critical areas and aims at overall improvement. It makes overall plans for training command, staff, flight and technical support personnel. It has fostered a group of core personnel with a good command of information technology and a contingent of new types of high-caliber personnel as represented by inter-disciplinary commanding officers, first-rate pilots, leaders in scientific and technological research, and technical experts.

To raise its integrated support capabilities, the Air Force attaches importance to the development of logistical and equipment support systems. It endeavours to improve the support facilities of airfields and positions; strengthen its logistical forces for rapid construction of air defence projects, bomb elimination at and rapid repair of airfields which have suffered attack, and aviation medical support; develop and deploy the second generation of specialized logistical equipment; create a storage and supply network for special-purpose materials; and build step by step bases capable of supporting multiple types of aircraft. The Air Force is also stepping up efforts to deepen the reform of the equipment support mode; improve the layout of support networks for the supply, maintenance and technical support of ammunition and material; and make support equipment smaller in size, more versatile in function and fitter for field operations.

AIR FORCE-SUPPORTED AIRCRAFT

The data on aircraft age and planned future replacements for aging aircraft that are maintained by the Air Force. During the course of this study the committee received briefings and written material on these aircraft. Some of the more significant structural problems encountered with these aircraft are discussed briefly below. Additional details on all the aircraft can be found. The B-2 bomber, the F-117 attack aircraft, and the C-17 airlifter are excluded because of their relatively recent introduction into the force. Also, because of time, budget, and technical considerations, the committee elected to exclude the H-1, H-53, and H-60 rotorcraft from this study. Helicopters are somewhat unique in that dynamic excitations in the rotor systems (i.e., causing combined high-and low-cycle fatigue) have been at the root of many past structural problems, and as such the committee suggests that this subject could best be addressed separately.

The Air Mobility Command's (AMC) airlifter and tanker aircraft were designed based on the fail-safe approach, and, as a result, the primary safety concern with regard to aging is the loss of this fail-safety from the onset of widespread fatigue damage (WFD). In fact, both the KC-135 and the C-5A had their original lower wing surfaces replaced in the 1970s and early 1980s because of WFD, and the wings of the C-141 have more recently undergone extensive modification because of WFD (i.e., use of boron composite doublers to repair and prevent further cracking at the weep holes in the lower wing surface risers). In addition, some C-141s are now experiencing WFD in the lower wing surface spanwise slices. Risk analyses performed by the aircraft manufacturer have shown that these splices reach the onset of WFD at about 37,000 flight hours. The current plan is to retire all of the C-141s within the next eight years; however, this plan was based on an aircraft retirement time of 45,000 flight hours. For any aircraft that must be flown more than 37,000 hours before retirement, extensive and burdensome inspections are required to protect the structural safety. These inspections involve inspecting more than 6,000 fastener holes per aircraft every 120 days. The committee is not aware of any data to indicate that the KC-135 or the C-5 will experience the onset of WFD in the near future. For example, a blue ribbon panel reviewed the KC-135 during 1996 and concluded that the current data indicate that the aircraft could likely be flown to beyond the year 2040 before encountering WFD. However, the panel recommended some additional actions to improve this estimate and emphasized the need to control the present corrosion and stress corrosion cracking problems.

The Air Combat Command's (ACC) fighter, bomber, and attack aircraft and the Air Education and Training Command's T-37 and T-38 trainer aircraft were either designed to be damage tolerant using the safe crack growth concept or were later analyzed on the basis of crack growth to establish safety limits and inspection requirements. This was accomplished during the durability and damage tolerance assessments (DADTAs) that were performed on these aircraft. Although some of these aircraft have some inherent fail-safety resulting from redundancy in load paths and crack arresting features or because of battle damage requirements, they do not meet the fail-safe standards of the large transport aircraft. As such, with increasing age the primary threat to their structural safety is the growth in fatigue-critical areas and the potential of missing one or more of these areas. There already has been a significant increase in the number of critical areas in the F-16 since its introduction into service in 1979. Also, based on the number of cracking locations currently being reported in the T-38 and A-10, it appears that this is also true for these aircraft.

The T-38 is of particular concern because of its single-plank lower wing skin, its very small critical crack sizes (i.e., 0.20 to 0.40 in.), and the age of the aircraft in terms of both calendar years and flight hours. Wing failure and

aircraft losses occurred during the 1970s when these aircraft were put into severe roles. The T-38 was used in the lead-in-fighter (LIF) role and the dissimilar air combat training role by the Tactical Air Command. The critical crack size that caused the wings to fail was also about 0.2 in. Since the 1970s it appears that the Air Force's San Antonio Air Logistic Center and their prime contractor, Northrop-Grumman, have done a good job of maintaining structural safety and preventing wing failures through the use of safety inspections, structural modifications, design changes, and lower wing surface replacements. Additional full-scale wing fatigue testing has also been performed to identify critical areas in the new and modified structure. Crack growth analyses have performed to establish inspection requirements. Further design changes, wing replacements, and full-scale testing are anticipated by the San Antonio Air Logistics Center. The committee concurs that these changes undoubtedly will be needed if the aircraft are to remain in the inventory for 25 years or more.

The ACC's other aircraft that are used in various missions involving electronic combat, surveillance, intra-theater airlift, and tracking of enemy air and ground forces. Except for the U-2, the structures of these aging aircraft are predominantly of a fail-safe design, in which the threat to safety is the onset of WFD. The E-3 and the E-8 are both derivatives of the Boeing commercial 707 aircraft. However, the E-8 airframes are old commercial airframes that have been modified, whereas the E-3 were new airframes based on the 707 design. In fact, several of the E-8s have airframes that exceed the original design life goal (i.e., 20,000 flights) and, a number of the aircraft are either at or are believed to be approaching the onset of WFD and will very likely require lower wing surface replacements in the near future.

The C-130 aircraft have been in production for more than three decades. The E models were delivered between 1961 and 1972 and they make up the majority of the active Air Force assets. The H model, which has been supplied since 1973, makes up the balance of the intra-theater airlift and EC-130 electronic combat capability. There have been a number of fatigue cracking and corrosion problems over the years that have led to the retirement of nearly all of the A models and outer wing replacements of the B and E models to the H configuration.

There have also been numerous center wing replacements on the B, E, and H models. The major uncertainty about the C-130E/H airframe is the probable service life of the fuselage and the associated future structural maintenance needs. During 1996 an Air Force Structural Review Team looked at this issue and made several recommendations, including the teardown inspection of a high-time aircraft to look for evidence of WFD and the performance of a DADTA to determine future safety inspection requirements.

ASSESSMENT OF CHINA'S MODERNISATION PLANS

The dichotomy between what China characterises as its "peaceful development" and its military ambitions, inevitably raises questions as to whether China's military build up is indeed benign. Even if the answer is yes, it is also worth asking whether such extensive military spending and modernisation can really be achieved exclusively of repercussions within the international system. On a global scale, realistically, the emergence of China as a hegemonic superpower with economic and military superiority, regardless of whether its intentions are peaceful or not, is also unlikely to go left unchecked. In its 2007 assessment of China's military capabilities, the US Department of Defence summed up this dilemma:

The outside world has limited knowledge of the motivations, decision-making, and key capabilities supporting China's military modernization. China's leaders have yet to explain adequately the purposes or desired end-states of the PLA's expanding military capabilities. China's actions in certain areas increasingly appear inconsistent with its declaratory policies. Actual Chinese defence expenditures remain far above officially disclosed figures. This lack of transparency in China's military affairs will naturally and understandably prompt international responses that hedge against the unknown.

The biggest question, therefore, comes down to what is China's long term intent? In the view of some critics, threats to international peace and security still tend to come second to considerations of national interest for China. From a security perspective those interests are currently very much regionally oriented. In the longer term, however, many analysts are concerned that China's national interests may take on a more global slant which, alongside high levels of military spending and modernisation of its armed forces, may result in China being able to mount a serious military challenge either to US interests in Asia or beyond its regional sphere of influence. This is particularly pertinent given China's increasingly global interests, including access to energy and resources.

China is building up its People's Liberation Army navy (PLAN) not only to achieve regional military dominance in Asia, but also to give Beijing increasing options for the global exercise of military power [...] Before the end of the decade, new Type 093 SSNs are likely to be able to carry out small scale but politically powerful power projection missions for the Chinese leadership.

The Economist in August 2007 agreed with this assessment, suggesting that "some Chinese officers want to fly the flag ever farther afield as a demonstration of China's rise". Richard Bitzinger of the Institute of Defence and Strategic Studies has also argued: Is Chinese defence spending simply defensive? Bull. The offensive-defensive argument is total nonsense because it's a theoretical argument.

The Chinese are engaged in buying large numbers of advanced weapon systems intended to improve the PLA's power projection, area denial, precision strike and battlespace knowledge. Such capabilities can be used in both offensive and defensive contexts. While China's military build up is causing alarm in some quarters other commentators have taken a more measured approach. According to one author: The Chinese accept [...] that they are functioning in a world dominated by a United States that in a globalised era is especially privileged [...] Moreover, while China has been increasing its military spending over the past several years, it is not about to exhaust itself in an unproductive arms race with the United States.

At a meeting of the EU Institute for Security Studies in March 2006 the view was also put forward that some of the developments in China's military posture "are either exaggerated or are a natural consequence of the rise in China's power and status". It was also argued that "looking at China as a potential threat could become a self-fulfilling prophecy". Indeed, John Ikenberry has also argued that China's rise, whilst inevitable, does not mean a violent power struggle for supremacy within the international order will ensue. Instead he has suggested that both the US and China have far more to gain from integrating the latter into the current liberal international order. Writing in the January 2008 edition of *Foreign Affairs* he argues:

The task now is to make it [the current international order] so expansive and so institutionalized that China has no choice but to become a fully fledged member of it. The United States cannot thwart China's rise, but it can help ensure that China's power is exercised within the rules and institutions that the United States and its partners have crafted over the last century, rules and institutions that can protect the interests of all states in the more crowded world of the future.

Conventional Procurement Priorities

The objective of conducting and sustaining what the Chinese have termed "informationized wars", at distance and in defence of China's increasingly global interests, will require assets that provide expeditionary capability and information superiority. Consequently, China's conventional procurement priorities have, thus far, appeared to focus on the development of an aircraft carrier capability, strategic lift, aerial refuelling capabilities and intelligence, surveillance and reconnaissance (ISR) assets. Analysts have also pointed to China's apparent development of asymmetric technologies that go beyond the traditional military sphere and into the non-traditional areas of space and cyberspace, as an additional cause for concern.

Expeditionary Capabilities : Since the mid-1980s China has expressed sporadic interest in the study and development of carrier technologies. More recently in October 2006 Lieutenant-General Wang Zhiyuan, Vice Chairman of the Science and Technology Committee in the PLA's General Armament Department stated:

The Chinese army will study how to manufacture aircraft carriers so that we can develop our own... aircraft carriers are indispensable if we want to protect our interests in the oceans. Indeed, progress in China's carrier programme is arguably more advanced than mere discussion about the PLAN's possible requirements in this area. For several years Russia is believed to have been not only assisting China in the completion of an aircraft carrier which was acquired from Ukraine in 2000, but has also been providing assistance in the construction of three Chinese-designed aircraft carriers. In March 2007 a Chinese Admiral of the PLAN was quoted as saying that the Chinese shipbuilding industry is actively conducting R&D in aircraft carrier construction and could be ready to build such a vessel by 2010. A number of analysts have thus predicted that China could have an operational carrier by 2015, while others have considered 2020 to be a more realistic timeframe.

China has also recently expressed an interest in acquiring weapons and technologies linked to aircraft carriers, including the possible purchase of up to 48 Russian Su-33 fighter aircraft. In contrast to the Su-30 already in-service in the Chinese Air Force, the Su-33 is carrier-capable. There have also been suggestions that China is exploring options for at least two carrier-based airborne radar platforms. Although there is a degree of uncertainty over China's exact carrier procurement plans. While open sources do not allow for an exact assessment of the future PLAN [PLA Navy] carrier air wing, it's increasingly clear that the Chinese have a number of options going forward. Which path they choose is less certain than their obvious desire to develop a capability.

In order to support operations, at distance, in 2005 China also ordered an additional 38 Il-76MD long-range transport aircraft and Il-78 tanker-transport aircraft from Russia in an attempt to supplement the PLAAF's strategic lift and aerial refuelling capabilities.

First deliveries of the aircraft were expected to begin in 2007. However, in March 2007 that contract was delayed due to an increase in production costs, after which most of the production was transferred from Uzbekistan to Russia. At present, it is unclear when delivery of those additional aircraft will now take place. The contract is reported to have been put on hold until a dispute over the price of the aircraft is concluded between the Russian and Chinese governments.

Intelligence, Surveillance and Reconnaissance (ISR)

In order for the PLA to achieve an end-state whereby they are capable of winning "informationized wars by the mid-21st century", the development of a sophisticated C4ISR architecture within which the PLA's assets are fully integrated, will be essential. To that end the PLA has dedicated considerable resources to developing its indigenous capabilities in this area. Indeed the level of progress achieved thus far has been notable, particularly with respect to its surveillance and reconnaissance assets. China is estimated to be developing around 15 types of satellite that include imagery reconnaissance, electronic intelligence and signals intelligence reconnaissance satellites; small and micro-sized satellites for imagery, navigation and communications roles; and anti-satellite weapons. It is estimated that China may have a requirement for as many as 200 military, civilian and dual-use satellites in the first two decades of the 21st century.

In its 2007 assessment the Pentagon also highlighted this upward shift in the PLA's surveillance, reconnaissance and communication abilities. Yet, the extent of modernisation in this sector has been regarded as unsurprising given the ability of the

PLA to exploit the skills, knowledge and expertise that is already available in China's relatively advanced commercial space and IT sectors, both of which are supported by significant State research and development assistance. As RAND has noted:

China's IT sector should be viewed as a civilian industry with links to the Chinese defence industrial establishment and the PLA. Certain IT companies supply finished command, control, communications, computers, and intelligence (C4I) equipment and related products to the PLA, facilitating a major modernization of China's military C4I infrastructure. Whereas China's defence-industrial system has long suffered from a wide-ranging set of structural problems that have impeded development of modern military equipment, the commercial IT sector carries none of these burdens.

As a result, the PLA has reportedly achieved significant improvements in its communications and operational security, as well as its capacity to transmit information... The indigenous development of these capabilities is also considered a potential strength if China is to pursue, over the longer term, fully networked military assets. In contrast to its previous approach to addressing its capability gaps, China has been considered, at least by some analysts, as unlikely to be able to source, on a large scale, such capabilities from overseas.

As ISR priorities for the future the Pentagon's 2007 report suggests: China is planning eleven satellites in the Huanjing program capable of visible, infrared, multi-spectral, and synthetic aperture radar imaging. In the next decade, Beijing most likely will field radar, ocean surveillance and high resolution photoreconnaissance satellites [...]

China may be developing a system of data relay satellites to support global coverage, and has reportedly acquired mobile data reception equipment that could support more rapid data transmission to deployed military forces and units [...] China is developing microsatellites – weighing less than 100 kilograms – for remote sensing, and networks of imagery and radar satellites. These developments could allow for a rapid reconstitution or expansion of China's satellite force in the event of any disruption in coverage.

Arguably, however, China's greatest challenge will not necessarily be the direct acquisition of ISR assets, such as satellites, UAV, airborne early warning or over-the-horizon radar. Rather it will be in the integration and networking of those new capabilities together with an array of technologically diverse and disparate legacy systems.

The fact that a substantial proportion of those legacy systems are second and third generation capabilities based on originally reverse-engineered technologies could be problematic given the limitations of the Chinese defence industry.

One of the main disadvantages of reverse engineering is that the detailed knowledge of how individual and often complex component systems that make up a platform operate is often not fully understood.

As a result 'quick fixes' are often incorporated into the 'copy' in order to achieve success. Effectively integrating a variety of platforms, for which China is not the original design authority, into an overarching network that provides effective command and control, information superiority and situational awareness of the battlespace in "real time", will be a real test of China's industrial capabilities. It will also require considerable financial resources. As RAND have pointed out: it is not clear whether this increasingly advanced information technology system in the military will only improve the handling of information, or will perform the much larger function of boot-strapping the PLA's much more primitive, much less "informationized" conventional forces into a more modern force.

Non-Traditional Technologies

The indications are that in the last few years China's military modernisation plans have not been focused exclusively on traditional areas of competence. Motivated by the fact that China's military capabilities are in no way a match for the technologically superior forces of the US, the PLA has thus been seeking to develop exploitative asymmetric capabilities that would offset the US' qualitative and quantitative superiority on the battlefield. What some analysts have referred to as the ancient martial art of "pressure point warfare".

THE SECOND ARTILLERY FORCE

The Second Artillery Force is a strategic force under the direct command and control of the CMC, and the core force of China for strategic deterrence. It is mainly responsible for deterring other countries from using nuclear weapons against China, and for conducting nuclear counterattacks and precision strikes with conventional missiles.

The Second Artillery Force sticks to China's policy of no first use of nuclear weapons, implements a self-defensive nuclear strategy, strictly follows the orders of the CMC, and takes it as its fundamental mission the protection of China from any nuclear attack.

In peacetime the nuclear missile weapons of the Second Artillery Force are not aimed at any country. But if China comes under a nuclear threat, the nuclear missile force of the Second Artillery Force will go into a state of alert, and get ready for a nuclear counterattack to deter the enemy from using nuclear weapons against China. If China comes under a nuclear attack, the nuclear missile force of the Second Artillery Force will use nuclear missiles to launch a resolute counterattack against the enemy either independently or together with the nuclear forces of other services. The conventional missile force of the Second Artillery Force is charged mainly with the task of conducting medium-and long-range precision strikes against key strategic and operational targets of the enemy.

THE PEOPLE'S ARMED POLICE FORCE

As a component of China's armed forces and subordinate to the State Council, the People's Armed Police Force (PAPF) is under the dual leadership of the State Council and the CMC. The PAPF consists of the internal security force and various police forces. The border public security, firefighting and security guard forces are also components of the PAPF. The PAPF is charged with the fundamental task of safeguarding national security, maintaining social stability and ensuring that the people live and work in peace and contentment.

DYNAMIC PLANNING AND EXECUTION CONTROL

Planning and Simulation

Dynamic Planning and Execution Control exploits the information derived through Global Awareness. It is not possible to increase the tempo of operations without increasing the tempo of planning. Planning time should be reduced from days to hours or even minutes. Joint planning will be essential. Reduction of planning time also reduces the time available for review and checking of plans, and the burden of verifying accuracy and effectiveness must shift to automatic systems. Verification of plans will be done by the continuous simulations of the plans using current information about all forces. Consistency checks should be part of all planning and command systems. Displays and planning tools will permit commanders to compare simulations and plans, and to change both easily and consistently. People and databases involved in the Planning and Control process may be separated by thousands of miles. The system will support collaboration through virtual meeting facilities.

Execution Control

We refer to Execution Control rather than Battle Management as a way of emphasizing that planning and control systems should integrate Mobility and Attack planning in both war and peace. Mobility resources are at least as limited as combat resources, and supply and use of supplies must be coordinated at the same rate as combat operations. Resources used to provide Global Awareness must be integrated into the Execution Control system to supply the information needed for planning and execution at the rate needed to support mobility and combat operations. In an integrated force, the tempo of operations can be no faster than the cycle time of the slowest component of the system. It may be necessary to automate the interpretation of voice commands and responses and to provide automatic translation from one language to another. Although automatic translation may appear to be a distant dream, one should realize that many situations use highly stylized language which should be amenable to machine interpretation and translation. We should not concentrate solely on producing plans and execution orders at the highest possible rate.

The planning and simulation facilities should provide long range estimates at all times. For example, the procurement of a replacement part and its shipment to the point of use may require days. A long range estimate of parts requirements should be produced days ahead of a projected use time. Building munition stocks requires time, but overbuilding stocks is an improper use of mobility resources. This does not mean that long-term plans will not change from, even, hour to hour, but estimates should be consistent and reasonably constant. The automatic systems should be aware of "commitment" times after which changes cannot be made. It is apparent that the execution control system will use expert system technologies extensively.

Processors and Communications

The computer and communication systems which are needed can be defined in a straight-forward way. The Air Force should be prepared to procure high speed parallel computing systems to make the Dynamic Planning and Execution Control system work. Parallel computing over networks is well along in development and will be perfected by the commercial world. The Air Force should take advantage of these developments. Distributed satellite systems, partly or wholly commercial, are a natural way to provide affordable connectivity where fiber is nonexistent. We depend more and more on commercial terrestrial communications networks, because they are redundant, reliable, survivable, and cost effective. We seem to insist, however, on developing military satcom systems in spite of their exorbitant cost and limited performance. During the next decade commercial satcom systems will exceed the capacity and reliability, if not the survivability, of the military systems. Commercial systems will have multiple ground stations which connect to the worldwide fiber system. They will eventually use laser crosslinks and downlinks that will dramatically increase redundancy of the systems. It is likely that the commercial systems, or DoD-owned commercial-like systems, can be used for military purposes more reliably than can completely unique military systems. This will be especially true if other nations develop anti-satellite systems. The Air Force should consider carefully before investing further in dedicated military satcom systems.

Digital communications to and from aircraft will be an important aspect of future warfighting. Links of interest include those for one-way broadcast and two-way command and control. For one-way broadcast, adoption of civilian satellite technology is an interim solution which will enable cheap one-way reception of information on a theater-wide basis. Such a wide-area broadcast service would permit all aircraft to receive critical warning messages, weather, and real time surveillance regardless of their location in the theatre.

Two-way links for high performance aircraft, whether to satellites, URAVs, or large air-craft, continue to present a challenge. Current systems (low cost modems and higher cost JTIDS) already permit digital links to fighters. Wide area networks can be established through use of gateways on URAVs or large aircraft (such as the Joint STARS or AWACS). The line of sight range between a relay transmitter and a fighter for various altitudes. A URAV at 60,000 feet can transmit line of sight to a fighter at 20,000 feet over a range of more than 400 nm. We recommend that technologies appropriate for direct satellite links to fighters be explored, but the Air Force should continuously evaluate the cost and utility of direct satellite links compared to links through aircraft.

Direct Satellite link to large aircraft and to URAVs is a much simpler and less expensive option. Certainly direct satellite links should be provided to all airlifters, AWACS, Joint STARS, URAVs and tankers. Commercial carriers will probably suffice for the airlifter links and, perhaps, for the tanker links.

User and Developer Interactions

The interaction of users with all systems must be flexible, secure, and situation dependent. Intelligent Agents 17 can be developed to support the interaction. Flexible connectivity can be achieved with commercial operating systems, network protocols, and programming languages. Some argue that only unique military operating systems and government standardization of equipment and protocols can guarantee security. Exactly the opposite is likely to be the case. Creation of a single unique universe increases the probability of a single point failure which can destroy the entire system. The folly of that logic was recognized millions of years ago in biological evolution, because the absence of biological diversity in a species makes the entire species susceptible to a single virus. The Air Force must beware the natural human tendency toward absolute standardization. It will be necessary to develop security and priority systems which overlay or integrate into commercial systems such as UNIX, the Internet, and C++. These additions should be constructed such that commercial software development tools can be used. The Air Force should not be in the software tool business. Nor should the Air Force be in the computer language and compiler development business. A capability for the use of Ada should be maintained for special cases where it is appropriate. In general, however, Ada has become irrelevant in the information world. Other languages are developing much faster. Insistence upon its use increases cost and development time of systems and reduces the availability of commercial software and tools. It is time that the use of arcane languages such as Ada be relegated to situations where nothing else will suffice.

Caveats

We have suggested what to do, but it is as important to say what not to do. At all cost the Dynamic Planning and Execution Control System must not be planned as a closed, finished product. If it is to utilize rapidly developing technologies it must be open ended. It should be a growing organism which incorporates advances naturally and gradually. The Air Force must avoid designs which demand permanent adherence to particular hardware, languages, or operating systems.

An organic, growing system can be planned and built one section at a time. It is now time to get on with it.

NATIONAL DEFENCE RESERVE BUILDUP

China firmly relies on the people for national defence, and seeks to strengthen the buildup of the national defence reserve incompliance with the requirement of being able to deal with both emergencies and wars.

Reserve Force Buildup

With active servicemen as its backbone and reserve officers and men as its foundation, the reserve force is an armed force formed in line with the unified structure and organization of the PLA. It is under the dual leadership of the PLA and local Party committees and governments.

The reserve force was founded in 1983. In August 1986 it formally became a part of the PLA. In May 1995 the NPC Standing Committee adopted the Law of the People's Republic of China on Reserve Officers. In April 1996 the CMC began to confer military ranks on reserve officers. The Law of the People's Republic of China on National Defence promulgated in March 1997 explicitly stipulates that China's armed forces consist of the active-duty force and the reserve force of the PLA, the People's Armed Police Force and the militia.

After 25 years of buildup and development, the reserve force has become an important component of the national defence reserve. It is made up of the Army Reserve, Navy Reserve, Air Force Reserve and the Second Artillery Force Reserve. The Army Reserve breaks down into infantry, artillery, antiaircraft artillery, antitank artillery, tank, engineering, chemical defence, signals, coastal defence and other specialized forces. The Navy Reserve is mainly composed of reconnaissance, mine-sweeping and mine-laying, radar observation and communications and other specialized forces. The Air Force Reserve mainly comprises ground-to-air missile, radar and other specialized forces. The Second Artillery Force Reserve mainly consists of the specialized missile support force and special equipment maintenance force.

In line with the unified structure and organization of the PLA, the reserve force has reserve divisions, brigades and regiments, and corresponding leading organs. Reserve units are organized mainly on a regional basis. Divisions are set up in provinces and brigades (regiments) in prefectures (autonomous prefectures or prefecture-level cities). A division (brigade) can be set up in a region covering more than one prefecture (autonomous prefecture or prefecture-level city), and a regiment in a region covering more than one county (county-level city or district).

In recent years, the reserve force has made new strides in organization building and military training. It has gradually enlarged the pool of reservists, improved its organizational methods, and actively explored new organizational models, such as industrial, trans-regional and community-based organizations. It conducts and manages training according to the training program and law, so as to regularize training. As stipulated in the Outline for the Military Training and Evaluation of the Reserve Force, one third of the authorized strength of a unit must undergo 30 days of training annually. Training tasks are based on possible wartime assignments and the caliber of the reservists. The reserve force is in the process of shifting its focus from quantity and scale to quality and efficiency, and from a combat role to a support role. The goal is to enable the reserve and active forces to cooperate closely with each other, to complement each other, and to develop in a coordinated way.

Militia Force Building

Militia work is under the unified leadership of the State Council and the CMC, and the leadership of local Party committees, local governments as well as the local military commands. The General Staff Headquarters supervises militia work nationwide. The military area commands are responsible for militia work in their respective jurisdictions. Provincial military commands, prefectural military commands and people's armed forces departments of counties (county-level cities or districts) are the organs of military leadership and command, and responsible for the militia work in their respective jurisdictions. The grass-roots people's armed forces departments established in town-ships (towns), urban sub-districts, enterprises and public institutions are responsible for organizing and carrying out militia work. Local Party committees and governments at all levels make overall plans and arrangements for militia work.

In recent years China has persisted in reform and innovation in militia force buildup, adjusted its size and structure, and upgraded its weaponry and equipment. The organizational structure has optimized to increase the capabilities of the militia to support combat and emergency response forces, and to gradually shift the centre of its responsibilities from rural areas to cities, areas along communication lines and other key areas. Importance has been attached to establishing militia organizations in emerging enterprises and high-tech industries to increase the technology content of the militia force. Investment in weaponry and equipment has been increased to systematically and organically provide a series of new types of militia air defence equipment such as air defence artillery and portable air defence missiles in key areas. Equipment for emergency response and stability-maintenance operations has been improved. Some types of weapons have been upgraded. During the Eleventh Five-Year Plan period (2006-2010) the number of militia personnel is scheduled to be reduced from 10 million to eight million.

In May 2007 the General Staff Headquarters released a new edition of the Outline for the Training and Evaluation of the Militia. The new outline adds over a hundred training tasks in dozens of categories covering specialties of the Navy, Air Force and Second Artillery Force, marking a shift from traditional single-service to multi-service/arm specialized militia training. Based on the principles of integrating resources, pooling strengths, organizing training level by level and conducting trans-regional training, the military training of the militia has a four-level organizational system: The provincial military commands are the backbone; the prefectural military commands are the main body; the people's armed forces departments are the basis; and the grass-roots people's armed forces departments are the supplement. The militia is improving its technology-based training, and promoting on-base, simulated and web-based training step by step. Prominence is given to such tasks as rapid mobilization of specialized detachments, coordination with active units and operations in complex electromagnetic environments. In addition, efforts are being made to enhance training in emergency response and rescue. The aim is to raise the militia's capabilities in combat operations, emergency rescue, disaster relief, crisis response and social stability maintenance.

AIR DEFENCE AND OFFENSIVE AIR OPERATIONS

The IAF has accepted for sometime that the increased costs of maintaining a modern and effective air force in the future would necessitate the need for a reduction in force levels. Consequently, procurement and upgrade programs since the late 1980s have emphasized the need to extract the maximum out of every aircraft. This means two things in practice. First, it means that all existing aircraft will be the subject of upgrades that make them more lethal and enhance survivability. The installation of new radar, avionics, weapons aiming system, electronic warfare suites are all consistent with the IAF's prevailing philosophy. Second, the IAF has decided that all new types of fighters added to inventory will be multi-role-the Su-30MKI and LCA are both designed to meet this requirement.

Where possible, existing platforms are being adapted to multi-role use. Indeed the extensive upgrade package for the MiG-21bis gives it a true multi-role capability. Similarly, trials are in progress to provide upgraded MiG-27s with a secondary air-air capability. The integration of the pod mounted Komar radar will allow the MiG-27 the ability to operate BVR AAMs such as the R-27 and R-77. With the imminent withdrawal of all three of Eastern Air Command's MiG-21FL squadrons, the MiG-27s will have to don the air defence mantle in the east, in the absence of any permanently based air defence units in the region. The quest for additional Mirage 2000s also fits this pattern. It is yet unclear whether the Mig-29 upgrades will bestow the type with multi-role capability.

The IAF's 1990s projection of a leaner meaner force for the beginning of the 21st century is likely to be quite accurate. The force will be meaner and more capable. It is also likely to be smaller. The last remaining MiG-21FL/M squadrons are likely to give up their aircraft in the near future, as is the solitary MiG-23MF squadron. Although the relative age of the latter unit's airframes and the training role that they fill, will likely allow them to outlive the older MiG-21s. If IAF decides to restrict the number of MiG-21bis upgrades to 125 airframes, we could expect to see a more substantial drop in number of operational squadrons. Hypothetically speaking, if procurement and modernization programs remain at present levels, by 2005 we could expect to see total numbers for fighter squadrons decline from the current peak of 39 to 32. The capabilities of newer aircraft ensure that the older MiG-21s need not be replaced one on one (even if cost permitted). For example, a single Su-30 can deliver as much ordnance as a squadron of MiG-21FLs and at greater ranges, and with greater accuracy.

The desire to reduce the multiplicity of combat aircraft types in IAF service is unlikely to produce any significant results for the next decade or so. The retirement of MiG-21 and MiG-23 variants will reduce the number of types in service from 10 to 7. Indeed, as is underscored by the extensive modernization programs, most of these aircraft remain too useful to discard. MiG-21/MiG-23/27/29, Mirage 2000, Jaguars, and Su-30 are likely to fly side by side well into the next decade. And while the multiplicity of types has not adversely affected the IAF's combat performance, it does make logistics more complicated. However, increased commonality between avionics and other sub systems across the fleet is expected to make maintenance and logistics easier than they have ever been. Not only will this fleet be capable of delivering larger amounts ordnance more accurately over greater distances, but can also expect a greater level of survivability thanks to the increasing availability of force multipliers.

Emphasis on Force Multipliers

The IAF has been slow to induct force multipliers. While quick to deploy sizeable numbers of EW, ECM, and Reconnaissance assets, the IAF lacked an in-flight refueling capability and AWACS for years. Until the arrival of the Su-30s, only two aircraft types came with plumbing for in-flight refueling – Jaguars and Mirage 2000s. However, the IAF had the refueling probes of these aircraft removed in service. Until the early 1990s, the IAF remained a largely tactical force in its outlook. The prevailing view was that in case of a war with Pakistan, all major targets could be reached without the need for in-flight refueling. It was envisioned that any conflict with China would remain largely localized, again putting all targets within easy range of its aircraft. However, nuclearization and an expansion in the size of the IAF supporting aircraft forced a reconsideration of this view. The need to deploy specialized aircraft for duties such as Suppression of Enemy Air Defences (SEAD) and the lengths of time that such aircraft would have to kept airborne created a pressing need for an in-flight fueling capability. The first in-flight refueling trials were conducted between IAF Jaguars and a RAF VC-10 tanker on loan as recently as 1996. Since then, the IAF has placed orders for a number of IL-78 tankers. It is expected that eventually eight such aircraft will be acquired. In the interim, the IAF has inducted UPAZ buddy refueling system for its Su-30s, Mirages, and Jaguars. The MiG fleet too is being equipped with in-flight refueling capability as part of their upgrades. In the context of nuclearization, the introduction of in-flight refueling provides the IAF with a rudimentary, if somewhat less than secure, deterrent capability against China.

The deployment of MiG-21s as airborne radar pickets in 1971, provided the IAF with an early introduction to the benefits of Airborne Early Warning (AEW). Unfortunately, an initial paucity of funds and an eventual inability to find a suitable platform set the IAF's efforts to acquire an AEW/AWACS back by many years. The IAF evaluated the Soviet A-50 in 1988 and rejected it for being incompatible with the existing air defence grid. Recent efforts to build a such a system indigenously has been hampered by the inadequacy of the trials platform (a Hs.748) and the loss of one prototype (of three) along with the R&D team. The need for an AWACS was sorely felt during the Kargil war in 1999. Consequently, the IAF has resumed its search with much vigour. A pair of A-50s with the new Shmel-2 radar was leased from the Russian AF in May of this year to help familiarize the service with operation of such systems. The IAF is reluctant to purchase the A-50 "as is" because, as in 1988, it would be a challenge to integrate the system with the Indian air defence set up. The IAF is also unhappy that some of the information processing for the A-50 has to be done via ground stations. The IAF would like to customize the system with Indian and non-Russian electronic subsystems so that it can be integrated with the Indian air-defence grid with less difficulty. For this reason, it will still be sometime before the IAF fields a viable AWACS/AEW force. The service has a requirement for up to six such aircraft.

There are two further dimensions to the IAF's quest for force multipliers – namely, EW and Reconnaissance. The IAF has rather extensive ELINT gathering and reconnaissance assets available. The bulk of the ELINT aircraft (B707, An-32, and B737) are operated under the auspices of the Aviation Research Center (ARC) and photographic reconnaissance assets are operated by directly by the IAF. Scores of MiG-21MRs and MiG-23BNs form the backbone of the tactical reconnaissance force. For strategic reconnaissance the IAF deploys squadron each of Canberra PR 57/67 and MiG-25Rs, complemented by a few Gulfstream III SRA-1s fitted with oblique cameras, which can look deep into enemy territory. Additionally several types of combat aircraft can be fitted with reconnaissance pods. It is expected that the MiG-21MRs are will be withdrawn in the near future. However, the IAF is looking at potential upgrade packages for the Canberras (both P 67s and B (I) 58 versions) in order to keep these forty-year old aircraft in service until 2010. Most recently, the IAF has acquired the Viten Vicon reconnaissance pods for use in strike squadrons, in order to give then an autonomous reconnaissance capability. The recent introduction of high altitude unmanned aerial vehicles (UAVs) gave the IAF its first significant experience with real-time reconnaissance capability. It is expected that in the next 5-7 years the defence forces will deploy dedicated satellites to enhance their intelligence gathering capabilities.

The IAF accepts the fact that losses in men and materials are to be expected during the course of combat operations. However, the IAF has invested quite heavily in trying to make sure that such losses are kept to a minimum. Budgetary constraints notwithstanding, the IAF has attempted, with some success, to create a comprehensive countermeasures force. Specialized aircraft have been acquired to support strike packages with ECM and ECCM cover. Stocks of anti-radiation systems – both missiles (ARMAT, Kh-25MP, Kh-59) and drones (Harpy) – have been diligently built up for this purpose. A number of MiG-23 airframes have been modified for SEAD duties with ARMs. It is also understood that the both of two-seat Jaguars currently under production will augment existing SEAD capabilities. The Jaguars greater endurance may have contributed to its selection as the primary EW support aircraft for the future.

Improvements in C4I and Land-based Air Defence

Nuclearization of the Indian subcontinent has important implications for the future of both C4I and land-based air defence. Cognizant of this, the IAF has been working continuously since the early 1990s to shield and harden its communication network/nodes against nuclear attack. This is critical because of the second strike doctrine adopted by India. As the principal operator of India's nuclear weapons, the IAF's C4I network must be able to survive a first strike. In addition to the radiation hardening, it is understood that several levels of redundancy have been built into the network. The IAF has also undertaken the task of incrementally upgrading the strike fleet with EMP shielding.

The IAF already fields a formidable (in a regional context) ground based air defence system. India's air defence network is essentially divided into two parts-the Air Defence Ground Environment System (ADGES) and the Base Air Defence Zones (BADZ). These two components are closely linked and share information relating to air defence tasks. The ADGES and BADZ along with their associated sensor network and SAM units provide India with an extremely potent defence against both Pakistani and Chinese manned aircraft. Additionally, SAMs and fighters of the Navy also defend sensitive nuclear installations along India's western coasts.

The ADGES is currently being upgraded with the new Indian and Israeli radar. The Pechora SAMs which form the backbone of the IAF's SAM units are also undergoing upgrades which will see them fitted with more sensitive seeker heads. The IAF is also looking at the Akash to provide it with the next generation SAM. The emerging challenge to the air defence network is defence against ballistic missile attack. Over the last two years, the Indian press has been awash with reports that the government has sanctioned the building of an ATBM defences. The IAF feels that the limited ability of the current sensor network to detect and track missile launches needs to be substantially upgraded. Furthermore, the Russian S-300 SAM is being considered to provide the backbone of ATBM defences. While the system has undergone several trials in India (and may even be deployed in limited numbers), the IAF and the government are wary of relying excessively on the baseline system which has been compromised. Negotiations are underway for Indian to acquire a transfer of technology for the indigenous production of an S-300 derivative with Indian developed electronics and subsystems. It is likely that technology developed for the Akash SAM will be incorporated into any Indian manufactured S-300 derivative. Indeed, it is believed that the Akash SAM and the associated Rajendra phase array radar have some ATBM capability. The creation of an effective ATBM screen is high priority for the IAF but it will be many years before such a screen is operational.

Transports and Helicopters

The IAF has a sizable fixed and rotary winged transport fleet. While not as glamorous as their counterparts in the fighter stream, the IAF transport and helicopter formations contribute more than half of the IAF's annual flying hours. Operating out of some of the world most dangerous and inhospitable airstrips, the IAF's transport and helicopter formations play a crucial role in keeping the Indian Army and Air Force supplied. During last the Kargil operations last year, transport pilots were the unsung heroes of the war-flying day in and day out to maintain an uninterrupted air-bridge to the world's highest battle zone. Indeed post-Kargil the transport squadrons are logging almost 30% more hours than their counterparts in the fighter stream. India's airlift capabilities are significant. The ability to airlift the equivalent of a brigade plus their equipment at a time easily gives the IAF the largest military lift capability in Asia.

Two squadrons of IL-76 provide the IAF with its heavy lift capability, some 1,080,000 kg in all. These aircraft regularly operate out airfields in Ladakh situated at over 10,000 ft above sea level. The IAF is considering replacing the engines of these aircraft with western engines with a view to increasing operating efficiency. Increased logistical commitments in the aftermath of Kargil have caused the IAF to revive plans to add to its IL-76 fleet.

The An-32 from the backbone of the IAF's medium lift capabilities. Originally equipping six operational squadrons and a training unit, several of the type has now been put into storage. The An-32s were hit hard by the chaos in the ex-USSR as spares became harder to obtain.

In response to these problems, the IAF successfully fitted several An-32s with An-12 power plants upon the retirement of the latter, and put a number airframes into storage. Although the spares problem is no longer as acute as in the early 1990s, the IAF has seen fit to keep the type flying with four operational squadrons and prevent wear & tear on the rest. The IAF still maintains one and a half squadrons of Hs.748 military freighters. The retirement of these aircraft in the near future is bound to affect the IAF airlift capabilities. It is not yet clear what aircraft the IAF considering as replacements for the type, although a fleeting interest has been shown in the ATR-42. The An-32s will also need replacements by the end of the decade as spares become harder to come by and airframe life will rapidly expire. The IAF Do-228 light transports are relatively new and the type is still in production in-country and one can expect the type to stick around well into the future.

The IAF helicopter fleet has come a long way from its humble beginnings. The IAF currently operates dozens of helicopter units, including three dedicated attack helicopter units. The "Hip" family is the workhorse of the IAF helicopter fleet. Hundreds of Mi-8/17s fly everything from liaison to assault missions. The Mi-17 fleet was quite active over Kargil and one of the type was lost in action. The recent deal to add 40 new Mi-17-1B helicopters to the IAF, is consistent with the IAF policy to replacing the older Mi-8s with its more modern and powerful stable-mate.

A number of Mi-17s are also to be upgraded with sensors such as Forward Looking Infra Red (FLIR) in order to help augment the attack helicopter fleet. The IAF's attack helicopter fleet comprises of between two and three Mi-25/35 units. The Mi-35 recently underwent a comprehensive upgrade in Israel. It is also understood that there is solitary Chetak unit for anti-armour operations. Additionally, the "Hip" family can be fitted with a range of guided and unguided weapons. The IAF flies several Cheetahs and Chetaks in the liaison, SAR, and training roles.

These types will eventually be replaced by Advanced Light Helicopter from Hindustan Aeronautical Limited, that has recently entered production. The IAF also operates a solitary unit of Mi-26 heavy-lift helicopters. The prohibitive cost of operating the type means that they are usually employed on special duties that are beyond the capabilities of other aircraft in the force. There is an ongoing tussle between the Army and IAF, over control of the attack & assault helicopter fleet. The former argues that the optimal deployment of these aircraft is only possible when ownership rests with the service that is expected to benefit from them.

Training

The IAF offers a very rigorous flying training schedule for its pilots. Before being assigned to operational squadrons, pilots are expected to log over 300 hours of flying at the basic, intermediate and advanced levels. However, maintaining the very high standards of training will pose a challenge for the air force in the new century. The problem is particularly acute at the advanced fighter training level. The problem arises form the age and unsuitability of the MiG Operational Flying Training Unit's (MOFTU) aircraft. As of now fighter pilots are expected to log 125 hours on the unit's MiG-21FL and UM before being assigned to squadrons. The some of these aircraft are now over 30 years old and in very poor state of repair. The MiG-21FLs were phased out of Indian production in the mid-1970s hence spares for the type are very difficult to come by. Whatever spares are available are second-hand. Furthermore the early generations of MiG-21s are unforgiving aircraft and pushing over a certain AoA at over 600 knots, sends the aircraft into an uncontrollable spin. Old airframes together with the fact that many IAF pilots go straight from basic training to MiG-21FL/UM explains the high accident rates for the type. In addition to the human cost, this has an unfavorable impact on morale for younger pilots. The IAF has been trying for years to purchase suitable Advanced Jet Trainers (AJT) to ease the transition to high performance aircraft. Both the Hawk and Alpha Jet were evaluated in the 1980s, but funding problems & dithering on the part of the government kept IAF from placing orders. More recently, the IAF has revised its interest in purchasing the Hawk (the Alpha Jet being long out of production). However, Britain's inability (and reluctance) to refurbish Indian Navy Sea Harriers in the face of a US arms embargo have thrown into doubt the UK's ability to provide support for any Hawks that may be purchased. With the acquisition of AJT hanging in the air, the IAF's training problems are likely to get more acute. It is unfortunate that neither the IAF nor the Ministry of Defence has shown any interest in turning the HJT-36 intermediate trainer, now in development, into an AJT.

After a bad patch in the early 1990s, the IAF has been able to restore training in operational squadrons to their normal levels. Increased use of simulators have made a substantial difference to IAF training programs in recent years by making enhancing safety and preserving airframe life. Advanced fighter training has received a boost with the acquisition of Air Combat Maneuvering Instrumentation (ACMI) systems for the Tactics & Air Combat Development Establishment (TACDE) at Jamnagar. TACDE now offers courses in EW and helicopter combat. It also provides Dissimilar Air Combat Training (DACT) facilities to the Sea Harriers of the Navy.

Manpower Issues

During the 1990s, India has experienced the highest levels of economic growth since independence. For the armed forces, this growth has had positive as well as negative consequences. On the positive side, economic growth has allowed them to benefit from larger budgetary allocations. On the negative side, an explosion in private sector jobs and salaries, have lured many away from careers in the armed forces. This is not a problem unique to India. Even wealthier countries, such as the United States military, have problems filling vacancies with suitable candidates. According to the Minister of Defence, the IAF was 500 pilots short of its authorized strength of 3347 in 1999. While the IAF still manages to maintain an adequate pilot to cockpit ratio and smaller force levels may yet alleviate some of the problems, the shortages are disturbing. The IAF will have re-visit its personnel policy not only for pilots, but also for the technical branches as these are also likely to be affected by a greater demand for technical skills in the civilian sector. The recent decision to recruit women into the technical and flying branches has been a step in the right direction. By enlarging the pool of applicants, the IAF is sure to raise the overall quality of entrants.

Some Recommendations

The IAF is a thoroughly professional and increasingly well equipped force. It has emerged stronger through very trying times at the beginning of the 1990s. One should, however, not underestimate the challenges that lie ahead. The IAF, I am sure, is quite conscious of its own operational deficiencies and a discussion of these issues is quite clearly outside the scope of this chapter. However, based on emerging trends one can offer a number of macro recommendations that can only benefit the IAF in the future.

The Kargil war demonstrated the importance of joint operations between the services. After some initial setbacks and disagreements, the Army and the Air Force evolved a satisfactory, if somewhat ad hoc, mechanism for joint operations. This, unfortunately, was a temporary arrangement brought on by demands of war. The lack of a more formal mechanism for inter-service co-operation hampers an optimal use of the armed forces.

The biggest challenge facing the armed forces in general, and the IAF in particular, is the recruitment of suitable manpower for future needs. It is inconceivable that the IAF, or any air force, can offer compensation packages on par with private sector in a fast growing economy. Nor should they try. To this end, the IAF should adopt more an imaginative recruitment policy. Instead of listing amounts for base salary, house rent allowance, flight pay, etc. in its recruitment brochures, as is the case now, the IAF should highlight the intangibles that the private sector could never provide. The promise of adventure, camaraderie, the lure of fast jets and a chance to serve one owns country is something that draws many young people towards the IAF. This is not to say that material benefits do not matter-they do. However, a professional air force can not be built on the size of compensation packets alone. Judging by the number of daily inquires that we at Bharat Rakshak receive, there are many dedicated young men and women who are interested in a career with the IAF – and not just in the flying branch! It is ultimately to the IAF to reach out and encourage such people. And this is only possible if the IAF raises the profile of its recruitment drive. Taking a leaf out of the Army's PR campaign would be step in the right direction. Backseat videos, documentaries and advertising campaigns in the media are the best way for the IAF to reach out to the public.

There are other measures that the IAF can introduce to tide over personnel shortages. These shortages should be expected to remain a perennial feature. The pyramidal structure of any armed force ensures that each year large numbers of qualified individuals are lost through a natural process of attrition. Many people leaving the service do so with between 10-15 years of service. These individuals retain the physical and mental capacity to carry out a variety of operational tasks. Many of these retirees are often still willing to help out, given the opportunity. The IAF should consider instituting a reserve system that can exploit this trained pool of manpower. The institution of a reserve system along the lines of the United States National Guard system merits some thought. In addition to helping fill peacetime shortages, a reserve system would enhance the IAF's war making potential. Additional ways in which manpower management can be improved includes the secondment of administrative and facilities officers to oversee the administration of facilities. This would allow the command and operational staff to remain focused on their primary task.

Overt nuclearization of the Indian subcontinent behooves the IAF to take up NBC training with greater urgency. While essential units are well versed with the procedures of dealing with an NBC attack, much more education is required. The air force has an important role to play in helping formulate disaster management policies in the face of unconventional attacks.

Last, but by no means the least, changed geo-political circumstances mean that the IAF should no longer rely on uninterrupted flows of arms and equipment from abroad. The spares crisis of the 1990s and recent Sea Harrier episode highlight the need for greater reliance on in house maintenance and production. More recently, the Israeli decision, under US pressure, to cancel the sale of a Phalcon AWACS to China highlight the dangers of excessive dependence on outside suppliers. While there are no quick fixes to the production dilemma, the IAF can do much by ensuring that it builds up substantial stocks of critical spares and ordnance. The co-production of PGMs, avionics, and engines should be encouraged where possible.

Bibliography

Alam, Aftab : *US Policy Towards South Asia: Special Reference to Indo-Pak Relations*, Raj, Delhi, 1998.

Allen Carlson, *Unifying China, Integrating with the World: Securing Chinese Sovereignty in the Reform Era,* Stanford: Stanford University Press, 2005.

Allison, Graham, *Nuclear Terrorism: The Ultimate Preventable Catastrophe,* New York: Times Books, 2004.

Alperovitz, Gar. *The Decision to Use the Atomic Bomb.* New York: Vintage Books, 1996.

Amitabh Sikdar: *India and China : Strategic Energy Management and Security,* Manas, Delhi, 2009.

Anil, K.C.: *Military and Democracy in South Asia : Challenges, Politics and Power,* Sumit Enterprises, Delhi, 2009.

Arend, A.: *International Law and the Use of Force,* London, Routledge, 1993.

Asha Gupta: *Military Rule and Democratization : Changing Perspectives,* Deep & Deep, Delhi, 2003.

Bhaskara Rao: *Military Conversion : Impact on Science and Technology,* Discovery, Delhi, 2003.

Bhat, T.P. : *India and China : Trade Complementarities and Competitiveness,* Bookwell, Delhi, 2008.

Bhattacharyya, S. K., *Genocide in East Pakistan/Bangladesh: A Horror Story,* A. Ghosh Publishers, 1988.

Boubel, Richard W.: *Fundamentals of Air Power,* San Diego, Academic Press, 1994

Bradley, John. *Learning to Glow: A Nuclear Reader*. Tucson: University of Arizona Press, 2000.

Brauer, J. and J.P. Dunne : *Air Arms Trade and Economic Development: Theory Policy and Cases in Arms trade Offsets,* London and New York: Routledge, 1973.

Bryner, Gary C. : *Blue skies, green politics : the Clean Air Act of 1990 and its implementation,* Washington, D.C., CQ Press, 1995

Buzan, Barry & Eric Herring: *The Arms Dynamic in World Politics,* London: Lynne Rienner Publishers, 1998.

Chakravarty, B C Dr.: *Indian Armed Forces - Official History of the 1965 Indo-Pak War.* Ministry of Defence.

Chandra, R.: *Judicial System in Mechanical Warfare*, Lucknow, Print House (India), 1992.

Chaturvedi, Air Marshal M. S.: *History of the Indian Air Force*. Vikas, Delhi, 1978.

Chitkara, M.G. : *China-Pak Relations Challenges Before New Millennium*, APH, Delhi, 2001.

Citino, Robert M: *Blitzkrieg to Desert Storm: The Evolution of Operational Art*, University Press of Kansas, Lawrence, 2004.

Digumarti Bhaskara Rao: *Military Conversion : Impact on Science and Technology*, Discovery, Delhi, 2003.

Dixit, A.K. : *Military Wars and Rescue Techniques*, Cyber Tech Pub, Delhi, 2010.

Dixit, Prabla: *Aviation: A Struggle for Power*, New Delhi, Orient Longman, 1981.

Douhet, Giulio: *The Command of the Air*. New York: Coward - McCann, 1942.

Erickson, Richard: *Legitimate Use Of Force Against State Sponsored Terrorism*. US Air War College, 1989.

Evelyn Goh, *Meeting the China Challenge: The U.S. in Southeast Asian Regional Security Strategies*, DC: East-West Center, 2005.

Friedman, G.: *The Future of War: Power, Technology and American World Dominance in the 21st Century*, N.Y., Random House, 1996.

Gao, Mobo: *The Battle for China's Past: Mao and the Cultural Revolution*, London, Pluto Press, 2008.

Gautam, P.K. : *Environmental Security : New Challenges and Role of Military*, Shipra, Delhi, 2010.

Ghosh, Ajoy : *Indo-Pak Conflict : Threat to South Asian Security*, Reference Press, Delhi, 2003.

Gray, Colin Spencer. *Understanding Airpower*, AFRI: Maxwell, March 2009.

Gupta, Asha: *Air Military Rule and Democratization : Changing Perspectives*, Deep & Deep, Delhi, 2003.

Gupta, SC: *History of the Indian Air Force 1933-45*, Pubications Division, Ministry of Defence, Delhi, 1961.

Halberstadt, Hans: *Army Aviation*. Novato, CA: Presidio Press, 1990.

Hans J. Morgenthau: *Politics Among Nations: The Struggle for Power and Peace*, New York, Knopf, 1960.

Heimanson, Rudolph: *Dictionary of Military*, N.Y.: Oceana Publications, 1967.

Hodson, H. V.: *The Great Divide*: *Britain-India-Pakistan*, Karachi, Oxford UP, 1993.

Holsti, K.: *The State, War, and the State of War*, Cambridge, Cambridge Univ. Press, 1996.

Huntington, S.P.: *The China Defence Modernisation Military and the State*, N.Y., Vintage Books, 1964.

Jagannath P. Panda: *China's Path to Power : Party, Military and the Politics of State Transition*, Pentagon, Delhi, 2010.

James Campbell: *Excursions, Adventures and Field-Sports in Ceylon : Its Commercial and Military Importance*, AES, Delhi, 2006.

James R Blaker: *Transforming Military Force : The Legacy of Arthur Cebrowski and Network Centric Warfare*, Pentagon Press, Delhi, 2008.

Janowitz, M.: *The Professional Soldier: A Social and Political Portrait*, N.Y., The Free Press, 1960.

Jha, Prem Shankar : *India and China : The Battle Between Soft and Hard Power*, Penguin Books India, Delhi, 2010.

Joel Moses: *The Computer Age, A Twenty-Year View.*Cambridge, MA, The MIT Press, 1979.

Jones, W.H.: *The Government and Politics of Indian Military*, London, Hutchinson, 1971.

Jordan, David: *Air and Space Warfare*, in: Jordan, David et al.: *Understanding Modern Warfare*, Cambridge: Cambridge University Press 2009, p.219

Juvale, R.P. : *Military Planning and Diplomacy*, Cyber Tech Publications, Delhi, 2010.

Kapila, AVM Viney: *The Indian Air Force : a balanced strategic and tactical application*, Ocean Books, Delhi, 2002.

Kapur, C.K. : *Chinese Military Modernisation*, Manas, Delhi, 2003.

Lovering, J.: *Labour and the Defence Industry: An Alliance for Globalisation.* Capital and Class, Delhi, 1998.

Major Donovan: *Air Defence Power*. Sampson Low. London, 1940.

Marie Lecomte : *Hindu Kingship, Ethnic Revival, and Maoist Rebellion in Nepal*, Oxford University Press, Delhi, 2009.

Mary, W.: *Asian Power and Politics: the Cultural Dimensions of Authority*, Cambridge, Belknap Press, 1985.

Miller, Richard L. *The U.S. Atlas of Nuclear Fallout, 1951-1962*, Woodlands, TX: Legis Books, 2001.

Montgomery, Bernard Law: *A History of Warfare*, World Publishing Company, New York, 1968.

Morris, W.H.: *The Government and Politics of India*, London, Hutchinson, 1971.

Nair, A. M.: *An Indian Freedom Fighter in Japan*, Bombay, Orient Longman, 1983.

Nayyar, K K : *National Security : Military Aspects*, Rupa, Delhi, 2003.

Peter G. Tsouras: *Dictionary of Military Quotations*, Manas, Delhi, 2006.

Peterson, B.R.: *The Sources of Military Space Force*, Cornell Univ. Press.

Posen, B.R.: *The Sources of Military Doctrine*, Ithaca, 1984, Cornell Univ. Press.

Pushpindar Singh: *Aircraft of the Indian Air Force, 1933-73*, English Book Store, Delhi, 1974.

Radhakrishna: *Handbook of Military and Defence Services*, Sumit Enterprises, Delhi, 2009.

Raj Kumar: *Weapons and Military Technology*, Sumit Enterprises, Delhi, 2009.

Randall Forsberg: *The Arms Production Dilemma: Contraction and Restraint in the World Combat Aircraft Industry*, Cambridge, Massachusetts: MIT Press, 1994.

Robert M Cassidy: *Counterinsurgency and the Global War on Terror : Military Culture and Irregular War*, Pentagon Press, Delhi, 2008.

Roopinder Singh: *Marshal of the Air Force Arjan Singh - Rupa Charitravalli series* , Rupa Publications, Delhi, 2002.

Rosen, P.: *Societies and Military Power: India and its Armies*, Ithaca, Cornell University Press, 1996.

Rothenberg, Gunther Eric: *The Art of Warfare in the Age of Napoleon*, Indiana University Press, Bloomington, 1978.

Rudolph, Heimanson: *Aviation Power*, N.Y.: Oceana Publications, 1967.

Samir Chopra: *The India-Pakistan Air War of 1965*, Manohar, New Delhi, 2005.

Samuel P. Huntington: *The Soldier and the State : The Theory and Politics of Civil-Military Relations*, Natraj Pub, Delhi, 2005.

Schroeer, Dietrich: *Science, Technology, and the Cyber Crimes*, Ontario: John Wiley & Sons, 1984.

Seth, Vijay: *The Flying Machines - Indian Air Force 1933-99*. Seth Communications, Delhi, 2000.

Shaun Narine, *Explaining ASEAN: Regionalism in Southeast Asia*, Boulder, CO: Lynne Rienner Publishers, 2002.

Simon, D. : *Public Administration and Policy of Indian Military*, New York, Knopf, 1950.

Singh Jadoan: *Military Geography of South East Asia*, Anmol, Delhi, 2001.

Singh, Y.K. : *Cyber Crime and Law*, Shree, Delhi, 2005.

Spector, Leonard S., *Going Nuclear*, Cambridge, MA: Ballinger Publishing Company, 1987.

Spengler, John D. : *Health Effects of Airborne Particles*, Cambridge, Harvard University, 1986.

Stear, L. : *Design of a Curriculum for Destination Studies*, Annals of Tourism Research, 1981.

Suresh Goel: *International Encyclopaedia of Military, Security and Intelligence Agencies*, MD Publications, Delhi, 2009.

Sutton, J., *Technology and Defence Market Structure*, MIT Press, Delhi, 1998.

Tanham, George K.: *The Indian Air Force: Trends & prospects*. Rand, Santa Monica, Delhi, 1995.

Tariq Quershi: *History of the PAF 1947-1982*. PAF Press, Masroor, Karachi 1982.

Tufail, Kaiser: *Great Air Battles of the PAF*. Ferozesons, Karachi 2004.

Venter, AL J.: *The Chopper Boys: Helicopter Warfare in Africa*. Gibraltar: Ashanti Publishing, 1994.

Verton, D. : *Black Ice: The invisible Threat of Cyber-terrorism*, New York: McGraw-Hill/ Osborne, 2003.

Vijaya Lakshmi Sharma : *Technology Tools and Appliances*, Shilpi Publications, Allahabad, 1997

William A.: *An Introduction to the International Criminal Court*. Cambridge: Cambridge University Press, 2007.

Index

A

B

C

D

E

F

G

I

K

L

M

N

O

P

S

T

W

❑❑❑